Contents

The TRANSFORMATIVE CONSTITUTION

A Radical Biography in Nine Acts

GAUTAM BHATIA

HarperCollins *Publishers* India

First published in India in hardback in 2019 by
HarperCollins *Publishers*
4th Floor, Tower A, Building No. 10, Phase II, DLF Cyber City,
Gurugram, Haryana –122002
www.harpercollins.co.in

First published in paperback in 2021 by
HarperCollins *Publishers*

2 4 6 8 10 9 7 5 3

P-ISBN: 978-93-5357-664-6
E-ISBN: 978-93-5302-685-1

Typeset in 11/14.2 Adobe Caslon Pro at
Manipal Digital Systems, Manipal

Printed and bound at
Replika Press Pvt. Ltd.

MIX
Paper from
responsible sources
FSC® C016779

This book is produced from independently certified FSC® paper
to ensure responsible forest management.

The

TRANSFORMATIVE CONSTITUTION

'A work of serious scholarship; also a social-democratic manifesto … *The Transformative Constitution* is a formidable achievement. Right at the start, Bhatia writes that his book doesn't claim to be the definitive reading of India's Constitution. This is mannerly, modest and untrue. This book's reason for being is the author's ambition to define the Constitution as a progressive charter and to choose the landmark cases that should determine its future interpretation. To this end he marshals a knowledge of history, political ideas and jurisprudence that would be demoralizing if it weren't so austerely deployed.

'Bhatia's commitment to lucidity and systematic argument, where every premise is stated and every argument outlined before being discursively made, is so far removed from the riddling opaqueness of desi academic writing that it feels foreign. If the book has an Indian ancestor it is Amartya Sen's *The Idea of Justice*. In its range, its social democratic moorings and its style of public reasoning, it earns the comparison.

'For liberal readers, *The Transformative Constitution* is a purpose-built arsenal. For conservatives, it is a guide to the best legal arguments liberals didn't know they had. For lawyers and lay citizens alike, this is an indispensable book.'

—Mukul Kesavan, *The Hindu*

'Gautam Bhatia is an excellent jurist—the best among the best. A joy to read. There is much to learn from him.'

—Rajeev Dhavan, *The Indian Express*

Celebrating
30 Years of Publishing
in India

'Gautam Bhatia's formulation ensures that the Constitution is not "frozen in time", nor does it give judges a blank cheque to rewrite the Constitution ... As a genre, *The Transformative Constitution* has more in common with Lenin's "What Is to Be Done?" than dry treatises on constitutional interpretation ... Despite throwing out both precedence and protocol, Bhatia is neither a revolutionary nor an apostate, what he offers is a set of interpretive tools and techniques to renew faith in the transformative vision of the Constitution.'

—Rohit De, *India Today*

'This biography of the Indian Constitution is not about the law today but about the ideal equilibrium. There are few practitioners and scholars who are better positioned than Bhatia to provide both insight and perspective. This book will help many in the path toward legal literacy and thus a fuller and more participative citizenship.'

—Nikhil Govind, *Scroll*

'Advances the argument that the Constitution, despite elements of continuity with a colonial administration, is a fundamentally "transformative" document. In pragmatic, calculated ways, it grounds Indian democracy in the principles of liberty, equality and fraternity, insulating it from the vagaries of electoral politics as well as oppressive social hierarchies.'

—Rihan Najib, *The Hindu BusinessLine*

'Makes a unique contribution to the literature on Indian constitutional law. The book's methodology has inspiringly adopted Edward Said's contrapuntal approach to identify the Constitution as a value-laden document beyond its tangible text. Interestingly, by the project's nature, *The Transformative Constitution* is comparable to Akhil Reed Amar's *America's Constitution: A Biography*.'

—Sandeep Suresh, *International Journal of Constitutional Law*

Acknowledgements

THE IDEA FOR THIS book took shape during a seminar course titled 'The Transformative Constitution' that I taught at the National Law School of India University (NLSIU), Bengaluru, in January 2015, and the National University of Juridical Sciences (NUJS), Kolkata, in June 2016. The students who took the course and their critical comments and interventions pushed me to think more deeply about the arguments in this book. I am grateful to them.

Many people gave generously of their time and energy to read and comment on various chapters of this book. I am grateful to Ramachandra Guha, Abhinav Sekhri, Vinita Govindarajan, Suhrith Parthasarathy, Timothy Fish Hodgson, Ninni Susan Thomas, Shreya Atrey, Bo Tiojanco, Malavika Prasad, Gulnar Mistry, Mridula Chari, and Vidushi Marda, upon whose shoulders I had thrust the unenviable task of peer-reviewing all or parts of this manuscript, sometimes even as I was writing the part under review. Nikhil Mahajan, whom I have not met nor know in person, read more than one draft chapter on SSRN (formerly known as Social Science Research Network), and sent me detailed and very helpful comments on email.

Litigation is notorious for its bad hours. When I began working on this book, I did not know if the demands of my profession would let me finish it. I could do it because, wherever I worked, my bosses believed in having a life, and in letting their juniors have one too. I am very grateful to Justice S. Ravindra Bhat, Jawahar Raja, and Chander Uday Singh, for creating workplaces where a young lawyer had the time, space, and privacy to carry on with his own projects alongside office work.

This book was written between 2014 and 2018—time that I spent as a practising lawyer in Delhi, when I was lucky to be involved in a number of cases where transformative constitutionalism leapt out of the pages of books and was a live issue, argued in the courtrooms. The arguments in this book have been shaped profoundly by my time in court, on a daily basis, for much of those four years, experiencing the Constitution in action. I do not have words enough to thank Arvind P. Datar, who, in the summer of 2015, brought me on board the National Judicial Appointments Commission (NJAC) challenge (the first of many cases that we have done together), and introduced me to the world of constitutional litigation. His openness, egalitarianism, and intellectual and personal generosity have meant more to a young first-generation lawyer than is possible to express. He may disagree with much of this book, but I also know that he will express his disagreement with a smile and many words of encouragement. Shyam Divan, K.V. Viswanathan, Rebecca John, and Anup Bhambani have been wonderful seniors to brief and learn from. My year and a half in the chambers of Chander Uday Singh was not only intellectually stimulating but also a daily lesson in personal integrity, professional rigour, and a commitment towards expanding rights. For someone who had initially ruled out legal practice as an option because of its hierarchical and nepotistic character, the insistence of every one of these seniors on treating briefing counsel as colleagues and equals was a revelation.

But you learn the most, of course, from your peers. It has been an extraordinary experience of togetherness—long nights and long briefings (often ending with midnight paneer parathas opposite the All India Institute of Medical Sciences; Version 11 of the written submissions; hurried lunch meetings in Library 2 during the breaks between a hearing; paginating files and arranging compilations; and, of course, the frantic, real-time commentary on WhatsApp as the case progressed. More than anything else, this book has been shaped by listening to and debating arguments with my friends and colleagues, as we stood on the same side of the bar, in and outside the courtroom, at a time when decades happened every week.

So, to Sahana, Chinmay, Rishi, and Vaibhav, for being wonderful chamber-mates; to Gulnar, for blunt and uncompromising feedback (including, when necessary, 'This is such drivel!'); to Mihir, for his penetrating and sardonic wit, utterly unafraid of authority; to Suhrith, who vocalizes my thoughts with an almost eerie accuracy; to Abhinav and Utkarsh, comrades and best friends over four years, for our fortnightly cathartic meetings ('Did you see what the heck the SC *JUST DID!?*'), and for preserving our sanity by venting about PILs to each other; to Siddharth and Arvind, for the frantic 2016 and 2018 rounds in *Naz Foundation*; to Prasanna, Apar, Rahul, Ujwala, Raman, Krittika, Praavita, Uday, and Samiksha, for solidarity and companionship over interminable Aadhaar-and-privacy cases; to Vrinda and Sai, for those manic four months—the best four months of my life—from January to May 2018, when the line between the Aadhaar arguments in the court and academic writing became so blurred that I momentarily lost track of whether we were articulating a culture-of-justification argument for a draft of our written submissions, or for a draft of this manuscript; to Maanav, Rupali, Prateek (PC), Shadan, Sarim, Satyajit, Karan, and to everyone else whose names I cannot readily recall, but with whom I have had the privilege of trying to live the Constitution every day in court—I am so very grateful.

It was not, of course, just the lawyers. I was taught, equally, by the coalitions that formed outside the courtroom: the women and men of the Peoples Union for Democratic Rights (PUDR) who campaigned against the Unlawful Activities (Prevention) Act (UAPA) (and some of whom were arrested under the UAPA three days before this book went to the publisher), Sudha *ji*, Shalini, and the others at Maati-Kanker, the technologists at Kaarana (Anand, Kiran, Srinivas, Srikanth, and everybody else), the right-to-information activists at Mazdoor Kisan Shakti Sangathan (MKSS) and the National Campaign for People's Right to Information (NCPRI), Reetika, Jean, and the others who documented Aadhaar exclusions on the ground and translated them into submissions for the court, and of course Usha *ji*—all were, in their own ways, exemplars of how to live transformative constitutionalism in its deepest sense.

In a very material and tangible way, writing this book would not have been possible without the existence of Libgen. Doing scholarly work outside the gated precincts of a university is like trying to swim with one arm and one leg. Dashing off email requests to friends with access to databases is not an ideal way to work. Libgen allowed me to access books that I could never have afforded, and I am very thankful for all those people who continue to doggedly push for an open knowledge commons, despite all the difficulties. I remain hopeful that those who have the privilege of being within the gated community of academia will understand one day quite how unjust and exclusionary the existing system of unaffordable research databases is, how it monopolizes knowledge and prevents those who cannot, or have chosen not to, enter academia from participating in the conversation. And I hope that they will take some concrete steps to remedy it.

I am grateful to the New India Foundation, whose grant enabled me to buy the books that I *could* purchase, and were essential for my work. The six-volume Shiva Rao edition on the drafting of the Indian Constitution was the first thing I bought with the money, and it became, of course, an indispensable source for this book. I would also like to thank Krishan Chopra, Siddhesh Inamdar, and the team at HarperCollins, for their editorial work on the manuscript. I am grateful, as well, to Rivka Israel of the New India Foundation, who painstakingly went through the text.

'The butterfly's footsteps leave no trace; but the butterfly's footsteps are never erased.' Every word of this book bears the butterfly-like, breath-on-glass imprint of three individuals: Justice Bhat, who showed me how empathy and rigour need not be mutually exclusive; Jawahar, who taught me the importance of doubt and scepticism (most importantly, to be sceptical about myself), and steered me away from the temptation of constructing a world to fit your theories instead of the other way round, all the while remaining a model of how to maintain an uncompromising commitment to thought and action; and Ninni, who was the touchstone for testing the intellectual and moral honesty of the arguments that follow. They have given this book a life and a soul.

Home has always been a sanctuary. It only remains to me to thank my parents, for three decades of that sanctuary.

Preface to the Paperback Edition

I FINISHED WRITING *THE Transformative Constitution* in September 2018. I ended the Epilogue by noting that the Constitution remained contested terrain, with two impulses warring for supremacy. There was a conservative and repressive impulse, marked by concentration of power, primacy given to restrictions and not rights, and a devaluing of the individual in her relationship with the State, and with social groups. But there was also a transformative and emancipatory impulse, which understood the Constitution as a site for interrogating power, for democratizing both public and private spaces, and for liberation.

In September 2018, there were reasons to be cautiously optimistic that the Constitution's transformative impulse promised to be something more than a 'contrapuntal canon', limited to the odd judicial dissent, or the rare civil rights victory. In the space of a month, Constitution Benches of the Supreme Court decriminalized same-sex relations, decriminalized adultery, and struck down the prohibition upon menstruating-age women from entering the Sabarimala temple. Each of these decisions deployed transformative and emancipatory reasoning, and—when considered in the light of the Supreme Court's nine-judge bench decision in 2017, holding that a fundamental right to privacy existed under the Constitution—the stage seemed set for a 'Constitution 3.0' to begin. As *A.K. Gopalan* had inaugurated *Constitution 1.0* and *Maneka Gandhi* had inaugurated *Constitution 2.0*, the privacy judgment and its immediate progeny heralded a third phase in Indian constitutionalism, a transformative phase.

Two years have passed since the (somewhat) heady days of September 2018. These two years have made clear that my prognosis was unduly optimistic.

By any standards, the last two years have seen a deep regression in the Supreme Court's role in our constitutional jurisprudence. The alteration of Jammu and Kashmir's constitutional status on 5 August 2019 demonstrated that the Supreme Court was unable—or unwilling—to enforce something as basic as the writ of habeas corpus (petitions went unheard for months, and the then Chief Justice of India made flippant remarks in court). The constitutional challenge to the alteration itself remains unheard this day. Challenges to statewide internet shutdowns were footballed for months, and were finally concluded with the court passing the buck to the state, instead of deciding whether or not the Indian Constitution permitted states to impose an internet blackout on eight million people.

The Supreme Court's role in the Kashmir cases has been documented extensively, both by this author and by others. *The Transformative Constitution* is not a book about the Supreme Court, and I will therefore not dwell too much upon that institution. The point I want to make is that the Kashmir cases reveal a particularly dangerous cocktail for constitutionalism: they reflect *judicial evasion* (the court does not hear a case, and its failure to do so benefits the state by maintaining the status quo) and *judicial abnegation* (the court refuses to decide legal issues involving the constitutional rights of people, and 'leaves it' to the executive to judge its own transgressions). It should be obvious that constitutionalism per se—

forget transformative or otherwise—cannot survive long when the highest organ of the judiciary acts in such a way. It is important to note that Kashmir is only a representative case: these problems persist elsewhere, ranging from the failure to hear the constitutional challenges to electoral bonds, severe conflicts of interest in cases such as the Land Acquisition hearing, the doctrinally dubious (at best) 'review' of the *Sabarimala* judgment, and so on.

What, then, is the future of transformative constitutionalism? In the Introduction to this book, I have warned against a vision of constitutionalism that limits it to courtroom battles. This is an impoverished vision, and risks an impoverished constitutionalism. As a terrain of liberation and emancipation, the Constitution is far more than what a court says at any given time, and—as movements around the Right to Information Act, the Forest Rights Act and, more recently, the Citizenship Amendment Act have shown us—the transformative Constitution is at its most powerful *outside* the courtroom, when it is a site of mobilization, of communication, and of *practices of liberation*.

It is that aspect of constitutionalism that I want to stress. Per force, this book is about courts and their judgments. In the courtroom, there is little doubt that the transformative canon is a contrapuntal canon: the last two years have suffocated the flicker that emerged in September 2018. But what the judgments in this book demonstrate is what the Constitution *can* be—in its best sense, in the sense that is most true to its origins, its histories, and the struggles that shaped it. And it is that transformative vision—the vision of liberty, equality, and fraternity—that we must preserve, beyond courtrooms and beyond lawyers.

Gautam Bhatia
December 2020

The Transformative Constitution

Author's Note

AS A PRACTISING LAWYER, I was professionally involved with four of the cases discussed in this book: the constitutional challenge to Section 377 of the IPC (Chapter 2), the right to privacy case (Chapter 7), the bail applications of Kabir Kala Manch before the Supreme Court (Chapter 8), and the constitutional challenge to Aadhaar (Epilogue). Readers may like to take my views on these judgements with a healthy dose of scepticism, given that I was an active participant in these cases, and held (and continue to hold) definitive views about them.

The Supreme Court judgements in the adultery challenge (Chapter 1), the Section 377 challenge (Chapter 2), and the Sabarimala temple entry case (Chapter 5) were delivered after I had finished writing this book. There was no time to integrate them into the body of the chapters. Because of their importance to the argument—and, more broadly, to the project of transformative constitutionalism—I have instead addressed them in brief postscripts to each chapter.

A version of Chapter 2 was published earlier as 'Equal moral membership: Naz Foundation and the refashioning of equality under a transformative Constitution', (2017) 1(2) *The Indian Law Review* 115 (Publisher: Taylor & Francis); of Chapter 4 as 'Horizontal Discrimination and Article 15(2) of the Indian Constitution: A Transformative Approach', (2016) 11(1) *The Asian Journal of Comparative Law* 87 (Copyright: Cambridge University Press); and of Chapter 5 as 'Freedom from community: Individual rights, group life, state authority, and religious freedom under the Indian Constitution', (2016) 5(3) *Global Constitutionalism* 351 (Copyright: Cambridge University Press). These have been slightly edited to fit the scheme of this book, and are reprinted with the permission of the publishers.

Prologue

The Past Is a Foreign Country

On 26th January 1950, India will be an independent country.

B.R. Ambedkar, in his closing speech to the Constituent Assembly (1949)

We have it in our power to begin the world over again.

Thomas Paine (1776)

IN MARCH 1948, THE ruler of Sant, a princely state in western India, granted to some of his subjects (the *jagirdars*[1]) rights over certain forests. It was to be one of the concluding royal acts in Sant's 700-year-long history. By June 1948, Sant had become one of the last princely states to accede to the newly independent Indian Republic.

Within a year, the State of Bombay—with which Sant had merged—reneged on the grant.

Various aggrieved parties (the respondents) moved court. After multiple rounds of litigation, the case came before a seven-judge bench of the Supreme Court in 1964.[2] The State's defence was simple: the Privy Council of the United Kingdom, which had been the highest court of appeal for colonial India, had repeatedly held that when a sovereign State acquires fresh territory, it could choose whether or not to recognize the rights enjoyed by the territory's inhabitants under the previous regime. In acquiring Sant, the government had exercised its sovereign prerogative and decided not to recognize the forest grant. This was an 'act of State' that was immune from judicial challenge.

The respondent-citizens objected strongly. They argued that 'this rule was a relic of the imperialistic and expansionist philosophy of ... British Jurisprudence, which is inconsistent with our constitutional set-up'.[3] It was inconsistent 'with the true spirit of our Constitution, which seeks to eschew all arbitrary authority, and establishes the rule of law by subjecting every executive action to the scrutiny of the courts'.[4] The respondent-citizens invited the Supreme Court to break with the doctrines of the Privy Council, and to hold that the State could not simply wipe out their rights when it assumed sovereignty over the state of Sant.

But by a wafer-thin 4–3 majority, the Supreme Court held in favour of the State. In his concurring opinion, Justice J.C. Shah addressed the constitutional argument of the respondent-citizens, and rejected it in the following words:

> There is no warrant for holding at the stroke of midnight of the 25th January, 1950, all our pre-existing political institutions ceased to exist, and in the next moment arose a new set of institutions completely unrelated to the past. The Constituent Assembly which gave form to the Constitution functioned for several years under the old regime, and set up the constitutional machinery on the foundations of the earlier political set up ... the process was not one of destruction, but of evolution.[5]

Justice Shah—like his colleagues in the majority—elected to follow the jurisprudence of the Privy Council, which had been 'the law laid down and given effect to … until India attained independence.'[6] In doing so, they overruled a judgement handed down by a five-judge bench of the Supreme Court, a decade before. In 1954, considering a very similar set of facts, Justice Vivian Bose had set his face firmly against the Privy Council's 'Act of State' doctrine. As with the respondent-citizens before the Supreme Court in 1964, he had founded his argument in the moment of constitutional framing:

> In our opinion, the Constitution … blotted out in one magnificent sweep all vestiges of arbitrary and despotic power in the territories of India and over its citizens and lands and prohibited just such acts of arbitrary power as the State now seeks to uphold … the past was obliterated except where expressly preserved; at one moment of time the new order was born with its new allegiance springing from the same source for all, grounded on the same basis: the sovereign will of the peoples of India with no class, no caste, no race, no creed, no distinction, no reservation.[7]

Ten years later, Justice Shah took direct issue with these words, labelling them 'assumptions … not supported by history or by constitutional theory'.[8] He insisted, instead, that the promulgation of the Constitution marked 'merely [a] change in the form of Government',[9] which was nothing more than the 'final step in the process of evolution towards self-government'.[10] This was evident from 'the continuance of the governmental machinery and of the laws of the Dominion',[11] even after the adoption of the new Constitution.

The disagreement between Justice Shah and Justice Bose was not merely over whether the jurisprudence of the Privy Council should be followed, but over *meaning*—what was the meaning of the historical event that was the framing of the Indian Constitution? For Justice Shah, that event signified continuity: marked by words and phrases such as 'continuance', 'evolution', 'gave shape', and 'change in form'. For Justice Bose, on the other hand, it marked transformation: a past that was 'blotted out', 'abandoned', 'obliterated'; and a 'new order' that was born.

That is why Justice Shah took the unusual step of attacking Justice Bose for his understanding of 'history and constitutional theory'. The judgements of Justices Shah and Bose reflected contesting views of history, and, based upon that history, contesting views about what the Constitution of India represented.

And the difference mattered. It mattered vividly in 1954 and 1964 in determining the legality of the State's refusal to recognize the pre-existing rights of its citizens. It had mattered before in 1950, when in its very first decision the Supreme Court had upheld the constitutionality of preventive detention laws that replicated their colonial antecedents. And it has mattered ever since, whether it is a landmark Supreme Court judgement upholding the fundamental right to privacy, or a barely noticed judgement of a high court applying the guarantee of gender equality to pregnancy-based discrimination. At the heart of every constitutional decision is the court's assessment of what the Constitution *means*, why it exists in the shape and form that it does, and, above all, what injustices it is meant to remedy.

This book advances Justice Bose's vision of the Constitution, a vision that understood both the historical moment of framing, and the Constitution itself, as fundamentally *transformative*. But it is a vision that, notwithstanding the Supreme Court's recent indications to the contrary,[12] remains marginalized in a judicial history that has overwhelmingly endorsed Justice Shah's view of conservatism and continuity.

I. The Conservative Constitution

In characterizing the Constitution as a conservative document, Justice Shah was not arguing in a vacuum. His references to the Constituent Assembly functioning under the old regime, to the earlier political set-up, and to a gradual evolution towards self-government, all tapped into an established intellectual tradition. This was the tradition of constitutional continuity.[13]

The purveyors of this tradition could count among themselves an authority as eminent as B.N. Rau, the Constitutional Advisor, who began his book, *India's Constitution in the Making*, by classifying the moment of Independence as 'transference of power'.[14] To justify the idiom of 'transfer' (as opposed to transformation), they could also call upon some formidable evidence.

First, the Constituent Assembly itself was no revolutionary body. It derived its own authority from the Cabinet Mission Plan of 1946, and its members were elected under the limited suffrage provisions of the existing colonial legal framework.[15]

Second, the Constituent Assembly borrowed heavily from the 1935 Government of India Act. As much as 75 per cent of the Indian Constitution was based on that colonial law.[16] So deep was its influence that, in 1958, Justice Venkatarama Aiyar observed that the provisions of the Constitution must be interpreted *in light* of the Government of India Act, because:

> … a Federal Constitution had been established under the Government of India Act, 1935, and though that has undergone considerable change by way of repeal, modification and addition, it still remains the framework on which the present Constitution is built …[17]

Where then was the break with the past, the rupture with the colonial regime, that Justice Bose had spoken about so lyrically?[18]

And, in particular, the Constitution replicated some of the very provisions that had been the subject of bitter protests during the course of the freedom struggle. These included preventive detention, granting the political executive the power to pass ordinances bypassing legislative procedure, as well as the power to effectively suspend the legal system by declaring an Emergency.[19] If the Constitution was meant to be transformative, surely it should have, at the very least, repudiated these hallmarks of arbitrary power instead of endorsing them?

Instead, specific proposals to incorporate some core civil rights (such as a guarantee against arbitrary searches and seizures) were considered and rejected by the Assembly.[20] All this has prompted scholars to argue that freedom was of secondary importance to the framers of the Constitution, relegated behind the overarching concerns of national integration and security, alleviation of economic and social ills, and India's international standing.[21]

Third, it is argued, even the system of government that the Constitution set up was neither new nor revolutionary. The Constitution established the Westminster system of parliamentary democracy,[22] but this was no abrupt break with an absolutist past. From at least the first decade of the twentieth century, there had been an incremental evolution of representative systems in India, which the nationalist movement had extracted from the colonial regime inch by inch. Parliamentary democracy under the Constitution did not replace a tyranny, but a system of 'responsible and *limited*'[23] government, which had been functioning under the 1935 Act. This included provincial legislative councils and ministries elected on the basis of limited franchise, which had limited law-making powers, often subject to the overriding authority of the Governor-General.[24] The representation might have been imperfect, but—so the argument goes—that was simply a question of degree.[25] The Constitution only marked a culmination of this incremental, but inevitable, process. So, as Justice Shah had observed, 'the process was not one of destruction but evolution.'[26]

These arguments about the character of the Constitution are nested within a broader narrative that denies any transformative character to the freedom movement. The Indian National Congress, it is argued, often pursued a strategy of containment. It actively discouraged and repressed popular movements, including agrarian and labour struggles, which did not come under its umbrella.[27] And Indian nationalism was itself a 'derivative discourse',[28] mirroring colonial institutions rather than seeking to abolish or transform them. These included colonial legal, political, and administrative institutions[29] and, indeed, the Constitution itself.[30]

Notwithstanding this broader argument, it is important to differentiate the nationalist movement from the framing of the Constitution. The framing was the culmination of the nationalist movement, inspired by its values, and had many of the same protagonists. That does not mean, however, that the two were equivalent.[31] Instead, I shall argue, there were discourses around liberty, equality, and fraternity which were part of the freedom struggle but were ignored, marginalized, or even rejected by the dominant nationalist movement. Nonetheless, they found their way into the Indian Constitution, and gave it its transformative character.

To understand and incorporate them into our constitutional vision, however, will require an act of imagination. We need to go beyond the narrow canon that is invoked in defence of constitutional continuity, a canon that is limited to a surface reading of the constitutional text, a surface comparison with colonial legal instruments, and a surface contextualization of the pre- and post-constitutional political framework. It entails a broader canvas that includes, in the words of the civil rights lawyer K.G. Kannabiran:

> … the social history of the period preceding the Constitution … the struggles of the people who fought for freedom, the repressive legal structures on whose altars people were sacrificed and their dreams shattered … [and] the aspirations of the people to build a better society for themselves.[32]

II. The Transformative Constitution

The litany of arguments advanced by the defenders of colonial continuity are not definitive. The Constituent Assembly might have owed its legal existence to the colonial regime, but one of its first acts was to declare itself sovereign, and frame the Constitution on its own terms.[33] In defending himself against the charge that he had simply copied the 1935 Act into the Constitution, Babasaheb Ambedkar, the principal draftsman of the Indian Constitution, insisted that it was only the 'details of administration' that had been borrowed.[34] This was not an unfair argument.[35] And while some measure of 'responsible government' existed in British India, it was scarcely comparable with the full-blooded parliamentary democracy, founded on universal adult franchise and equality of citizenship, which the Constitution brought into existence.[36] As Uday Mehta points out, for all the surface similarities with the colonial past, there was much in the Constitution that was a radical departure:

> Here was a document which granted universal adult franchise in a country that was overwhelmingly illiterate; where, moreover, the conditionality of acquiring citizenship made no reference to race, caste, religion, or creed ... which committed the state to being secular in a land that was by any reckoning deeply religious; which evacuated as a matter of law every form of prescribed social hierarchy under extant conditions marked by a dense plethora of entrenched hierarchies; that granted a raft of fundamental individual rights in the face of a virtually total absence of such rights ... [and] most importantly, the Constitution created a federal democracy with all the juridical and political instruments of individual, federal, local, and provisional self-governance, where the nearest experience had been of imperial and princely authority.[37]

These words lay the foundations for the argument of this book: that the Indian Constitution was a transformative constitution.[38] But what did it seek to transform? To answer this question, I begin with Ruti Teitel's important insight: 'As a state undergoes political change, legacies of injustice have a bearing on what is deemed transformative.'[39] I shall argue that there were two clear 'legacies of injustice' that the Constitution sought to repudiate and transform.

First, the Constitution transformed the legal relationship between the individual and the State. It transformed the subjects of a colonial regime into citizens of a republic. It replaced the colonial logic of governing and administering a population[40] with the democratic logic of popular sovereignty, public participation, and limited government. Apart from the guarantee of universal adult franchise and the structures of parliamentary democracy, this transformation was expressed through the fundamental rights that embodied citizenship and made democracy possible: the freedom of speech, expression, association, and conscience; the right to life and personal liberty; and the right to equality before law.[41] These fundamental rights, alien to the 1935 Government of India Act, represented 'a tectonic shift in constitutional philosophy'.[42]

So far, so familiar. This is the story of constitution-making the world over, most famously told through the American Revolution. Yet, that was not all. The Indian Constitution was transformative in a second sense. It sought a thoroughgoing 'reconstruction of State and society itself'.[43] In its horizontal—or comprehensive—transformative avatar, the Constitution recognized that the State had never been the only locus of concentrated power in Indian society. Unlike the modern West, which understood sovereignty in centralized and unitary terms, Indian society had always been characterised by 'layered sovereignty'.[44] Hierarchies were established and maintained by 'self-regulating communities' taking multifarious forms (primarily, caste), and the State had 'rather limited powers to interfere with [a] social segment's internal organisation'.[45]

Consequently, in India, freedom and equality were suffocated not merely by 'a despotic government, but also by embodied traditional authority and … domestic or religious practices'.[46] The freedom struggle that culminated in the framing of the Constitution was at one end a movement for liberation from political servitude, but it was *equally* 'a struggle for self-determination against multi-layered oppressive structures' of the feudal order as well as the structures that constituted colonial domination.[47] This story is reflected in the Constitution's horizontal rights provisions (i.e., fundamental rights enforceable against groups, communities and private parties), a rarity in constitutions even today, let alone in 1950: Article 15(2), which bans discrimination in access to restaurants and roads, Article 17, which abolishes untouchability, and Article 23, which proscribes forced labour.

To defend this vision of the transformative Constitution, it is imperative to go beyond the sterile and deadlocked academic debates surrounding the bare text of the document, and (some of) the legal instruments that preceded it. The words of the Constitution, I suggest, come alive only in the context of a broader canon. For example, we cannot understand the constitutional guarantee of equal protection of laws without taking into account the 'enormously influential'[48] *Samya* (Equality) (1879), Bankim Chandra Chattopadhyay's nineteenth-century political treatise on equality. We cannot understand the Constitution's repudiation of gender discrimination without listening to the voices of the women who used the language of equal rights to publicly intervene in the nineteenth-century debates surrounding the restitution of conjugal rights, the twentieth-century controversies over the Child Marriage Bill, and the equally *public* struggle of the suffrage movement. It is only when we read the speeches of Congress presidents Motilal Nehru and C.R. Das, savaging the colonial regime's arbitrary executive authority, that the austere right to 'life and personal liberty' will begin to speak to us. It is the writings of B.R. Ambedkar, from his Report to the Southborough Committee to *Annihilation of Caste* and the story of the Mahad Satyagraha, that will allow us to understand how the Constitution was committed to erasing social and economic hierarchies. And it is Gandhi's uncompromising approach to civil rights and his defence of all speech—even 'revolutionary speech'—that will enable us to understand the transformative potential in the simple words: 'all citizens shall have the right to freedom of speech and expression'.[49]

That is just the beginning. For more than a hundred years, in their struggle against alien colonial rule and against indigenous social and economic domination, Indians imagined, conceptualized, and articulated a vocabulary of rights, of equality and freedom, and of dignity, a vocabulary rooted in the lifeworld of India. We do that struggle a disservice if we erase it from our consideration when interpreting the charter of fundamental rights that, finally, *constituted* an independent India.

In particular, it was a struggle that found utterance in the curtain-raiser to the Constitution: the Preamble, with its three words which, over the course of almost two centuries, had acquired the force of an incantation: liberty, equality, fraternity.[50]

III. Liberty, Equality, Fraternity: The Framework of Democratic Politics

The trinity of liberty, equality, fraternity was a familiar one, from the time of the French Revolution. But in his closing speech to the Constituent Assembly on 25 November 1949, the day before the Constitution was adopted, B.R. Ambedkar articulated what these words meant to him:

> Political democracy cannot last unless there lies at the base of it social democracy. What does social democracy mean? It means a way of life which recognizes liberty, equality, and fraternity as the principles of life. These principles of liberty, equality, and fraternity are not to be treated as separate items in a trinity. They form a union of trinity ... liberty cannot be divorced from equality, equality cannot be divorced from liberty. Nor can liberty and equality be divorced from fraternity. Without equality, liberty would produce the supremacy of the few over the many. Equality without liberty would kill individual initiative ... Without fraternity, liberty and equality could not become a natural course of things. It would require a constable to enforce them.[51]

In this paragraph, I contend, Ambedkar distilled the heart and soul of the Indian Constitution. Liberty, equality, and fraternity were the three mutually reinforcing pillars upon which the edifice of the Constitution was erected. All three were equally integral. Each of them could be understood only in the context of the other two.

A. The Constitutional Trinity

Liberty was simple enough. In its classic sense, it referred to that threshold of individual freedom that the State could not cross. And so, we had our Rights to Freedom, guaranteed by Articles 19 to 22 of the Constitution. But in order to ensure that the fruits of liberty were accessible to all, the government would also have to commit to equality of status. This was especially true where the laws themselves had long sanctioned discriminatory and unequal treatment: between men and women, rich and poor, white and brown, caste and caste, and the loyal and the disloyal.[52] And so we had our 'Equality Code', contained within Articles 14 to 18.

But in a country where the most invidious discrimination had been the product of community sanction, where the social and economic boycotts had been the chosen methods to discipline and to punish, and where society was defined by a system of 'graded inequality'[53] (Ambedkar's words), it was never going to be enough to direct the State to act by the principles of liberty and equality. Fraternity was the bridge that would make liberty and equality become 'the natural course of things'. As Ambedkar visualized it, the principle of fraternity would interrogate, undermine, and eventually break down the hierarchical *social* relations that, over the course of centuries, had come to be treated as 'natural'.[54] Fraternity would reject 'forms of domination',[55] characterized by 'social patterns, power relations, and other systematic (structures)'.[56] These forms were not imposed by an authoritarian and visible State, but owed their force to silence and slow time, to the insidious and often invisible social processes that, having accumulated over millennia, sometimes by coercion and violence, and sometimes by co-option and hegemony, now possessed the immovability of mountains.[57]

What was the purpose of the State guaranteeing liberty if, at the first attempt at exercising their new-found freedom, communities faced excommunication, boycott, and violence? What was the point of promising equality and non-discrimination if the force of convention continued to restrict women to the 'private sphere'? And what would liberty and equality do for a labour force that remained bound by exploitative and unequal workplace relationships? This was where fraternity came in: to liberate and equalize the individual, not from or with respect to the State, but with respect to her community, her family, and her workplace, so that the guarantees of liberty and equality meant something more than a rope of sand. This fundamental truth was enunciated by Dr S. Radhakrishnan in his opening speech to the Constituent Assembly as early as December 1946. While commending the Objectives Resolution (the blueprint of the Constitution) to the Assembly, Radhakrishnan observed, 'We wish to bring about a fundamental alteration in the structure of Indian society ... to abolish every vestige of despotism, every heirloom of inorganic tradition'.[58] And so we had a right against economic exploitation (Articles 23 and 24), the prohibition of untouchability (Article 17), and a guarantee against economic and social boycotts (Article 15[2]).

While fraternity was the bridge that would make liberty and equality meaningful, its role was not merely auxillary. Ambedkar's reference to the 'union of trinity' reflected the insight that the *content* of liberty and equality (which were otherwise abstract terms) would be shaped by fraternity. For example, when the State guaranteed to all the 'equality of opportunity', could it ignore the many centuries of social discrimination that had left some individuals in a far better position to take advantage of this 'equality' than others? Would the constitutional commitment to equality, therefore, be better understood as a commitment to *affirmatively* overcoming the structural and institutional barriers that had existed, and continued to exist, between India's citizens and the promise of equal treatment? Similarly, could the venerable principle of the 'freedom of contract', as an aspect of personal liberty, continue to remain oblivious to the imbalances of social and economic power that defined the relationship between employers and employees?

And the dependence was mutual. Fraternity itself could not be defined in isolation from liberty and equality. In particular, fraternity was not—as some of the French revolutionaries imagined it, and as some Indian judges have understood it recently[59]—about promoting a one-for-all-and-all-for-one vision of the nation, where the State itself became personified as 'a common endeavour'.[60] Rather, the role of fraternity was to ensure that, in India, liberty and equality would come to mean something *real*. Indeed, this understanding of fraternity was put to the test as early as 1948. When the Draft Constitution was published in February of that year, it was thrown open for public comment. Led by B. Pattabhi Sitaramayya, seven members of the Constituent Assembly wanted to rephrase the fraternity clause of the Preamble to put the words 'unity of the nation' before 'dignity of the individual' instead of the other way around. B.N. Rau, who was charged with vetting all the suggestions, rejected the proposal. He argued that 'the reason for putting the dignity of the individual first was that unless the dignity of the individual is assured, the nation cannot be united'.[61] Following his advice, the original phrasing—'FRATERNITY, assuring the dignity of the individual and the unity of the nation'—was retained by the Drafting Committee, and finally adopted by the Constituent Assembly.

To avoid being ambushed by attractive, but ultimately doubtful, interpretations of liberty, equality, and fraternity, it is crucial to understand, as B.N. Rau did in 1948, that despite its numerous references to 'groups' and 'denominations', it is the *individual* that is placed at the heart of the Constitution's Fundamental Rights chapter. The framers of the Constitution were aware of the fallacy—which Western political theory would discover a few decades later[62]—of treating individuals as abstract and disembodied beings, existing in a world without communal ties.[63] They were aware that human beings only made sense of themselves and the world around them through the bonds they forged with others, and through the communities to which they belonged. For this reason, the Fundamental Rights chapter contains explicit safeguards for minorities to preserve their culture and way of life and for religious denominations to manage their own affairs. That does not mean, however, that the Constitution treated groups and communities on a par with the individual. Indeed, specific proposals to that effect were rejected, and Ambedkar expressed his relief that 'the draft Constitution has ... adopted the individual as its unit'.[64] And it was this sentiment that was expressed most eloquently by Justice Vivian Bose (again) in his dissenting opinion in *Krishnan v. State of Madras*:

> Is not the sanctity of the individual recognized and emphasized again and again? Is not our Constitution in violent contrast to those of States where the State is everything and the individual but a slave or a serf to serve the will of those who, for the time being, wield almost absolute power? I have no doubts on this score.[65]

This basic point is reflected in the Preamble. The Preamble promises to secure to all the *citizens* of India liberty, equality, fraternity (and justice).[66] It makes no mention of peoples, nations, groups, communities, denominations, or religions. The three pillars of liberty, equality, and fraternity hold up an elaborate constitutional structure that places the individual front and centre. *That* is how we must understand and interpret the transformative Constitution.

B. Beyond Liberalism

In its commitment to the trinity of liberty, equality, and fraternity, the Indian Constitution and its Fundamental Rights chapter departed from the template that had been established by the United States Constitution in 1776, and that has served as the global default ever since. Defined by scholars as the structural-liberal approach to constitutionalism, this template holds that the primary goal of a constitutional bill of rights is to secure individual freedom, and individual freedom is to be secured by limiting *State power*.[67] This creates a set of binaries that are now treated as fundamental to constitutionalism: the State and the individual; the public sphere (subject to constitutional norms of liberty and equality) and the private sphere (of the family, the workplace, and so on, where these norms are inapplicable); the vertical relationship (between State and individual, characterized by fundamental rights) and the horizontal relationship (between individuals and individuals, or groups and corporations, where the Constitution has no say); and so on.

However, there is nothing natural or inevitable about this characterization of constitutionalism.[68] The US Constitution took the form that it did because it was driven by an ascendant bourgeoisie class, arose out of a reaction against an absolutist monarchy, and was designed to guard against the threats to freedom posed by centralized and concentrated power. Its focus on associating individual freedom with limitations upon the government was a product of its time and place.[69] But the India of 1947 was a very different place and a very different time, and it chose a different form of constitutionalism. As I shall argue throughout this book, the constitutional trinity challenged the simple polarities between the categories of the State and the 'public' on the one hand and the 'private' on the other. The framers were clear that 'private' structures and private institutions were often sources of domination and authoritarianism, and, therefore, 'private regimes of power'[70] had to be tackled *constitutionally*.[71]

Additionally, while the constitutional trinity defined individual freedom in relation to equality and fraternity, other parts of the Constitution supplemented this vision by viewing the State not merely as a threat to individual freedom, but as a necessary enabler of it, as a vehicle of social transformation.[72] This was expressed most clearly in Part IV of the Constitution, the Directive Principles of State Policy (DPSPs). Framed as exhortations to the legislature,[73] the DPSPs embody many of the principles of a social-democratic welfare State: equitable distribution of resources, special solicitude towards vulnerable sections of society, strong labour protections, and other socio-economic rights.

But an important clarification is due here. Despite their vision of an enhanced role for the State, the framers of the Constitution ensured it didn't collapse into only a vehicle for achieving distributive justice.[74] The DPSPs were designed to facilitate and enable the State to carry out programmes designed to achieve economic and social justice, yet not to be equated with the set of judicially enforceable fundamental rights guaranteed by the Constitution. Indeed, despite his earlier enthusiasm for writing socialism into the Constitution, by the end of the drafting process, Ambedkar was clear that it was not the Constituent Assembly's prerogative to impose an economic philosophy, or an economic system, upon future generations.[75] The Indian Constitution was compatible with a socialist government, and in some respects (especially through the DPSPs) it even encouraged socialism. It was not, however, a *socialist* Constitution.[76] While the constitutional trinity travelled well beyond classical liberal constitutionalism's focus upon limiting State power, it did not quite travel far enough to determine economic and social policy. As we shall see, that remained the prerogative of democratic politics.[77]

C. PILs: The Wrong Turn

This clarification becomes important in order to briefly, but critically, assess that segment of Indian constitutional jurisprudence which, in popular and scholarly imagination, is taken to represent the Constitution's transformative character: Public Interest Litigation or PIL or 'social action litigation', as one of its votaries insists that it must be called.[78] For the first twenty-five years of its history (or so the popular argument goes), the Supreme Court was a conservative institution, aligning with landed and propertied interests to thwart the ambitious reform agenda of successive governments. This avatar of the Court reached its nadir with the notorious Emergency-era judgement in *ADM Jabalpur v. Shivakant Shukla*. After the Emergency was lifted, a chastened Court decided to make it up to the country for its past sins. So was born the PIL, whose principal features now include a loosening of locus standi requirements, procedural innovations designed to ensure responsive governance (ranging from elaborate, near-legislative 'guidelines' filling legal vacuums to the 'continuing mandamus'), and an expansion of Article 21's guarantee of life and personal liberty to include a host of socio-economic rights (many of them incorporated from the DPSPs).

I have no quarrel with the original purpose of PILs as a mode for giving voice to those unable to approach the courts by themselves. Nor do I take issue with invoking the directive principles to infuse socio-economic content into our fundamental rights, to the extent that this is consistent with the text.[79] However, PIL today is no longer recognizable by these purposes. Through the substantive expansion of Article 21 (and Article 142), and the removal of procedural constraints in order to enable 'justice', it now involves the courts in playing an active role in governance, and taking both quasi-legislative and executive actions. But to defend *this* as 'transformative jurisprudence', we must ignore the Constitution's text, structure, drafting history, and underlying philosophy. This is a problem. Beginning with the judgement in *Maneka Gandhi v. Union of India*,[80] when the Court decided to rewrite the text of the Constitution because it felt that it was insufficiently progressive, a large part of the history of PIL has been the history of judges and academicians substituting an *ideal* of justice for the concrete articulation of justice actually in the Constitution.

The problem with PIL, however, is not simply that it no longer maintains fidelity to the Constitution. Rather, in doing so, it misunderstands the role of the courts in our constitutional scheme vis-à-vis popular democracy. The Constitution is a transformative document, but its transformative vision has several components.[81] Courts are not automatically entrusted with giving effect to the entire constitutional vision on their own.[82] On the contrary, the Constitution has consciously selected different *vehicles* to carry out the separate items of its transformative agenda. To the courts is entrusted the task of breathing life into the Fundamental Rights chapter. And to popular democracy—through the Parliament and the executive—is assigned the task of achieving distributive justice, the attainment of independent socio-economic rights, and that boundlessly manipulable phrase: good governance.[83] When it comes to these goals, the courts must not stand in the way of the other organs of State acting to achieve the Constitution's transformative goals;[84] but nor must they make themselves the vehicles for achieving the goals.[85] As K.G. Kannabiran correctly recognized, 'the attempt [of the framers] was to have a Constitution which would enable the people to cope with and transform India's social reality within a liberal framework'.[86]

D. The Framework of Democratic Politics

But if transformative constitutionalism is neither merely about constraining State power, nor about guaranteeing socio-economic rights and securing distributive justice, then what *is* it about? The rest of this book is devoted to answering that question. Here, I shall attempt a brief summary: through a transformative understanding of liberty, equality, and fraternity, the Constitution is committed to creating the *framework* for a rich and substantive vision of democracy;[87] in other words, the framework that makes democratic politics possible.

By democratic politics, I mean a rough correspondence between State policies (including economic and social policies) and the popular will, expressed through constitutionally established channels such as periodic elections and the parliamentary structure, and with adequate safeguards against majoritarian tyranny.[88] One of the greatest impediments to a thriving democratic politics is asymmetry of power: between individual and State, individual and community, and individual and individual (especially in skewed institutional contexts, such as the family and the workplace). Asymmetries in power enable domination and subordination at the point *prior* to participation in democratic politics, thereby skewing participation itself and, by extension, choking fair democratic outcomes.

The liberty-equality-fraternity trinity aims to guarantee the preconditions that make possible any meaningful participation in democratic politics. It does so by deepening democracy in the public sphere, where it insists upon a 'culture of justification',[89] i.e., every act of public power be justified by the touchstone of the Constitution. It also does so by expanding our notion of *what* constitutes the public sphere, and by democratizing the very spaces (such as the household and the family) that liberal constitutionalism has long deemed to be off-limits, because those institutions are as crucial in shaping individual participation in democratic politics as the State is.

And that is where it stops. Transformative constitutionalism does not seek to interfere with the democratic process itself, or to determine outcomes. This is what separates the transformative constitutionalism that is articulated and defended in this book from the dominant, PIL vision of contemporary jurisprudence, which *does* involve the courts in shaping substantive outcomes.

IV. The Nine Judgements

It is not the aim of this book to glorify the courts as agents of constitutional transformation, or to place the language of rights that they speak upon a pedestal. The limitations of both are well known.[90] Neither do I accord to courts normative priority over individuals, citizens, communities, and social movements in determining constitutional meaning or articulating constitutional truth.[91] The Constitution is for all to interpret, for themselves, and 'whichever story the Court chooses, alternative stories still provide normative bases for the growth of distinct constitutional worlds through the persistence of groups who find their respective meanings [elsewhere]'.[92]

Nonetheless, in India and in many other parts of the world, it is the courts alone whose interpretations are authorized as *legally* final, and backed up (when necessary) by the force of the State. 'Historical truth is hardly ever more than a descriptive hypothesis,' the Italian oral historian Alessandro Portelli remarked wryly, '[but] legal truth, on the other hand, has a performative nature, measured in years in jail.'[93] The transformative Indian Constitution is by no means limited to the courtroom (nor should it be), but the court remains an integral part of the story. Keeping that in mind, this book elects to tell the story of the transformative Constitution in the courtroom. It tells that story through nine judgements, ranging across our constitutional history, and selected from both the Supreme Court and the high courts. Together, these nine judgements articulate, in concrete terms, the transformative vision of the Indian Constitution.

The first set speaks to the Equality Code (Articles 14 to 16 of the Constitution). The cases engage with gender equality, the decriminalization of sexual orientation, and the justifications for affirmative action and reservations. Taken separately and taken together, these judgements understand equality to be about overcoming institutional and structural barriers that have kept individuals and groups in a state of subordination. The text of the Equality Code, born out of more than a century of struggles for equal status and equal moral membership of the polity, locates and identifies *sites* of historical and current discrimination. It then commits the Constitution and the State to overcoming them, whether by the removal of discriminatory laws or by positive (affirmative) action. To use familiar shorthand—the Equality Code enshrines a vision of *substantive* equality as opposed to a merely *formal* (likes should be treated alike) one.

The second set of cases engages with the concept of fraternity, and interprets those articles of the Constitution that have remained marginalized, both in judicial and in academic discourse. In dealing with economic exclusion (Article 15[2]), social boycotts and religious excommunication (Article 17), and workplace exploitation (Article 23), these judgements recognize that liberty and equality are threatened not only by concentrated State power but also by 'private' orderings (including religion and 'custom') that nonetheless have the potential to dominate individuals and block their access to the basic goods that are necessary to sustain a dignified life. This has been especially true in Indian history, where social and economic sanctions have often operated with far greater force than the coercive power of the State. The principle of 'fraternity' commits the Constitution and the courts to overcoming these 'spheres of personal subordination'.[94]

The last set of cases takes us back to the relationship between the individual and the State, and the Constitution's 'liberty code' (Articles 19 to 22). These judgements interrogate the State's role in *upholding* oppressive structures (in this case, family structures) that threaten individual freedom and the right to privacy. They examine the extent to which core civil liberties can be subordinated to claims of the 'public welfare' (especially in cases of an 'Emergency'). And lastly, they look at how—by guaranteeing a right against self-incrimination—the Constitution stands between an individual accused of a crime, and the State in its most violent avatar: that of an interrogator and enforcer of laws. Together, these judgements indicate how the purpose of the Constitution is to transform a culture of authority under the colonial regime into a culture of justification in a free, open, and democratic society.

And as we have seen, liberty, equality, and fraternity are not hermetically sealed off from each other. So, while these judgements are each worth studying individually, their transformative potential only shines through when we read them together: as integral elements of the three pillars of the constitutional trinity, mutually reinforcing and creating the necessary foundation for a free and egalitarian democratic politics.

V. Emotion Recollected in Tranquillity: The Interpretive Approach

What interpretive theory underlies this vision of the transformative Constitution? The contemporary, dominant approach to constitutional interpretation is that of the 'living tree':[95] the Constitution is treated as an evolving document, with judges bearing the responsibility of 'updating' it so that it keeps pace with changing times. The living-tree approach is invoked to justify the expansion of Article 21, as well as the expansion of judicial power beyond what was contemplated by the framers[96] (or is permitted by the text). However, without an explanation of the basis for evolution, and the direction in which the Constitution is meant to evolve,[97] living-tree constitutionalism remains little more than an incantation, and a vehicle for judicial ideologies to masquerade as constitutional evolution. With a few exceptions,[98] the Supreme Court is yet to provide us with a conceptual grounding for its evolutionary approach.

By contrast, the intellectual opponent of living-tree constitutionalism, i.e., constitutional originalism, is discredited in India. Any reference to it draws derisive and fearful comments about a 'return to the *Gopalan* era'[99]—the Supreme Court's early, text-bound days. Trapped between the historical unacceptability of originalism and the boundless manipulability of the living tree, constitutional interpretation seems to be at an impasse.[100]

Transformative constitutionalism takes seriously the text of the Constitution, its structure, and the historical moment of its framing. In order to glean the meaning of the Constitution's provisions, it examines the discussions of the Drafting Committee, where these provisions were first proposed and given shape, and then the Constituent Assembly Debates, where they passed through the furnace of fierce opposition before being moulded into their final form. While conceding that this is by no means a definitive enquiry, transformative constitutionalism rules out interpretations that simply cannot be reconciled with a historically informed reading of the constitutional text.[101] For instance, it rules out the judicial pyrotechnics that rewrote Article 21 in *Maneka Gandhi v. Union of India*—the jewel in the crown of living-tree constitutionalism. In that sense, transformative constitutionalism shares some of the commitments of originalism.

Unlike the prominent variants of originalism, however, transformative constitutionalism is not *frozen* at the moment of framing. While taking text, structure, and history as crucial building blocks of constitutional meaning, it does not accord an overriding veto power to any of them. It does not bind itself to a mythical 'original intent'[102] of the framers, and nor does it tie itself to the 'original meaning' that the words used by the Constitution carried in 1950. Transformative constitutionalism recognizes that the framers were building a Constitution meant to last for generations. They were careful and conscious about the words they chose, and the words they chose (for the most part) expressed *principles* that would endure, not concrete commitments that would soon lose their salience and become antiquated in a rapidly changing world.[103] Transformative constitutionalism's task is to identify and express these founding principles that constitute the framework within which constitutional interpretation is to be carried on.[104]

How are these principles to be identifed? It is here that transformative constitutionalism decisively parts company with both constitutional originalism and living-tree constitutionalism by embracing a more ecumenical interpretive canon, as discussed above. Transformative constitutionalism takes seriously Kannabiran's insight that:

> … a constitution framed after a liberation struggle or a struggle for independence is like poetry, emotion recollected in tranquillity … there cannot be, there should not be two social histories, one for political theorizing and another for legal theorizing … the people who met in the Constituent Assembly were not mere technicians who had gathered there to prepare a handbook for running the government. They had participated in the struggles and, short of holding elections, every effort had been made to give their gathering a representative character.[105]

To give expression to this 'emotion recollected in tranquillity', transformative constitutionalism examines the historical roots of the Fundamental Rights chapter in the liberation struggles: not just the dominant *nationalist* avatar of the freedom movement, but the plurality of liberation struggles that preceded the drafting of the Constitution, in the course of which Indians gave shape to their aspirations in the language of liberty, equality, and fraternity. For transformative constitutionalism, the Congress party's 1931 Karachi Bill of Rights is as important as Rukhmabai's letters to the *Times of India* in 1885, arguing for marital equality within the family; and Jyotirao Phule's *Gulamgiri* is as relevant as the work of the Sub-Committee that drafted the Fundamental Rights chapter. Ultimately, it is a combination of all of these—text, structure, drafting history, and broader social and political history, including non-dominant dissenting strands of that history—that locates the constitutional document within its complete context and yields constitutional meaning. The task of this book, through the nine judgements that it examines, is to demonstrate how this approach to constitutional interpretation might work in practice.

But to this interpretive approach, two objections may be raised. First, that colonial India had no vocabulary of 'rights' (whatever existed was merely derivative of Western conceptions). Therefore, any history-driven approach is anachronistic. This popular objection, which treats the concept of rights as a Western import that is somehow alien to India, is deeply misguided. To start with, it ignores language. As Anderson and Guha point out, the existence of words such as '*insaf* [justice], *hak* [right], *nyaya* [justice], and *adhikara* [right]' should give pause before lazily subscribing to colonial scholarship (and its postcolonial variants) that holds that 'South Asian "societies base their social structure on duties and obligations rather than on rights"'.[106]

It also ignores the thriving discourse on rights that existed in colonial India, both within the formal channels of the nationalist movement[107] and beyond.[108] This included the domain of culture (such as the mediaeval *Bhakti* movement, which was translated by nineteenth-century reformers into the modern idiom of 'equality' and 'justice'[109]). As this book will demonstrate, whatever the (Western) origins of the discourse of rights in colonial India, it arose out of the specific circumstances of the subcontinent,[110] and assumed a shape that was far more than merely derivative. Whether it was Jyotirao

Phule's critiques of caste by using the vocabulary of slavery and freedom, Tarabai Shinde's critique of gender relations in the language of equality, the Ad-Dharmi Movement's 'communal egalitarianism', B.R. Ambedkar's framing of his anti-boycott movement in terms of access to the public sphere, Gandhi's uncompromising advocacy of the freedom of speech, and many more—Indians excavated the concept of rights, framed it to respond to the circumstances of the time, and made it their own.[111]

The second objection is that transformative constitutionalism takes a historical approach without undergoing the full rigours of the historical method. To an extent, this peril exists with any approach to legal and constitutional interpretation. The nature of the legal enterprise requires the interpreter to draw conclusions from history and, to a lesser extent, from political philosophy, sociology, and other disciplines. This remains a fraught enterprise. As Alessandro Portelli observed, while discussing Italian terror trials of the 1970s:

> … the magistrates were thus involved in reconstructing the past, redefining its meaning, and attempting an overall interpretation. These are historical tasks, and it is appropriate to examine the way they were performed from the point of view of the theory and method of history …[112]

The criticism is well taken, and, as will be clarified in the next section, transformative constitutionalism makes no claim to superior truth, whether legal or historical. It is also important to point out, however, that the form of interpretation is constitutional, not historical. Transformative constitutionalism does not seek to engage in a purely historical enquiry. Rather, it takes the constitutional text and the principles embedded in it as its starting point, and attempts to place them in their extended *historical context* in order to understand their meaning. This form of 'contextual interpretation' is the staple feature of numerous constitutional courts (such as those of Canada and South Africa). While it must, of necessity, remain *sensitive* to historiography and the historical method, it need not be judged on precisely the same yardstick that we would judge a claim that is made *within* the discipline of history.[113]

VI. The Contrapuntal Canon

Finally, to reiterate, this vision of the transformative Constitution does not make any claims to universal truth. It does not set itself up as *the* correct interpretation of the Constitution, or necessarily even as a superior interpretation of the Constitution. That would be a perilous claim, given the polyphony of the Constituent Assembly, the sheer diversity of its voices, as well as the silences and absences (of the Muslim League, the Socialist Party, and Gandhi, to name just three) that surrounded the Constitution-making process.[114] Besides, grand narratives have a tendency towards becoming totalitarian.[115] Any historically grounded interpretation must therefore acknowledge its own potential to exclude and marginalize voices from the past, and commit to remaining both open-ended and subject to revision. Otherwise, it risks stifling the very Constitution that it intends to liberate.[116] So, my aims are more modest: I seek only to advance one reading of the Constitution that, when viewed in light of its text and context, is compelling on its own terms.[117]

Indeed, any attempted task of imposing a single truth upon the Constitution would be a futile one. As Robert Cover pointed out in a famous essay, 'no set of legal institutions or prescriptions exists apart from the narratives that locate it and give it meaning'.[118] And narratives are never singular. Through the course of his essay, Cover explored the proliferation of legal meanings and narratives through a range of examples taken from US history. For instance, in the mid-nineteenth century, the 'radical constitutionalists' challenged the US Supreme Court's interpretation of the relationship between slavery and the constitution. They advanced an insurgent, alternative reading of the constitution that used the constitutional structure and a broader interpretive canon (including the Declaration of Independence) to argue that slavery was not just a moral wrong, but that it was *unconstitutional*.[119] There is thus an inevitable plurality of 'meanings' that circulates around the constitutional text, as well as a plurality of 'narratives' within which the text comes to be located. Legal and moral tensions arise when dominant meanings and narratives, as selected by courts, are challenged by dissident individuals and communities who build alternative systems of meaning.

But, in this book, that dissent comes from *within* the courtroom. The nine judgements are not part of the traditional 'constitutional canon', as taught in law schools or found in popular writing—the canon that is defined by *Kesavananda Bharati*, *Maneka Gandhi*, *Minerva Mills*, *Vishaka*, and so on. Instead, they include high court judgements that were reversed by the Supreme Court, dissenting opinions, and Supreme Court judgements that remain good law but are rarely relied upon or even cited by the contemporary Court. This is a contrapuntal canon.

I borrow the term contrapuntal from Edward Said, who counselled us to read any textual tradition 'with an effort to draw out, extend, give emphasis and voice to what is silent or marginally present'.[120] From the detritus of the Indian constitutional canon—the dissenting opinions, the overruled high court judgements, and the ignored or marginalized Supreme Court decisions—there shines forth the vision of the transformative Constitution, and the trinity of liberty, equality, and fraternity. By reading our constitutional history against the grain,[121] it is a vision that is open to us to retrieve and reclaim.[122] That is the task of this book.

Part One
Equality

Article 14

The State shall not deny to any person equality before the law or the equal protection of the laws within the territory of India.

Article 15

(1) The State shall not discriminate against any citizen on grounds only of religion, race, caste, sex, place of birth or any of them.

...

(3) Nothing in this article shall prevent the State from making any special provision for women and children.

(4) Nothing in this article or in clause (2) of Article 29 shall prevent the State from making any special provision for the advancement of any socially and educationally backward classes of citizens or for the Scheduled Castes and the Scheduled Tribes.

Article 16

(1) There shall be equality of opportunity for all citizens in matters relating to employment or appointment to any office under the State.

...

(4) Nothing in this article shall prevent the State from making any provision for the reservation of appointments or posts in favour of any backward class of citizens which, in the opinion of the State, is not adequately represented in the services under the State.

1

Sex Discrimination: *Anuj Garg* and the Anti-Stereotyping Principle

NO EYEBROWS WERE RAISED when, in 1914, the colonial government enacted the Punjab Excise Act—a dry-as-dust, eighty-section legislation regulating the transport and sale of liquor in Delhi. Tucked away unobtrusively in the middle of the Act was Section 30, part of a bouquet of prohibitions and penalties:

> No person who is licensed to sell any liquor or intoxicating drug for consumption … shall … employ or permit to be employed … any man under the age of 25 years or any women in any part of such premises in which such liquor or intoxicating drug is consumed by the public.[1]

It took eight decades before an eyebrow was finally raised. The constitutionality of Section 30 was challenged in 1999. The Delhi High Court held that it was discriminatory against women and struck it down. In 2008, the case proceeded to the Supreme Court (*Anuj Garg v. Hotel Association of India*).[2] The Government of Delhi contended that the law had been framed to protect women from the hazards of employment in the liquor industry. A bemused Supreme Court did not need too many words to reject this argument, noting in conclusion that the law resulted in 'invidious discrimination perpetuating sexual differences'.[3]

Striking down a law excluding women from an entire industry may seem easy.[4] *Anuj Garg*, however, was more than just that. It was the first time that the Supreme Court seriously engaged with the meaning of the constitutional imperative contained in Article 15(1): 'The State shall not discriminate against any citizen on grounds only of religion, race, caste, sex, place of birth or any of them.' In doing so, I will argue, it initiated a jurisprudence whose impact extended far beyond the Punjab Excise Act, and which could become the foundation for a transformative constitutional vision of gender equality.[5]

I begin by excavating the sparse text of Article 15(1) of the Constitution (I) and then examine the history of Indian sex discrimination jurisprudence in the six decades leading up to *Anuj Garg* (II). This history can broadly be divided into two intellectual traditions. The first is a 'formal reading', which justifies differential treatment of men and women on the basis of presumed 'natural differences' between the sexes. It also holds that discrimination results only from conscious, hostile intentions of lawmakers. Set against this approach is the 'transformative reading', which rejects the notion of 'natural differences'. It understands discrimination as a product of social, economic, and cultural structures and institutions that create 'patterns of ... exclusion'.[6] The judgement in *Anuj Garg* is the culmination of this second tradition.

Then, in (III), I trace the roots of gendered stereotypes to a social and political consensus that divided the colonial Indian society into two 'separate spheres': a public sphere to be occupied by men, and a private sphere—representing the 'community'—that was the domain of women. I argue that this idea of separate spheres was challenged by the political movement for women's right to vote, a movement whose vision triumphed with the framing of the Constitution (IV). Consequently, *Anuj Garg* was correct in rejecting the conception of 'natural differences'. I conclude by discussing the transformative potential of the reasoning in *Anuj Garg* for sex discrimination jurisprudence in the years to come (V).

I. 'Shall not discriminate … on grounds only of … sex …'

Let us tentatively define 'discrimination' as an unequal and unjustifiable distribution of benefits and burdens between people or groups of people.[7] Immediately, however, we run into problems. For example, racial segregation in the West was defended for many years on the faulty basis that the facilities offered to whites and blacks were 'separate but equal'. Closer home, we can imagine that if the State were to provide public facilities (for example, separate public toilets) based on caste, it would be presumptively unconstitutional. On the other hand, separate toilets for men and women do not appear to raise any constitutional concerns.[8] It, therefore, seems that in some cases, the mere *act* of classification creates constitutional problems, while in other cases this is not so.[9]

Further, notice that the act of classification precedes differential allocation of benefits and burdens. Therefore, the problem is not material but expressive in at least some cases. Whatever the actual distribution of tangible or material benefits, certain kinds of classifications by their very nature communicate a *social message* of separation and segregation. This is inextricably connected with superiority and inferiority, exalting certain groups and demeaning others. When we consider sex discrimination under Article 15(1), therefore, the first question that we must ask ourselves is whether all sex-based classifications are at least presumptively discriminatory (they might still ultimately be constitutional if the State can justify them), or whether something more than mere classification is needed to make out a claim of discrimination.[10]

The word 'grounds' is equally slippery. On one reading, 'grounds' might refer to someone's subjective reasons for holding a set of beliefs, or acting in a certain way. For example, consider the question, 'What are the grounds upon which you acted?' which roughly translates to 'Why did you act in this way?' On this reading, under Article 15(1), the phrase 'on grounds only of … sex' *qualifies* the phrase 'The State shall not …' and translates into the following injunction: the grounds of sex, race, caste, etc. cannot be what *motivates* the State to discriminate against anyone.

The word 'grounds', however, need not only translate into 'reasons for'. It could also be understood to refer to the personal attributes of sex, caste, race, religion, and place of origin set out in the latter part of Article 15(1). On this reading, Article 15(1) does not ask us to locate the root of discrimination in the reason or motivation for State action, but asks us to focus on how an act of discrimination, in its effects, might involve one of the grounds listed under Article 15(1). For example, a hypothetical law that requires people to relinquish their employment on pregnancy might be motivated by reasons of efficiency, and would thus not be discriminatory in the first sense of the word 'grounds'. But it is also part of a broader institutional structure of workplace norms that disadvantage women from achieving parity with men. Therefore, it can be argued to be discriminatory in the second sense of the word 'grounds'.[11] As the Canadian Supreme Court put the point, the distinction between the two approaches is a distinction between locating discrimination in the 'moral blameworthiness' of individual actors and their actions (in this case, the State) on the one hand, and on the other locating it in 'policies and practices' whose effect is discriminatory 'even if that effect is unintended and unforeseen'.[12]

This dual understanding of the word 'grounds' acquires particular salience when read alongside two words that follow: 'only' and 'sex'. Does the placement of the word 'only' after 'grounds' allow the State to get away with discriminatory action if it can demonstrate the existence of grounds additional to sex?[13] And does 'sex' itself refer only to the observable, physical distinctions between men and women, or does it also include social norms and assumptions that are often superimposed upon physical difference, and which make that physical difference *salient*?[14] For example, the fact that women can become pregnant and men cannot is a physical difference. However, that difference acquires salience only in the context of workplace regulations which, by default, require a certain number of days of attendance in the year, and therefore disadvantage pregnancies.[15]

Lastly, Article 15(1) cannot be separated from Article 15(3):

> Nothing in this article shall prevent the State from making any special provision for women and children.[16]

Textually, Article 15(3) is framed as an exception to Article 15(1), saving State action that would otherwise have violated the non-discrimination clause, as long as it is a 'special provision for women …'[17] However, does the phrase 'special provision' provide a carte blanche to the State? That seems unlikely because, structurally, Article 15(3) is nested not only within Article 15 (that deals with discrimination), but within the broader Equality Code of the Constitution (Articles 14 to 18).[18] Its purpose seems to be obvious: to allow the State to make laws removing existing social or cultural barriers that prevent women from achieving genuine equality with men in various fields.[19] Consequently, to fall within Article 15(3), State action would need to bear some relation to the above goal. What that leaves open, however, is the nature and degree to which the State might be called upon to demonstrate that relation.[20]

II. Article 15(1): The Courts and the Constitution

A. The Formalist Approach

Soon after the Constitution came into force, the High Court of Calcutta was asked to decide the scope of the sex discrimination clause. Order XXV, Rule 1 of the Code of Civil Procedure (1908) outlined the conditions under which plaintiffs in a legal proceeding could be required to furnish a security to the court. This was to guard against the eventuality that they lost the case, were ordered to pay the costs of litigation to the other party, and were unable to do so. Security could be taken from male plaintiffs in case they were residing outside India and did not possess sufficient immovable property in India. From female plaintiffs, on the other hand, security could be taken merely if they did not possess sufficient immovable property, regardless of where they were living.

In *Mahadeb Jiew v. B.B. Sen*,[21] the High Court of Calcutta rejected a challenge to this provision, holding that the discrimination wrought by the provision was not on grounds of sex alone, but of sex *and* property.[22] So, even though Order XXV, Rule 1 treated men and women who were otherwise in an identical position (non-propertied and resident in India) differently, the Court held that Article 15 barred only *'discriminations on the grounds of sex alone and on no other grounds'*.[23]

In *Mahadeb Jiew*, the Calcutta High Court did three things. First, it read the word 'only' in Article 15(1) to mean 'that and no other'. Legislation would be held not to violate Article 15(1) as long as the State could demonstrate that its discriminatory classification took into account at least one feature other than those listed under Article 15(1).[24] Second, it did not examine the legislation's effect (which was to place a burden upon non-propertied resident women but not their male counterparts), but limited itself to examining the formal basis of the legislative classification (sex + property). And third, the Court made no attempt to undertake a deeper examination into the foundations of the impugned legislation. *Why* was it the case that resident, non-propertied female plaintiffs could be required to pay security for costs, but resident, non-propertied male plaintiffs could not? The answer is clear: the law rested on assumptions or stereotypes about women's financial acumen (or lack thereof), and their (in)ability to earn and pay on demand. A formal reading of Order XXV, Rule 1 that stopped at noting that the legislative classification was drawn along sex and property simply ignored the fact that 'sex' and 'property' were not analytically distinct and separate categories.

Rather, 'sex' and 'property' together advanced a legislative vision (and a legislative result) that relegated the financial capacities of women to a lesser sphere than those of men, with no other justification than the fact that they were women.

The logic of the Calcutta High Court was taken one step forward by the High Court of Punjab and Haryana in *R.S. Singh v. State of Punjab*,[25] a case challenging the governor's order disqualifying women from being appointed to any post in a men's jail (apart from clerk or matron). Rejecting a claim brought to it by a woman who had been refused appointment as the superintendent of a men's jail, the Court held that sex, along with 'other factors', could be a legitimate basis of legislative classification. These factors included:

> patent physical disparities ... [differences] in the structure of body, in the functions to be performed by each, in the amount of physical strength ... [in] the influence of vigorous health upon the future well-being of the race .... [in] *the self-reliance which enables one to assert full rights, and in the capacity to maintain the struggle for subsistence.*[26]

Further, women's 'physical structure and the performance of maternal functions' were two 'conditions' cited that placed them at a 'disadvantage in the struggle for subsistence.' The Court held that as long as legislation was founded upon these 'natural differences' between the sexes, even if it drew a clear line privileging men over women, it could be justified. It then upheld the challenged order because 'it needs no great imagination to visualize the awkward and even the hazardous position of a woman acting as a warder or other jail official who has to personally ensure and maintain discipline over habitual male criminals'.[27] Here, the 'natural differences' that the Court outlined in the paragraph above were transformed into salient differences in the context of prison hiring. Presumably because of the disparities in physical strength, self-reliance, and so on, the State could legitimately discriminate against women in contexts where such disparities were relevant considerations.

Read together, *B.B. Sen* and *R.S. Singh* advance what Ratna Kapur calls the 'formalist reading' of Article 15(1).[28] Broadly, the formalist reading consists of three prongs. First, State-sanctioned differential treatment between men and women does not amount to 'discrimination' if it is based on 'natural differences' between men and women. These natural differences are presumed to exist between all men and all women (or at least between enough men and enough women that the blunt instrument of law can assume them to be universal when it makes classifications). Second, the word 'grounds' is to be read as referring predominantly to the form of the legislative classification under challenge (e.g., sex + property), and not its impact. And third, the phrase 'only ... of sex' in Article 15(1) is to be read to mean 'sex alone, and nothing else'.[29]

The formalist reading culminated in the three-judge bench decision of the Supreme Court in *Air India v. Nargesh Meerza*,[30] decided in 1982. *Nargesh Meerza* involved a constitutional challenge to Regulations 46 and 47 of the Air India Employees' Service Regulations. These regulations created significant disparity between the pay and promotional avenues of male in-flight cabin crew (Air Flight Pursers or AFPs) and their female counterparts (Air Hostesses or AHs). For example, while the retirement age for AFPs was fifty-eight years, AHs were compelled to retire at the age of thirty-five years, *or* on marriage (if they married within four years of joining the service), *or* on their first pregnancy, whichever occurred first. After many lengthy and complex rounds of litigation before different forums, the Supreme Court finally upheld the Regulations in part, modified them in part, and struck them down in part. The Supreme Court's judgement involved some problematic reading of service law jurisprudence, but more importantly the Court endorsed the *Sen-Singh* line of reasoning. It upheld the Regulations because the disparities were based 'on the grounds of sex coupled with other considerations'.[31] The marriage regulation, for instance, was upheld because:

> … the Regulation permits an AH to marry at the age of 23 if she has joined the service at the age of 19 which is by all standards a very sound and salutary provision. Apart from improving the health of the employee, it helps a good deal in the promotion and boosting up of our family planning programme. Secondly, if a woman marries near about the age of 20 to 23 years, she becomes fully mature and there is every chance of such a marriage proving a success, all things being equal. Thirdly … if the bar of marriage within four years of service is removed then the Corporation will have to incur huge expenditure in recruiting additional AHs either on a temporary or on ad-hoc basis to replace the working AHs if they conceive …[32]

Later in the judgement, while the Court refused to accept compulsory retirement on first pregnancy, as a 'reasonable compromise' it endorsed a proposal by Air India to amend the Regulation and replace 'first pregnancy' with 'third pregnancy', along with a series of requirements such as unpaid pregnancy leave and regular physical check-ups. This, the Court observed, was reasonable because:

> [it] would be in the larger interest of the health of the AH concerned as also for the good upbringing of the children. Secondly … when the entire world is faced with the problem of population explosion it will not only be desirable but absolutely essential for every country to see that the family planning programme is not only whipped up but maintained at sufficient levels so as to meet the danger of overpopulation …[33]

Read together, these two paragraphs constitute the foundation of the stereotype approach to sex discrimination, which, in turn, is based on a social vision known as the 'separate-spheres theory'. Broadly, the separate-spheres theory holds that because of certain natural differences between the sexes, while the public sphere is the appropriate arena of action for men, the private sphere—the home, the family, and domestic life—is the appropriate arena for women. In *Nargeesh Meerza*, the separate-spheres theory formed the backbone of the Court's sex discrimination analysis: differential treatment between men and women was held not to be discriminatory, and was justified by invoking 'family planning', 'successful marriage', 'upbringing of children', and 'control of population explosion', *each of which was deemed to be the specific responsibility of women.*[34] Hence, the structure of the Regulations, aimed at achieving this by disincentivizing women from early marriage and too many pregnancies, was held to be constitutional.[35] *Nargeesh Meerza* represents, therefore, the apogee of the formalist approach to Article 15(1), combining all the elements that we have discussed above.[36]

Furthermore, this reading of Article 15(1) has also spilt over into the interpretation of Article 15(3). In *Yusuf Abdul Aziz v. State of Bombay*,[37] the constitutional validity of Section 497 of the Indian Penal Code was challenged. Under Section 497, in an extramarital affair, *only* the man could be held guilty of the offence of adultery. When this section was challenged as being discriminatory *against* men, the Supreme Court upheld it in a very short judgement, holding that since Article 15(3) authorized the State to make 'any special provisions for women',[38] a criminal provision exempting women from liability for precisely the same act that a man could be punished for was nonetheless constitutional. However, this surely cannot be right: if Article 15(3) is to be read as providing a carte blanche to the State in this fashion, then the prohibition upon 'sex discrimination' under Article 15(1) becomes redundant (the provision might as well have read,'The State shall not accord favourable treatment to men'). More importantly, however, what the Supreme Court failed to analyse was that Section 497—while ostensibly for the benefit of women—was nonetheless based upon gendered stereotypes: in this case, the stereotype that, when it comes to sexual relations, women are passive and devoid of agency, always the seduced, and never the seducers.[39] In fact, three decades later, in another challenge to the adultery provisions, the Court articulated the stereotype and accepted it as a legitimate basis for the law: 'it is commonly accepted that it is the man who is the seducer and not the woman'.[40] *Yusuf Abdul Aziz*, therefore, highlighted the important insight that Articles 15(1) and 15(3) cannot be separated. Our approach to understanding what constitutes 'discrimination on grounds only of sex' will also structure our approach towards what 'special provisions' the State can make, ostensibly for the benefit of women.

B. The Transformative Reading

In 1954, just three years after the judgement in *B.B. Sen*, the High Court of Allahabad was faced with a similar situation. The Uttar Pradesh Courts of Wards Act allowed the local government to declare that persons suffering from certain specific conditions, such as physical or mental 'defects', conviction for non-bailable offences, failure to discharge debts, and so on, were 'incapable of managing their property'. The Act also, however, allowed the Government to declare any woman incapable of managing her property, whether or not any of the above conditions existed. In *Rani Raj Rajeshwari Devi v. State of UP*,[41] the Act was defended on the basis that, as in *B.B. Sen*, the legislative classification was not drawn solely along the lines of sex, but along the lines of sex and property. And like *Yusuf Abdul Aziz* (which was decided the same year), it was argued that the provision was a 'benign' one, designed to protect women from unscrupulous predators of their property ('... women generally are not such competent managers of property as men and are much more liable to be led astray ...'[42]).

The Allahabad High Court, however, was having none of it. It swiftly held that whatever the manner in which the legislative classification had been drawn, the fact remained that it treated (otherwise) identically placed men and women differently. In other words, if the legislation's *effect* was to treat men and women differently, its *form* (i.e., the precise character of the classification) or *reason* was irrelevant. Equally brusque was the Court's rejection of the Government's plea that because women were more liable to be led astray, they could be treated as 'a class by themselves' for the purpose of drawing legislative distinctions:

> ... evasion of the Constitution can[not] be permitted merely by calling an act classification and not discrimination ... A classification which the Constitution forbids cannot possibly be said to be reasonable.[43]

This observation is crucial. The Allahabad High Court effectively rejected the argument that legislative differentiation founded upon 'natural differences' was not discrimination but only 'classification'. On the contrary, in the teeth of Article 15(1), it was not open to the State to treat men and women as separate 'classes' by themselves by attributing certain stereotypical or generalized characteristics to all men or all women (competent management of property, physical weakness, maternal functions, etc.)

The Allahabad High Court's analysis was followed by the High Court of Orissa in 1969. The Orissa Civil Service Rules allowed the state government to disqualify married women from employment if the 'efficiency of the service' required it.[44] Men were placed under no similar disqualification. The justification for this was provided in the Indian Administrative Rules, which stated that 'marriage brings about certain disabilities and obligations which may affect the efficiency or suitability for employment'.[45] Once again, the State defended its law by arguing that the legislative classification was not based 'only' on grounds of sex, but that it had a 'reasonable nexus in relation to ... the maintenance of the efficiency of the service'.[46] The role played by 'sex plus physical weakness' in R.S. Singh and 'sex plus obligations of motherhood' in *Nargesh Meerza* was now played by 'sex plus efficiency'. The Orissa High Court was as swift in rejecting this line of reasoning as the Allahabad High Court had been, observing that:

> ... marriage does not operate as a disqualification for appointment ... in the case of men, whereas in the case of married women,

> by Rule 6(2), they are being excluded from appointment. Such a disqualification being thus based on sex is unconstitutional.[47]

Both the Allahabad and the Orissa High Courts intuitively grasped that what was being defended as 'sex plus another ground' was little more than stereotype-based justification of laws that discriminated against women. However, neither of those cases examined the stereotypes in any detail. A move towards this was first made by the Delhi High Court, in a case where the claim of sex discrimination was brought by a man. In *Walter Alfred Baid v. Union of India*,[48] Lady Irwin Hospital's Recruitment Rules permitted only women to be appointed as senior nursing tutors. Striking this down, the High Court held that:

> … it is difficult to accept the position that a discrimination based on sex is nevertheless not a discrimination based on sex 'alone' because it is based on 'other considerations' even though these other considerations have their genesis in the sex itself … while it is true that there are patent physical disparities between the two sexes, yet it is not possible to justify a conclusion … that all women or all men, as the case may be, would be unfit … for a particular class of work.[49]

Taking one step further along the road, the Delhi High Court correctly identified the fact that the State's 'sex plus' justification meant nothing more than assumptions about what sex entailed. The Court made it clear that existing physical differences between men and women could not be made legislatively salient in this manner. In other words, the State could not take differences between men and women that existed in some, or even most cases, and frame laws as if that difference was what *defined* the sexes. To put it another way: while in the *Sen-Singh* line of cases, the Courts had (implicitly) held that the word 'sex' under Article 15(1) carried with it an entire constellation of physical and social characteristics that attached themselves to the sexes, the Delhi High Court rejected any reading of 'sex' that went beyond the biological.

This emerging jurisprudence was consolidated by the Kerala High Court soon afterwards. In *A.N. Rajamma v. State of Kerala*,[50] women were denied appointment in the Last Grade Service by invoking 'the arduous and special nature'[51] of the duties (including late office hours and touring). Invalidating the disqualification on the basis that what mattered was the *effect* of the law, here, for the first time, a court explicitly identified what had been at play in the *Sen-Singh* line of cases and, drawing from American jurisprudence, gave it a name—'romantic paternalism':

> [Under romantic paternalism] the social thinking and the approach to the question of the role women had to play in society was … tradition bound.[52]

As opposed to the formalist approach to Article 15(1) and sex equality, I characterize this as the transformative approach. The hallmarks of the transformative approach are: first, that it focuses not on the particular manner in which the legislative classification is drawn (its object or its form), but upon its impact, or effects, upon men and women (or sub-classes of men and women); second, it rejects any State justification that relies upon the trope of 'natural differences' between the genders;[53] and third, as a corollary, it no longer allows the word 'only' to be used to limit the scope of Article 15(1) by granting safe harbour to laws that have not formally disadvantaged women, or have done so on the presumption of natural differences. And it was in *Anuj Garg v. Hotel Association* that this second judicial tradition found its culmination.[54]

Recall that in *Anuj Garg*, the State justified the ban on women's employment in the liquor industry on the basis that it was a benign legislation (perhaps even a 'special provision' under Article 15[3]) for their own security. Rejecting this argument and observing that the burden of providing adequate security lay upon the State (and not upon women), the Court went on to note:

> The impugned legislation suffers from incurable fixations of stereotype morality and conception of sexual role. The perspective thus arrived at is outmoded in content and stifling in means.[55]

In this way, the Court rejected the stereotype-based justification that would have upheld the law as either a non-discriminatory benign classification, or saved by Article 15(3). But in any event, the State's reasoning could not be accepted, because:

> Legislation should not be only assessed on its proposed aims but rather on the implications and the effects … No law in its ultimate effect should end up perpetuating the oppression of women.[56]

I want to focus closely on this, because both parts of the Court's formulation are important. In the first sentence, the Court affirmed the effects-oriented test (as opposed to the formal, classification-based test) of discrimination under Article 15(1). But 'effects' upon what? In the second sentence, the Court answered this question by highlighting that it would scrutinize whether laws perpetuated the oppression of women. In other words, the Court endorsed a view of discrimination that understood it as something both ongoing (perpetuation) and institutional (oppression).

A significant consequence of adopting an institutional, effects-based view of discrimination is the impact of the role of the word 'only' in Article 15(1). Recall that previous judgements had invoked the word 'only' to deny discrimination claims in two contexts: first, where the State invoked reasons other than sex to justify a straightforward discriminatory classification that impacted women; and second, where the classification itself was drawn along the lines of 'grounds' other than sex, and therefore did not result in burdening only and all women, but only some women in an indirect manner. A straightforward example is pregnancy; but consider also, for example, a law that set educational barriers for contesting elections in a society where women are disproportionately denied access to education.[57]

A simple effects test, with nothing more, would be able to deal with the first kind of claim, because the reasons for State action would now drop out of the picture. However, only an institutional view of discrimination could deal with the second kind of claim, where legislative classification did not single out 'women' *qua* women for unfavourable treatment, but nonetheless, in a broader institutional context, contributed to 'perpetuating the oppression of women'.[58] This is particularly important because, in modern times, it will be rare to find the State *expressly* invoking stereotypes to justify discriminatory laws. What will be far more common, as we shall see, is that legislative form, which will appear to be worded neutrally, will nonetheless be *founded* on stereotypical assumptions that have disadvantaged women and continue to do so at a structural and institutional level. The importance of *Anuj Garg* was to decisively shift the enquiry from the former to the latter.

Anuj Garg, therefore, brought together the two disparate strands of the transformative approach to Article 15(1) that had been present to varying and scattered degrees in previous decisions. Under Article 15(1), legislation would have to be tested on the basis of its systematic and institutional effects, and not on the basis of the goals or aims that the State sought to invoke; and secondly, in no circumstances could discriminatory legislation be justified by resorting to stereotypes about the roles, abilities, or capacities of the sexes. These two strands, when brought together, yielded a powerful jurisprudence of sex equality, which not only adopted the perspective of those whose actions, identities, and lives were actually impacted by the law, but also ruled the entire justificatory logic of 'natural differences' constitutionally invalid.

To understand what is at stake, let us briefly return to our discussion in Section I. The disagreement between the formal and the transformative approaches, it should now be clear, is a disagreement over the meanings of the four words at the heart of Article 15(1):

'grounds', 'discriminate', 'only', and 'sex'. The formal approach reads 'grounds' to mean the bases, or objects, of legislation, and equates it with the manner in which the legislature has gone about drawing the line of classification along which benefits or burdens are distributed. The transformative approach, on the other hand, understands 'grounds' to refer to the five indices of discrimination set out under Article 15(1), and consequently assesses legislation for its impact, or effect, upon those indices (in our case, the index of sex).

Secondly, the formal approach holds that if legislation tracks supposed or assumed 'natural differences' between men and women, then it isn't discriminatory at all, but merely a 'reasonable classification'. The transformative approach, on the other hand, holds that basing legislation on assumed 'natural differences' is precisely *what it means* to discriminate. In framing a guarantee against discrimination, the Constitution was ruling out the use of 'natural differences' as a factor in classification groups of individuals for the allocation of differential benefits and burdens.

Thirdly, the formal approach holds that the word 'only' in Article 15(1) exempts State action that can be justified by reasons other than sex, or legislative classifications that are not directly and frontally drawn along the lines of sex. On the other hand, the transformative reading, which focuses on discrimination as involving institutional patterns, does not accord any such limiting role to the word 'only'.

And lastly, as a corollary, the formalist approach is wedded to an understanding of sex that attaches a whole range of physical, mental, and emotional attributes to men and women as a class. This is why, if an unequal law is based on these attributes, the formalist approach treats it not as (impermissible) discrimination but as (valid) classification. And it is this understanding of sex that the transformative approach rejects. Importantly, the transformative approach is not committed to denying the existence of differences between men and women. What it is committed to is rejecting the manner in which these differences are often given legal *salience*, as the bases of laws that permit or sanction discrimination.

In their approach to sex equality and discrimination, these two approaches are polar opposites of each other. Which of them is correct? The bare-bones language of Article 15(1) gives us no answers. We must therefore turn to constitutional structure and constitutional history.

III. Separate Spheres

The division of the world into gendered public and private spheres was a staple feature of the subcontinent's social and political thought from the second half of the nineteenth century. It was influenced by a combination of Enlightenment and Victorian morality on the one hand[59] and appeals to an authentic 'Indian tradition' on the other.[60] For instance, in his examination of the 'woman question', as framed and taken up by the Indian nationalist movement, Partha Chatterjee identifies the division of social space into:

> ... *ghar* and *bahir*, the home and the world. The world is external, the domain of the material: the home represents one's inner spiritual self, one's true identity. The world ... is also typically the domain of the male. The home in its essence must remain unaffected by the profane activities of the material world—and woman is its representation.[61]

This was both a physical division of space (the 'home' and the 'outside') and a division of functions. While the outside was the realm of politics and economics, the domestic space was characterized by 'enlightened childcare, cookery, accounts, and family education'. And furthermore, the relationship between the two was hierarchical, because 'the male world of work and public intervention carried more prestige and status than the female world of domesticity'.[62]

The gendered division between the public and the private spheres was reflected in numerous ways: in educational policy, for example, both in terms of the justification for women's education ('... a good grounding in health and hygiene in order to raise robust children ...'[63]), as well as in the framing of separate curricula for boys and girls, with a focus on the 'domestic virtues' for the latter;[64] in laws, where an 1827 rule barred women from inheriting *watan* (a specific kind of property), and a 1904 Bombay Regulation granted local administrators the power to 'declare a female landholder incapable of managing her property "on grounds of sex"';[65] in the sphere of employment, where it found its support in no less a figure than Gandhi, who famously remarked that the 'equality of sexes does not mean equality of occupation';[66] and so on. So pervasive was this view that echoes of it continued to resound well into the twentieth century, and within women's forums. At its first gathering in 1927, the All India Women's Conference (AIWC) passed multiple resolutions on education that endorsed sex segregation so as to prepare men and women for 'their different tasks in life', as well as highlighting motherhood and social service as the core values of women's education.[67] In its initial years, the AIWC followed the nationalist movement by drawing a clear line of separation between the 'political' and the 'social', and accepting that the former was the domain of men and the latter of women.[68]

However, while this was the dominant view, it was by no means an unchallenged one. In *Samya*, perhaps the first Indian political text on equality to come out of the colonial period, the famous writer and thinker Bankim Chandra Chattopadhyay devoted a full chapter to sex discrimination. He began his analysis by quoting the theory of natural difference, before rejecting it entirely:

> ... the areas in which there are differences in rights between men and women do not correspond to sufficient natural differences between them. The evident differences are due to faulty social rules. The basic idea behind notions of equity is to amend these social rules.[69]

What were these 'faulty social rules'? Bankim cited disparities in education, in the right to remarriage, and in the right to move outside the four walls of the house, each of which corresponded to the gendered division of the public and private spheres.[70] Having located the root of the disparity in the assumption of gender roles, Bankim then argued that the task of equality was to demolish such rules:

> An equal society is built out of several different and interdependent strands. If it is true that men and women should be entitled to equal rights everywhere, then it is equally true that the woman's lot is not that of rearing and feeding the child, or at least, that is not her responsibility alone. If there is true equality, both men and women must bear an equal share in what is called the duties of the household. One partner will tend to the household and be deprived of education, the other partner will escape such onerous duties and become learned—regardless of whether this is natural or not, is against the principles of equality … [and] inequality leads to inequality.[71]

At the heart of Bankim's argument for sex equality were three crucial insights, which placed him at odds with the 'natural differences' school of thought. First, he delinked whatever natural differences that existed between men and women from differences in rights. In other words, while he acknowledged the *fact* of differences, he rejected their *salience* (or, in other words, their social relevance). Second, he rejected the relevance of natural differences in fixing social roles for men and women. Finally, and perhaps most importantly, he located the root causes of gender equality not in individual acts, but in the *design* of social institutions and rules. And he then argued that the role of equality was to 'amend' precisely those social rules that made natural differences salient in fixing social roles and in the allocation of rights to men and women—if necessary, through active intervention. Here, in a proto-form, we can vividly see the transformative jurisprudence of sex equality that would be endorsed by the Supreme Court in *Anuj Garg*, almost 130 years later.

While Bankim's was a minority voice, it was by no means the only one. Right from the early social reform movements in various parts of colonial India, scholars and activists argued that the perceptible differences (in education, awareness, and even character) between men and women were rooted not in any natural state of affairs, but in social 'prescriptions, demands, and the disciplinary order'.[72] This case was made both by notable male reformers such as Raja Ram Mohan Roy and Ishwar Chandra Vidyasagar, as well as by the few women writers who carved out a presence for themselves in the public sphere of letters. In an early version of an argument that gender hierarchy was a product not of 'natural differences' but of social construction, Rukhmabai (who would later attain fame as one of the first Indian women to qualify as a doctor) noted that 'reduced to [a] state of degradation by the dictum of the shastras, looked down upon for ages by men, we have naturally come to look down upon ourselves'.[73] The 'essentialist nature of womanhood' was further challenged, in their writings, by Rokeya Sakhawat Hossain,[74] Krupabai Satthianadhan,[75] and Soonderbai Powar,[76] and in actual conduct by Pandita Ramabai, who taught carpentry and masonry in a school that she founded for orphaned widows and girls.[77] Subsequently, in the early twentieth century, ideas of natural difference and social roles were rejected both by a nascent women's movement in Maharashtra,[78] as well as the more radical Self-Respect movement in Tamil Nadu.[79]

These arguments were eventually to find their way into official political discourse, in the form of the Indian National Congress-sponsored National Planning Committee's 1939 report, titled 'Women's Role in a Planned Economy'.[80] This document began by noting that 'woman shall have an equal status and equal opportunities with man ... the State while planning shall consider the individual as the unit ... marriage shall not be a condition precedent to the enjoyment of full and equal civic status, social rights and economic privileges ...'[81] It specifically went on to demand, among other things, 'a full and equal share in the economic life of the community'[82] and expressly rejected any separation of educational curricula on the lines of sex.[83] As we have seen above, both these issues, i.e., participation in economic life and the structure of educational curricula, were at the base of the separate-spheres model. And, like Bankim and

Rukhmabai, the 1939 report argued that inequality was the result of existing social institutions, and that the remedy entailed changing those institutions. Concrete proposals to do just this included crèches in all workplaces and local bodies, prohibiting retrenchment upon marriage, maternity-oriented schemes of social insurance, and financial compensation for housework.

Thus, out of the rejection of the separate-spheres theory, we have also a proto-critique of gender discrimination as a result of institutional and structural patterns of exclusion and subordination, and consequently a call for remedies to be shaped around understanding and mitigating this reality. In constitutional language—or, what would become constitutional language later—Bankim and, after him, Rukhmabai as well as other thinkers, and then the 1939 report, were simultaneously advancing a version of the anti-stereotyping principle to rule out separate-spheres-based justifications of discrimination, and also affirming an understanding of discrimination that focused upon the impact and effect of institutions upon the lives of people, rather than upon the conduct or hostile intentions of individual actors. It was this two-pronged argument, framed as an interpretation of Article 15(1), which ultimately came to be at the heart of the judgement of the Supreme Court in *Anuj Garg*.

IV. Sex Roles, the Indian Franchise Movement, and the Constitution

In the previous section, I have attempted to demonstrate that the dominant idea of separate spheres, present in colonial India, was at all times challenged by an oppositional tradition of ideas that rejected it root and branch. And it is in this context—amidst the battle of conflicting sets of ideas about the very meaning of equality—that we must now consider the Indian franchise movement. It is through the battles around women's right to vote, I argue, that the transformative vision of equality was written into the Constitution. Voting is the quintessential *public* act, the most basic affirmation of equal citizenship. The link between voting and the fate of a separate-spheres account of society, therefore, is intuitively obvious.

Unsurprisingly, at the time that the colonial regime first contemplated granting a restricted franchise to Indians, the two conflicting visions of gender differences and sex equality spilt over into the debates over whether, and on what terms, to extend the vote to women. The debate began during the Indian visit of Edwin Montagu, the British Secretary of State, whose plans of introducing institutions of limited self-government for India included an expansion of the franchise. Montagu was met by a deputation of women, representing the newly formed Women's Indian Association (WIA), who submitted a demand for a limited vote. This demand, however, was rejected, both by Montagu and by the Southborough Committee on the Franchise, which followed a year later.[84] However, after some intense campaigning by women's organizations, a compromise was arrived at, allowing provincial legislatures, if they so wanted, to pass resolutions allowing women to vote, on whatever terms they saw fit.[85] Over the next decade (the 1920s), in response to public pressure, provincial legislatures progressively began to remove the sex disqualification from the franchise.[86]

What is particularly important, however, is the justification advanced for extending the vote to women. On one side, the demand was structured in a manner that placed the separate-spheres theory at its heart. The argument was summed up in the pages of the *Anand Bazaar Patrika* by Kumudini Bose:

> … it is said in the first instance that woman's place is in the home. I do not deny it. No woman ever does … by getting the suffrage she is not going to be ousted from her home; on the other hand, she will, by her vote, influence and control the legislation that is likely to be passed in the Council affecting her home …[87]

The argument then was not that women deserved the vote because they had an equal right to participate in the public realm.

Rather, the argument was that because politics impacted the private realm, the voice of women was important to ensure that legislation was adequately responsive to the concerns of the home. These concerns included (in the words of the proponents of suffrage) children, sanitation, and morality,[88] and temperance and the laws of property.[89] Indeed, as some scholars note, women advocates for the vote went out of their way to assure their male counterparts that they were *not* aiming to undermine traditional gender roles.[90]

In the initial years, as the provincial legislative councils began to incrementally expand the franchise to women, this understanding—now known as social feminism—formed the basis of the demand for the vote.[91] Organized groups such as the WIA and the All India Women's Conference on Educational and Social Reform invoked issues of child marriage and *devadasis* to justify the nomination of women to the legislature, while Margaret Cousins, one of the earliest proponents of extending the franchise to women, cited 'education, health, morality, prohibition, children bills, etc.' as 'specific interests relating to women's interests'.[92] This view was also supported by prominent political figures such as Sarojini Naidu (also one of the leaders of the franchise movement), who unambiguously stated that 'men and women have separate goals and separate destinies and that just as men can never fulfil the responsibility of a woman, a woman cannot fulfil the responsibility of man'.[93]

The argument that men and women represented separate constituencies, with separate 'natural' interests, both sets of which needed to be represented in the political arena, had an obvious corollary: a legislative model based either on special reservations for women, or on separate electorates of the kind that existed on the lines of religion, and which B.R. Ambedkar tried, and failed, to achieve for 'the Depressed Classes'.[94] The stated logic underlying separate electorates on religious lines was precisely that of communal representation: just as there existed such a thing as a religious community, defined by specific and distinct interests, and which could only be represented effectively by members of that community, there existed 'a women's constituency that represented women's issues and was embodied by the candidate'.[95] Indeed, at the First Round Table Conference at London, the British-nominated representatives[96] of the Indian women's movement, Begum Shahnawaz and Radhabai Subbarayan, specifically argued that the 'division of responsibilities' between men and women required separate reservations for women in the legislatures.[97] And in 1935, following upon the recommendations of the Lothian Committee, the Government of India Act—a proto-constitutional document—along with providing a restricted franchise for women based on property and educational qualifications, also provided for the reservation of seats on the lines of gender.[98] This, then, was the culmination of the social-feminist argument for the franchise.[99]

Social feminism, however, was not the only argument invoked to support votes for women. There was another, simpler argument. Although in their private interview with Montagu, the Sarojini Naidu-led deputation focused on legislation dealing with children, sanitary conditions, and morality, the actual text of the deputation itself read differently:

> Our interests, as one-half of this country's population, are directly affected by the demand that 'The members of the Council should be elected directly by the people on as broad a franchise as possible', and in the Memorandum that 'the franchise should be broadened and extended directly to the people'. We pray that, when such a franchise is being drawn up, women may be recognized as 'people', and that it may be worded in such terms as will not disqualify our sex, but allow our women the same opportunities of representation as men.[100]

Significantly, this part of representation grounded the vote not in the special roles or capacities of women, but as a simple question of political parity, and 'opportunities of representation'.

As Mrinalini Sinha puts it:

> … the political demands of women were also beginning to be articulated by means of a new set of concepts – equality, rights, representation – that were associated less with the imperatives of enduring cultural or national 'difference' than with a liberal political discourse of women as themselves rights-bearing subjects.[101]

Further, in 1918, the same year as the women's deputation met Montagu, Saraladevi Chaudharani, speaking at a session of the Indian National Congress, rejected the 'fanciful division of intellect and emotion being the respective spheres of men and women',[102] endorsed an equal right to self-determination, and specifically stated, 'the sphere of women [included] comradeship with men in the rough and tumble of life and to being the fellow-workers of men in politics and other spheres'.[103] At the heart of this argument was not a role-based model of political participation, where men and women brought their different forms of expertise to the framing of policies, but an affirmation of *individual self-determination*: the right for every person to choose their role and their sphere. This was necessarily inconsistent with any vision of culturally ordained, unchangeable separate spheres.[104] More specifically, as Rajkumari Amrit Kaur argued at the time of the framing of the 1935 Government of India Act, the right to vote itself was based upon a 'republican tradition going back to the Greeks that understood citizenship in terms of active participation in the life of the community'.[105] This was a tradition that directly contradicted the separate-spheres approach to sex roles.

The vocabulary of Chaudharani's argument was also replicated during the Second Round Table Conference in 1931, between the colonial government and Indian representatives. Here, representatives of the women's movement insisted that they sought the vote not in the name of a specific constituency (of women), but 'as a unit of humanity', and therefore 'demanded only universal adult suffrage and a declaration of fundamental rights in the new constitution that removed sex, along with caste, class and religion, as the grounds for any political disqualification'.[106] The linking of suffrage with non-discrimination is particularly significant, and in fact followed upon the famous Karachi Resolution of 1931, where the Indian National Congress had adopted a bill of rights that included both a right against sex discrimination, as well as a guarantee that 'the franchise will be on the basis of universal adult suffrage'.[107] Both the framing of suffrage as a fundamental right, as well as its universality, directly contradicted the social feminism basis for voting.[108]

Furthermore, in a memorandum after the Second Round Table Conference, the WIA opposed British plans to introduce a 'wifehood qualification' (i.e., extending the franchise to wives or widows who met either a property or an educational qualification), called for universal adult franchise, and agreed to countenance reservations only as a 'transitional measure' until the broader legal structure was made more equal—including, crucially, laws of inheritance and laws of marriage.[109] That the link between *universal* suffrage and equality was drawn explicitly and would continue to be drawn through the course of the suffrage movement[110] is crucial. This is because, if the demand for universal suffrage, as a question of *right,* represented a repudiation of the separate-spheres theory, it followed that it also repudiated any vision of equality and non-discrimination that continued to have, at its base, any form of that theory. And equally crucial was the opposition to the wifehood qualification:[111] the social feminist justification for the vote relied upon women's role within the private sphere, which, invariably, was a role they played in their capacity *as* wives or as mothers. In fact, the Franchise Committee, in its 1932 report that recommended the wifehood qualification, made exactly this argument:

> We recognise that the principle of enfranchising a woman on her husband's qualification did not find favour with the representatives of some women's organisations and others who gave evidence before us, on the grounds that it would perpetuate the idea of the dependency of the women on the men … we think, however … that marriage gives a community of interest, and that in it a woman enters into a partnership with her husband which may well confer civic rights as well as domestic duties.[112]

A wifehood qualification, therefore, was entirely in line with social feminism, and express opposition to it, at least implicitly, reflected some measure of repudiation of the separate-spheres theory.

In terms of history, this is obviously a simplified account. Some of the participants in the women's franchise movement changed their own views over the course of time;[113] others rejected separate electorates while affirming social feminism;[114] still others framed their arguments against special electorates from a purely pragmatic perspective, unwilling to put forward points of view that might have jeopardized the nationalist movement's campaign for political independence;[115] and finally, the issue of women's right to vote often intersected with religious community-based separate electorates.[116] This is hardly surprising. Social movements have always been ideologically riven, messy, and diverse, with different and even self-contradictory goals jostling for space within the overall structure.[117] They are also often intensely pragmatic, with participants concerned primarily about achieving their goals, and not about intellectual consistency.[118] My aim, therefore, is not to parcel the franchise movement into two cleanly opposed camps, but to identify the conflicting ideas that were at its base, and then to ask which of these ideas are represented in the Indian Constitution.[119]

We must begin by noting that the Indian Constitution both repudiated the concept of separate electorates, as well as enshrined voting as a right.[120] Article 326 of the Constitution (taking on from the 1931 Karachi Resolution[121]) states:

> The elections to the House of the People and to the Legislative Assembly of every State shall be on the basis of adult suffrage ...[122]

As the discussion above illustrates, framing suffrage as a *right* is entirely inconsistent with the separate-spheres theory. Of course, it is not my claim that the framers of the Constitution were consciously and deliberately rejecting the separate-spheres theory. Just as many of the women who argued for universal franchise also supported separate spheres, there is evidence that many of the framers were in agreement with that viewpoint.[123] It is my claim, however, that in the historical context of the two opposed intellectual traditions that demanded the vote for women, the text of the Constitution (in granting the vote as a right that was delinked from status and delinked from community) was simply irreconcilable with the separate-spheres theory and broadly consistent with its repudiation. The reasons for that—from separate electorates to the wifehood qualification—have been discussed above.

However, once it is accepted that the Constitution's voting provisions repudiate separate spheres, it must necessarily follow that separate spheres can no longer be a valid interpretive approach towards the justification of any kind of discrimination between men and women. A Constitution, a document laying down political principles, cannot repudiate separate spheres when it comes to voting, while endorsing it as an underlying basis, or justification, for other forms of legislative classification that are challenged under Article 15(1). This is the lesson of the contested history of the Indian women's suffrage movement, its clear link with the issue of sex equality, and its culmination in the final text of the Indian Constitution.

Lastly, this argument is buttressed by two other structural features of the Constitution. The first is found in an unlikely place. Article 39(e) of the Constitution—part of the Directive Principles of State Policy—commands the State to ensure that 'that the health and strength of workers, men and women, and the tender age of children are not abused and that citizens are not forced by economic necessity to enter avocations unsuited to their age or strength'.[124] In the Constituent Assembly, three specific amendments to add the word 'sex' after 'age' and 'strength' were moved. One was withdrawn for lack of support, and two were voted down by the Assembly. In fact, H.V. Kamath, the mover of one of the amendments, specifically stated that what he had in mind was to save women from having to take up 'occupations which may not be suitable to the conditions imposed on them by nature'.[125] He withdrew. Lakshminarayan Sahu, another of the movers, stated that 'the condition of the women of our country is rather deplorable and I do not like that they should work day and night in the mines and be obliged to adopt some such profession which may spoil their home life'.[126] His amendment was rejected by the Assembly. Both Kamath and Sahu invoked variants of the separate-spheres theory to justify the addition of the word sex to the clause. Both failed. And while it is always a perilous enterprise to read too much into the failure of an amendment that is rejected through a straight yes-or-no vote, the final text of Article 39(e), what it omits, and the history of that omission, goes at least some way towards supporting a constitutional rejection of the separate-spheres theory.

The second structural feature may be located in a more straightforward place: a closer reading of Article 15(1) itself. Recall that that article reads, in full:

> The State shall not discriminate against any citizen on grounds only of religion, race, caste, sex, place of birth or any of them.[127]

Article 15(1), therefore, lists five grounds: religion, race, caste, sex, and place of birth. It is also a 'closed list' of grounds, i.e., a law can be challenged under Article 15(1) only on one of these five grounds, and no others. If we take a close look at the four *other* grounds, viz., religion, race, caste, and place of birth, it is immediately obvious that for any of them, an argument justifying legislative differentiation by invoking 'natural' or 'inherent' differences would not only sound discordant but positively contradictory. Across the world, racial and religious discrimination has existed by attributing certain 'natural' characteristics that define or typify racial and religious groups, and then by invoking those characteristics to justify discrimination.[128] In India, more specifically, that tactic has been used to justify discrimination based on caste or place of origin.

Words and phrases in the Constitution cannot be studied in isolation. They must be interpreted as complementary parts of a holistic document, a document laying down a set of political and social principles. The framers' conscious and deliberate choice to place the word 'sex' in the company of 'religion', 'race', 'caste', and 'place of birth', within a broader guarantee against discrimination, suggests a comprehensive rejection of a long tradition of thought that justified discrimination by invoking natural differences, whether between races, castes, or sexes. Any other interpretation would leave sex as the odd word out, the only word out of five still in thrall to the 'natural differences' school of thought. That might still be a correct interpretation if there was none other available.[129] What I have attempted to show, however, is that political history, the Constitution's structure, and the text of Article 15(1) together make an unanswerable case for a transformative understanding of the constitutional vision of gender equality.

V. *Anuj Garg* and the Future of Transformative Constitutionalism

The transformative vision of *Anuj Garg* represented another step forward along a long path that had been waymarked over many decades. Bankim's *Samya*, the objections of the suffragists to the wifehood qualification, the 1939 Congress Document, the deliberations of the Constituent Assembly, and the judgements of various high courts in the years after Independence, all represented an evolving tradition of thinking about gender and equality. And it was this tradition that culminated in *Anuj Garg*, with the acknowledgement that the constitutionality of discriminatory laws must be tested by their systemic and institutional effects rather than by their intentions.

As we have seen, however, throughout history, the transformative tradition has had to contend with another, more conservative, approach to gender and equality, an approach rooted in the separate-spheres understanding of sex roles, and which draws upon an entirely different reading of Article 15(1) of the Constitution. And so, even today, the statute books are littered with gender-discriminatory provisions. These cover a range of issues—civil procedure, criminal law, family law (spanning divorce, succession, and maintenance), property law, tax law, and employment law. Particularly blatant examples include inheritance laws (across all religions), 'limited polygamy' in Goa,[130] and, absurdly, the barring of women from open prisons.[131] They even include provisions that ostensibly benefit women, but are motivated by exactly the same kind of stereotypical reasoning that is antithetical to the transformative vision of equality. These provisions have survived challenge and continue to hold the field today.[132]

Anuj Garg provides us with the judicial and constitutional template to rethink such laws, and review the decisions that have upheld their constitutionality on the basis of a formal reading of Article 15(1). In its synthesis of precedents into one coherent transformative vision of equality, moreover, it opens up a new space for further argumentation. For example, in the summer of 2017, there were strong protests against the government's decision to tax sanitary pads at a high rate.[133] Under the formal approach to sex discrimination, this would present no constitutional problems: sanitary pads are used only by a percentage of menstruating women, so it is not discrimination on grounds only of *sex*; the objective is to raise revenue, so it is not discrimination on *grounds* only of sex; it is a tax on sanitary pads, not on women, and so it is not discrimination on grounds *only* of sex; and lastly, there is no equivalent tax that men are exempted from, and therefore it is not *discrimination* on grounds only of sex.

The transformative approach, however, would have something very different to say. It would begin by noting the well-documented social, cultural, and economic roles played by perceptions of menstruation in upholding (unequal) gender roles in society, as well as the physiological effects of menstruation upon women's participation in the workplace on equal terms with men. It would argue that taxation regimes, being systems of financial incentives and disincentives, are among the State's foremost vehicles to shape patterns and ways of life. And it would then argue that the State's decision to legislatively burden an activity (menstruation) that, when juxtaposed with social and cultural norms, has placed significant barriers to women's participation in the public sphere on equal terms with men, is an 'invidious discrimination perpetuating sexual differences'.[134]

That, however, is far in the future. For now, it is the conflict that remains. Although it is rare to see express judicial endorsements of the separate-spheres theory any more, courts still apply the formal reading, without noticing that gender stereotypes continue to exist as undercurrents beneath formally 'neutral' or benign legislative classifications. Consequently, the formal and transformative approaches to gender equality continue to coexist in an uneasy tension, even after *Anuj Garg*. For example, in October 2016 a division bench of the Bombay High Court rejected a constitutional challenge to Section 56 of the Code of Civil Procedure, which states, 'the court shall not order the arrest or detention in the civil prison of a woman in execution of a decree for the payment of money'[135] on the basis of Article 15(3).[136] The Court advanced no argument, however, that would illuminate the purpose of Section 56, or the basis for the 'special provision'; in fact, it relied upon *Yusuf Abdul Aziz*—the Supreme Court's six-decade-old adultery judgement—to hold that once a 'special provision' existed, there was no need for any further judicial analysis. Had it done so, it might have found that it was impossible to defend Section 56 on any grounds other than the very stereotypes about men and women that *Anuj Garg* had categorically rejected.

In contrast, a year before this, the Delhi High Court was asked to rule upon the denial of seniority in promotion to a female inspector by the Central Reserve Police Force (CRPF). The inspector had missed a 'Pre-Promotional Course' because of a pregnancy (she later attended and completed it), and this was deemed to be evidence of her 'unwillingness to attend'. The Court noted:

> Unlike plain unwillingness on the part of an officer to undertake the course … the choice exercised by a female employee to become a parent stands on an entirely different footing … A seemingly 'neutral' reason such as inability of the employee, or unwillingness, if not probed closely, would act in a discriminatory manner, directly impacting her service rights.[137]

In holding that pregnancy-based burdens violated the guarantee against sex discrimination, Justice Ravindra Bhat of the Delhi High Court built upon the foundations laid in *Anuj Garg* (which itself had only been dealing with formal sex-based discrimination). But what was more important was how he did that. In observing that 'a seemingly "neutral" reason such as inability of the employee, or unwillingness, if not probed closely, would act in a discriminatory manner, directly impacting her service rights', the Court acknowledged that the discrimination occurs not through the individual hostile acts of legislators, but through seemingly neutral norms that end up reproducing existing social inequalities and hierarchies.[138]

In fact, the placement of 'neutral' within quotes was particularly interesting, because, in effect, the Court pointed out that our intuitive ideas about the existing baseline, the 'normal' from which we judge deviations, is a political and social construct. Or, in other words, the 'neutral' is constructed from the perspective of a privileged subject position. In the context of the case, the baseline was that of the 'normal' worker who, being male, was not expected to become pregnant. Consequently, the baseline rules (penalization for 'unwillingness' to attend the promotional course) were construed from his perspective.[139]

Thus, by de-mythologizing 'normalcy', the Delhi High Court recalled, in constitutional language, Bankim's original argument: entrenched power structures, which, over decades and even centuries of sedimentation, have attained the status of facts of nature, should no longer be treated as immutable in the very existence of things, but as human-caused instances of injustice. The point of a Constitution was to actively dismantle this appearance of immutability. And in doing so, the Court demonstrated what *Anuj Garg's* transformative jurisprudence of gender equality might look like in practice.

The judgements of the Bombay and the Delhi High Courts reveal that the meanings of Article 15(1) and of gender equality under the Constitution remain contested battlegrounds. In this chapter, I have advanced a transformative reading of this austere constitutional guarantee, grounded in a dissident political tradition that, nonetheless, provides us with a more plausible way to understand and interpret the Constitution's text and structure. To sum up, this reading, flowing from the text of Article 15(1), is three-pronged. First, the constitutionality of potentially discriminatory legislation is to be tested by its effects, especially by placing its effects in the context of existing institutions and social rules that skew a perceived 'normal baseline' against women (or specific groups of women, such as workers, or pregnant women). Second, discrimination cannot be justified by invoking natural differences, or immutable, gendered social rules. Formally neutral provisions that have the effect of disadvantaging women should be closely scrutinized for whether, underlying the formulation of the law, there is a continuing presence of the separate-spheres vision of society. And third, 'special provisions' under Article 15(3) can be justified only if they bear some connection with the underlying bases of Article 15(1).[140] In particular, 'special provisions' that simply perpetuate precisely the kinds of stereotypes and role conceptions Article 15(1) was designed to eliminate cannot stand the test of constitutional scrutiny. This approach, I have argued, is what I consider to be faithful to the Constitution's transformative purpose.

* * *

Postscript—The Adultery Judgement

On 27 September 2018, in *Joseph Shine v. Union of India*, a Constitution Bench of the Supreme Court unanimously overruled *Yusuf Abdul Aziz* and struck down the adultery provision as unconstitutional.[141] Some of the concurring judgements made explicit reference to the anti-stereotyping analysis. For instance, Justice Chandrachud observed, 'It is the duty of this Court to break these stereotypes and promote a society which regards women as equal citizens in all spheres of life'.[142] On similar lines, Justice Malhotra observed that as the logic of the adultery provision was based on treating the wife as the property of the husband, it could no longer stand scrutiny under Article 14.[143] She also endorsed the interpretation of Article 15(3) that has been advanced in this chapter, namely, 'the true purpose of affirmative action is to uplift women and empower them in socio-economic spheres. A legislation which takes away the rights of women to prosecute cannot be termed as "beneficial legislation"'.[144]

With the imprimatur of a five-judge bench of the Supreme Court, the transformative vision of gender equality articulated in this chapter has now attained a firm constitutional platform.

2

Equality Before Law: *Naz Foundation* and Equal Moral Membership

One important condition for the due maintenance of equality is that no restriction be placed in such matters on any human being on the grounds of sex, race, speech, creed, or colour. All these have in the past been used as excuses for exclusiveness, which must go if equality is to be real and effective for all persons.

K.T. Shah, 'A Note on Fundamental Rights' (December 1946)

Words are magic things … but even the magic of words sometimes cannot convey the magic of the human spirit.

Jawaharlal Nehru, speech on the Objectives Resolution (December 1946)

WHEN JAWAHARLAL NEHRU INTRODUCED the Objectives Resolution—the 'outline of a plan' for the Constitution—to the Constituent Assembly, he urged the framers not to examine its words 'like lawyers … [which would] produce only a lifeless thing'.[1]

Yet, sixty-two years later, it was in a courtroom, amidst lawyers, that the Objectives Resolution found powerful utterance. In *Naz Foundation v. NCT of Delhi*,[2] a division bench of the Delhi High Court held that the colonial-era Section 377 of the Indian Penal Code, popularly known as the 'sodomy law', which criminalized 'carnal intercourse against the order of nature',[3] was unconstitutional to the extent that it penalized same-sex intercourse between consenting adults in private. At the end of a detailed analysis of how the sodomy law contravened the LGBT community's right to equal treatment before the law (Article 14), right against discrimination on grounds of sex (Article 15[1]), and right to privacy (Article 21), the Court wove all its arguments together within the overarching web of the Objectives Resolution. 'If there is one constitutional tenet that can be said to be [the] underlying theme of the Indian Constitution,' wrote Chief Justice of the Delhi High Court A.P. Shah, 'it is that of "inclusiveness" ... this was the "spirit behind the Resolution" of which Nehru spoke so passionately. It cannot be forgotten that discrimination is [the] antithesis of equality and that it is the recognition of equality which will foster the dignity of every individual.'[4]

Inclusiveness. Discrimination. Equality. Dignity. These four words underpin the judgement of Chief Justice Shah and Justice Muralidhar in *Naz Foundation v. NCT of Delhi*. In this chapter, I will argue that *Naz Foundation* was a transformative judgement, not merely, or even primarily, because of its much-celebrated outcome (the decriminalizing of homosexuality), but because of its radical reimagination of the Constitution's promise that 'the State shall not deny to any person equality before the law or the equal protection of law'.[5] *Naz Foundation* moved away from a formalistic vision of equality, which only asked the State to 'rationally justify' the different treatment of individuals and classes, and which had crippled Indian constitutional equality jurisprudence since its very inception.[6] Instead, it chose to ask a different question altogether: did not the roots of *inequality* and *discrimination* lie in the denial of full *inclusiveness* within the polity, and in the undermining of *human dignity*?

In reframing the question in this way, *Naz Foundation* initiated a rich and complex jurisprudence of equality, which was truer to the Indian Constitution's transformative purposes than what had come before. Specifically, *Naz Foundation* understood that in promising non-discrimination and equal treatment before the law, the Constitution spoke to a past and a present, where certain personal characteristics had become the sites of exclusion, marginalization, disadvantage, and indignity. The jurisprudence of *Naz Foundation* was an attempt to fulfil the constitutional purpose of redressing this reality.

I begin by highlighting the origins of Section 377 of the Indian Penal Code, and the judicial interpretations that led up to the Delhi High Court's 2009 judgement (I). I then outline the Indian Supreme Court's dominant approach(es) towards understanding Article 14 of the Constitution—the 'classification test', the 'arbitrariness test' and the 'legitimate purpose test'—and address their shortcomings (II). I go on to argue that while *Naz Foundation* did apply the classification and legitimate purpose tests, staying within the bounds of existing precedent, it nevertheless infused them with a novel, transformative content (III). I take a quick look at how the transformative potential of *Naz Foundation* was subsequently snuffed out by the Supreme Court, first in its reversal of the Delhi High Court judgement in *Suresh Kumar Koushal v. Naz Foundation*, and subsequently in its 2015 judgement in *Rajbala v. State of Haryana*. These two judgements present an alternative understanding of Article 14, but one that cannot be defended using the touchstone of transformative Constitution (IV). I conclude by examining what promise the *Naz Foundation* judgement holds for the future of Indian equality law (V).

I. 'Carnal intercourse against the order of nature': Colonial Antecedents, Postcolonial Interpretations

Any challenge to a law on grounds of unequal treatment must begin by identifying *whom* the law treats unequally. On its face, Section

377 does not single out a person, or a group of persons, for unequal treatment. It only criminalizes 'carnal intercourse against the order of nature.'

What kinds of carnal intercourse may be against the order of nature? For Thomas Macaulay, who drafted the first version of the Indian Penal Code in 1837, and for his colonial successors who based the final language of Section 377 on Edward Coke's seventeenth-century compilation of English law,[7] the issue was too disgusting to even permit an explanatory discussion.[8] It was left to the courts to put their own gloss to the meaning of 'carnal intercourse against the order of nature'. Naturally, differences arose. The High Court of Sind, in 1925, observed that 'the natural object of carnal intercourse is that there should be the *possibility of conception* of human beings'.[9] A few decades later, however, the Gujarat High Court drew a fine distinction between sexual acts of cunnilingus or fellatio that were performed to excite the sexual organs for coitus, and the same acts performed as *substitutes* for coitus. The Court classified the latter as 'sexual perversions' and against the order of nature.[10] In the facts of the case, it held that a man inserting his penis into the mouth of another performed 'an imitative act of sexual intercourse for the purpose of his satisfying the sexual appetite [sic]'.[11] Since the 'orifice of the mouth is not, *according to nature*, meant for sexual or carnal intercourse',[12] Section 377 was applied. The phrase 'sexual perversity' was repeated by the Supreme Court a few years later, although without any further elaboration.[13]

While the Delhi High Court in *Naz Foundation* found these decisions to be in conflict, and observed a 'shift' from a procreation-oriented view of Section 377 to a view focused on 'sexual perversity', what is clear is that at the heart of all these judgements was the view that the 'natural' way of conducting 'carnal intercourse' is through penetrative, penile-vaginal sex.[14] Sexual acts that could reasonably be categorized as part of a prelude leading up to coitus would escape the sting of Section 377, but all 'non-procreative sexual acts'[15] would fall within its scope. On this reading of the Section, every sexual act performed by homosexual people would necessarily violate Section 377, since it could not possibly lead to penile-vaginal sexual intercourse.[16] On the other hand, non-penile-vaginal sex acts between heterosexuals would be illegal only if they were intended to provide sexual satisfaction *in their own right*, rather than merely 'excite' the sexual organs for eventual coitus.[17]

Consequently, the legislative distinction drawn by Section 377 through the phrase 'carnal intercourse against the order of nature' did not *precisely* map onto a distinction between homosexuals and heterosexuals. Rather, it penalized some forms of sexual expression among heterosexuals,[18] while necessarily prohibiting *any* sexual intimacy between homosexuals. The challenge to Section 377 on the grounds of Article 14, therefore, would have to address the point—as argued by those supporting its retention[19]—that Section 377 did not single out only homosexuals for burdensome and discriminatory treatment.

II. Article 14: The Traditional Approaches

A. Classification and Its Discontents

Article 14 of the Constitution provides that 'the State shall not deny to any person equality before the law or the equal protection of laws within the territory of India'.[20] At the dawn of Indian constitutionalism, when the early Supreme Court was faced with the task of interpreting the equal protection clause for the very first time, it noted that the first part of Article 14 (equality before the law) was borrowed from the Irish Constitution, while the second part (equal protection of laws) was identical to the US Constitution's Fourteenth Amendment.[21] Consequently, relying heavily upon the US precedent,[22] the Supreme Court commenced its Article 14 journey by holding that equality required similar treatment of those who were similarly situated, while allowing for differential treatment between those who were different 'in fact'.[23] In other words, the equality guarantee prohibited 'class legislation', but permitted 'reasonable classification'.[24]

What did this mean? It meant that legislative classification would have to be tested on two grounds: First, was there an 'intelligible differentia' between the things brought within the scope of the legislation and those left out? And second, was there a 'rational nexus' between the intelligible differentia and the legislative goal?[25] However, this basic test leaves many questions unanswered. And in highlighting some of them, the Supreme Court has relied upon a highly influential article written in 1949 (coincidentally, only a few months before it handed down the first of its Article 14 decisions) by the American scholars Joseph Tussman and Jacobus tenBroek.[26]

Tussman and tenBroek outlined four issues that a court would have to address while applying the standard to concrete legal problems.[27] The first was the problem of over-inclusiveness and under-inclusiveness. The world was too complex a place, and language too imperfect an instrument, for there to be *perfect* correspondence between the legislative goal and the legislative classification (the 'intelligible differentia'). There could be no divine exactitude in the drawing of a line: some persons would always find themselves on the wrong side. The court would have to decide how much slack to allow the State before a 'rational nexus' became irrational.[28]

Second, while deciding the question of rationality, the court would also have to decide the extent of *deference* that it would accord to the legislature. This question of deference, in turn, had two components. Which of the parties—the individual challenging the law, or the State defending the law—bore the *burden* of convincing the court that a particular classification was irrational (or unreasonable)?[29] Also, could the court independently scrutinize the legislature's claim that there existed facts that justified a rational nexus between the legislative goal and the law's classification? Could the court go into the question of whether such facts existed, whether they were true, and if so, whether they justified the law?

Third, Tussman and tenBroek proposed that equality, by its very nature, *excluded* certain kinds of classifications from being invoked in defence of a particular legislative purpose: 'the assertion of human equality is closely associated with the denial that differences in colour or creed, birth or status, are significant or relevant to the way in which men should be treated ... [these] are some classifications which can never be made no matter how reasonably they may be related to a legitimate public purpose.'[30] Or, if 'never' was too strong a word, at the very least, laws employing such traits for classification would be 'presumptively unconstitutional',[31] and would need to pass 'rigid judicial scrutiny'[32] (as opposed to the more relaxed 'rational review' standard).

Finally, Tussman and tenBroek argued that not only ought certain kinds of classifications be excluded under an equal protection enquiry, but so ought certain legislative *purposes*. In particular, laws motivated by 'hostility' or 'discriminatory intent' towards specific groups had been stated by the courts to be illegal.[33] Tussman and tenBroek proposed a wider set of 'legislative purposes' that might also be illegal, while cautioning against the inevitable dangers that such an approach carried, in particular involving the judiciary in impermissible policy-oriented assessments of legislative purpose.

Within this four-pronged conceptual universe, the Indian Supreme Court's equality jurisprudence, as it evolved in the first decade after Indian independence, can be best characterized as minimalistic. In the very first Article 14 case before it, viz., *Chiranjit Lal Chowdhury v. Union of India*, the Court announced that the legislature was to be accorded substantial leeway in challenges of over-inclusiveness and under-inclusiveness. Upholding a law that authorized government takeover of a factory on grounds of mismanagement, the Court rejected the petitioner's argument that there were numerous other factories that were also mismanaged, which the law had not targeted (classic under-inclusiveness). Citing American precedent, a majority of the Supreme Court held that 'the Legislature is free to recognise degrees of harm and it may confine its restrictions to those cases where the need is deemed to be the clearest'[34] (and that if there were any factories in an *identical* situation, the petitioner bore the burden of proving it). In subsequent judgements, the Court justified under-inclusiveness by stating that it would be wrong to force the legislature to 'choose between inaction and perfection'.[35] It also invoked 'administrative necessity'.[36]

This approach to Article 14 allowed the State great leeway when it came to the 'fit' between legislative purpose and legislative distinction. It also placed the burden of proof on the petitioner while deferring to legislative judgement. It was consolidated by the Supreme Court in succeeding judgements,[37] and continues to be accepted law today.[38]

At the same time, Tussman and tenBroek's third and fourth constraints, viz., impermissible grounds of classification and impermissible purposes, did not feature on the Court's radar at all. While impermissible purpose would find its way into Article 14 jurisprudence decades later,[39] the Constitution's structure presented an immediate, intuitive barrier towards incorporating impermissible grounds into Article 14. This barrier was Article 15(1) of the Constitution, which prohibits the State from discriminating on grounds only of 'religion, race, caste, sex, place or birth, or any of them'.[40] Tussman and tenBroek's 'suspect grounds', which would have to be developed in the United States through incremental judicial interpretation,[41] seemed to have been already codified in the Indian Constitution under Article 15(1). This precluded the addition of further 'grounds' under Article 14. Although the Court did not have an occasion to address this question directly, Chief Justice Patanjali Shastri hinted at such a reading in his majority judgement in *Kathi Raning Rawat*, where he observed:

> The expression 'discriminate against' is used in Article 15(1) and Article 16(2) ... [and] involves an element of unfavourable bias ... if such bias is disclosed and is based on any of the grounds mentioned in

> Articles 15 and 16, it may well be that the statute will, without more, incur condemnation as violating a specific constitutional prohibition ... *but the position under Article 14 is different*. Equal protection claims under that article are examined with the presumption that the State action is reasonable and justified. This presumption of constitutionality stems from the wide power of classification which the legislature must, of necessity, possess...[42]

On this reading of the Constitution's Equality Code, Article 15(1) provided a closed list of five grounds, which could not serve as the basis for any unfavourable or unequal classification. For all *other* bases of classification, Article 14's rational review test would apply.[43]

B. The Arbitrariness of 'Arbitrariness'

In 1989, the Canadian Supreme Court handed down its first judgement under Section 15, the equality and non-discrimination clause of the recently enacted Charter of Rights and Freedoms. The Court explicitly rejected the reasonable classification formula for adjudicating equality claims.[44] Labelling the test 'seriously deficient' because of its mechanistic formalism, its reduction of equality to a 'categorization game', and its blindness to systemic disadvantage, the Supreme Court focused its enquiry, instead, on the universal right to 'equal concern and respect'.

Canada was not alone. Through the last three decades of the twentieth century, various jurisdictions understood that the traditional classification test was insufficiently sensitive to social context and to the very purpose of equality law.[45] For instance, the United States responded by developing a system of 'tiered scrutiny' under the Fourteenth Amendment, where certain 'grounds' of classification (such as race) would automatically place a more rigorous duty of justification upon the State than rational review.[46] In the late 1990s, the South African Constitutional Court followed the Canadian example, and made 'dignity' the basis of equality and non-discrimination jurisprudence under its new Constitution.[47]

Meanwhile, the Indian Supreme Court fashioned its own judicial response to the inadequacy of the rational classification test, and called it 'arbitrariness'.

From the very beginning, the word 'arbitrariness' had featured in Article 14 judgements. In *Chiranjit Lal Chowdhury*, Justice Fazl Ali, in his concurring opinion, observed that 'any classification which is arbitrary and which is made without any basis is no classification'.[48] This was echoed in the majority opinion and in subsequent judgements.[49] In *E.P. Royappa v. State of Tamil Nadu*, however, the Supreme Court decoupled arbitrariness from reasonable classification, and set it up as a free-standing Article 14 test for testing the validity of executive action:

> Equality is a dynamic concept with many aspects and dimensions and it cannot be 'cribbed cabined and confined' [sic] within traditional and doctrinaire limits … equality is antithetic to arbitrariness.[50]

Scholars have hailed *Royappa* as the decision that freed Article 14 from the 'traditional and doctrinaire' classification test, and inaugurated an era of 'substantive equality'.[51] The serious problem with *Royappa*, however, is that the word 'arbitrariness', as defined by the Court in the passage excerpted above, is neither self-evident nor self-interpreting;[52] and in the thirty-seven years after *Royappa*, the Court has never clarified what, precisely, is *meant* by the word.[53] In recent years, the constitutional status of the arbitrariness standard itself has been contested,[54] and apart from a brief attempt by a concurring opinion in 2017, there has been no serious effort by the Court to clarify its content.[55]

C. 'Illegitimate' Purpose and Its Incoherence

In *Dipak Sibal v. Punjab University*,[56] a State university limited admission to its evening law classes only to employees of government and semi-government institutions. This exclusion was challenged by rejected private-employee applicants on the basis of Article 14. The

State produced multiple arguments in defence, such as the problem of bogus certificates and the possibility of wasted seats, all of which, the Court held, failed the test of rational scrutiny. Then, finally, the State argued that its goal was exactly what its *classification* was: to provide legal education to government and semi-government employees. After observing that it failed to see what specific public interest was served by imparting legal education to government employees, the Court went on to note:

> If the objective [of the classification] be illogical, unfair, and unjust, necessarily the classification will have to be held as unreasonable.[57]

In other words, after having run out of arguments, the State could not simply contend that it drew a legislative distinction in favour of government employees because it wished to benefit government employees. In the context of public education, this objective was *itself* an illegitimate one.

As Tussman and tenBroek had recognized, adjudicating legislative purpose is an inevitable part of the classification test, in order to prevent the State from simply restating classification as its purpose.[58] Faced with such a situation, a court could do one of two things. It could reject the State's restatement of classification as purpose, go behind the law, and reconstruct the most convincing legislative purpose in the circumstances, which it could then subject to the test of rational scrutiny.[59] Or it could hold that the purpose, as stated, was invalid because, for example, it was motivated by 'hostile intent' towards a class of people.[60] This would apply in a hypothetical case where a law sentencing all brown-haired people to prison was justified by the State on the basis that it disliked brown-haired people and wished to imprison them.[61]

In *Dipak Sibal*, the Court took the latter option. In doing so, however, it did not specify the *legal basis* upon which it was sitting in judgement over the State's legislative policy of preferring government employees for admission into law classes. The adjectives 'illogical', 'unfair', and 'unjust' only beg the question. There is nothing 'illogical' about the State preferring government employees; and 'unfairness' and 'injustice', without further elaboration, remain expressions of subjective judgement. Unless the Court could locate its finding of 'unfairness' and 'injustice' in a deeper legal or constitutional principle, the question of legal basis would remain unanswered. To date, it awaits clarification.[62]

III. Naz Foundation and the Reimagination of Equality

Consequently, when *Naz Foundation* came to be heard by the Delhi High Court in 2009, constitutional equality jurisprudence was in a deeply unsatisfactory state. The traditional rational classification test had been carrying on unaltered since 1950. However, it had long been recognized that it was simply unequipped to cope with situations of complex inequalities. Nonetheless, the alternatives—arbitrariness and illegitimate purpose—were scarcely better. The former was applied untethered from any discernible constitutional principle, while the latter faced serious doubts about its very legitimacy. If *Naz Foundation*, then, was to find that Section 377 of the IPC violated Article 14, it would first have to refashion the fundamentals of constitutional equality, while maintaining fidelity to Supreme Court precedent.

A. Classification: Proportionality, Burden of Proof, Deference

Before the High Court, the State, through the Ministry of Home Affairs,[63] justified the retention of Section 377 on two grounds. The first was public health. The State argued that the homosexual community was particularly susceptible to AIDS. Consequently, the criminalization of same-sex conduct through Section 377 was designed to protect and promote public health.[64] Under the traditional classification test, coupled with the presumption of constitutionality, the Court would have been expected to defer to the State's position on this question of fact, while also granting the

State a substantial amount of leeway to tailor a remedy for it. And this was precisely what the State urged the Court to do.[65]

The Court, however, did nothing of the sort. Instead, through the course of fourteen detailed paragraphs,[66] drawing upon material placed before it by the parties,[67] it conducted its *own* assessment of the validity of the public health argument. From the point of view of Article 14, what is remarkable about these paragraphs is the degree to which the Court scrutinized the State's public health defence and found it wanting. It cited comparative law; evidence supplied by the National AIDS Control Organization; the 2001 Declaration of Commitment on HIV/AIDS in the UN General Assembly's special session; the (Indian) National Human Rights Commission's National Conference on Human Rights and HIV/AIDS; and a UNAIDS Declaration—the import of all of which was that the real cause of the spike in AIDS rates among homosexuals was the *criminalization* of homosexuality, which drove persons underground and undermined safe sex practices.[68] When the Additional Solicitor-General (ASG) cited his own sources, the Court rejected his arguments as being both *scientifically incorrect* ('the understanding of homosexuality, as projected by [ASG] ... is at odds with the current scientific and professional understanding')[69] and *internally inconsistent* ('the submission of ASG ... is in contrast to that of NACO [National Aids Control Organization], a specialized agency of the government entrusted with the duty to formulate and implement policies for prevention of spread of HIV/AIDS').[70]

In sum, the Court marshalled comparative jurisprudence, the work of international bodies, and scholarly medical research to override the State's public health justification for Section 377. The level of detail into which the Court went and its refusal to accord significant deference to the State's position suggest a departure from the classical 'rational review' standard under Article 14, which was defined by its minimalism. What standard, then, *did* the Court advocate? An answer may be found towards the conclusion of its Article 14 analysis, where the Court observed:

> The state interest 'must be legitimate and relevant' for the legislation to be non-arbitrary and must be proportionate towards achieving the state interest.[71]

This is a crucial statement. A relationship of 'relevance' between the legislative goal and the legislative classification is akin to a 'rational review' standard. It is the bare minimum required of the State, a demonstration that there exists *some* intelligible connection between what the legislation aims at accomplishing and how it seeks to go about accomplishing it.[72]

But in addition to 'relevance', or rationality, the Court then added another requirement—*proportionality*. This is a term of art,[73] and is used as an element of rights review by courts in many jurisdictions,[74] including, among others, two that the High Court relied upon in particular: Canada[75] and South Africa.[76] A far more exacting standard than rational review, proportionality requires not only that the challenged law should have a rational connection with legislative policy, but also 'while regulating exercise of fundamental rights, the appropriate or least restrictive choice of measures [should be made] by the legislature ... so as to achieve the object of legislation'.[77] In cases involving personal autonomy, proportionality does not require the Court to defer to the State's claims.[78] Instead, it places the onus upon the *State* to demonstrate that its curtailment of a right is proportionate and meets the required standard.[79]

Was this the meaning of 'proportionality' that the Court meant to incorporate into Article 14? The High Court attempted to clarify its position further by citing the judgement of the Supreme Court in *Anuj Garg*[80] (which we had discussed in the last chapter), to invoke 'deeper judicial scrutiny' of laws that encoded 'oppressive cultural norms that especially target minorities and vulnerable groups'[81] (call this 'deeper scrutiny review').[82] The Court summed up *Anuj Garg*'s holding as requiring 'a measure that disadvantages a vulnerable group defined on the basis of a characteristic that relates to personal autonomy must be subject to strict scrutiny'.[83]

Why 'personal autonomy'? Because, the High Court held, it was the concept of personal autonomy that united the five 'grounds' stipulated under the provision adjacent to Article 14 in the Constitution—Article 15(1), which prohibited discrimination on the basis of religion, race, caste, sex, or place of birth.[84] Drawing a link between Articles 14 (equality) and 15(1) (non-discrimination), the High Court then held:

> The grounds that are not specified in Article 15 but are analogous to those specified therein, will be those which have the potential to impair the personal autonomy of an individual ... Section 377 IPC in its application to sexual acts of consenting adults in privacy discriminates [against] a section of people solely on the grounds of their sexual orientation which is analogous to prohibited grounds of sex.[85]

Deeper scrutiny review, therefore, was justified on the basis that Section 377 brought into play grounds (sexual orientation) that were *analogous* to the five listed under Article 15(1), where analogousness was to be determined by their potential to impair an individual's personal autonomy.[86] In other words, the High Court advanced an interpretation of the Constitution that read the equality (Article 14) and non-discrimination (Article 15[1]) provisions *together*. It did so by incorporating the governing principles of the non-discrimination clause—which was more specific, but limited to a closed list of five 'grounds'—into the equality clause, which was more abstract, but covered all potential instances of disadvantageous or discriminatory legislative classification.

B. Purpose: Constitutional Morality

The State's second defence of Section 377 was even more straightforward. Public morality, it argued, was strongly opposed to homosexuality.[87] Section 377 simply reflected this social reality. And the Court's response was equally straightforward. It held that public morality, without anything more, could not constitute a 'legitimate state purpose' under Article 14.

It is important to qualify this point. Drawing from judgements of the European Court of Human Rights,[88] the Constitutional Court of South Africa,[89] and the US Supreme Court,[90] the petitioners argued that 'the desire to enforce a certain morality'[91] cannot constitute 'public interest', and that criminal law cannot enforce 'private morality'.[92] Framed in this manner, the argument is clearly pitched too high. It can be nobody's case that the State is per se barred from giving effect to its understanding of public morality through law.[93] In fact, as the State correctly argued, criminal legal systems (and especially sentencing provisions) are, at least in part, based upon the legislature's sense of public morality.[94]

The argument, therefore, could not have been that public morality was, by itself, an illegitimate purpose under Article 14. And indeed, this was not the Court's argument. What was illegitimate was not the fact that the State was invoking public morality, but that public morality in this case was equated with bare hostility against the LGBT class, *and* severely affected its rights and interests. It was this *form of public morality* that was simply not a valid and defensible purpose that the State might be permitted to invoke.[95] Why? Because, the Court held, it was directly contrary to the morality that was grounded *within* the Indian Constitution, which expressly 'recognizes, protects, and celebrates diversity'.[96] Stigmatizing homosexuals on the basis of their sexual identity violated 'constitutional morality',[97] which was the only kind of morality that was relevant for constitutional adjudication.[98]

What is constitutional morality? Perhaps its clearest statement can be found in a judgement of the Ontario Court of Appeal, which noted, 'When governments define the ambit of morality, as they do when they enunciate laws, they are obliged to do so in accordance with constitutional guarantees, not with unwarranted assumptions'.[99] In similar terms, the Delhi High Court, drawing from both B.R. Ambedkar and the Constitutional Court of South

Africa, defined constitutional morality as 'morality derived from constitutional values', distinct from 'popular morality ... [which is] based on shifting and subjective notions of right and wrong'.[100]

This, then, suggests another crucial conceptual advance under Indian equality jurisprudence. Legislation that justified inequality by invoking public hostility towards a class of people, based upon characteristics related to personal autonomy, and which had the effect of stigmatizing them and undermining their dignity, could not survive Article 14 scrutiny. This was *because*, and only because, its very purpose contravened constitutional morality's requirement of inclusiveness and tolerance of diverse ways of living. The constitutional commitment to diversity, in turn, could be derived from multiple constitutional provisions such as the freedom of conscience and religion,[101] the rights of minorities to preserve their culture,[102] and the freedom of speech, association, and assembly.[103] The legitimacy of purpose would be measured not on a sliding scale of the policy-based evaluation of a challenged law, without any judicial explanation of *what* made legislative purpose illegitimate, but would be firmly anchored to the Constitution.[104]

C. Impact and Effect

As pointed out earlier, Section 377 did not *directly* criminalize homosexual intercourse. What it did criminalize was carnal intercourse against the order of nature. Judicial interpretation indicated that the offence could be committed by both homosexual and heterosexual persons as long as they were engaging in non-penile-vaginal intercourse. Therefore, the petitioners had to cross a preliminary hurdle: if Section 377 only criminalized 'conduct', how was Article 14—which guaranteed equal protection to all *persons*—attracted in the first place?

The question had been raised before other Courts, and had been answered. In *Lawrence v. Texas*, the US Supreme Court had held that the 'conduct' in question 'is closely correlated with being homosexual ... there can hardly be more palpable discrimination against a class than making the conduct that defines the class criminal'.[105] Likewise, the South African Constitutional Court held that 'it is not the act of sodomy that is denounced by the law, but the so called sodomite who performs it'.[106] While superficially similar, and leading to the same result, the two approaches are nonetheless very different. According to the US Supreme Court, a homosexual's very identity is *defined* by the (same sex) sexual conduct that he chooses to engage in; according to the South African Constitutional Court, anti-sodomy laws *construct* a homosexual identity by criminalizing a set of acts.[107]

In *Naz Foundation*, the Delhi High Court selected the latter interpretation, but went one step further. Apart from citing scholarship about how anti-sodomy laws created a regime of surveillance and stigma centred around the homosexual identity,[108] the Court also took on record affidavits filed by Voices Against 377 (Respondent No. 8) that chronicled the actual experiences of the *victims* of Section 377, experiences that included custodial rape and torture, social stigma, and incarceration.[109] Using this evidence, the Court found that while, formally, Section 377 criminalized conduct, *in effect* it created a systemic pattern of disadvantage and indignity, the target of which was the LGBT community.[110]

As an analytical approach, the Court's focus on the effect of a law, rather than on Parliament's intent, was not novel.[111] What was novel, however, was its argument that Article 14 was attracted because a law's effect was to target and stigmatize a community, perpetuate its social exclusion, and rob it of its dignity. In other words, the *focus* of the Court's preliminary enquiry determining the applicability of Article 14 shifted from examining the *nature of the classification* (whether it treated similarly situated persons similarly, and dissimilarly situated persons dissimilarly) to examining whether the law *disadvantaged* a group (or groups) based on their personal characteristics. Or, to use terms developed by the German scholar and constitutional court judge Susanne Baer, the Court shifted from viewing equality as an issue of 'comparatability', to viewing it as a 'right against hierarchy'.[112] And this interpretive shift was crucial, because, once again, by citing disadvantage and indignity, the Court brought the form, language, and import of Article 15(1)'s non-discrimination clause into Article 14's equality clause.

D. In Defence of Naz: Equality as Inclusion and Dignity in the Transformative Constitution

I have argued that *Naz Foundation* changed course from the traditional classification test, and effectively read into an Article 14 (equality) enquiry a judicial approach that was normally reserved for Article 15(1) (non-discrimination). Where did this novel analysis come from? The answer is found in Naz Foundation's own written submissions before the Court, paragraph 119 of which stated:

> The purpose of Article 14's equal protection clause is to offer redress to vulnerable groups assailed by discriminatory practices.[113]

Crucially, 'vulnerable groups' and 'discriminatory practices' is precisely the language of Article 15(1), which explicitly protects groups marked by five personal characteristics that have been historic and present sites of vulnerability.

To appreciate the transformative force of the petitioner's arguments, we must note that the Supreme Court has always referred to Articles 14, 15(1) and 16 as the Constitution's Equality Code, and has specified that they should be read together.[114] The relationship, however, has been one-way, flowing *from* Article 14's abstract declaration of equality *to* Articles 15 and 16, which flesh out that guarantee in specific circumstances.[115] In *Naz Foundation*, the petitioner asked the Court to reverse the logic: instead of reading Article 15(1) as applying the principle of equality to sites of discrimination, to read Article 14 as encoding the principle of non-discrimination into the guarantee of equality.

Why did this matter? It mattered because under the traditional, equal-protection-oriented classification test, the petitioner would have faced two hurdles: first, to show a connection between classification of *conduct* (carnal intercourse with or against the order of nature) and classification of *persons* (homosexuals and heterosexuals) in order for Article 14's guarantee of equal protection of laws to all *persons* to apply at the threshold level; and second, to get around the presumption of constitutionality and the high degree of deference accorded to the State in the standard classification enquiry. But by framing Article 14 in terms of non-discrimination, both hurdles were cleared. The classification attracted Article 14 as long as the petitioner showed that homosexuals, *as a class*, were disadvantaged by Section 377 (which, as we have seen, they certainly were). And because the correct lens for understanding this issue was discrimination and disadvantage, the Court could focus more on the question of whether the State was able to adequately justify its discriminatory conduct, rather than the question of whether the classification bore a 'rational nexus' to the State's goal.

We are now in a position to reconstruct the Court's argument in full. Article 15(1) prohibited all discrimination, i.e., unfavourable treatment on the basis of five stated grounds. What united these grounds was that they were, historically, sites of group disadvantage and vulnerability, and were closely connected with personal autonomy. Article 14, which was a general restatement of Article 15(1)'s guarantee of non-discrimination, equally prohibited discrimination on the basis of *analogous grounds*—personal characteristics not among the five named in Article 15(1), but which were also sites of disadvantage and had the potential to impinge upon personal autonomy.

Where such analogous grounds were concerned, therefore, a court would depart from the traditional Article 14 classification test and apply a framework closer to Article 15(1). This was to be done in three ways: first, the court was not to look at the formal terms of the classification but at what *effect* the classification had on a vulnerable group, in terms of their dignity and social inclusion; second, legislative purposes that specifically sought to entrench or perpetuate disadvantage on *those very analogous grounds* were invalid as contrary to constitutional morality—this explained why the Court refused to acknowledge 'public morality (against homosexuals)' as a legitimate legislative purpose; and third, instead of the rational nexus test, a deeper scrutiny, requiring the State to defend its actions on a proportionality standard, was to be applied. This three-pronged test—that effectively merged Articles 14 and 15 in cases where analogous grounds were concerned[116]—finally exorcized the ghost of Justice Patanjali Shastri's off-the-cuff remarks about the stark separation of the two Articles, made so many years ago, and which had haunted equality jurisprudence ever since.

So much for what the Court did. Was it correct to do so? Was it correct to equate the guarantee of equal protection and the guarantee of non-discrimination in this manner?

I will argue that it was, and that the strongest defence for the Court's approach is historical. Recall that in its early decisions, the Supreme Court incorporated the classification and rational-review test from US law on the basis that the text of Article 14 was nearly identical to the US Fourteenth Amendment. But that is only part of the story. This is what Section I of the Fourteenth Amendment states, in full:

> No state shall make or enforce any law which shall abridge the privileges or immunities of citizens of the United States; nor shall any state deprive any person of life, liberty, or property, without due process of law; nor deny to any person within its jurisdiction the equal protection of the laws.[117]

The 'due process' and the 'equal protection' clauses together constituted a broad rule-of-law guarantee for the protection of citizens, upon which is based the rational review test for legislation.[118] The history of the drafting of the Indian Constitution reveals, however, that the US analogy is not quite as simple as the early Supreme Court believed it to be. Instead of combining an equal protection clause and a due process clause, in the initial stages of the drafting of the Indian Constitution, the equal protection clause was linked with the *non-discrimination clause*. The Fundamental Rights Sub-Committee's proposed draft of 24 March 1947 contained an equal protection guarantee, and within the same clause, a guarantee of non-discrimination:

> All persons within the Union shall be equal before the law. No person shall be denied the equal protection of laws within the territories of the Union. There shall be no discrimination against any person on grounds of religion, race, caste, language, or sex.[119]

While this was carried over to the Sub-Committee's Draft Report of April 1947, in the final draft text that was put to the Constituent Assembly for it to begin its discussion and debate, the equal protection clause had disappeared. There was now only a simple non-discrimination guarantee, which had no equivalent in the US Constitution. Clause 4(1) of the April 1947 draft stated:

> The State shall not discriminate against any citizen on grounds of religion, race, caste, or sex.[120]

The equal protection clause, however, had only shifted its location. Clause 9 read:

> No person shall be deprived of his life or liberty without due process of law, nor shall any person be denied equality before the law within the territories of the Union.[121]

Readers will note that this Clause is virtually identical to a significantly larger chunk of the US Fourteenth Amendment than the final version of Article 14. Like the Fourteenth Amendment, Clause 9 links the due process clause with the equal protection clause. Had this been the final text of the Constitution, the Supreme Court's reliance on the US precedent for construing the equal protection guarantee might have been justified. However, towards the end of the Constitution-making process in 1948, the Drafting Committee (which was tasked with revising the Fundamental Rights Sub-Committee's proposals in light of the Constituent Assembly Debates) *delinked* the two, provided the equal protection clause with a stand-alone status (Article 14), *and* shifted it seven articles before, to stand beside Article 15(1)'s non-discrimination clause. In other words, the Drafting Committee separated equal protection and due process (departing from the US model) and linked equal protection and non-discrimination (the new Indian model). This was the final form of the Constitution: Article 14 (equal protection), Article 15(1) (non-discrimination), and Article 21 (life and personal liberty).

While the Drafting Committee did not record detailed reasons for the shift, its significance is unmistakable. As we have seen, at first, the Fundamental Rights Committee's 1947 sub-chapter titled *Rights of Equality* had only a non-discrimination clause, suggesting that equality was understood *in terms of* non-discrimination. The equal protection clause was within the sub-chapter titled 'Rights of Freedom', along with a due process guarantee of life and liberty. But one year later, the Drafting Committee chose to rearrange the Articles *by shifting equal protection from* 'Rights of Freedom' to 'Rights of Equality'. This suggests strongly that primacy in understanding the constitutional commitment to equality was always meant to be in terms of non-discrimination, an understanding that was meant to be supplemented by bringing in a more generally worded equality clause.[122]

And what did it mean to think of equality in terms of non-discrimination? An answer is to be found, once again, in the Fundamental Rights Sub-Committee and, in particular, in the 'Notes on Fundamental Rights' submitted by K.T. Shah and B.R. Ambedkar (who ultimately chaired the Drafting Committee), two of the most vocal members of the Constituent Assembly. K.T. Shah noted:

> ... equality is not merely equality of treatment before the established system of Law and Order but also of opportunity for self-expression

> or self-realization that may be inherent in every human being. One important condition for the due maintenance of such equality is that no restriction be placed in such matters on any human being on the grounds of sex, race, speech, creed, or colour. All these have in the past been used as excuses for exclusiveness, which must go if equality is to be real and effective for all persons.[123]

Ambedkar submitted a draft bill of rights, which stipulated:

> All citizens are equal before the law and possess equal civic rights. Any existing enactment, regulation, judgement, order, custom or interpretation of law by which any penalty, disadvantage, or disability is imposed upon or any discrimination made against any citizen shall, as from the day on which this Constitution comes into operation, cease to have an effect.[124]

It is here that we see the language of *Naz Foundation*: the linkage between equality and non-discrimination, the identification of sites of group exclusion, the focus on disadvantage, disability, and self-realization ('dignity'), and the attention to the actual experiences of the subjects of a law ('real and effective equality'). Here was a deep, rich, and substantive understanding of equality, grounded in an understanding of the structural and systemic hierarchies of exclusion and subordination that had historically characterized Indian society, and the determination to remedy them. And the careers of the equality and non-discrimination clauses—their initial linking, then delinking with only the non-discrimination clause remaining under the sub-chapter of equality, and their final relinking in two separate Articles *under* the sub-chapter titled 'Equality' reflect, according to me, the triumph of Ambedkar's and K.T. Shah's exhortation to understand equality *as* non-discrimination, instead of the American classification approach to the concept.[125]

This reading is borne out by other provisions of the Constitution. While the Supreme Court has stopped at Articles 14, 15, and 16 as the Equality Code, that is not all that the Constitution has to say. Article 17, for instance, prohibits the practice of 'untouchability' *in any form*.[126] Untouchability, the caste-based practice of exclusion and subordination that was at the heart of the discriminatory social order, was prohibited in a clause that was *also* placed within the sub-chapter 'Rights of Equality'.

So was Article 18, which prohibits the taking of titles by Indian citizens, and was framed as a specific response to the British practice of rewarding loyalty by exalting some Indians above others.[127] Both Articles 17 and 18 speak to *specific* historical situations of subordination, which the Constitution was attempting to remedy. And suddenly, it is Article 14's overarching 'classification test' that seems the odd one out. Articles 15, 16, 17, and 18 are all aimed at the Constitution's transformative purpose—as invoked by several members of the Constituent Assembly[128]—of doing away with the hierarchies of subordination and exclusion based on personal characteristics which characterized the pre-constitutional polity.

Nor did the work of the Drafting Committee, and Ambedkar and Shah's visions of equality, spring from a vacuum. The Constitution's Equality Code was the culmination of more than half a century of Indian theorizing about equality in the grammar and vocabulary of 'rights'. In *Samya*, which we discussed in the previous chapter as perhaps the first important modern Indian political text on equality, Bankim Chandra Chattopadhyay organized his discussion not around an abstract principle of classification and formal equal treatment, but around three specific group-based sites of discrimination: caste, sex, and race/class (all of which finally found their way into Article 15[1]).[129] In Bankim's view, thinking about equality could not be divorced from social hierarchies that had been created on the basis of 'artificial differences' between individuals and groups. Instead, the core of his argument was structured upon the premise of *inclusion*: 'There must be equality in access to rights. No one should be deprived from access to a right, even though that individual does not possess the strength.'[130]

Bankim's understanding that a guarantee of equality must address questions of *access to rights*, i.e., questions of exclusion and inclusion, was reflected in the many constitutional documents composed during the early twentieth century on the long march towards Independence and the Constituent Assembly. The Congress party's Karachi Resolution of 1931—a sustained and detailed attempt at an Indian Bill of Rights[131]—guaranteed that 'all citizens are equal before the law, irrespective of religion, caste, creed or sex',[132] and followed it up immediately with 'no disability attaches to any citizen by reason of his or her religion, caste, creed or sex, in regard to public employment, office of power or honour, and in the exercise of any trade or calling'.[133] A few years later, the famous 1935 Government of India Act eschewed the equal protection guarantee altogether, and limited itself to a non-discrimination/non-disability promise of access.[134] And all of this must be understood in the context of decades of prior reflection and action, which did not speak the language of constitutions and rights, and might not be construed as *political thinking* in the way we understand it today, but nonetheless conceptualized equality in terms of *anti-hierarchy*. This conceptualization, in turn, was responding directly to a polity and society that was deeply stratified in terms of access to public goods and the right to full participation in the economic and social life of the community, primarily upon the grounds of caste and sex.[135]

It is therefore clear that the tradition the Constituent Assembly was tapping into was one that perceived equality before law as a question of non-discriminatory inclusion. However, questions might then be asked: if that was the case, why did Article 14 take the specific form that it did? Why did the framers borrow the specific language of the US Fourteenth Amendment if they did not wish it to be interpreted as the Fourteenth Amendment was? How *did* they wish it to be interpreted?

Any answer to these questions must be speculative but, based on the material outlined above, my answer would be this: the five 'grounds' of Article 15(1), viz., race, religion, caste, sex, and place of birth, were grounds that were known and salient in *1950* as sites of unjustified discrimination. The framers, however, were experienced individuals, who were surely aware that they had no eternal monopoly over wisdom. They were aware that new grounds might come into existence or, with new generations and new struggles, acquire a salience and a valence that they never had before.[136] For this reason, they provided a closed list of grounds under Article 15(1) to deal with the present. And they also brought in the equal protection clause under Article 14 to leave courts to deal with the future on the basis of the principles underlying Article 15(1) ('analogous groups'). Any other reading would have committed the Constitution to a completely rigid vision of non-discrimination, which would be entirely at odds not only with its structure, but also with the experiences of the men and women who drafted it. Justice Kennedy expressed this when he concluded his judgement in *Lawrence v. Texas*:

> Had those who drew and ratified the Due Process Clauses of the Fifth Amendment or the Fourteenth Amendment known the components of liberty in its manifold possibilities, they might have been more specific. They did not presume to have this insight. They knew times can blind us to certain truths and later generations can see that laws once thought necessary and proper in fact serve only to oppress. As the Constitution endures, persons in every generation can invoke its principles in their own search for greater freedom.[137]

As Ronald Dworkin argues, the very fact that Bills of Rights are framed in abstract language implies that they lay down *concepts* (of equality, freedom, and so on), and not specific *conceptions* of how those concepts are to be applied in concrete situations.[138] Interestingly, the framers of the Indian Constitution, when dealing with equality and non-discrimination, chose to take *both* paths: Article 14 embodied the *concept* ('equal protection'), while Article 15 instantiated the *conception* ('non-discrimination on five specific grounds'). This, I suggest, is because the framers recognized that there would be countless situations where the equal protection clause *was* attracted, but no question of discrimination against analogous groups arose. For these situations, what better standard than the tried and tested 'classification' standard?

This explains the final structure of the 'Equality' sub-chapter: within the overall theme of remedying structural subordination and disadvantage, the equal protection clause—with its US-inspired language, redolent of the classification test—had a stand-alone Article to itself. But at the same time, it did not enjoy an altogether separate existence (as it did when part of the 'life and liberty' clause in the 'Right to Freedom' sub-chapter). The understanding of Article 14 could not be segregated from the principles of non-discrimination underlying the rest of the sub-chapter. In this sense, the relationship between Articles 14 and 15 is better understood as being akin to the non-discrimination clauses of the Canadian and South African constitutions, which of course came much later. For instance, Section 15 of the Canadian Charter of Rights and Freedoms reads:

> Every individual is equal before and under the law and has the right to the equal protection and equal benefit of the law without discrimination and, in particular, without discrimination based on race, national or ethnic origin, colour, religion, sex, age or mental or physical disability.[139]

The use of the connector 'in particular' has allowed the Canadian Supreme Court to jettison the classification test. Instead, it has developed an extensive jurisprudence of 'analogous grounds' under the equal protection part of the clause, which do not fall within the listed grounds, and on the basis of which laws are subjected to a broad proportionality review.[140] Similarly, S. 9(1) of the South African Constitution reads:

> Everyone is equal before the law and has the right to equal protection and benefit of the law.[141]

S. 9(3) adds:

> The state may not unfairly discriminate directly or indirectly against anyone on one or more grounds, including race, gender, sex, pregnancy, marital status, ethnic or social origin, colour, sexual orientation, age, disability, religion, conscience, belief, culture, language, and birth.[142]

Inspired by, and similar to, the Canadian Charter, the South African Constitutional Court conducts a proportionality review for discriminatory conduct based on listed or analogous grounds, and a rationality review for other cases of claimed equality violations.[143] *Broadly*, these constitutions are structured similar to India's, but with a few important differences, of course: an equal protection clause followed by a non-discrimination, listed-grounds clause, which may or may not be part of the same sentence. The Canadian and South African courts have used the phrases 'in particular' and 'including' to open up the protection of non-discrimination, respectively, to 'analogous grounds', the analysis of which now forms an integral part of their equality/non-discrimination jurisprudence. I have argued that the Indian Constitution provides a model for our courts to do the same under Article 14's equal protection guarantee, and that such a reading is structurally and historically justified, and true to the Constitution's transformative purpose.

It was this reading that *Naz Foundation* resurrected after fifty-nine years of stillbirth. That is what makes it a truly transformative decision.

One last point remains: *Naz Foundation* was extremely careful in articulating the underlying basis of the Article 15(1) grounds as a combination of group disadvantage and infringement of personal autonomy. This was not the only option open to the Court. In Canadian law, for instance, the relevant basis at present is 'immutability'[144] (attributes that are either unchangeable [age] or changeable only at great and unjustified cost [religion]), while South

Africa focuses on 'dignity'.[145] Both these approaches have been criticized: immutability, because it traps individuals into categories in terms of which they may not wish to define themselves,[146] and is insufficiently sensitive to how 'grounds' of non-discrimination have been the sites of disadvantage and exclusion; and dignity, for its conceptual emptiness.[147] *Naz Foundation* avoided the temptation of both these intuitive approaches to 'analogous grounds'. Rather, it kept the focus on a two-pronged approach: defining the basis of non-discrimination as remedying group disadvantage by identifying the sites on which that disadvantage takes place on the one hand, while specifying that the manner of disadvantage must be linked to personal autonomy on the other. Dignity, while discussed extensively, was part of a broader enquiry into vulnerability and disadvantage.[148] And it is this approach, I have attempted to show, which was ultimately true to the Constitution's text, structure, history, and transformative purpose.[149]

IV. The Aftermath: *Koushal* and *Rajbala*

On 11 December 2013, in *Suresh Kumar Koushal v. Naz Foundation*,[150] a two-judge bench of the Supreme Court reversed the Delhi High Court's verdict. Section 377 was reinstated as it had been before *Naz Foundation* was decided.

The judgement in *Koushal*, authored by Justice G.S. Singhvi, is difficult to interpret. This is primarily because its ninety-eight pages consist almost entirely of recapitulating the submissions of counsel and the position of law, with neither an analysis nor a definite finding on most of the issues before the Court.[151] With respect to Articles 14 and 15, what passes by way of analysis is found in paragraph 42:

> Those who indulge in carnal intercourse in the ordinary course and those who indulge in carnal intercourse against the order of nature constitute different classes and the people falling in the latter category cannot claim that Section 377 suffers from the vice of arbitrariness and irrational classification. What Section

377 does is merely to define the particular offence and prescribe punishment ...[152]

In concluding that Section 377 merely defined an offence, and by virtue of that was *automatically* shielded from scrutiny under Articles 14 and 15, the *Koushal* bench evidently failed to engage with any of the arguments advanced by the High Court on issues of impact and effect under Article 14, the link between targeting conduct and targeting groups, rigorous scrutiny for analogous grounds, and the anti-stereotyping principle.

Two years later, when two Indian states passed laws requiring a minimal educational qualification (among other things) for contesting local government elections, the Supreme Court had the chance, once again, to advance *Naz Foundation*'s vision of equality and non-discrimination. The challenged laws disproportionately affected women and disadvantaged castes, who for myriad reasons had been unable to access primary education. Here was an ideal opportunity to apply standards of impact and effect, anti-stereotyping, and exclusion from core public goods. Furthermore, given that the challenge was to an electoral law, and therefore to the very basis of the system that *granted* laws their presumptive legitimacy,[153] it was a chance to apply rigorous scrutiny under Article 14. Once again, however, in *Rajbala v. State of Haryana*,[154] the Supreme Court declined the opportunity, upholding the law under an Article 14 rational review standard, simply by making the unsubstantiated observation that 'it is only education which gives a human being the power to discriminate between right and wrong, good and bad'.[155]

Koushal and *Rajbala* mark a temporary closure of the transformative potential of Articles 14 and 15(1) of the Constitution. In both cases, the Supreme Court failed to engage at all with the arguments in *Naz Foundation*. Consequently, the High Court's transformative reasoning in *Naz Foundation* exists, at present, in a strange limbo: the judgement itself was reversed, but its reasoning has yet to be frontally met and addressed by the Supreme Court.

V. Conclusion: *Naz Foundation* and the Future of Article 14

> The Constitution of India is one of the great emancipatory charters, lifting, as it does, from the status of wretchedness and subordination – communities, castes, tribes, and women – to full Citizenship.
>
> Outline of Arguments, Voices against 377 (Respondent No. 8), *Naz Foundation v. NCT of Delhi* (on file with the author)

As early as 1952, Justice Vivian Bose expressed his unease at the direction the Constitution's equal protection clause was taking. Concurring in *State of West Bengal v. Anwar Ali Sarkar*, he formulated his own understanding of Article 14, questioning:

> … whether the collective conscience of a sovereign democratic republic can regard the impugned law … as the sort of substantially equal treatment which men of resolute minds and unbiased views can regard as right and proper in a democracy of the kind we have proclaimed ourselves to be.[156]

What was 'a democracy of the kind we have proclaimed ourselves to be'? In *Naz Foundation,* Respondent No. 8 (Voices Against 377) proposed an answer to this question: a democracy that abhorred subordination, and promised 'full citizenship' to all. It was an answer that the High Court accepted.

Let us go back to the four words with which we began the chapter, the words that constituted the heart and soul of *Naz Foundation*: inclusiveness, discrimination, equality, dignity. If the constitutional guarantees of Article 14 (equal protection) and Article 15 (non-discrimination) meant anything, the Court held, they meant that the Constitution stood as a bulwark against laws and policies that excluded individuals or groups, or denied and undermined their dignity. This was what it meant for the Constitution to be a charter of emancipation, and this was what was meant by the promise of full citizenship. Or, to put it another way, 'equal moral membership' of the polity.

The High Court's reasoning, however, had consequences beyond *Naz Foundation*. In its written submissions before the Court, the Union of India expressed the worry that if homosexuals were to be treated as a protected class for the purposes of non-discrimination law, 'then in India there will be lakhs of minorities, men who are bald, men who suffer from other ailments like old age problems, suffer from leprosy or other ailments'.[157] Keeping aside the example of 'bald men' as a frivolous one,[158] the answer to the Union's concern is, '*Yes, and that is precisely the point!*' The 'analogous grounds' reasoning would open the door for similar challenges to discriminatory laws that were not covered by Article 15(1): age, physical or mental disability (in fact, the Union's invocation of leprosy is particularly poignant, because of the widespread discrimination—codified in laws—against people suffering from this disease),[159] and perhaps even economic class.[160] It would also ensure that the equality and non-discrimination clauses remained dynamic and forward-looking, able to identify and redress discrimination as it arose in a rapidly changing world.

Interestingly, the reasoning in *Naz Foundation* was echoed by the Supreme Court in July 2013, just a few months before *Koushal*. In *State of Maharashtra v. Indian Hotel & Restaurants Association*,[161] the Supreme Court struck down a ban on 'bar dancing' that was restricted to hotels below the 'three-starred' category. Rejecting the State's argument that lifting the ban would lead to moral corruption and exploitation of women, the Court held that the sole basis of the classification was the 'classes of persons' who frequented the establishments:

> We are of the firm opinion that a distinction, the foundation of which is classes of the establishments and classes/kind of persons who frequent the establishments and those who own the establishments can not be supported under the constitutional philosophy so clearly stated in the Preamble of the Constitution of India and the individual Articles prohibiting discrimination on the

> basis of caste, colour, creed, religion or gender ... Taking away of these rights of equality by any legislation would require clear proof of the justification for such abridgment.[162]

What we see here, in proto-form, are the arguments advanced by the High Court in *Naz Foundation*, applied to the grounds of *economic status*. The Supreme Court held that classification motivated *solely* by assumptions about the moral character (or otherwise) of poor people failed on the legitimate purpose grounds, because it was opposed to the 'constitutional philosophy' stated in the Preamble ('equality of status and opportunity and the *dignity* of the individual').[163] Crucially, the Court invoked the specific grounds of Article 15(1) to substantiate its claim, *and* to hold the legislature to a standard of 'clear proof of justification' under Article 14. While the Court did not develop these propositions in as much detail, the power and force of the argument is evident. However, it did note that the State's arguments were based on stereotypes instead of on empirical data—another key link of the reasoning in *Naz Foundation*.

In sum, therefore, *Naz Foundation* struck a powerful blow for the liberation of a group that had long been stigmatized and discriminated against, in public and in private. It also did something more: through its focus on non-discrimination, equality, inclusion, and dignity, it also liberated Indian equality jurisprudence from its six-decade-old fetters of 'intelligible differentia' and 'rational nexus'. From 'equals must be treated equally and unequals unequally' to 'inclusion', 'dignity', and 'equal moral membership'; from a vision of equality bounded in a nutshell to infinite space. The Delhi High Court revived the hopes that K.T. Shah and B.R. Ambedkar nurtured while formulating the equal protection and non-discrimination clauses, and restored to them Nehru's 'magic of the human spirit'.

Will the High Court's judgement itself be revived by the 'intelligence of a future day when a later decision ... correct[s] the error'[164] into which the *Koushal* Court was betrayed? Only time will tell.

Postscript—Navtej Johar

The intelligence of a future day was not too long in coming. On 6 September 2018, a few months shy of five years since *Koushal*, a Constitution Bench of the Supreme Court overturned that judgement, and largely restored the judgement of the Delhi High Court in *Naz Foundation*. In *Navtej Johar v. Union of India*, Section 377 was read down to exclude consensual same-sex relations between adults.[165]

While the judgements of the Chief Justice and Justice Nariman respectively proceeded on the bases of individual choice and the manifest arbitrariness of Section 377, the concurring opinions of Justices Chandrachud and Malhotra have some resonance with the arguments advanced in this chapter. Justice Chandrachud, for example, explicitly agreed with the shortcomings of the classification standard, and indicated that a disadvantage-based interpretation of Article 14 signalled a possible way forward.[166] And Justice Malhotra argued that legislation discriminating on the basis of an 'intrinsic and core trait' of an individual was, ipso facto, a breach of Article 14.[167] Although the Justices did not go further down this road in *Navtej Johar*, the foundations for future transformative constitutionalism around the Articles 14/15 axis have now been laid.

3

Equality of Opportunity: *N.M. Thomas*, Group Subordination, and the Directive Principles

I am glad that the draft Constitution has ... adopted the individual as its unit.

B.R. Ambedkar, speech in the Constituent Assembly, November 1948

We cannot have equality because in trying to attain equality we come up against some principles of equality.

Prime Minister Nehru, speech in Parliament on the First Amendment, May 1951

'EQUALITY,' AS THE SUPREME Court reminds us every few years, 'forbids class legislation, but does not forbid reasonable classification.' Intuitively, this makes sense—a Constitution that places the individual at its heart cannot permit laws that allocate benefits and burdens based on class. Articles 15(1), 16(1), and

16(2)—the concrete embodiments of the Constitution's Equality Code—substantiate this view. Article 16(1), for instance, guarantees to all citizens the 'equality of opportunity ... in matters relating to employment or appointment to any office under the State', while Article 16(2) prohibits discrimination in State employment on grounds of 'religion, race, caste, sex, descent, place of birth ... [or] residence'. Reading Articles 16(1) and (2) together, we derive a vision of equality that mandates '[State] indifference to ascriptive characteristics'[1] in public employment. Or, in other words, a person's race, caste, class, etc. cannot feature in decisions about public employment. In some quarters, this is called 'colour-blind equality'.[2]

A closer look at the constitutional scheme, however, complicates matters. Article 16(4) states:

> Nothing in this article shall prevent the State from making any provision for the reservation of appointments or posts in favour of any backward class of citizens which, in the opinion of the State, is not adequately represented in the services under the State.

Article 16(4) is mirrored in Article 15(4), which authorizes the State to make provisions for 'the advancement of socially and educationally backward classes of citizens or for the Scheduled Castes and the Scheduled Tribes'. But if equality's slogan is 'no class legislation', then Articles 15(4) and 16(4), which explicitly use the word 'class', seem to be pulling in an entirely different direction. Are these provisions departures from the constitutional vision of equality? Is their existence testimony to the fact that in a deeply riven society, there must be some limited compromise with equality in order to guarantee meaningful social justice? Or is their presence a signal for us to revise our initial presumption about the very meaning of 'equality' under the Constitution?[3]

The history of the Supreme Court's 'reservations' jurisprudence is the history of a struggle between two competing visions of equality. In 1975 (*State of Kerala v. N.M. Thomas*), the Court decisively embraced one vision and rejected the other. More than forty years after, however, the transformative character of that judgement has yet to be articulated. That is the task of this chapter.[4]

I begin with a survey of a few of the Supreme Court's initial judgements on Articles 15 and 16 (I). In its first two decades, the Court held that Articles 15(4) and 16(4), which allowed class-based affirmative action, were constitutionally mandated 'exceptions' to the Equality Code. In *State of Kerala v. N.M. Thomas*,[5] however, a narrowly divided Supreme Court reversed that view. In their complementary majority opinions, Justices Mathew and Krishna Iyer advanced a vision of equality according to which individual disabilities were *embedded* in class identity and, consequently, within a set of social hierarchies that the Constitution's Equality Code was created to surmount (II).

After discussing the judgement(s) in *N.M. Thomas*, I articulate and defend the transformative understanding of equality that emerges out of a combined reading of the majority opinions (III). The majority, I argue, grasped the insight that in India, 'differential access to life chances corresponded in large measure to membership in different *communities*'.[6] To take community membership into account, therefore, was not to depart from the principle of individual equality, but to abide by it in its deepest sense.

I then contend that *N.M. Thomas* was also transformative in a second, important way (IV). It was the first judgement to articulate the role of Part IV of the Constitution, i.e., the Directive Principles of State Policy, as a system of framework values that gave life to the abstract concepts outlined in the Fundamental Rights chapter. In conclusion, I argue that the vision of equality articulated in *N.M. Thomas* had, and continues to have, the potential to transform how the law addresses subtle and often hidden social hierarchies (V).

I. 'Caste-Blindness' and the Early Supreme Court

The concept of reservations did not spring forth from a vacuum at the time of the framing of the Constitution. At the turn of the twentieth century, there was increasing awareness that an individual's opportunities for educational, economic, and social advancement were heavily determined by her membership of different social groups, and, in particular, by her caste. Influenced by the writings of the radical egalitarian thinker Jyotirao Phule, the ruler of the princely state of Kolhapur (Shahuji Maharaj) first introduced affirmative action in 1902, reserving 50 per cent of government and administrative posts for backward castes. Setting out his justification for reservations, Shahuji noted that despite an active attempt to foster the education of all classes in the state, there had been a lack of success because 'the rewards for higher education are not sufficiently widely distributed'.[7] The phrasing is noteworthy because it reflects Shahuji's acknowledgement of the structural and institutional barriers that prevented an equitable distribution of opportunities *right from the beginning of life*. Following Kolhapur's example, by the 1920s, numerous princely states, as well as provincial legislative councils under colonial rule, had instituted quota systems for admission into educational institutions and for recruitment to government posts.[8] These quotas were aimed at ensuring the representation of 'backward classes' in spaces that they were unable to access.

Under the colonial regime, which unapologetically viewed Indian society as an agglomeration of communities,[9] distributing benefits on a group-wise basis was quite normal. After all, the centrepiece of colonial legal policy was the existence of separate, communal electorates, on the grounds that the interests of different communities could be represented only by members of those communities. However, with the passage of the Constitution, which decisively rejected communal electorates in favour of universal adult *individual* suffrage, and guaranteed to all *citizens* a right against discrimination and a right to equality of opportunity, could the regime of 'communal quotas' continue?[10]

When the Supreme Court was first asked that question, it responded with a decisive 'No'. The State of Madras had a pre-constitutional reservation policy for admission to medical institutions, which allocated seats among 'non-Brahmin Hindus', 'Backward Hindus', 'Brahmins', 'Harijans', 'Anglo-Indians', and 'Muslims', on a quota basis. Soon after the Constitution came into force, this policy was challenged by Champakam Dorairajan, an aspiring Brahmin medical student, who argued that the government's reservation policy violated her right to non-discrimination under Article 15(1), and her right to non-discriminatory access to State educational institutions under Article 29(2)[11] (Article 15[4] did not exist at the time). In *State of Madras v. Champakam Dorairajan*,[12] the Supreme Court agreed, holding that 'the right to get admission into any educational institution of the kind mentioned in clause (2) is a right which an individual citizen has as a citizen and not as a member of any community or class of citizens'.[13] A policy that made admission conditional upon class membership, therefore, was unconstitutional.

The State argued that, under Article 46 of the Constitution, which was part of the Directive Principles, it was mandated to 'promote ... with special care the educational and economic interests of the weaker sections of the people ...'[14] The Constitution itself, therefore, envisaged policies aimed at *sections*, or groups, that had suffered, and continued to suffer, from various disadvantages. The Court swiftly rejected this argument, observing that 'the directive principles of the State policy, which ... are expressly made unenforceable by a court, cannot override the provisions found in Part III'.[15]

Champakam Dorairajan was both the first and the clearest exposition of a constitutional philosophy of equality that I shall call 'caste-blind'. These were the building blocks of the philosophy: first, that the rights under Article 15(1), 16(1), and 29(2) were *individual* rights; second, that Article 46's mandate to uplift weaker sections, framed in the language of groups and group rights, was merely a political exhortation to the government; and third, that group-based policies were constitutional only if they came within a specific, enabling provision, like Article 16(4), which was a group-oriented exception to the constitutional principle of individual equality. However, in a circumstance where Article 16(4) was not applicable, and where (as the Court concluded its judgement by noting) 'the classification proceeds on the basis of religion, race and caste … [it is] opposed to the Constitution and constitutes a clear violation of the fundamental right guaranteed to citizens under Article 29(2)'.[16] In short, the Constitution was caste-blind because it required that, except where specifically provided otherwise, '*… government must treat citizens as individuals and not as members of racial, ethnic, or religious groups*'.[17]

Even as the Supreme Court was deciding *Champakam Dorairajan*, the Parliament was moving to amend the Constitution. Through the First Amendment, Article 15(4) was inserted, stipulating that:

> Nothing in this Article … shall prevent the State from making any special provisions for the advancement of any socially and educationally backward classes of citizens or for the Scheduled Castes and the Scheduled Tribes.

The First Amendment reinforced the vision of a caste-blind Constitution. If Parliament had to amend the Constitution and add a fresh article whenever it wanted to make a provision for groups, then it made sense to view these fresh provisions as departures from, or exceptions to, the idea of caste-blind, individual-focused equality, as expressed by Articles 14, 15(1), 16(1), and 16(2).[18]

The Supreme Court doubled down on caste-blind equality after *Dorairajan*. In *General Manager, Southern Railway v. Rangachari*,[19] it held that Article 16(4) covered only 'reservation of appointments or posts'. Consequently, in those aspects of public employment that did not fall within this phrase—'such as salary, increment, gratuity, pension and the age of superannuation'[20]—there could be no reservation, because 'these matters … do not form the subject-matter of Art. 16(4)'.[21] In other words, as *Rangachari* made starkly clear, 'equality of opportunity' and 'reservation' were antithetical concepts. The latter existed only because, and to the extent that, Article 16(4) allowed for it.

There were, furthermore, two important corollaries to this principle, which were evolved by the Supreme Court soon after. First, in *M.R. Balaji v. State of Mysore*,[22] the Court capped reservations at a maximum of 50 per cent, on the grounds that the exceptions (Articles 15[4] and 16[4]) could not 'swallow up' the rule (of equality and non-discrimination).[23] This was reaffirmed soon after in *T. Devadasan v. Union of India*,[24] where the Court prohibited the State from 'carrying forward' unfulfilled reserved vacancies into succeeding recruitment years. And secondly, if the legitimacy of reservations was solely due to Articles 15(4) and 16(4), then no person could claim them as a matter of right.[25]

This puzzle, however, misses one last piece. Any method for selection of individuals—whether for educational admissions or government recruitment—would have to follow some kind of classification.[26] An admission test, for example, would use marks as the basis for decision, separating applicants into two 'classes': those who cleared the cut-off and those who didn't. This takes us back to the Supreme Court's well-worn aphorism that the Constitution's Equality Code permits 'reasonable classification' but not 'class legislation'. But what is the difference between these two terms? Or, to frame the question another way, what kinds of 'classes' fall within the prohibition of 'class legislation'?

Early on, the Court answered the question by referring back to the classic two-pronged test under Article 14 of the Constitution, which guaranteed the 'equal protection of laws': a 'classification' would be reasonable if there was an intelligible differentia between the two classes, and if it bore a rational nexus with a State goal.[27] However, while this answer might suffice for an Article 14 challenge, it would not be enough under Article 16(1). The State might simply argue that its goal *was* just to increase representation of 'backward classes' in State employment. Then, class-based reservations would have a rational nexus with this goal, and the tests of Article 14 would be met. The Court got around this problem by ascribing a set of normative commitments to the term 'equality of opportunity'. The very concept of individual equality of opportunity, held the Court, ruled out goals such as levelling class-based representation. The only goals the State could legitimately base its recruitment or admissions policies on were goals *internal* to the institution in question, related only to the 'demands and needs of the office';[28] for example, increasing efficiency[29] or selecting the best candidates.[30] An admission test met this criterion; reservations did not.

What links the vision of the caste-blind Constitution with this understanding of equality of opportunity is a philosophical individualism that distinguishes between an individual's 'personal characteristics'[31] (her religion, caste, gender, socio-economic class, and so on) and her 'personal qualities' (merit).[32] Classification on the basis of the former (such as a reservation scheme) is presumptively illegitimate and antithetical to equal treatment, both because personal characteristics are not within the individual's control, and because they should be morally irrelevant to determining individual worth.[33] For the opposite reasons, classification schemes that take into account personal merit and qualities are consistent with the principle of equal treatment and equality of opportunity.[34] Although the Supreme Court never articulated this philosophical commitment that underlay its early Article 16 jurisprudence, as I have argued, it is this vision that explains both its focus on a caste-blind Constitution as well as its distinction between merit- or efficiency-oriented selection procedures on the one hand and group-oriented reservations on the other.

II. *State of Kerala v. N.M. Thomas*

However, even amidst this near-uniform consensus, there was a note of disagreement. In *T. Devadasan*, the question was whether the State could 'carry forward' unfilled reserved vacancies into the succeeding recruitment year. To put it in concrete terms: suppose the State reserved 30 per cent of seats, but in year X only 20 per cent were actually filled up by reserved category candidates, could the State 'carry forward' the remaining 10 per cent into the succeeding year, and reserve 40 per cent of the seats in order to bring the total representation of reserved category candidates back to 30 per cent?

Following the *Balaji* rule of capping reservations at 50 per cent, a majority of the Court rejected the 'carry-forward principle'.[35]

Justice Subba Rao dissented. His dissent, however, was not limited to reservation caps, but presented a serious challenge to the entire philosophical structure that the Court had erected over its first decade. After surveying the constitutional provisions, he observed:

> If [Article 16(1)] stood alone all the backward communities would go to the wall in a society of uneven basic social structure; the said rule of equality would remain only an [sic] utopian conception unless a practical content was given to it.[36]

The crucial philosophical shift initiated by Justice Subba Rao was this: in his view, ascriptive group markers such as class were not to be understood as 'personal characteristics' alone, but as personal characteristics embedded within an 'uneven basic social structure'. The concept of equality of opportunity had to take into account how these personal characteristics interacted with social structure. To illustrate the point, Justice Subba Rao took the example of a race between a racehorse and an ordinary horse, noting that if they both started together, it would only be a 'farce of a competition'.[37] A handicap was necessary to ensure 'real competition' and, by extension, genuine equality of opportunity. Transposing the example into Article 16(1), he went on to note:

> Centuries of calculate [sic] oppression and habitual submission reduced a considerable section of our community to a life of serfdom.[38]

This took the argument one step further, locating the different conditions of sections of the community to 'calculated oppression' and 'habitual submission'. In other words, the racehorse was not a racehorse by nature but as the result of many generations of conscious breeding and a lifetime of painstaking care—advantages not available to the ordinary horse. By attributing the condition of the 'backward classes' to a history of structured and institutional oppression, Justice Subba Rao was laying the ground for the moral and constitutional argument that would follow: that any meaningful conception of equality and equality of opportunity must necessarily take this history into account:

> That is why the makers of the Constitution introduced clause (4) in Art. 16. The expression 'nothing in this article' is a legislative device to express its intention in a most emphatic way that the power conferred thereunder is not limited in any way by the main provision but falls outside it.[39]

The shift was complete: Article 16(4) was no more an exception to Article 16(1) but an 'emphatic' expression of the same intention. Articles 14, 15, and 16 constituted a comprehensive Equality Code whose philosophy was to take into account, and surmount, inequalities generated by social and institutional structures over time. Where the site of such inequalities mapped onto class, equality could be served only by fashioning policies that identified persons *on the basis* of class membership, and then allocated benefits and burdens accordingly. Readers will note that it was strikingly similar to the justification offered by Shahuji Maharaja when he introduced the concept of reservations into the Indian polity for the first time.

It was twelve years later, in *N.M. Thomas*, that Justice Subba Rao's proto-formulation of this more substantive conception of equality was given a rich and detailed articulation. In *N.M. Thomas*, a governmental order granted provisional promotions to members of Scheduled Castes (SCs) and Scheduled Tribes (STs) who did not have the requisite qualifications to be eligible for such promotion, along with a two-year grace period for them to gain such qualifications. This was challenged. The key contention of the aggrieved parties was that the classification was clearly void under Articles 16(1) and (2), and *not* covered by Article 16(4). Under existing precedent, this ought to have been a simple case. *If* Article 16(4) did not apply, then special provisions for SCs and STs clearly violated Articles 16(1) and (2).

Not so, said a divided Court, splitting 5–2. In paragraph 31, Chief Justice Ray, writing the majority opinion, began with the basics:

> … the question of unequal treatment does not really arise between persons governed by different conditions and different sets of circumstances.[40]

As we have seen, until now, using characteristics external to the context of employment, viz., an absence of representation of certain classes, had been held not to be reasonable. Chief Justice Ray, however, turned this on its head:

> … equality within Articles 14 and 16(1) will not be violated by a rule which will ensure equality of representation in the services for unrepresented classes *after satisfying the basic needs of efficiency of administration.*[41]

Consequently, following Justice Subba Rao, Chief Justice Ray propounded the view that Article 16(4) was not an exception to Article 16(1) but existed as 'one of the methods of achieving equality embodied in Article 16(1)'.[42]

Standing by itself, however, this is not enough. Taken on its own, the phrase 'unrepresented classes' used by Chief Justice Ray is much too broad. For example, it cannot be that the children of ministers have an enforceable right to government employment, in case at any time, as a class, they were 'unrepresented'.[43] Examples can be multiplied, but the crucial point is to understand that what matters is not simply class-based representation but a method for ascertaining the circumstances in which representation (or the lack thereof) becomes salient for the principle of equality of opportunity.

The issue was sharpened in Justice Khanna's dissenting opinion, where he put the point simply: preferential treatment, by definition, was a negation of equality.[44] Of course, the word 'preferential' is a fraught one. As we discussed above, in a slightly different context, every admission or recruitment test that makes use of general standards is 'preferential'. A written exam, for example, 'prefers' people with better test-taking skills, a better command over language, a better knowledge of the subject, and so on. Well aware of this, Justice Khanna went on to clarify: 'reasonable classification', he argued, allowed you to take into account only those factors that were required for ensuring effective employment; or, in other words, factors *other* than personal characteristics.[45] That is, the kind of 'preference' implicit in written, subject-oriented tests was permitted under equality of opportunity, but 'preference' in terms of 'personal characteristics' was not.

This argument was buttressed by Justice Beg in a partially concurring and partially dissenting opinion, where he noted that Article 16(4), in allowing reservations, departed from the 'principle of absolute equality of opportunity in the application of uniform tests of competence'.[46] The phrase 'uniform tests of competence'—which Justice Beg tacked onto the definition under Article 16(1)—is an important one, and requires some unpacking.

The word 'uniform', like the word 'preferential', is not self-explanatory. There is nothing inherently more 'uniform' about a recruitment test than there is about a reservation quota. What makes a 'test of competence' *seem* 'uniform', however, is that it doesn't take into account personal characteristics, i.e., it treats individuals as unencumbered selves, detached from the features that mark them out as members of groups ('impersonal').[47] In other words, you take people as you find them: if an individual fails a 'uniform test of competence', it is not because of something *about them* (a personal characteristic such as sex or religion or class), but because of something they *were unable to do* (score high enough).

This goes back to a point made above. Reservations seem antithetical to the principle of equality of opportunity because they allocate benefits and burdens on the basis of that which individuals cannot control (their membership of a group). An entrance test, however, is the opposite of that—it depends entirely on factors within the individual's control (or so the argument goes). Consequently, at the heart of the clash between Chief Justice Ray on the one hand and Justices Khanna and Beg on the other was a conflict over the relationship between principles of equality and personal (or group-oriented) characteristics, within the framework of a Constitution that, ostensibly, was committed to the individual. And it was this clash that set the stage for the concurring opinions of Justices Mathew and Krishna Iyer, which advanced a new and transformative vision of equality.

Justice Mathew began his opinion by identifying the clash at the heart of the case. Everyone agreed that equality entailed treating equals equally and unequals unequally. But what did it mean for people to be 'equal' or 'unequal': that is, 'what is to be allowed as a significant difference [between people] such as would justify differential treatment'[48] As we have seen, prior Supreme Court decisions and the dissenting judgements in *N.M. Thomas* had answered this question by drawing a distinction between differences relevant to the State's goal (in this case, recruiting for public employment) and irrelevant 'personal characteristics'. As Justice Mathew himself conceded, 'in distributing the office of a state, not any sort of personal equality is relevant; for, unless we employ criteria appropriate to the sphere in question, it would turn out that a man's height or complexion could determine his eligibility or suitability for a post … candidates for office should possess those qualities that go to make up an effective use of the office.'[49]

But while prior judgements had also *limited* their understanding of 'relevant differences' to this narrow conception, Chief Justice Ray had broadened it to include inadequate representation *itself* as a relevant difference, as we have seen. As we also saw, however, this was insufficient. It was Justice Mathew who took the idea further. And he began his analysis with a crucial interpretive move:

> The notion of equality of opportunity is a notion that a limited good shall in fact be allocated on the grounds which do not, a priori, exclude any section of those that desire it. All sections of people desire and claim representation in the public service of the country, but the available number of posts are limited and therefore, even though all sections of people might desire to get posts, it is practically impossible to satisfy the desire. The question therefore is: on what basis can any citizen or class of citizens be excluded from his or their fair share of representation?[50]

Whereas, until now, the Supreme Court had asked whether a particular mode of recruitment was consistent with the goals of State employment, Justice Mathew turned this on its head, starting with the presumption that everyone was *entitled* to the public good of State employment. However, given that this public good was scarce, the State would have to devise some method of selecting some people and excluding others. The question then became: on what basis could the State exclude persons, or groups of persons, from their share of representation? Once the question had been framed in that manner, Justice Mathew was able to escape from the conceptual framework that limited equality of opportunity to tracing a rational relationship between the goals of public employment (efficiency, skill, etc.) and the mode of recruitment:

> What, then, is *a priori* exclusion? It means exclusion on grounds other than those appropriate or rational for the good (posts) in question. The notion requires not merely that there should be no exclusion from access on grounds other than those appropriate or rational for the good in question, but the grounds considered appropriate for the good should themselves be such that people from all sections of society have an equal chance of satisfying them.[51]

As we can see, the first part of this analysis echoed the old jurisprudence. The second part added an additional requirement, which flowed from Justice Mathew's starting presumption of a basic entitlement to public goods. To illustrate his argument, he cited an example drawn from the British philosopher Bernard Williams: imagine a warrior society where the position of a soldier carried prestige and power. Up to a point, this was also a slave-owning society, and slaves were barred from becoming soldiers. Imagine that the slaves were then emancipated, and the formal bar removed. However, because they had been kept systematically weak and malnourished during their period of slavery, they were unable to pass the physical tests that were required to qualify as a soldier. Bernard Williams argued that the ostensibly neutral physical tests did not, in any genuine way, further the principle of equality.[52] Invoking this example, Justice Mathew then observed:

> What one is doing there is to apply the same criteria to X as affected by favourable conditions and to Y as affected by unfavourable but curable conditions. Here there is a necessary pressure to equal up the conditions. To give X and Y equality of opportunity involves regarding their conditions, where curable, as themselves part of what is done to X and Y and not part of X and Y themselves. Their identity for this purpose does not include their curable environment, which is itself unequal and a contributor of inequality.[53]

This paragraph was at the heart of Justice Mathew's transformative vision of equality, a vision that involved a fundamental shift from viewing 'personal characteristics' as part of *who you are* to viewing them as part of a *humanly* constructed environment that can facilitate or hinder your access to basic public goods. A person's membership of a Scheduled Tribe, for example, was to be understood not as a mark of personal identity (and which, therefore, could not be privileged under the doctrine of equality), but as a socially constructed fact that severely limited her access to opportunities.[54]

While Justice Mathew's opinion laid out the philosophical foundations of the new vision of equality, it remained incomplete. At the beginning of his judgement, he noted that '[Equality] is a symbol of man's revolt against chance, fortuitous disparity, unjust power, and crystallized privileges'.[55] But as a constitutional proposition, this is both too vague and too broad. Does Article 16(1) actually aim to compensate people for bad luck or 'fortuitous disparity'? Perhaps not. Later, Justice Mathew went on to note that what Article 16(1) required was 'equality of results', because 'formal equality of opportunity simply enables people with mere education and intelligence to capture all the posts and to win over the less fortunate in education and talent even when the competition is fair'.[56] If, however, Article 16(1) was designed to compensate even for differences in 'intelligence', then it's difficult to see what, if any, differences *couldn't* be invoked to compensate for. As we had discussed earlier in this section, such a totalizing approach to Article 16(1) would make it more or less unworkable. Justice Mathew's opinion, therefore, failed to answer the question that he himself posed: what differences between persons were to be treated as *relevant* for the purposes of compensatory treatment under Article 16(1)?

Justice Krishna Iyer answered that question in his concurrence. Drawing upon the history of India's hierarchical society, the Directive Principles of State Policy, and the Constitution's commitment to the 'untouchable' community in several of its Articles, he noted that:

> ... 'equal opportunity' for members of a hierarchical society makes sense only [through] a strategy by which the underprivileged have environmental facilities for developing their full human potential ... the distinction would seem to be between handicaps imposed accidentally by nature and those resulting from societal arrangements such as caste structures and group suppression. Society being, in a broad sense, responsible for these latter conditions, it also has the duty to regard them as relevant differences among men and to compensate for them whenever they operate to prevent equal access to basic, minimal advantages enjoyed by other citizens.[57]

Here was a workable definition of the 'relevant differences' between people and classes of people. The kind of differences that the doctrine of equality is meant to take into account, and compensate for, are those imposed by social and institutional structures (over time), and which have the effect of denying people 'equal access' to basic goods.

Of course, this is by no means a perfect definition. The difference between disadvantages that society is 'responsible' for and those that are imposed 'accidentally by nature' is often blurred and unclear.[58] Consider, for example, an illness that is curable but the government's budgetary priorities preclude it from providing affordable access to the medicine. Is 'society' responsible, or is 'nature'?[59] This same problem, of course, lies in Justice Mathew's alternative approach, which focused on the word 'curable'. Between the incurability of death and the curability of caste-based social boycotts, there is a vast, uncertain spectrum where it is unclear where society's 'responsibility' begins and where it ends. But while the specific content of the nature/society distinction remains to be critically scrutinized, it is at least clear that Justice Krishna Iyer provided us with *a* plausible answer to the question that Justice Mathew posed: what distinctions between persons count as 'relevant' for the purposes of equality of opportunity?

We are now in a position to appreciate the transformative constitutional vision of equality based on a combined reading of the concurring opinions of Justices Mathew and Krishna Iyer in *N.M. Thomas*. According to this vision, every individual had an equal right to access basic public goods and resources, including State employment. In cases where these goods were scarce, the State would have to devise a procedure of selection, of exclusion and inclusion. Any State process would have to take into account both internal rationality (efficiency and merit) as well as external circumstances, such as historical and present-day social and institutional discrimination. Equality meant taking into account, and compensating for, historical and social circumstances that impeded an individual's access to the basic public goods important to sustain a dignified life.[60] As we have seen in a number of different ways, this more substantive vision of equality departed from what had come before.

III. *N.M. Thomas* as a Transformative Decision—A: Equality of Opportunity

In *N.M. Thomas*, a majority of the Supreme Court held that Article 16(4) was not an exception to Article 16(1) but a facet of it.[61] However, the 'reading in' of Article 16(4), with its specific commitment to 'classes', into Article 16(1), which guaranteed equality of opportunity to all 'citizens', raised some further interpretive problems. In particular, it meant that there were two distinct ways in which the new Article 16(1)/(4) combination could be understood. Under the first interpretation—call it the 'group subordination principle'[62]—the point of the special measures authorized by 16(4) is to achieve equality between *groups*.[63] In other words, the site of constitutional action is the group, and the right (to equality) that is being vindicated is that of the group's. The justification for this approach is that, historically, injustice has been meted out to certain groups (women, Dalits, etc.), and thus it makes sense for remedial action to be focused on them.

The second interpretation is also sensitive to the realities of historical discrimination, but even so it insists that ultimately the right to equality is an *individual* right. However, because historically the individual has been discriminated against *in virtue of* her membership of a particular group (e.g., *as* a woman, or *as* a Dalit), it might be necessary to take group identity into account in order to achieve genuine equality.[64] Notice that both these approaches support reservations, based on a historical understanding of the way in which discrimination has worked in our society, but for radically different reasons. The first, i.e., group-subordination approach, is geared towards *preserving* group identities by equalizing groups qua groups.

The second approach aims at eventual *elimination* of group identity, accepting group-based classifications as a necessary set of evils on the road to a society in which all individuals are brought to a position of genuine equality.[65]

In *N.M. Thomas,* the majority opinions did not address this issue in detail, although Justices Mathew and Krishna Iyer did nail their colours to the individual-right mast. The former began his opinion by noting that equality of opportunity was an individual right,[66] while Justice Krishna Iyer clarified that the ultimate purpose of reservations was to break down and eradicate caste groups (instead of preserving and equalizing them).[67] But neither Justice provided any further reasons justifying this interpretation of the Equality Code.[68]

A preliminary justification, of course, is located in the text of Article 16(1), which guarantees the equality of opportunity to all 'citizens' (not to all 'classes of citizens'). This also yields the important point that, by holding that Article 16(4) was a facet of Article 16(1), Justices Mathew and Krishna Iyer were making it clear that even the reservation provisions were, ultimately, about vindicating individual rights, even though the rights holders were defined in the language of 'backward classes.'

I will suggest, however, a deeper justification lies in constitutional history that speaks both to the argument that the right under Article 16(1) remains vested in the individual, and to the argument that under the Equality Code, Article 16(4) is a facet of Article 16(1). This is because the Constitution's Equality Code was a recognition of a long social history in which individuals had been singled out for discrimination and disadvantage because of their group identity (primarily caste): a social structure that, in the words of Marc Galanter, was built upon a 'complex pattern of exclusion, separation, and restricted use'.[69] Importantly, this was a social structure that existed parallel to, and often in complicity with, the colonial legal regime, which was supposedly based on principles of formal equality. For example, Eleanor Zelliot highlights an instance as early as

1856, where a Bombay school's refusal of admission to a Mahar student was upheld by the education department on the basis that it would not be right to 'force' caste-students into association with the Mahar, and thus 'mak[e] the institution practically useless to the great mass of natives'.[70] This was not a one-off situation. Schools segregated based on caste, and even segregated classrooms within integrated schools, were a reality for much of the late-nineteenth and early-twentieth centuries under an ostensibly equal formal public schooling system.[71]

School segregation is but one instance of a broader social structure in which a series of interdicts and prohibitions, both formal and informal, explicit and implicit, served to effectively deny certain groups access to basic public goods, whether roads and wells, or educational institutions. Ameliorative efforts proceeded on precisely this understanding. In 1931, the Census Commissioner, J.H. Hutton, proposed nine tests for determining 'untouchable groups' (subsequently 'Scheduled Castes' in the Constitution), most of which revolved around questions of disabilities and access (ability to use public conveniences, ability to access the services of barbers, water carriers, etc., access to temples, and so on).[72] With a few differences, this method was replicated by the 1932 Franchise Committee.[73]

The political thought of the rising nationalist movement reflected a similar understanding. For instance, following a nearly identically worded resolution passed in a Depressed Classes meeting at Bombay, the Indian National Congress in 1917 accepted the necessity of 'removing all disabilities imposed by custom upon the Depressed Classes'.[74] The 1928 Nehru Report provided, as a fundamental right, that 'no person shall by reason of his religion, caste or creed be prejudiced in any way in regard to public employment, office or power or honour and the exercise of any trade or calling'.[75]

This principle was then refined in the 1931 Karachi Resolution, the proto-Bill of Rights whose importance we have discussed in the previous chapter. The 1931 resolution's non-discrimination principle stipulated that 'no disability attaches to any citizen by reason of his or her religion, caste, creed or sex, in regard to public employment, office of power or honour, and in the exercise of any trade or calling'.[76] The use of the phrase 'no disability attaches' (instead of 'the State shall not discriminate') demonstrates an understanding of how the denial of equality of opportunity was primarily the result of entrenched social sanctions rather than any specific act of exclusion by the State.

More importantly, however, the succeeding phrase—'to any citizen by reason of his or her …'—anticipated Justices Mathew and Krishna Iyer's formulation in *N.M. Thomas*: the task of equality was to ensure that one's group membership did not become a *reason* for disability or exclusion. The 1928 Nehru Report used the phrase 'no person', and the 1931 Karachi Report used the phrase 'any citizen'. Consequently, the right remained individual (whether belonging to a person or to a citizen), while group membership was a salient factor in ensuring that the individual right could be genuinely and effectively exercised. The idea, in other words, was to achieve individual equality *through the means of* 'a national commitment to reduce invidious distinctions among groups, coupled with a conviction that it was permissible and perhaps necessary to employ these discredited caste notions to effectuate … equalizing policies …'[77]

This understanding is visible in the Constituent Assembly's Fundamental Rights Sub-Committee's first draft bill of rights. This first draft did not have anything resembling what eventually became Article 16(4). What it did have, as part of its equality clause, was the following:

> Any enactment, regulation, judgement, order, custom or interpretation of law, in force immediately before the commencement of this Constitution, by which any penalty, disadvantage or disability is imposed upon or any discrimination is made against any citizen on any of the grounds aforesaid (i.e., religion, race, caste, language or sex) shall cease to have effect.[78]

As in the earlier proto-constitutional drafts, the use of the broad words 'disadvantage' or 'disability' demonstrated a sensitivity to barriers that went beyond formal prohibitions (which were covered by the word 'penalty'); and the use of the word 'custom' signified 'disadvantages' and 'disabilities' whose origins were social and structural. Most importantly, once again, the fulcrum of the clause was the citizen. It was the (individual) citizen who, by virtue of her group identities, was subjected to disadvantages and disabilities, and it was the (individual) citizen whom the new Constitution was meant to emancipate through its commitment to equality.

Interestingly, in a subsequent version of the draft, this provision disappeared. What did come in was a proto-version of Article 16(4): 'Nothing herein contained shall prevent the State from making provision for reservations in favour of classes who, in the opinion of the State, are not adequately represented in the public services.'[79] Although this was not a direct substitution, the new provision was effectively doing the work of the old one, but in a clearer, more explicit fashion. Instead of the ambiguous prohibition of 'disabilities', there was now a mandate for affirmative action.

When the Constituent Assembly debated the clause, first in April 1947 and then during the reading of the draft Constitution in November 1948, there was little argument over the necessity for having it in the Constitution, and no discussion about its underlying philosophy. The debate centred primarily around the addition of the word 'backward' before 'classes', which was added by the Drafting Committee between the 1947 and the 1948 debates. Critics of the provision attacked it as being vague and indefinable. It was in his speech responding to these criticisms that B.R. Ambedkar offered some insight into the principles that grounded the clause. Noting that there existed 'three points of view' in the Assembly, which had to be 'reconciled', he observed that:

> ... the view of those who believe and hold that there shall be equality of opportunity has been embodied in sub-clause (1) of Article 10. It is a generic principle. At the same time, as I said, we had to reconcile this formula with the demand made by certain communities that

> the administration which has now – for historical reasons – been controlled by one community or a few communities, that situation should disappear and that the others also must have an opportunity of getting into the public services.[80]

Three aspects of this speech are important. The first is Ambedkar's insistence that Draft Article 10(1)—which would eventually become 16(1)—was only a 'generic principle'. By implication, therefore, the phrase 'equality of opportunity' did not, by itself, connote any concrete content. The second was his deliberate use of the word 'opportunity' to characterize the claims of the 'backward classes' as well. And the third was his characterization of the Draft Article as a 'reconciliation' between formal equality of opportunity and equitable representation. This reconciliation, Ambedkar went on to argue, was achieved by the addition of the word 'backward' before 'classes'. This would prevent a constitutional requirement to accede to *all* claims of prior insufficient representation, an eventuality that could 'destroy' the principle of equality of opportunity.

To substantiate his point, Ambedkar then took the example of a situation where 70 per cent of government posts were reserved, and stated that this would not be 'satisfactory from the point of view of … equality of opportunity'.[81] Such a situation, he argued, would be prevented by the addition of the word 'backward'. However, if Ambedkar's concern was purely numerical, then it would surely have been far easier to place a cap on reservations within the Article itself (as the Supreme Court did in *M.R. Balaji*). The use of the word 'backward' suggests not a quantitative constraint upon reservations but a qualitative one. It suggests a *normative* basis for distinguishing between claims of representation that could be constitutionally sustained and those that could not. And it is that normative basis that would constitute the moral foundation of the Constitution's Equality Code.

It is here that the link between 'social disabilities'—the pre-constitutional understanding—and 'backwardness' becomes salient.

The phrase 'backward class' had a long pre-constitutional history, starting, as we have seen, with the princely state of Kolhapur, after which it was taken up by other provincial governments. It was also used in numerous colonial documents, such as the Starte Committee[82] and the Franchise Commission. As Galanter observes, it had no fixed meaning. Its use had changed and varied widely according to local contexts, ranging from being synonymous with the untouchable classes, to being applied to classes that did not suffer from the stigma of untouchability but were nonetheless, in the view of the State, in need of 'special treatment'.[83] It had never been clarified, however, what precisely was the principled justification for 'special treatment', and Ambedkar's own defence of the provision in the Constituent Assembly effectively left the matter to the discretion of local governments.

That, however, is not the whole story. As Chandrika Ram pointed out during the Constituent Assembly debate on 30 November 1948, the phrase 'backward classes' had been defined in the census reports of 1921 and 1931,[84] where the criteria of 'backwardness', we have seen above, had been group-based, socially imposed disabilities of access. And, as we have also seen, preparatory drafts of the Advisory Committee specifically sought to overcome individual 'disability' and 'disadvantage' experienced 'by reason' of group membership, as part of a broader, substantive vision of equality.

We have, therefore, an incipient and incomplete link between the pre-constitutional groping towards equality, the drafts and debates in the Constituent Assembly, and the final text of what became Article 16: a 'reconciliation', as Ambedkar put it, between the claims of formal equality of opportunity on the one hand and equitable representation on the other. This reconciliation was achieved through a more nuanced vision of individual equality that contained within it the mandate to overcome disadvantages and disabilities that had an enduring societal, institutional, and structural character.[85] It was this vision that, as we have seen, first motivated Shahuji Maharaj in 1902. And it was this vision that was completed by the majority in

N.M. Thomas, and articulated most clearly in the concurring opinions of Justices Mathew and Krishna Iyer.[86]

IV. *N.M. Thomas* as a Transformative Decision—B: Directive Principles of State Policy

The historical arguments outlined above are indicative, but certainly not conclusive. The genealogy of the term 'backward class' was inconclusive, making it unclear what exactly was the normative basis of determining who was entitled to reservation under Article 16(4). After all, in the course of the same speech, Ambedkar referred both to 'reconciling' equality of opportunity and claims of representation as well as ensuring that the 'exception' (of reservations) did not swallow up the 'rule' (of equality of opportunity)—which, of course, was precisely how the pre-*Thomas* court understood the constitutional scheme.[87] The distinction is important: the rule-exception language suggests that Articles 16(1) and 16(4) contain opposed principles, and the judicial task is to balance (or 'reconcile') them by marking out their respective, separate domains. The *N.M. Thomas* understanding, however, is that the 'reconciliation' is achieved in Article 16(1) itself, through a vision of individual equality that is sensitive to group disadvantage, and that 16(4) is only a concrete restatement of this reconciliation.[88]

While some of the speakers in the Constituent Assembly adhered to the second understanding, specifically arguing that Article 16(4) was meant to provide 'equality of opportunity' in its genuine sense to members of backward classes,[89] other speakers categorically viewed it as a departure from the principles underlying the Equality Code, including Article 16(1).[90] Ambedkar's own ambivalence supports the idea that in the Constituent Assembly there was perhaps no genuine consensus about the nature of the relationship between Articles 16(1) and 16(4).

The text of Article 16(1) itself, as we have seen, is open to both interpretations. Consequently, with an ambiguous text and an inconclusive history, Justices Mathew and Krishna Iyer had to turn elsewhere to substantiate their reading of the Equality Code. They did so by looking beyond Article 16, beyond the Fundamental Rights chapter itself, and to another part of the Constitution—the Directive Principles of State Policy (Chapter IV). The opening clause of the DPSPs states:

> The provisions contained in this Part shall not be enforceable by any court, but the principles therein laid down are nevertheless fundamental in the governance of the country and it shall be the duty of the State to apply these principles in making laws.[91]

Recall that Article 46 of the Constitution, part of the DPSPs, commits the State to promote the interests of the 'weaker sections' of the people. In *Champakam Dorairajan*, the State had invoked this Article to defend its communal quotas. The Supreme Court had rejected this defence, holding that, because they were expressly unenforceable, DPSPs could have no role to play in the constitutional enquiry. In *N.M. Thomas*, however, Justice Mathew observed that:

> … if we want to give equality of opportunity for employment to the members of the Scheduled Castes and Scheduled Tribes, we will have to take note of their social, educational, and economic environment. Not only is the directive principle embodied in Article 46 binding on the law-maker as ordinarily understood but it should equally inform and illuminate the approach of the Court …[92]

Justice Krishna Iyer put the point more pithily:

> … Article 46 has to be given emphatic expression while interpreting Article 16(1) and (2).[93]

Therefore, Justices Mathew and Krishna Iyer held that Article 46, as a directive principle, was meant to inform the decision about which conception of equality of opportunity the Constitution was committed to. Article 46—with its mandate to the government to promote the interests of 'weaker sections' and to protect them from 'exploitation'—was to be 'read into' Article 16(1)'s guarantee of equality of opportunity and give it enforceable content. In other words, the DPSPs were to be treated as framework values, which would play a role in helping the Court to clothe the abstract principles of Part III (the Fundamental Rights chapter) with the flesh and blood of concrete constitutional commitments.

In making this claim, Justices Mathew and Krishna Iyer were joining issue in a long and contested battle about the precise constitutional relationship between fundamental rights and directive principles. The battle had raged in the Constituent Assembly, where one set of members failed to see the purpose of including within the Constitution a set of unenforceable principles, little more than 'pious wishes', and called for the entire Chapter to be scrapped. Other sets wanted some or all of the directive principles to be made enforceable fundamental rights. Against both camps, Ambedkar argued for the validity of a set of principles that, for various reasons, could not be judicially enforced, but were nonetheless 'binding'[94] and were intended to be 'the basis of all executive and legislative action'.[95]

The early Supreme Court, supported by H.M. Seervai,[96] took the position that 'unenforceability' meant 'legal irrelevance', and that Part IV could play no role in constitutional interpretation. By the end of the 1950s, however, the Court came around to the view that fundamental rights and directive principles had to be construed 'harmoniously'. This could mean invoking Part IV to hold that a law was a 'reasonable restriction' upon a fundamental right, or interpreting ambiguous statutes in a manner that advanced the goals of Part IV. Neither of those views, however, was entirely satisfactory or developed with any rigour. It was in *N.M. Thomas* that, for the first time, the Court understood the 'harmonious relationship' between Parts III and IV in the fashion outlined above: that Part IV expressed a system of political, social, and economic values that gave concrete shape to abstract fundamental rights and helped the Court to determine which of the many possible concrete interpretations of those rights to select in any given case (in *N.M. Thomas*, it was the right to equality).[97]

I have argued elsewhere that in doing so, the Supreme Court was correct, for many reasons. The use of the word 'enforceable' in Article 37 was deliberate (it replaced the word 'cognizable' from an earlier draft), and was meant only to prevent courts from striking down laws on the basis that they did not comply with the DPSPs. The framers did not, at any point, plan to make Part IV a vestigial organ of the Constitution. In fact, the use of the DPSPs as framework values was consistent with an important current of Indian political thought that came to fruition in the late 1930s and 1940s, in the build-up to the drafting of the Constitution: that the civil and political rights (which would be guaranteed by Part III of the Constitution) could not be meaningfully enjoyed without the concomitant provision of socio-economic rights (found in what finally became the Directive Principles chapter).[98]

Ambedkar himself, in a 1947 memorandum, pointed out the meaninglessness of civil and political rights to the unemployed, starving, and economically powerless.[99] There was, therefore, intellectual support for the proposition that, even if socio-economic rights could not be made directly enforceable, 'meaningful civil and political rights could not exist without being conceptualized in a way that took into account socio-economic considerations'.[100] This position was further endorsed by Ambedkar in the Constituent Assembly, where he argued that the Constitution was committed to the principle of 'economic democracy' as a complement to 'political democracy').[101] And this, of course, was exactly the position taken by Justices Mathew and Krishna Iyer in *N.M. Thomas*, as evidenced, in particular, by this paragraph:

> … if we want to give equality of opportunity for employment to the members of the Scheduled Castes and Scheduled Tribes, we will have to take note of their social, educational, and economic environment.[102]

Or, as the Supreme Court would observe a few years later:

> [The framers] had themselves made provisions in the Constitution to bring about a socio-economic transformation. That being so, it is reasonable to infer that the Constitution makers employed a broad phraseology while drafting the fundamental rights ...[103]

N.M. Thomas, therefore, was transformative in two senses. It was transformative in replacing the caste-blind vision of equality with a richer, more substantive vision. This vision retained the focus upon the individual, but also postulated the goal of equality as overcoming structural and institutional barriers that prevented individuals from accessing basic public goods because of their membership of certain groups. And it was transformative in articulating a new relationship between Parts III and IV of the Constitution: the socio-economic commitments of the directive principles were meant to serve as framework values for interpreting fundamental rights, especially where fundamental rights, couched in abstract principles, were susceptible to more than one interpretation.[104]

V. Conclusions: Problems and Prospects

To briefly recapitulate, the transformative vision of equality advanced by the Supreme Court in *N.M. Thomas* has three salient features. First, the rights to equality, and to equality of opportunity, are individual rights. Second, that these are substantive rights, designed to overcome asymmetrical social and institutional barriers to accessing basic public goods. And third, because in India these structural disadvantages and disabilities have been imposed largely on the basis of group (especially caste) membership, the equality provisions of the Constitution need to take groups into account, even though the rights remain individual rights.

This articulation helps to understand one of the most well-known and controversial doctrines evolved by the Supreme Court in the post-*N.M. Thomas* era. In *Indra Sawhney v. Union of India*, the Supreme

Court held that the benefits of reservation could not accrue to the 'creamy layer' among the backward groups; that is, those individual members who had managed to escape the markers of backwardness to an extent enough for them to no longer count as 'members' of that group in any meaningful way.[105] It will be immediately obvious that the existence of the creamy layer doctrine is consistent *only* with an individual-centric view of the right to equality of opportunity. If the right was that of groups, then it would make no sense to undertake an investigation of the relative backwardness of individuals within those groups.[106] Furthermore, we can also now understand another doctrine that is, in many respects, the opposite of the creamy layer: in *R.K. Sabharwal v. State of Punjab*,[107] the Supreme Court held that even if a certain number of reserved category candidates managed to compete successfully with the general pool, this would not lead to a proportionate *decrease* in the number of available reserved seats. However, if reservation is a *group* right, meant to uplift a historically subordinated group to a level of substantive equality, then it makes perfect sense to stop once the prescribed percentage of representation has been achieved—whether through the general pool or through the reserved quota. On the other hand, if the right is an individual right that is instantiated through the individual's membership in a group, *then* the Court's holding was understandable: the fact that some members of the subordinated group have achieved parity with the rest of society doesn't affect the scope of the right held by *other* members of the group.

However, perhaps more important are the implications of a clear understanding of *N.M. Thomas*—implications that have remained unexplored by the Court even until today. These implications are not limited to an analysis of Article 16, but pervade the entire Equality Code of the Constitution.[108]

A. Groups

In 1955, in *Sukhnandan Thakur v. State of Bihar*, a divided full bench of the Patna High Court struck down job reservations for persons who, during the colonial era, had been punished by the British regime for participating in the freedom movement.[109] Hewing to the logic of *Champakam Dorairajan*, the Court held that the reservations could not be traced to Article 16(4), and clearly violated the rule of equality of opportunity under Article 16(1).[110] Despite the legitimate claims of political sufferers to government solicitude, the State would have to find some other way of accommodating their needs. The Court's holding came over a strong dissent by the Chief Justice, who expressed the view that the State did have the power to make reservations in cases of 'underserved want'[111] (a phrase borrowed from Article 41), and that doing so amounted to a 'reasonable classification' under Article 16(1).

Two decades later, in a very similar case, Punjab's decision to provide job reservations for ex-armed forces personnel was challenged. In *Jagdish Rai v. State of Punjab*, relying upon the Supreme Court's recent decision in *N.M. Thomas*, the High Court of Punjab and Haryana upheld it, holding that Article 16(4) was no longer the exclusive source of the power to make reservations.[112] Noting the decision in *Sukhnandan Thakur*, the Court observed that the dissenting judgement had got it right. Therefore:

> ... while the best and the most meritorious of those seeking appointment under the State should be selected, it is also equally fair and equitable that a just proportion of the posts should be given to those who, because of a peculiar handicap, may not stand a chance against those not so handicapped. It would be an extension of the principle of Article 16(4) to those that do not fall under Article 16(4). Defence Personnel who on account of their service with the Army, the Navy, and the Air Force over the years have lost opportunities for entering Government service and have also lost contact with ordinary civilian life may find it extremely difficult, on demobilization, to compete with civilians for civilian jobs despite the qualities of discipline, sacrifice, sense of public duty, initiative, loyalty, and leadership which they would have undoubtedly acquired as members of the Defence Forces.[113]

What *N.M. Thomas* did, therefore, was to turn the reasoning of the dissenting opinion in *Sukhnandan Thakur* into the judgement of the Court in *Jagdish Rai*, and open up Article 16(1) to a range of group-oriented affirmative action measures. Importantly, *Jagdish Rai's* formulation of 'underserved want' was substantially wider than *N.M. Thomas*'s focus on socially imposed disabilities. Depending on how the word 'undeserved' is interpreted, it could expand the reach of Article 16(1) to encompass situations covered by Justice Mathew's broadest formulation, requiring the State to compensate individuals for bad luck or a lack of fortune or talent.

The basic point remains, however: 'classification' under Article 16(1), after *N.M. Thomas*, is not limited to 'uniform tests' aimed at selecting the most 'meritorious' or the most 'efficient', but includes measures that take into account the personal characteristics (or group membership) of people, and how those personal characteristics interact with the social environment in ways that could facilitate or limit an individual's chances in an open competition. As *Jagdish Rai* shows, the groups in question need not be limited to the traditional subjects of Article 16(4), viz., Scheduled Castes, Scheduled Tribes, and Other Backward Classes, but can include any set of persons who share a characteristic that has, in the past or the present, been a site of, or reason for, disadvantage.

Notably, a final corollary of this is that Article 16(1) permits further sub-classification which is sensitive to disadvantage *within* groups, and the Supreme Court has been wrong in rejecting the State's power to do so.[114]

B. Power and Duty

Secondly, the immediate impact of holding that Article 16(4) is a facet of Article 16(1) is that, contrary to the Supreme Court's holding in *Rajendran*, the principles underlying Article 16(4) are now enforceable rights. Group-oriented substantive equality is no longer only a matter of the State exercising its discretion in deciding whether and how to compensate for structural inequalities. Indeed, if the principles underlying Article 16(4) are now 'facets' of Article 16(1), then it must follow that—as Galanter realized immediately after the judgement in *N.M. Thomas* was delivered[115]—an individual who feels that she has been substantively disadvantaged by reason of her group membership has a *right* to approach the Court and demand that this inequality be mitigated.

Of course, this radically transforms the relationship between individual and the State, when it comes to questions of structural inequalities and substantive barriers to access. After *N.M. Thomas*, the State does not merely have the *power* to remedy these inequalities, but has a *duty* to identify and remedy them—a duty for which it is answerable in a court.[116]

This duty is not limited to the groups that are the subjects of reservation policies, i.e., the Scheduled Castes, the Scheduled Tribes, and the Other Backward Classes, following the 1992 Supreme Court judgement in *Indra Sawhney*. While the *N.M. Thomas* judgement was delivered in the context of reservations, and was an interpretation of Article 16(4), its formulation of equality as requiring the overcoming of structural and institutional barriers to access is constrained neither by the subject group of Article 16(4) (backward classes) nor by its chosen mode of redressal (reservation in appointments).[117]

After *N.M. Thomas*, any individual or group of individuals is entitled to bring a claim under Article 16(1), based only on demonstrable structural or institutional discrimination. *N.M. Thomas*, therefore, makes the Equality Code dynamic: instead of tying substantive equality to a fixed category of backward classes, it envisages a constantly evolving situation, where groups that are the sites of social and institutional disadvantages can change over time, and even new groups can be added as times change.[118]

Although the Supreme Court had inconsistently rejected the 'power + duty' formulation of Article 16(1) even after *N.M. Thomas*,[119] there are recent signs that it has begun to understand the issue. For instance, in its famous *National Legal Services Authority* or *NALSA* judgement, it directed reservation for members of the transgender community in State employment.[120] After cataloguing a long history of institutional discrimination and violence 'in all spheres of society'[121] (including denial of recognition, access to healthcare and employment, and access to public spaces), in its final directions to the State, the Supreme Court specifically noted that the transgender community would be entitled to reservations *as* a 'socially and economically backward class' under Article 16(4) of the Constitution.[122]

Although *NALSA* has faced problems in implementation, it nonetheless remains an important judgement that advanced the logic of *N.M. Thomas* in the two directions discussed above. First, *NALSA* expanded the reach of Article 16 to a group that did not fall within the traditional category of backward classes, by using the underlying transformative logic of the Constitution's Equality Code (i.e., that of overcoming structural barriers that had been thrown up around entire groups of people because of their group membership). Second, once it had been established that the transgender community did have the markers of a backward class, it followed that it also had a *right* to an equality-achieving remedy from the government. No longer was Article 16(4) simply an enabling provision under which the government could choose to act, or refrain from acting, in aid of backward classes. The logical conclusion of *N.M. Thomas* reading Article 16(4) into 16(1) was precisely that groups facing structural inequalities now had an enforceable right against the State, grounded in the idea of equality.

C. Disparate Impact

This leads us to the next important implication. As the Supreme Court has often held, Articles 14, 15, and 16 together constitute the Equality Code (along with Articles 17 and 18), and embody one coherent philosophy of equality under the Constitution. We have seen that courts have used this dictum to read Article 14's classification test into Article 16(1) and, occasionally, Article 15. However, if Articles 14, 15, and 16 constitute the Equality Code, then surely the relationship is two-way. Just as the principles under Article 14 can illuminate and inform the interpretations of Articles 15 and 16, the concrete content of Article 16(4)—now, after *N.M. Thomas*, a facet of Article 16(1)—ought to be read back into the abstract principles of Articles 14 and 15(1).

As Justice Mathew pointed out in *N.M. Thomas*, one important aspect of Article 16(4) is that its test for inequality is an effects-oriented test.[123] That is, according to Article 16(4), inadequate representation in State employment is an indicator that this state of affairs is the result of social or institutional inequality, which requires to be remedied *via* the doctrine of equality of opportunity.[124] Justice Mathew's own example, borrowed from Bernard Williams, supports this view. The fact that the descendants of erstwhile slaves are overwhelmingly unsuccessful in qualifying as soldiers under a seemingly neutral test of strength is evidence to suggest that the test is not quite neutral. And a little digging reveals that the 'neutral' test is so constructed that the past socially imposed disabilities that the erstwhile slaves suffered from will put them at an extreme disadvantage in the 'open competition' of the present.

In equality jurisprudence, the approach of focusing on the 'disproportionately exclusionary impact'[125] of policies rather than their formal character or their motive is known as 'disparate impact'. It is based on the premise (as we discussed in Chapter 1) that inequality and discrimination result not from individual hostile acts, but from structures and institutions. As a corollary, discrimination does not necessarily occur through a set of identifiable and discrete acts, but can be seen through results—for example, when a particular group's participation in the workforce is found to be far smaller than its share in the population.[126]

Disparate impact of this kind raises a presumption of inequality, which must then be rebutted. For example, in a Canadian case, it was necessary to pass an aerobics test in order to get a job as a firefighter. It was found that, statistically, and for physiological reasons, far fewer women passed this test than men. Even though the test made no reference to gender, and was perfectly 'neutral' in that regard, the doctrine of disparate impact raised a presumption that the test was gender-discriminatory. The State was called upon to demonstrate that the physical test was necessary for fulfilling the duties of a firefighter. It failed to do so, and the test was struck down.[127]

As we discussed in previous chapters, the Indian Supreme Court has never *explicitly* accepted disparate impact as being a part of its equality and discrimination law toolkit. However, a necessary implication of *N.M. Thomas* is the incorporation of disparate impact analysis into equality law. This is because Article 16(4) is based entirely on that principle. The lack of representation in government services raises the initial presumption of inequality, which is then substantiated by investigations into backwardness. Until *N.M. Thomas*, Article 16(4) remained an exception to the Equality Code, along with whatever principles that underlay it. However, once it is accepted that 16(4) is a facet of 16(1), it becomes clear that disparate impact is contained not only within the meaning of equality of opportunity under Article 16(1), but must also be 'read back' into Articles 14 and 15(1), and into the broader jurisprudence of equality and non-discrimination.

Part Two
Fraternity

Article 15

(2) No citizen shall, on grounds only of religion, race, caste, sex, place of birth or any of them, be subject to any disability, liability, restriction, or condition with regard to–

(a) access to shops, public restaurants, hotels, and places of public entertainment

Article 17

'Untouchability' is abolished and its practice in any form is forbidden. The enforcement of any disability arising out of 'Untouchability' shall be an offence punishable in accordance with law.

Article 23

(1) Traffic in human beings and *begar* and other similar forms of forced labour are prohibited and any contravention of this provision shall be an offence punishable in accordance with law.

(2) Nothing in this article shall prevent the State from imposing compulsory service for public purposes, and in imposing such service the State shall not make any discrimination on grounds only of religion, race, caste, or class or any of them.

Article 25

(1) Subject to public order, morality, and health and to the other provisions of this Part, all persons are equally entitled to freedom of conscience and the right freely to profess, practise, and propagate religion.

(2) Nothing in this article shall affect the operation of any existing law or prevent the State from making any law–

(a) regulating or restricting any economic, financial, political, or other secular activity which may be associated with religious practice;

(b) providing for social welfare and reform or the throwing open of Hindu religious institutions of a public character to all classes and sections of Hindus.

Article 26

Subject to public order, morality and health, every religious denomination or any section thereof shall have the right—

...

(b) to manage its own affairs in matters of religion.

4

Civil Rights: *Indian Medical Association* and Horizontal Discrimination

The issue is not entry [into temples] *but equality.*

B.R. Ambedkar (quoted in Anupama Rao, *The Caste Question*)

The teacher had allotted us a place in a corner near the door from where we could not move until school was over for the day. The blackboard would be in another corner.

Baby Kamble, *The Prisons We Broke*

IN EARLY 2014, THE Indian government mooted an 'Equal Opportunities Commission' (EOC).[1] This move was based upon the Sachar Committee Report of 2006, which had found that the Indian Muslim community was significantly disadvantaged on a host of parameters, including access to social and physical infrastructure, standards of living, and literacy. According to the report, the task of the EOC, like its counterparts in the US and European countries,[2] would be to check discrimination against minority communities in employment, housing, accommodation, and so on.[3]

The EOC was necessitated by the existence of *horizontal discrimination*, i.e., discrimination suffered by private entities at the hands of other private entities (individuals or corporations) on the basis of constitutionally proscribed markers, viz., sex, race, caste, religion, place of birth, etc. Horizontal discrimination can take a variety of forms: restrictive covenants, denial of access to public spaces, exclusion from economic transactions, and so on. These disparate ways of discrimination all involve, in some manner, a clash between the associative rights of private individuals (including their right not to associate with others, and to exclude others from associating with them) on the one hand, and the rights of individuals and groups against non-discrimination and to full participation in the economic and social life of the community on the other.[4]

In this chapter, I examine horizontal discrimination in the form of one particularly invidious avatar: housing discrimination on the basis of religion. This is because housing discrimination has become a pervasive feature of the Indian social landscape in recent times.[5] In some states it has even received legal sanctity through laws that allow State agencies to prohibit sale of property along inter-religious lines.[6] More importantly, however, the Supreme Court's most detailed and, as I shall argue, incorrect engagement with horizontal discrimination arose in the context of a housing case, and provides us with a point of departure from which to analyse the constitutional questions at issue and how the Court dealt with them.

At first blush, housing discrimination appears to be a straightforward violation of Articles 14 and 15(1) of the Constitution. Of course, matters are complicated because most housing societies[7] are private, while the equality and non-discrimination guarantees are addressed to the State. In the first part of this chapter, I examine various possible solutions to this problem by looking to the decisions of other constitutional courts (I). I then examine the greatest obstacle that lies in the way of similar legal developments in India—

the 2005 Supreme Court decision in *Zoroastrian Cooperative*—and argue that its reach must be narrowly limited to its specific factual matrix (II). I go on to analyse the Supreme Court's landmark 2011 decision in *Indian Medical Association* (*IMA*) *v. Union of India*, and argue that it lays the groundwork for a constitutional, horizontally applicable civil rights jurisprudence grounded in an expansive reading of Article 15(2) of the Constitution which goes *beyond* the solutions advanced in other jurisdictions (III). I end by discussing how this interpretation, an apparent departure from the principles of classic political and constitutional liberalism, is philosophically and historically justified, given the transformative character of the Constitution (IV).

I. The Problem of Restrictive Covenants

Housing discrimination is often carried out through exclusionary covenants, which restrict the sale, transfer, or occupation of property on the bases of race, caste, religion, ethnicity, sex, nationality, or other such grounds that are normally considered discriminatory.[8] Exclusionary covenants present a troublesome legal problem because they fall at the intersection of the private right of contract and the evil of discrimination. Often, the groups at the receiving end of the exclusionary covenant have, until recently, been *formally* treated as second-class citizens in law and/or fact, and only lately been legally emancipated.[9] Exclusionary covenants then become a substitute for official state-perpetrated discrimination and other direct forms of suppression that are no longer permitted by law. They contribute to perpetuating second-class status on a now *informal* plane, ensuring that the social disadvantages and disabilities (that we discussed in the last chapter) continue to endure.

Comparative constitutional jurisprudence (drawn from jurisdictions that broadly respect the freedom of contract while also enshrining a constitutional guarantee of non-discrimination) reveals that courts have been acutely aware of this problem and have devised creative solutions. Arranged along a spectrum of horizontality between one end where the sanctity of contract is given great deference and the other where the constitutional value of non-discrimination is accorded priority, three distinct solutions emerge, viz., non-enforcement, invalidation on the contractual grounds of vagueness and public policy, and invalidation on the grounds of public policy as drawn from the constitutional guarantee of non-discrimination. These solutions track each jurisdiction's differential understanding of the relationship between private actors, private law, and the Constitution, which in turn is often drawn from specific textual provisions.[10]

A. Non-Enforcement

Shelley v. Kraemer[11] is a 1948 US Supreme Court decision concerning a covenant that prohibited certain property from being 'occupied by any person not of the Caucasian race', and signalled an express intent to exclude 'people of the Negro or Mongolian race'. Notwithstanding this, a parcel of land was sold to the Shelleys, the petitioners, who were black. The respondents (parties to the original restrictive covenant) invoked the restrictive covenant to argue that this contract was void. The petitioners argued, on the other hand, that the covenant violated their Fourteenth Amendment constitutional right to the equal protection of laws.

At the outset, the Court clarified, 'the Fourteenth Amendment erects no shield against merely private conduct, however discriminatory or wrongful'.[12] Consequently, it refused to invalidate the covenant. Nonetheless, here it was the *Court*, one wing of the State, that was being asked to *enforce* the terms of the exclusionary covenant.[13] As the Court observed, because 'the owners of the properties were willing sellers; and contracts of sale were accordingly consummated … it [was] clear that but for the active intervention of the state courts, supported by the full panoply of state power, petitioners would have been free to occupy the properties in question without restraint'.[14] Consequently, this was a clear case of state action, and the Court was able to find that judicial enforcement of the exclusionary covenant would violate the constitutional requirement of equal protection of laws. The covenant was held to be unenforceable.

Shelley has been criticized by commentators on the grounds that it invalidated mere State *acquiescence* in a voluntary, private system.[15] Laurence Tribe, however, provides an alternative, narrower reading. He argues that *Shelley* can be distinguished from ordinary cases of State acquiescence, such as the judicial enforcement of facially neutral trespass laws to allow a bigoted homeowner from excluding only blacks from his property. In *Shelley*, on the other hand, the exclusionary covenant created an *exception* to the general property law principle requiring that there can be no general constraints upon a person's right to transfer or alienate her property. And this exception was founded in racial discrimination.[16] Consequently, *Shelley* was not a case of the State *facilitating* permissible private discriminatory conduct but an instance of *active* State discrimination. This distinction, as we shall subsequently see, is crucial in assessing the Indian position on restrictive covenanting.

B. Contractual Solutions

In *Re Drummond Wren*, a 1945 Canadian case, a restrictive covenant prohibited land from being sold to 'Jews or persons of objectionable nationality'.[17] It was argued before the Ontario High Court that this exclusionary covenant was void as it was in violation of public policy, a common law exception to the freedom of contract. On a survey of international law as well as domestic, anti-racist legislation, Justice Mackay held that 'nothing could be more calculated to create or deepen divisions between existing religious and ethnic groups … than the sanction of a method of land transfer which would permit the segregation and confinement of particular groups to particular business or residential areas'.[18] Thus, the crucial point was that the exclusion of certain groups from geographical areas would, in a stratified society, invariably mean their exclusion from economic and social life. Ghettoization could not but lead to discrimination and deepening inequality, both of which were contrary to public policy. And because contracts that violate 'public policy' cannot be sustained, Justice Mackay held the covenant void. He also held it void on more familiar common law grounds—for restraining the freedom of alienation[19] as well as being impermissibly vague and uncertain.[20]

It was this last, more conservative argument, that was picked up by the Canadian Supreme Court six years later in *Noble v. Alley*.[21] At issue was an exclusionary covenant restricting the sale of land to 'any person of the Jewish, Hebrew, Semitic, Negro or colored race or blood'. The majority held the covenant void. Three judges specifically held it void for uncertainty, holding that 'it is impossible to set such limits to the lines of race or blood as would enable a court to say in all cases whether a proposed purchaser is or is not within the ban'.[22]

C. Constitutional Public Policy

Lastly, consider the 2010 South African case of *The Curators v. University of Kwa-Zulu Natal*.[23]At issue was a will creating a charitable trust, which was to be administered solely for the benefit of white women seeking a tertiary education. The will was defended on the grounds that the freedom of testation—as an aspect of the freedom of property—was a fundamental right guaranteed by the South African Constitution. Both the High Court and the Supreme Court of Appeal rejected this argument and invalidated the offending provision. In its decision, the Supreme Court of Appeal referred to the equality provisions in the South African Constitution,[24] and the Preamble of the 2000 Promotion of Equality Act, which called for 'the eradication of social and economic inequalities, especially those that are systemic in nature, which were generated in our history by colonialism, apartheid, and patriarchy.'[25] That Act specifically prohibited racial discrimination in educational institutions, leading the Court to observe that the principle of equality obtained even in person-to-person relations.

In a language reminiscent of German constitutional doctrine, the Court then held, 'public policy "is now rooted in our Constitution and the fundamental values it enshrines, thus establishing an objective normative value system"'.[26] In other words, a constitution not only lists out a set of rights and corresponding State obligations, but also expresses an *objective order of values* (e.g., dignity, equality, etc.). These values are not to be invoked only against State action, but also have a 'radiating effect', serving as background interpretive principles for adjudicating private law disputes.[27]

The South African Supreme Court of Appeal directly linked public policy with the objective order of values embodied within the constitution, observing that 'in considering questions of public policy ... the Court must find guidance in "the founding constitutional values of human dignity, the achievement of equality, and the advancement of human rights and freedoms, non-racialism and non-sexism"'.[28] These public-policy concerns, grounded in constitutional values, overrode the freedom of testation, and did not unjustifiably deprive the individual of his property.

To sum up, exclusionary covenants are private contractual acts; nonetheless, for reasons explained above, there are strong interests in preventing them when they are used to discriminate against historically marginalized and subordinated groups. Because of the respect for private contracts, and a general hesitation to apply fundamental rights horizontally against individuals, Courts in various jurisdictions have not *directly* held them constitutionally invalid, but have searched for other remedies. These include judicial non-enforcement, weak contractual remedies such as vagueness, and stronger contractual remedies such as voidness for public policy, where public policy may be drawn from constitutional values. Thus, the constitution is not invoked *to directly invalidate private contractual acts*, but is invoked *indirectly to interpret private law* in a manner that achieves the same result.

II. *Zoroastrian Cooperative* and Its Discontents

The remedies discussed above have their parallels in the Indian Constitution. Our Fundamental Rights chapter, as we discussed in the Prologue, is, for the most part, only applicable against the State. But akin to *Shelley* (and going far beyond), the Supreme Court has found State action to be implicated in the State's *failure* to protect the rights to equality and personal liberty by passing meaningful legislation to deal with sexual harassment in private workplaces.[29] Akin to Canada, it has expanded equity-based public policy exceptions to the law of contract.[30] And akin to South Africa and Germany, it has interpreted and modified common law to bring it in consonance with constitutional values.[31] Consequently, when dealing with horizontal discrimination and restrictive covenants, Indian constitutional jurisprudence would allow the Court to place itself on any of the points of the spectrum discussed above.

With this in mind, consider *Zoroastrian Cooperative v. District Registrar*,[32] a 2005 two-judge decision of the Supreme Court. The facts of this case closely resemble *Shelley v. Kraemer*. The Zoroastrian Cooperative Housing Society was a registered society with its own by-laws under its parent legislation, the Bombay Cooperative Societies Act. According to the by-laws, only Parsis (adherents of Zoroastrianism) could become members of the society. Since housing shares could be transferred only to members, effectively only Parsis could buy plots under the aegis of the cooperative society. Nonetheless, Respondent No. 2 (a member) entered into negotiations with Respondent No. 3, a (non-Parsi) builders' association, to sell them its property. After a series of decisions in the tribunals, a High Court single bench and a High Court division bench—*all* essentially holding that the by-laws were invalid as a restriction on alienation of property (an argument used, as we have seen, by the Canadian courts)—the matter came before the Supreme Court. The decisions of the lower courts reflect Tribe's understanding of *Shelley*: this was not merely State facilitation of a private arrangement, but an active departure from the general principle against restrictions on alienability *in favour* of constitutionally impermissible, religion-based discrimination. As we shall see, unfortunately, this distinction was lost on the Court.

The cooperative society argued that their private covenant was authorized by the by-laws, which in turn were authorized by the parent statute. The Constitution had no role to play in adjudicating upon such private conduct. In fact, the society actually invoked the Constitution to *support* its conduct. It argued that under Article 19(1)(c), which guarantees to all citizens the freedom of association, Parsis' right to association could not be infringed by imposing upon them members they did not wish to accept. It also relied upon Article 29, which guaranteed minorities the right to preserve their own culture. On the other hand, the respondents raised a familiar argument: this kind of restrictive covenant was invalid because it violated public policy, as drawn from various constitutional provisions (in particular, Article 15 and other non-discrimination clauses).

The Court embarked upon an elaborate history of cooperative society legislation in India. It found that, 'running right through these enactments [is the] *the concept of* restricted membership'.[33] The reason for this, the Court held, was that as far as a housing society is concerned, 'there should be a bond of common habits and common usage among the members … in India, this bond was most frequently found in a community or caste or groups like cultivators of a village.'[34]

This reasoning is problematic, because one of the whole purposes of the Constitution, as reflected in Article 15(1)'s non-discrimination clause, was to ensure that the invidious modes of identification such as caste were to be made legally irrelevant as far as possible. The error was then compounded when the Court examined the public policy argument and, unlike the decisions of other jurisdictions, rejected by noting that 'the concept of public policy in the context of the Cooperative Societies Act has to be looked for under the four corners of that Act'.[35]

This is unconvincing. Following established principles of common law, the Indian Contract Act, under Section 23, has a public policy exception[36] that can be invoked to invalidate contracts. Courts have utilized this to hold void, for example, marriage brokerage contracts[37] and letting of a property for sex work,[38] neither of which are found within the 'four corners' of the Contract Act. Indeed, as the Court had held in *Delhi Transport Corporation v. DTC Mazdoor Congress*,[39] the whole point of a public policy clause is to serve as an exception to the enforcement of statutory rules. To look for public policy *within* the statute whose provisions are impugned is viciously circular. Matters, admittedly, would have been different if there had been an *express* statutory provision, designed to carve out an exception to the operation of public policy. The Cooperative Societies Act, however, did no such thing. Consequently, the Court was incorrect to equate *statutory policy* (the policy embodied in the statute) with *public policy* (grounds for invalidating contracts).

The Court then responded to the constitutional challenge on the grounds of non-discrimination, holding that the society's by-laws were in the nature of the articles of association a company; that is, not like a statute, but only 'binding between the persons affected by them'.[40] In other words, rejecting the radiation approach of indirect horizontality, followed in Germany and South Africa, and in its own cases on defamation law, the Court held that a private, contractual agreement is not subject to general fundamental rights scrutiny, but *only* under the parent legislation (if it was a contract, it would be the Indian Contract Act; here, it would be the relevant Cooperative Societies Act). The Court went on to make the contract analogy even clearer, by holding that the Fundamental Rights chapter did not, in any way, interfere with citizens' rights to enter into contracts. Responding to the contention that the Constitution's guarantee of non-discrimination *should* be held to prohibit certain *kinds* of contracts which directly discriminated on proscribed grounds, the Court's answer was somewhat elusive:

> Running through the Cooperative Societies Act is the theory of area of operation. That means that membership could be denied to a citizen of this country who is located outside the area of operation of a society.[41]

This in its own right makes perfect sense, since limiting membership by area does not discriminate on any prohibited head, and is also, not coincidentally, perfectly in consonance with the point of housing societies. *That* logic, however, says nothing about restrictive covenanting based on *constitutionally* prohibited grounds such as sex or religion. This also explains why the Court's numerous examples of other cooperative societies—of agricultural workers, labourers, and even vegetarians[42]—are irrelevant, because there again there is no discrimination on the basis of a prohibited category.

On these grounds, the Court refused to find the agreement void. But then, it went even further, holding that:

> It is also not open to the authorities under the Act to relieve [the contractual party] of his obligations in the guise of entering a finding that discrimination on the basis of the religion or sex is taboo under the Constitution in the context of Part III thereof.[43]

In this, the Court went even beyond the weak *Shelley v. Kraemer* doctrine in not just refusing to invalidate the agreement, but even requiring State *enforcement of it*. This is surely incorrect. Even if it is argued that the Court is not the 'State' for the purposes of Part III, statutory authorities tasked with implementing the Cooperative Societies Act most definitely are. Keeping in mind Tribe's critique of *Shelley*, it is at least arguable that in *requiring* the State to directly enforce a covenant that discriminates on the basis of a prohibited Article 15 category, the Court effectively compelled it to perform an unconstitutional action.

Yet, consider the Court's ancillary invocation of Article 19(1)(c), which guarantees the freedom of association, as an independent *constitutional* reason to support the society's claim. As we have seen above, part of the Court's public policy arguments appears to turn upon the unconstitutionality of requiring persons to 'associate' with others that they do not want to associate with. According to the Court, this would have been the outcome had the exclusionary covenant been left unenforced.

However, there is a problem with this argument. The statutory right to contract—which is what the by-laws of the Cooperative Societies Act authorized—*is not the same as the constitutional freedom of association.* This is self-evident, because the Indian Contract Act places numerous restrictions upon the freedom to contract that go beyond the permissible limits upon the constitutional freedom to associate under Article 19(4).[44] More importantly, a quick glance at the Constituent Assembly Debates reveals, unsurprisingly, that the freedom of association was considered to be an essential aspect of personal civil liberty, akin to the freedom of speech and the freedom of movement, with contractual rights mentioned nowhere.[45] Historically, the freedom of association has been about protecting the rights of labour unions, religious minorities, and other disadvantaged or persecuted groups to organize and defend their rights or their ways of life, as the case may be.[46] The important Indian cases have also understood the freedom of association to be about such purposes.[47]

This confusion went to the heart of the Court's judgement, when it observed:

> An aspirant to membership in a co-operative society is at arms [sic] length with the other members of the society with whom he enters into the compact or in which he joins, having expressed his willingness to subscribe to the aims and objects of that society. In the context of Section 23 of the Contract Act, something more than possible or plausible argument based on the constitutional scheme

> is necessary to nullify an agreement voluntarily entered into by a person.[48]

The reasoning is flawed because, as far as the Court speaks about arm's-length transactions and holds membership in a cooperative society akin to a contract, Article 19(1)(c)'s constitutional freedom of association is not in play. But once the Article 19(1)(c) argument fails, we fall back upon the original, flawed statutory-policy-equates-public-policy argument. We are therefore faced with the following situation: to the extent that *Zoroastrian Cooperative* is based on principles of contract law, the two major bases for the decision, viz., public policy and freedom of association, are incorrect. The case, therefore, can be saved only by arguing that it is not, after all, about contract law. Therefore, it is not precedent for the unconstitutionality of unenforceability of exclusionary/restrictive covenants *generally*, but about something else that elevates it to the level of the constitutional principle of the freedom of association. What might that be?

I believe that the strongest argument in favour of the covenant is grounded in Article 29 of the Constitution, which the Court incidentally alluded to at the very end of its judgement, when it observed:

> ... it is open to [a] community to try to preserve its culture and way of life and in that process, to work for the advancement of members of that community by enabling them to acquire membership in a society and allotment of lands or buildings.[49]

Article 29 of the Constitution guarantees the rights of 'any section of citizens ... having a distinct language, script or culture of its own ... to conserve [it]'. This provision, I would argue, helps us to grasp the only possible justification for *Zoroastrian Cooperative*. While explaining the purpose of the provision during the Constituent Assembly Debates, Ambedkar clarified that it was meant for the protection of communities that were minorities in the 'linguistic and cultural sense'.[50] Ambedkar's specific concern was to ensure that groups of people who migrated between provinces could 'keep their connections ... [but] if this protection was not given to them ... and [if] the local Legislature were to deny them the opportunity of conserving their culture, it would be very difficult for [them] to go back to their province and to get themselves assimilated to the original population to which they belonged'.[51]

At the heart of Ambedkar's formulation was the idea that as far as language and culture go, minorities should have the option of *refusing* to completely assimilate with the majority group. In independent India, the controversy around cultural and educational rights has focused upon the extent to which minorities may establish and control access to their own educational institutions.[52] In *Zoroastrian Cooperative*, the Supreme Court, arguably, was extending that logic to establish that voluntarily choosing to live together as an exclusive, geographically bounded community might be another way of preserving the Parsis' language and culture. Such an argument is known in philosophical literature,[53] and is not unfamiliar in the Indian constitutional context. The Fifth and Sixth Schedules to the Constitution, for instance, empower the State to prohibit the sale of certain tribal land to non-tribals. In *Samatha v. State of Andhra Pradesh*, the Supreme Court cited sociological studies to note the link between land and the preservation of culture, observing that 'tribals had held large tracts of lands as masters and had their own rich culture with economic status and cohesiveness as compact groups'.[54]

However, if *that* was the underlying reasoning of the Court, then surely something more was needed: in particular, evidence that a distinct way of life was central to the preservation of Parsi culture, and this way of life might be jeopardized by living in physical proximity with non-Parsis. This the Court made no attempt to establish.

Yet, *even if* the Court was justified in invoking Article 29 as the legitimating provision for the exclusionary covenant, then the same constitutional provision limits the nature of the covenants that can take its shelter. There are two essential requirements that must be fulfilled under Article 29. The first refers to *whom* it applies to: a 'section of citizens having a distinct language, script, or culture of its own.' The second determines *what* it applies to: conservation of said language, script, or culture. Conceivably, the Parsi community, as a besieged minority, might rely upon the combination of Articles 19(1)(c) and 29 to argue that living together in groups is a crucial way in which it can preserve its distinct culture. The same argument, clearly, will not apply to exclusionary covenants where these specific circumstances are not present.

The claim of the exclusionary covenant in *Zoroastrian Cooperative* to not just validity (contra legitimate public policy concerns), but actual enforcement, must surely rest upon this basic idea. That is, to the extent that a community believes that the survival of its own set of cultural values depends on its members living together exclusively with each other (and not upon a politically illiberal conception of race/cultural/religious superiority, the eradication of which is the whole point of Article 15), the principles of Article 19(1)(c) and Article 29 are attracted, and the contrary non-discrimination principle of Article 15 is not. In such cases, the exclusionary covenant is both valid and may be judicially enforced. Of course, this will be a complex question and the Court must look into whether the claim in question is actually justified in fact. In *Zoroastrian Cooperative*, as I have attempted to argue, it did not do so.

III. *IMA* and Article 15(2) of the Constitution

I will now argue that in *general* cases of horizontal discrimination, the Indian Constitution contains the tools to go one step beyond the solutions advanced in other jurisdictions. Article 15(2) of the Constitution, on my proposed reading, provides a horizontally applicable constitutional remedy for holding racially/religiously restrictive covenants void. Unlike the jurisdictions we have studied, therefore, the Constitution can be brought to bear *directly* upon the issue of horizontal discrimination, in the sense that it doesn't just apply to private *law* (such as the law of contract) that might be at issue in a dispute between two non-State actors, but it applies also to private *action*.

Article 15(2) states, in relevant part:

> No citizen shall, on grounds only of religion, race, caste, sex, place of birth or any of them, be subject to any disability, liability, restriction or condition with regard to … access to shops, public restaurants, hotels and places of public entertainment …

In *IMA v. Union of India*,[55] decided by the Supreme Court in 2011, the question was whether a private, non-minority higher *educational institution* that admitted students only on the basis of their scores in an entrance test violated Article 15(2). The claim was based on the disparate impact of test-based admissions upon educationally underprivileged castes. But before the Court could even reach that question, it had to decide whether, on its terms, Article 15(2) was attracted in the first place. How did educational institutions fit within 'shops, public restaurants, hotels and places of public entertainment'?

The Court held that Article 15(2) was indeed applicable, because educational institutions were covered by the term 'shops'. It quoted and endorsed Ambedkar's speech in the Constituent Assembly Debates, where he had observed:

> To define the word 'shop' in the most generic term one can think of is to state that 'shop' is a place where the owner is prepared to offer his service to anybody who is prepared to go there seeking his service … I should like to point out therefore that the word 'shop' used here is not used in the limited sense of permitting entry. It is used in the larger sense of requiring the services if the terms of service are agreed to.[56]

In other words, the Court rejected the standard uses of the word 'shop', i.e., a store, 'a building or room where goods are stored', 'a building stocked with merchandise for sale', 'a small retail establishment or a department in a large one offering a specified line of goods or services',[57] in favour of a more abstract and 'generic' usage, to fit educational institutions into the definition.

What is this 'generic' meaning that allows a school to count as a shop? There can be only one answer: a shop, as Ambedkar understood it in 1949, and as the Supreme Court interpreted it in 2011, is any place where an abstract seller x offers an abstract thing y to an abstract buyer z. Or, in other words, a shop is merely the concrete expression of the *idea of the impersonal, abstract market of the modern liberal-capitalist economy*. This is the only way that the Court could succeed in bringing educational institutions within the ambit of 15(2). But, once the Court did so, obviously, the reach of shop isn't limited to educational institutions. If shop merely embodies the abstract market, then the reach of 15(2) extends to *private economic market transactions generally*, and not just the business of education. And covenants for the lease of property are examples par excellence of such transactions. The logic of *IMA v. UoI*, therefore, inescapably brings such covenants under Article 15(2), which applies horizontally. If such covenants discriminate against persons on prohibited grounds, viz., race, religion, sex, etc., they are unconstitutional.

This conclusion isn't as radical as it sounds. While we have argued for a broad reading of the word 'shop', clearly, its scope is not limitless. The word itself, which indicates a commercial relationship as well as Ambedkar's focus on 'terms of service', suggests that Article 15(2) is limited to *economic transactions* (which, in any event, in accordance with classical economic theory from the time of Adam Smith, are supposed to take place at arm's length). It would not apply to non-economic, associative relationships. For instance, if I wanted to sell or supply certain goods or services on the market, Article 15(2) would apply to prohibit me from discriminating on the basis of the proscribed markers; but if I wanted to *gift* the same goods or services to someone, it would not.[58] Apart from the nature and history of the word 'shops', it must also be noted that a broader mandate for the intervention of Article 15(2) would also run up against Article 19(1)(c) of the Indian Constitution, which, as we have seen above, guarantees the freedom of association. Restricting the scope of 15(2) to commercial relationships is one way of harmoniously reading the two provisions.

Furthermore, there are good philosophical reasons for this: as Tarunabh Khaitan has recently argued, and as cases from the United States and Canada demonstrate,[59] the imperative of non-discrimination has to be balanced against the legitimate right to autonomy in private relationships.[60] According to Khaitan, therefore, it is only certain kinds of private relationships that discrimination law should reach (e.g., relationships of service providers and consumers, landlords and tenants, etc.). The criteria for determining this is the extent to which such relationships have a 'public character', as well as the extent to which they can potentially affect people's ability to lead a dignified life by cutting off access to important physical and social infrastructure.[61] And, as we shall see below, the rationale for applying and limiting the scope of Article 15(2) to economic transactions of a certain type is grounded in some unique aspects of Indian constitutional and political history that speak to precisely this concern.

IV. 'Shops', Horizontal Discrimination, and the Transformative Constitution

Is there any warrant for the Court's rather creative reading of Article 15(2)? I argue that there is. To start with, let us consider the most basic objection: the constitutional text. If the framers wanted to apply Article 15(2) to all market transactions, why didn't they simply say so? Why did they use concrete terms—and not just one concrete term, but *shops, restaurants, hotels*—to express the abstract concept of the market? To answer that question, let us examine the history and circumstances under which this provision has come into being.

The meaning of shops was debated in the Constituent Assembly on 29 November 1948.[62] S. Nagappa, a close associate of Ambedkar, expressed a wish that the clause could have been made 'more expansive and explanatory', and by way of clarification asked specifically whether shops included not just places where goods were bought, but also places where *services* were contracted for. 'When I go to a barber's shop or a shaving saloon,' he observed, 'I do not buy anything concrete, but I purchase labour.'[63] The debate then turned to a host of private, discriminatory practices, the amelioration of which was the objective of Article 15(2), *as a whole* (not simply as the sum of its isolated terms). Indeed, Shibban Lal Saksena *objected* to the provision precisely on the basis of its far-reaching character, one that would compel Hindus to go against their religious practices involving food. In his words:

> I may also point out the revolutionary character of this article. I know that there are hundreds of Hindu shops where food is served to Hindus only. Food is a matter where Hindus have got special habits and they generally will not allow anybody to enter the place where they eat food ... [but] anybody can now claim entry to any place where food is sold. I therefore think that we must prepare the ground to give effect to this change which is of a far-reaching character.[64]

Ambedkar then answered Sardar Nagappa in the quotation that the Supreme Court in *IMA v. UoI* extracted—about 'shop' being used in its 'generic' sense. Specifically, Ambedkar was asked whether shop included a doctor's and a lawyer's chambers. His answer: 'It will include anybody who offers his services ... the word 'shop' used here is not used in the limited sense of permitting entry. It is used in the larger sense of requiring the services if the terms of service are agreed to.'[65]

The debate made it clear, therefore, that the word shop was not understood in its narrow, *spatial* sense, but in a broader sense of a place *defined* by an arm's-length transaction on the basis of previously agreed terms and conditions. This is buttressed by the fate of a proposed amendment by K.T. Shah, who wanted to replace the two sub-clauses of the horizontal non-discrimination provision with a single omnibus clause, focused on *public spaces*. His amendment sought to protect 'places dedicated to the use of the general public', such as theatres and cinemas, parks, gardens, museums, etc.[66] Shah's amendment was rejected, making it clear the article was not based upon the concept of guaranteeing access to space, but of ensuring that nobody was excluded from *participation* in the basic economic life of the community. In terms of outcomes, this would often overlap with a spatial idea of the public, but it was, obviously, very different in its thrust and intent.

And lastly, when, on 22 November 1949, during the third and final reading of the Draft Constitution, Ajit Prasad Jain discussed the provision, he did so by grounding it in a long history of horizontal, societal, and *economic* discrimination against women, scheduled castes, untouchables, and other groups, which had blighted Indian society.[67] We can thus see that both the supporters and the opponents of what eventually became Article 15(2) were united in their understanding that the purpose of the provision—as expressed through its language—was to reverse this history, a history in which a part of society was *systematically excluded* from the normal functioning of economic life.

This argument is buttressed by the fact that, when the non-discrimination clause was first drafted in the Fundamental Rights Sub-Committee, 'schools' were expressly included within its ambit.[68] This is scarcely surprising, since caste-based segregation in schools had been a staple feature of colonial life (Ambedkar himself began his education sitting outside in the verandah of the classroom). The word 'schools' was taken out on the recommendation of the Sub-Committee on Minorities,[69] *not* because it was proposed that schools be exempted from the non-discrimination clause, but because, as the framers specifically recognized, the Constitution authorized *denominational* schools that by definition existed to serve specific religious communities.[70] Naturally, such schools would have to set (discriminatory) criteria for admission; however, as we have seen, the forms of discrimination that Article 15(2) sought to tackle were much broader and more far-ranging. Put in this perspective, the Fundamental Rights Sub-Committee's initial decision to include schools within the ambit of (what became) Article 15(2) testifies to its transformative character, a character that is not diluted by its subsequent removal for certain very special reasons.

It is with this background that we can now understand that *IMA v. UoI's* interpretation, far from being untenable, infused transformative content into Article 15(2).

To understand precisely the manner in which Article 15(2) was meant to be transformative, as discussed in the Prologue, recall that, traditionally, civil liberties have been exercisable vertically, i.e., individuals against the State. The vertical nature of bills of rights—which arose from the American and French revolutions—goes hand-in-hand with a separation between State and market, and between the public and private spheres.[71] Critical theorists argue that the State/market and public/private distinction encoded into classical bills of rights reflects the fact that these revolutions were driven by a rising bourgeoisie class, and targeted at absolutist and centralized State power.[72] Thus, by addressing bills of rights exclusively to state action, and by creating protected zones under the rubric of the 'private sphere', those liberal constitutions ensured that all action within the protected private sphere was deemed off-limits, subject to no scrutiny, and beyond the field of politics. Naturally, this meant that inequalities of power, structural violence, and relationships of domination and subordination *within* the private sphere (which included the market) went untouched and unregulated.

As a related point, when bills of rights were first conceptualized (in particular, in the aftermath of the American revolution), they were conceptualized in the context of a distinctly Western idea of *sovereignty*: the idea that sovereignty was single, indivisible, and ultimate, and resided at *one place* in the polity.[73] Initially, sovereignty was believed to be concentrated in the figure of the sovereign, but through the American and French revolutions, it came to be thought of as residing in the *people*. The basic idea of the inherent unitary and unified nature of sovereignty, though, remained intact. Thus, when the American revolution culminated in a system of representative republican democracy, through which sovereign power was delegated by the people to their elected representatives, it made sense to draft a bill of rights designed to check the *State*, because it was there where the locus of sovereign power, albeit delegated, resided.[74]

As we saw in the Prologue, however, sovereignty in India was always understood very differently: it was inherently decentralized and had its locus at multiple points, *especially* in the economic sphere.[75] In addition, as the works of the subaltern historians has shown, forms of authority *in the marketplace* (even during the colonial period) unlike in the West, instead of being governed by the impersonal, vertical market forces of liberal capitalism, continued to be horizontal, person-to-person and tradition-based, in continuance of the multiple, decentralized centres of power-and-sovereignty that had characterized the old Indian polity.[76]

This understanding of authority as decentralized, horizontal, and consisting of multiple foci was mirrored by the evolution of the concept of rights, which were never understood exclusively as bulwarks against *State* power. For instance, as the historian Tanika Sarkar argues, while examining the three great social reform movements of the nineteenth century that were aimed at women (i.e., the age of consent for sexual intercourse, widow remarriage, and outlawing the custom of *sati*), the vocabulary of a woman as a rights-bearing individual was first framed *horizontally*, in opposition to the 'community as a culture-bearing entity'[77] (and not in opposition to the State). Similarly, even as the nationalist movement was articulating a set of vertical civil and political rights against the colonial authority through a series of constitutional charters,[78] Ambedkar himself invoked the vocabulary of rights against the horizontal structures of the caste system, which excluded Dalits from the social and religious life of the community—an exclusion that, not coincidentally in the context of our reading of Article 15(2), was founded upon *spatial and social segregation*. In particular, and in response to the segregated social and economic order, Ambedkar led movements to guarantee the right to take water from public watering places (horizontal social exclusion), while other leaders of the 'Depressed Classes', with the support of Gandhi, led movements to enter Hindu temples, on parity with other Hindus (horizontal religious exclusion).[79] As we shall see below, both these rights would ultimately be incorporated into the Constitution.

Indeed, Ambedkar's own arguments were the culmination of decades-long discourse, in which the representatives of the 'Depressed Classes' (as they were then referred to in the public sphere) located the greatest deprivation of their freedom (as we saw in the previous chapter) within social and economic practices of exclusion. As early as 1890, Gopal Baba Walangkar, a retired army officer, wrote a petition highlighting 'exclusion from dharmshalas [pilgrims' and travellers' guest-houses], discrimination while travelling, bans on participation in trade, [and] social stigma',[80] which the Mahar caste was subjected to. Walangkar was responding to practices that formed part of daily living, including, perhaps most notoriously, schoolroom segregation, where 'untouchable' students were made to sit outside the class, in the verandah, in order to maintain adequate physical distance from upper-caste students.[81]

The truth of Walangkar's allegations was formally affirmed four decades later in the report of the Starte Committee, set up by the Bombay Legislative Council. The Starte Committee Report highlighted the fact that the single, dominant feature that defined the relationship between the Depressed Classes and the rest of society was *exclusion*, which, as we discussed above, variously took the form of physical segregation (including residential segregation), socially sanctioned prohibitions from undertaking certain trades or professions, and exclusion from the use of common or public utilities.[82]

Beginning with Walangkar's petition, every level of response initiated by the Depressed Classes recalled this fundamental reality: one of the first organizations dedicated to the welfare of the Depressed Classes was called the 'Bahishkrit Hitkarini Sabha', and Ambedkar's journal was called *Bahishkrit Bharat*.[83] The word 'Bahishkrit', depending on the specific nuance, means either excluded or boycotted. As we have seen, by the 1920s, this had evolved into a specific language of *rights and remedies*: a right against horizontal discrimination, as expressed in the resolutions passed during the Mahar Satyagraha,[84] and the remedy—expressed in a Settlement arrived at by the Minorities Committee at the Second Round Table Conference in London—that required the 'invalidation' of 'any custom or usage' (as opposed to any 'law') that discriminates.[85]

What this tells us is that, unlike the American and French revolutions, the Indian pre-Independence discourse of freedom had twin focal points, viz., political independence from an authoritarian colonial power (which explains the predominance, in the Fundamental Rights chapter, of classic liberal civil and political rights against the State), *as well as* horizontal independence from exclusionary systems of authority and control, manifested most clearly in various reform movements aimed at the emancipation of women and the eradication of the caste system.[86]

The vocabulary of rights was central to both foci. *Within this framework,* the Constituent Assembly Debates, discussed above, make it clear that one of the characteristic features of oppression that the Constitution sought to address was, precisely, the horizontal exercise of power relations in an exclusionary manner, including in the sphere of economic transactions. As Ambedkar specifically pointed out in his Memorandum to the Fundamental Rights Sub-Committee in the early days of the Constituent Assembly, the following paragraph, that had been recorded in the Starte Committee Report of 1929, continued to hold true even as the Constituent Assembly deliberated:

> We have heard of numerous instances where the orthodox classes have used their economic power as a weapon against those Depressed Classes in their villages, when the latter have dared to exercise their rights, and have evicted them from their land, and stopped their employment and discontinued their remuneration as village servants. This boycott is often planned on such an extensive scale as to include the prevention of the Depressed Classes from using commonly used paths and the stoppage of sale of the necessaries of life by the village *bania*.[87]

Ambedkar then cited a letter that he had received from an 'untouchable' in a Punjab village to argue that 'the general use of the boycott' remained a staple feature of Indian life.[88]

Therefore, the very different Indian experience with political and civil rights movements leading up to, and influencing the framing of, the Constitution indicates that there is enough warrant for the Court to strike the balance between autonomy and social democracy in a manner that is more skewed towards the latter. This further buttresses the broad reading that the Court provided to Article 15(2) in *IMA*.

In the next two chapters, we shall discuss how this understanding of the Constitution's role is borne out by other guarantees under the Constitution—specifically, the horizontally applicable provisions guaranteeing the abolition of untouchability and of forced labour. For now, it is sufficient to note that this commitment is reflected by the other parts of Article 15(2) itself. In addition to shops, Article 15(2)(a) guarantees access to 'public restaurants, hotels, and places of public entertainment'. Article 15(2)(b) does the same for 'wells, tanks, bathing ghats, roads and places of public resort maintained wholly or partly out of State funds or dedicated to the use of the general public'. In the face of all this, it makes perfect sense that the framers, through Article 15(2), which is also clearly transformative, were attempting to do away with traditional discriminatory practices that pervaded the private economic realm. Their use of the word 'shops', including Ambedkar's clarification of its meaning, was one way of doing so, and fulfilling the transformative promise of India's Constitution.

V. Conclusion

In his famous poem *Begampura*, the sixteenth-century Bhakti poet Ravidas imagined a utopia: a city without taxes, [private] property, or torture, a city of equality. Apart from these familiar themes, common to utopian thinking, one other stands out: in Begampura, Ravidas and his kin were free to 'walk where they want to'.[89] What this casual, almost throwaway, line demonstrates is that the struggle for social justice in a society riven by caste has always included a focus on *access* and *exclusion*.

In 1991, the state of Gujarat passed the Disturbed Areas Act.[90] The Act authorizes the government to declare areas in the state to be 'Disturbed' (ostensibly because of riots or mob violence), and then effectively prohibit the transfer of property within those areas. Under the guise of maintaining public order in times of communal stress, the Act, in effect, has become a State-wielded weapon of segregation and ghettoization, and has created colonies 'exclusively' for Hindus and for Muslims.[91]

Ravidas' Begampura and the Gujarat Disturbed Areas Act belong in separate universes: ethical, moral, and political. The dream of the Indian Constitution was to create Begampura; the Gujarat Disturbed Areas Act shows us how far we have wandered in the opposite direction. *IMA v. Union of India* is a transformative judgement because it allows us a glimpse of how, one day, the Constitution may be invoked to bridge the chasm between the dream and the reality.

In summary, Article 15(2)(a) contains an inbuilt framework broadly akin to a civil rights law, which prohibits discrimination even within the private economic realm, to the extent that such discrimination operates to exclude persons from access to core economic, social, and physical infrastructure. It makes the right to non-discrimination horizontally enforceable. This interpretation turns upon a historically grounded reading of shops, which understands that word to be embodying the abstract market of arm's-length economic transactions. The specificity of the text of Article 15(2) is not an insurmountable bar against a broad reading of shops. The Constituent Assembly Debates support a broad reading. The structure of Part III supports it. And finally, the uniquely transformative nature of India's Constitution justifies the use of horizontal constitutional rights against discriminatory economic transactions in the private sphere. As a corollary, it hardly needs to be said that laws like the Gujarat Disturbed Areas Act, which authorize the *government* to impose communal housing segregation, can no longer withstand constitutional scrutiny.

IMA v. UoI's transformative interpretation of the Constitution is faithful to the structure and philosophy of India's bill of rights. It ought to be upheld, and its reasoning taken to its logical conclusion.

5

Religious Freedom and Group Identity: *Saifuddin* and the Anti-Exclusion Principle

You can never separate social life from religious life.

Alladi Krishnaswami Ayyar, debates on Fundamental Rights in the Advisory Committee (April 1947)

IN AUGUST 2016, THE High Court of Bombay upheld the right of women to access the inner sanctum of the Haji Ali Dargah.[1] A year later, the Supreme Court referred to a Constitution Bench the question of whether Kerala's famous Sabarimala Temple could deny access to women between the ages of ten and fifty. The case was fiercely contested by the Travancore Devaswom (temple) Board and various religious groups, and was heard by the Supreme Court in July 2018.[2]

But before that, in January 2016, the case (pending for thirty years) of *Central Board of the Dawoodi Bohra Committee v. State of Maharashtra* was listed (although it wasn't heard) before a five-judge bench of the Supreme Court. More directly even than the right-to-worship cases, *Dawoodi Bohra* heralded a reopening of a fraught constitutional question: in what manner should a Constitution that guarantees the freedom of religion to both individuals and communities mediate the claims of religious groups *against* the claims of their constituents?

Dawoodi Bohra involves a request to the Court to reconsider and, if necessary, reverse a fifty-year-old judgement: *Sardar Syedna Tahir Saifuddin v. State of Bombay*.[3] *Saifuddin* was about a constitutional challenge to the Bombay Prevention of Excommunication Act, 1949, which outlawed the practice of excommunication within religious communities. The petitioner was the 'Dai' or head priest of the Dawoodi Bohra community, an offshoot of Shia Islam. He argued that, by taking away his power of excommunication, the Act violated his right to religious freedom under Article 25(1) of the Indian Constitution, and the Dawoodi Bohras' right to regulate their own affairs in matters of religion under Article 26(b) of the Constitution.

By a 4–1 majority, the Supreme Court agreed with the Dai, and struck down the Act. Writing for the three judges, Justice Das Gupta held that Articles 25 and 26 of the Constitution protected practices that were *essential*, or *integral*, parts of religion. Surveying the authorities, he found that excommunication was needed for preserving community solidarity, cohesiveness, and discipline, and, therefore, fell within Articles 25 and 26. He then held that, since the Act only purported to bar excommunications made on religious grounds, it could not be saved by Article 25(2)(b), which allowed the State to override religious freedom in the interests of 'social welfare or reform'. In his concurring opinion, Justice Ayyangar went one step further, and held that even if the Act was a measure of social reform, it could not be allowed, under the Constitution, to 'reform a religion out of existence'.[4]

Chief Justice Sinha dissented. According to him, an excommunicated person 'is excluded from the exercise of rights in connection ... with places of worship ... from burying the dead in the community burial ground and other rights to property ... which are ... of a civil nature and are not purely religious matters'.[5] The Act was actually furthering the underlying objectives of Article 25(1) and of the Constitution by guaranteeing human dignity and the individual freedom to dissent without the price of ostracism, and of being 'treated like a pariah'.[6] He therefore upheld the Act.

The three judgements in *Saifuddin* represent three radically different understandings of the right to, and limits of, religious freedom under the Indian Constitution. In particular, they differ on the relationship between the individual member of a religious community, the community itself, and the State—a relationship that has always been underdetermined by the sparse constitutional text. The attempt to have the Supreme Court review its judgement in *Saifuddin*, therefore, is not simply about a single case, but a challenge to a sixty-year-old judicial practice of interpreting the Indian Constitution's religious freedom guarantees.

In this chapter, I argue against the majority and concurring opinions, and in support of CJI Sinha's dissent. I begin by unravelling the web of textual provisions that characterizes the right to freedom of religion under the Indian Constitution and, in particular, the tension between individual religious freedom and group autonomy (I). I then argue against the 'essential religious practices' test, which was the basis of the majority and the concurrence in the *Dawoodi Bohra Case* (II). However, the Court's invocation of this test stems from the 'thick' role played by religion in Indian public life, which underscores the need for an approach that is different from the one adopted in Western liberal constitutional jurisdictions (III). Nonetheless, CJI Sinha's dissent and the 'anti-exclusion principle' that I will develop out of it provide an alternative that is equally cognizant of the reality of the State-religion-community relationship in India. The anti-exclusion principle limits religious group autonomy in the interests of securing individual access to basic material and cultural goods (IV). It is more faithful to Indian history, to the structure of the Indian Constitution, and to the Constitution's transformative purpose of limiting powerful group affiliations in the interests of individual freedom (V). It should be the blueprint that the Court adopts in future cases dealing with religious freedom and secularism (VI).

I. Individual, Community, State: The Textual Web of Indian Constitutional Secularism

The Constitution's Fundamental Rights chapter comprises diverse, and possibly conflicting, sets of rights-holders, duty-bearers, and juridical relationships. There are individual rights against the State, direct horizontal rights, and also group rights, such as the rights of minorities to conserve their language, script, and culture. Further, the Constitution also allows the State wide regulatory powers over both individuals and groups, with a view to social reform, for instance, through reservations. Consequently, it is a mistake to understand the Constitution's religious freedom clauses (as academic and judicial debates tend to have done) as though they constitute a self-contained code.[7] An understanding of religious freedom under the Constitution is incomplete without acknowledging that the provisions are *nested* within a Fundamental Rights chapter that, in various contexts and ways, attempts to grapple with the relationship between three actors, viz., the individual, the community and the State.

What do these provisions say? Article 25(1) guarantees that 'subject to public order, morality and health and to the other provisions of this Part, all persons are equally entitled to freedom of conscience and the right freely to profess, practise, and propagate religion'. This language of personal freedom is similar to liberal-democratic constitutions all over the world.[8] Immediately after that, however, Article 25(2)(a) permits the State to make laws for 'regulating or restricting any economic, financial, political or other secular activity which may be associated with religious practice'. Article 25(2)(b) follows, allowing laws 'providing for social welfare and reform or the throwing open of Hindu religious institutions of a public character to all classes and sections of Hindus'.

Two things stand out. First, the Constitution expressly distinguishes between religion and secular activities that might be 'associated with religious practice'. Implicitly, therefore, it tasks the courts with drawing the dividing line between the religious and the secular.[9] Second, it allows the State to intervene in, and recalibrate, the relationships within religious groups or communities, in the interests of 'social welfare and reform', an instance of which is requiring public Hindu religious institutions to be open to all Hindus. Once again, the Constitution makes the courts the ultimate arbiters of the question.

Article 26(b) permits a 'religious denomination' to 'manage its own affairs in matters of religion', while also allowing it to administer property that it owns or has acquired 'in accordance with law'. Two things, again, stand out. First, Article 26 *directly* makes groups the bearers of rights. And second, like Article 25, Article 26 invites law, and the courts, to draw a distinction between matters of religion and secular questions, illustrated by the express textual provision that property may be administered only in accordance with law.

Articles 25 and 26, taken together, guarantee the rights of individuals and groups to religious freedom, while allowing the State to regulate secular matters that might take a religious form, and to frame reform-oriented laws that might impinge upon the internal autonomy of religious communities. Read plainly, the text seems to represent conflicting impulses, attempting to achieve a 'simultaneous commitment to communities and equal citizenship'.[10] Scholars have disagreed about whether it manages to achieve a workable modus vivendi between competing claims,[11] or only succeeds in setting up an irreconcilable contradiction.

Finally, note what is left unsaid. Articles 25 and 26 do not provide a *principle* to distinguish between the religious and the secular. Furthermore, they do not clarify whether Article 26(b) guarantees only a group right against State intervention, or whether it also guarantees to groups rights *against* their own constituents (and vice versa).[12] Article 26(b) does not directly speak to situations where the individual and the community might clash with each other over issues of religious freedom. The wide powers given to the State under Article 25(2)(b) suggest the answer might not be as easy as it has been in other jurisdictions, where individuals have few antecedent constitutional rights against their communities.[13] As we shall see, the majority's error in *Saifuddin* lay in its failure to address any of these questions in the comprehensive manner that they required.

II. 'Essential Religious Practices'—Tracing the Genealogy of a Phrase

In *Saifuddin*, the majority and concurrence both struck down the Excommunication Act on the grounds that excommunication was an integral, or essential, part of the Dawoodi Bohra faith. As held by the majority, 'what constitutes an essential part of a religious or religious practice has to be decided ... with reference to the doctrine of a particular religion'.[14] Once that was established, curtailing the power of excommunication was deemed to be interference into a purely religious matter, and, therefore, not saved by the social reform clause of the Constitution.

The term 'essential religious practices' as the trigger for invoking the protection of Articles 25 and 26 has long been criticized. The objection is well known and has been made throughout the Court's history: it is not for the judiciary to pronounce on the importance of specific doctrines or beliefs internal to a religion.[15] This criticism is familiar to other liberal constitutional jurisdictions. Constitutional courts in the US,[16] Canada,[17] and Europe[18] have established limits upon the extent to which individuals or groups can engage in religious practices that might conflict with the civil law of the State. But, for the most part,[19] they have refused to impose an external point of view upon whether a practice is religious or not, and how important it is to its adherents. This refusal is part of a deeper commitment to constitutional liberalism, which declines to impose particular substantive visions of the good upon individuals.[20] As *Saifuddin* illustrates, this approach is not the approach of the Indian Supreme Court.

What is the genesis of the phrase 'essential religious practices'? An answer, of sorts, is found in the Constituent Assembly Debates. While discussing the religious freedom clauses, Ambedkar observed:

> ... the religious conceptions in this country are so vast that they cover every aspect of life, from birth to death ... I do not think it is possible to accept a position of that sort ... we ought to strive hereafter to limit the definition of religion in such a manner that we shall not extend beyond beliefs and such rituals as may be connected with ceremonials which are essentially religious. It is not necessary that ... laws relating to tenancy or laws relating to succession should be governed by religion.[21]

Ambedkar, therefore, was speaking to a very specific concern, a concern that scholars have located in the difference between the 'thin' and 'thick' role of religion.[22] In Western liberal democracies, where religion has (largely) been relegated to the sphere of private worship and ceremony, religious autonomy is unlikely to seriously jeopardize the State's legislative programme, or, for that matter, to affect individual rights in any meaningful way. In India, however, according to Ambedkar, religion, the private life of the individual, and the public life of the community are inextricably bound together (in T.N. Madan's words, religion is 'constitutive of society').[23] Consequently, the State would have no choice but to restrict the operation of religious freedom to matters that are essentially religious, and not those that are secular in character but over whom religion nonetheless claims dominion. As we have seen, the Constitution explicitly contains this division, in the very text of the numerous sub-clauses of Articles 25 and 26. Indeed, Ambedkar's original formulation seemed to be precisely oriented towards denying religious groups sweeping powers over their constituents.

What Ambedkar and the constitutional text did not do, however, was to provide a test, or a set of principles, for distinguishing the religious from the secular. Both provided examples—Ambedkar of tenancy and succession law, the Constitution of administration of property—without actually answering the question. And so the battle moved to the courts.

As early as 1954, the Supreme Court acknowledged the 'thick' conception of religion by rejecting a definition that would have limited it to private matters of thought, conscience, and belief. It accepted, instead, that the religious freedom clauses would also protect action and practice. In *Lakshmindra Swamiar*, a case that dealt with State control over the administration of religious denominations, the Court held:

> ... if the tenets of any religious sect ... prescribe that offerings of food should be given to the idol at particular hours of the day, that periodical ceremonies should be performed in a certain way at certain periods of the year ... all these would be regarded as parts of religion and the mere fact that they involve expenditure of money or employment ... would not make them secular activities partaking of a commercial or economic character.[24]

The Court went on to hold that under Article 26(b), religious denominations had complete autonomy to decide what rites and ceremonies were essential to the religion.

The Court therefore began by adopting an internal point of view to distinguish between the religious and the secular: look to the religion itself. This doctrine nonetheless fails to solve Ambedkar's poser. If religion itself claims such a vast domain, making religion the arbiter of what falls within its domain seems illogical. The position was, however, affirmed in a similar case that same year.[25] In both cases, the Supreme Court employed the 'essential practices' formulation—borrowed from Ambedkar—to distinguish between the religious (free from regulation) and the secular (subject to regulation).

However, three years later, there was a sudden change of tack, when the Allahabad High Court was asked to decide whether government regulations prohibiting bigamy violated Article 25(1).

It was argued that, because of the special religious duties performed by Hindu sons, bigamy was required in case no male children were forthcoming from the first marriage. In response, the Court analysed certain important Hindu religious texts and held that 'polygamy ... [is not] an essential part of the Hindu religion'.[26]

Here is the key shift: the word 'essential' went from qualifying the *nature of the practice* (whether it is religious or secular) to qualifying its *importance* (within the religion), i.e., from whether something is *essentially religious* to whether it is *essential to the religion*. It was a minor semantic shift but with significant consequences, because it allowed the Court to address questions internal to religion in a judicial enquiry, and thereby define the nature of religion itself. Towards the end of the decade, this test was affirmed by the Supreme Court in upholding a law prohibiting cow slaughter.[27]

At the turn of the Court's first decade, therefore, there appeared to be two distinct tests under Article 25 and 26 of the Constitution. First: was the practice of a religious or secular nature? And second: was it essential to the religion? The first enquiry was conducted to decide which aspects of temple or religious trust management could come within State control. The second was to decide whether specific religious practices which the State sought to prohibit or regulate met the threshold test for constitutional protection at all. As we have seen above, while the distinction between religious and secular was set up by the Constitution itself and in Ambedkar's framing speech, the distinction between essential and inessential *religious* practices was nowhere to be found in the text or history.

While the Court was yet to recognize, let alone explain, the dichotomy, it is easy to see how and why it came about. The original sin lay in *Lakshmindra Swamiar*. That case had set up two propositions in tension with one another: first, that the scope of the religious freedom clauses extended to practice and conduct; and secondly, what practice or conduct was protected was to be judged from the internal standpoint of the religion itself. When placed in the context of Ambedkar's acute observation about the influence of religion in Indian public life, no Court could have faithfully followed both propositions. However, instead of rethinking *Swamiar*, the Court's response was to tweak the test in a subtle but far-reaching direction, one that effectively gave it substantial powers of intervention into religious faith—a direction that had clearly not been contemplated by the constitutional framers.

In the 1960s, however, in a series of judgements delivered by Justice (and then Chief Justice) Gajendragadkar, the systematic distinction between the two tests was dissolved. While deciding upon the constitutionality of an Act stipulating control over the managing committee of a Muslim dargah, Justice Gajendragadkar observed in *obiter*:

> [for] the practices in question … [to] be treated as a part of religion they must be regarded by the said religion as its essential and integral part; otherwise even purely secular practices which are not an essential or an integral part of religion are apt to be clothed with a religious form … Similarly, even practices though religious may have sprung from merely superstitious beliefs and may in that sense be extraneous and unessential accretions to religion itself …[28]

In this paragraph, Justice Gajendragadkar ran together the two distinct tests. In the first part of the first sentence, he equated 'being part of a religion' with being an 'essential and integral part' of it, for the purposes of constitutional protection. He then observed that the *reason* for this distinction was to differentiate between the merely secular claiming the mantle of religion and the actually religious. But that wasn't all; he then argued that 'similarly', there was a distinction between the religious and the merely 'superstitious'.

There is, however, nothing 'similar' between the two! The religious/secular distinction, however it might be drawn, does not involve the court in external *normative* value judgements about the religious practice in question. In addition to combining the two tests, Justice Gajendragadkar was making another innovation.

Effectively, he was clothing the judiciary with the power to achieve, *by interpretation,* what the Constitution had allowed Parliament to do, through *legislation*: implement 'social reform' by erasing supposedly regressive religious practices by labelling them as mere superstition. Earlier, when the Court had taken upon itself the task of deciding what constituted an essential or integral aspect of a religion, it had already assumed the power of erasure. Now, that power was coloured with the brush of normativity. And the very next year, the two (equated) tests were merged into two succeeding steps of a single test. In *Govindlalji v. State of Rajasthan*, Justice Gajendragadkar held that 'the Court may have to enquire whether the practice in question is religious in character and, if it is, whether it can be regarded as an integral or essential part of the religion'.[29]

Finally, in *Sastri Yagnapurushadji v. Muldas*, the appellants tried to circumvent the operation of a Bombay temple entry law, which required public Hindu temples to open themselves up for worship to all castes, by arguing that the 'Swaminarayan sect' did not consider itself to be Hindu at all. This contention was rejected by now Chief Justice Gajendragadkar, who devoted reams of text to prove that the Swaminarayan sect was, indeed, Hindu (contrary to its own self-identification), by isolating a few core concepts that formed the bedrock of 'Hinduism'.[30] The Chief Justice's vision of Hinduism, as many scholars have remarked, was that of a rationalistic and progressive religion, implicit within which was the further notion that the appellants, in trying to continue to deny certain castes the right to worship in their temple, had themselves misunderstood the principles of Hinduism.[31]

To sum up, therefore: through the 1960s, CJI Gajendragadkar combined the two distinct tests, viz., religious/secular and essential/inessential, into a single one. With respect to the first test—now the first 'step'—he continued to pay formal obeisance to the internal point of view, i.e., to the religious community's determination of the scope of what constituted religion, while actually determining the question by judicial fiat; and to the second, he added a normative prong, which allowed the Court to cleanse and uniformize disparate religious practices in an—allegedly—socially 'progressive' direction, again by judicial fiat.[32]

Doing so had two further consequences: as the Court increased its own power in this manner, the use of Article 25(2)(b)—which granted the *State* the power of religious intervention for social reform—began to decrease.[33] And secondly, at times, the Court was led to record seemingly absurd conclusions. In *Commissioner of Police v. Acharya Jagdishwarananda Avadhuta*, it refused to accept a practice (in this case, a war-like public dance performed on the streets) as an essential religious practice even when the sect's founder had stipulated it in the sect's holy book, *precisely* so that it could be accorded constitutional sanctity.[34]

Indeed, in that case, the absurdity of the conclusion was recognized by Justice Lakshmanan in a strong dissenting opinion. As a first of any judge formally noting thus, Justice Lakshmanan observed that Justice Gajendragadkar's observations in *Durgah*, distinguishing the 'superstitious' from the 'essential religious practices' and calling for close judicial scrutiny to determine the content of 'essential religious practices', were at variance with the original dictum of the Court in *Swamiar*. Justice Lakshmanan, instead, swung the pendulum to the other end: 'to allow any authority to judge the truth or falsity of a religious belief or practice is to destroy the guarantee of religious freedom in the Constitution.'[35] Justice Lakshmanan's opinion parallels that of Justice Ayyangar's concurring opinion in *Saifuddin*, and provides a counter-point to the dominant 'three-step test'. This counterpoint goes back to the original formulation in *Swamiar*. By adopting the internal point of view and a deferential approach towards what constitutes constitutionally protected 'religion', it tips the balance back towards maintaining the integrity of religious groupings over social-reformatory purposes of the parliament and the judiciary.

III. The Three-Step Test and Its Discontents

The Supreme Court itself, on occasion, has evinced awareness of the tensions created by its jurisprudence. In late 2015, Justice Gogoi observed that the 'performance of such tasks, i.e., determination of essential religious practices, is not enjoined in the court by virtue of any ecclesiastical jurisdiction conferred on it but in view of its role as the Constitutional arbiter ... [and] on the touchstone of constitutional necessity.'[36] These words are interesting, suggesting that the Constitution has *necessarily* entrusted the task of determining essential religious practices to the Court. This necessity would seem to stem from Ambedkar's observation in the Constituent Assembly about the pervasive role of religion in Indian public life.

For this reason, the argument goes, the Constitution *itself* exhibits a 'reformist intention',[37] and in interpreting it, Indian courts cannot adopt the hands-off, deferential approach to religion that is the hallmark of other constitutional courts. This is why the Supreme Court, in its first ever decision in *Swamiar*, appeared to do two contradictory things: extend the scope of Articles 25 and 26 to religious conduct and practice, giving it, in theory, a vast jurisdiction, while at the same time placing a limit upon what counted *as religion*, and restricting its influence. And this is why the alternative approach, in Justice Ayyangar's concurring opinion in *Saifuddin*, and Justice Lakshmanan's dissent in *Avadhuta* (II), while seemingly elegant and attractive, are nonetheless inconsistent with the constitutional text and purpose.

The 'three-step test', however, comes at a high cost. First, unlike the religious/secular distinction, it has no root in the constitutional text or history.[38] Second, the Court has failed to develop a rigorous methodology for determining the content of essential religious practices.[39] It has relied upon English-language sources,[40] colonial writings[41] (in stark contrast, for instance, to the approach of the South African Constitutional Court),[42] and has even decided cases without taking testimony from the affected parties.[43] The Court's enquiry privileges a certain set of sources and has the effect of uniformizing and homogenizing religious meaning at the cost of dissident and marginalized traditions.[44] This, of course, is part of the broader critique that questions the Court's competence *and* legitimacy to adjudicate religious truth.[45]

Third, as cases like *Avadhuta* show, the enquiry itself seems to destroy the balance between secular intervention and religious autonomy. If it is true that religious communities are essential for self-determination by providing the 'contexts of choice' within which individual autonomy becomes meaningful, then the determination and imposition of religious meaning by an external authority seems to defeat the purpose entirely.[46]

And fourth, the justifications for this approach seem to rest not in constitutional principles but in consequentialist considerations. Galanter argues, for instance, that the Court's reliance on the three-step test instead of the social reform clause is because regulating a practice that has been pronounced as non-religious, or inessentially religious, enjoys more presumptive legitimacy than granting threshold constitutional protection and *then* upholding the State's coercive power to regulate.[47] This also explains CJI Gajendragadkar's efforts to hold that religion, *truly* understood, is in harmony with the reformatory ideals of the Constitution. However, as Galanter himself acknowledges, there is no empirical evidence to substantiate this claim.[48]

The other consequentialist justification has been that of necessity, as Justice Gogoi observed. The three-step test is required because it is the only way the judiciary can stay true to the broader constitutional vision of regulating and limiting the vast scope of religion in Indian life in the interests of social reform. As mentioned above, the constitutional text itself exhibits reformist intentions; and scholars of Indian secularism have repeatedly differentiated it from its liberal Western counterpart, noting its 'ameliorative'[49] or 'contextual'[50] nature, which specifically envisages State intervention into religion in order to achieve certain substantive values.

However, is the three-step test the only way to achieve this? This claim too is doubtful. Each of the cases (referred to above) in which the three-step test was applied could have been decided on alternative, textual grounds. In *Ram Prasad Seth*, the Court upheld bigamy prohibition *both* on the touchstone of Article 25(2)(b), and on the grounds that it wasn't an essential religious practice. In *Qureshi*, while upholding a ban on cow slaughter, the Court spent a lot of time on the public health benefits of preserving the bovine population, and could have, therefore, upheld the prohibition upon the 'public health' prong of Article 25(1), instead of holding, as it did, that cow slaughter during Eid was not an essential part of Islam. *Sastri Yagnapurushadji* could have been decided under Article 25(2)(b), which expressly allows the State to legislate for temple entry.[51] In *Seshammal*, the abolition of hereditary priesthood was expressly defended by the State on the grounds of social reform, an argument ignored by the Court. And similarly, in *Ismail Faruqui*, the State takeover of the disputed land in Ayodhya was expressly defended on the grounds of preservation of public order, a permitted basis of restriction under Article 25(1)—again, ignored by the Court.

It is in this context that I now argue that CJI Sinha's dissenting opinion in *Saifuddin* articulated an alternative to the three-step test. This alternative provides a more coherent understanding of the relationship between individual, community, and State, and one that I believe is truer and more faithful to the constitutional vision.

IV. Civic Equality and the Transformative Constitution

Chief Justice Sinha's dissenting opinion in *Saifuddin* was woven out of three strands. First, locating the Excommunication Act within a long history of social welfare legislation, he observed that its purpose was to ensure 'individual freedom to choose one's way of life and to do away with all those undue and outmoded interferences with liberty of conscience, faith and belief. It is also aimed at ensuring human dignity…'[52] Second, echoing Ambedkar's distinction between the essentially and the incidentally religious, he noted that the effect of excommunication was to deprive an individual of basic civil rights, such as the rights to worship, community burial, community property, and so on. And *third*, traversing beyond the contours of Articles 25 and 26, he linked the Excommunication Act with the prohibition of untouchability under Article 17. Observing that excommunication enjoined other members of the community from having any contact, social or religious, with the outcast, he held that 'the position of an excommunicated person becomes that of an untouchable in his community ... the Act in declaring such practices to be void has only carried out the strict injunction of Art. 17 of the Constitution ... to do away with all that mischief of treating a human being as a pariah ... of depriving him of his human dignity.'[53]

It is this last argument that I want to consider first. It is true that Article 17 of the Constitution prohibits untouchability. However, 'untouchability' is a term that refers to a specific practice of caste-based structural and systemic oppression and exclusion which operates simultaneously in the political, social, and economic spheres, and whose defining characteristic is an injunction against any form of physical contact between untouchables and touchables.[54] Beyond surface resemblances, there is little similarity between untouchability and community ostracism. In equating social ostracism with Article 17, therefore, CJI Sinha chose to adopt an interpretation of untouchability that went beyond its *concrete* meaning, and embraced a wider understanding of social and community exclusion, the 'mischief of treating a human being as a pariah ... of depriving him of his human dignity'.

On what basis did CJI Sinha select the more expansive, abstract definition of untouchability? It is important to note that this choice was indicated not only by the text of the clause, which abolishes the practice of untouchability 'in any form',[55] but also by the history of its framing. While the communities constituting 'untouchables' had been specifically enumerated in the Government of India Act of 1935 (the predecessor of the Indian Constitution), as Ambedkar pointed out, the Constitution itself had elected not to operate at that level of specificity.[56]

Indeed, an amendment moved by Naziruddin Ahmed to restrict the scope of the Article to untouchability only on account of 'religion or caste'[57] was specifically rejected by Ambedkar and voted down by the Assembly.[58] Furthermore, even though K.M. Munshi pointed to the fact that the word 'untouchability' was contained within quotation marks, making it clear that the intention was to 'deal with it in the sense in which it is normally understood',[59] many members called for providing a clearer definition of the term on the grounds of vagueness.[60] In fact, K.T. Shah specifically 'warned' that it might even be extended to cover women, who at various times had been treated in the manner of untouchables by the society.[61]

Specifically, while some of the members of the Assembly undoubtedly understood untouchability in its narrow, concrete sense,[62] they did not do so to the exclusion of its broader sense. Meanwhile, other members expressly linked the provision to Article 15(2),[63] and repeatedly argued that *their* understanding of Article 17 included the right of everyone to enjoy 'equal social conditions',[64] 'equal rights',[65] 'social equality',[66] the abolition of 'social inequity … social stigma and … social disabilities',[67] and as a remedial clause for 'those who have been left behind in social and economic matters'.[68] Therefore, it seems clear that between both the supporters *and* the opponents of Article 17, as it stood, there was agreement on the *breadth* of its meaning.

Consequently, CJI Sinha's adoption of untouchability in its broad sense, in the sense of social ostracism, had its foundation in both the text of the Constitution and the debates surrounding it. What, however, did that choice entail? To answer this question, let us look again at the first two strands of his argument. The purpose of the Act, he held, was to guarantee individual freedom, remove interferences with liberty, conscience, and faith, and guarantee human dignity and freedom of choice.

But this is the crucial question: freedom from *what*? CJI Sinha was not talking about *State* coercion and interference with freedom. Rather, he was talking about the coercive freedom-interfering acts of communities (such as social ostracism) against their members. In other words, as discussed above, CJI Sinha believed that Articles 25 and 26 not only guaranteed *group-differentiated rights* to religious denominations in the interests of preserving their integrity, but also provided for the rights of individuals *against* their groups in the interests of individual freedom, liberty of conscience, and human dignity. It was in this context that the balance between group integrity and social reform, set out textually within the scheme of 25 and 26, was to be understood.

As in the previous chapter, such a strong statement of horizontality might sound counter-intuitive.[69] However, I shall argue that CJI Sinha's understanding of horizontality and his construction of Articles 25 and 26 are faithful to the constitutional value of fraternity. And fraternity, as part of the transformative Constitution, is committed to a rich vision of substantive equality and freedom both between and within communities.

To understand this, recall our discussion of *IMA v. Union of India*, which had held that Article 15(2) guaranteed non-discriminatory access to schools.[70] At the heart of the judgement was the historical awareness that the economic and social *boycott* practised by dominant castes in India had been one of the most effective ways of discrimination and subordination.[71] The exclusionary effect of the boycott had been recognized by the 1929 Starte Committee, which had cited the examples of preventing the boycotted persons from using common paths, as well as stoppage of sale of the necessaries of life, and recommended outlawing the practice.[72]

Thus, the boycott served as both a means of exclusion from material resources, such as schools, water tanks, and other civic amenities, as well as reinforcing existing social hierarchies through stigmatizing the excluded.[73] It was this understanding, and the will to ensure that the newly framed Constitution could guarantee a remedy against community practices whose result was the material and symbolic exclusion (and thereby, the subordination) of individuals from the economic and social life of the polity, that saw the formulation of the oddly worded Article 15(2) and its 2011 interpretation by the Supreme Court.[74]

The story of Article 15(2), in its historical context, reinforces the argument that the Indian anti-colonial movement had two distinct aims: against the despotism of colonial rule, *and* against the far-reaching (pre-colonial) grip of caste and community upon individual life. As discussed in the previous chapter, simultaneously with the Congress party's agitation against British rule in the 1920s and '30s, there were mass movements of the 'Depressed Classes' to access drinking water from community wells, and the right to enter Hindu temples.[75]

Crucially, these movements were framed within the vocabulary of *civil rights* (of individuals against communities) and *civic equality* (within communities), and *against* the claims of the religious integrity of communities.[76] As Anupama Rao puts it, the focus of the movements was an expanded and inclusive idea of the 'public' that covered important material and symbolic *community spaces* (whether religious or secular), and asked for equality of access to those spaces.[77] And most crucially for our interpretive purpose, as we have seen, *both* issues, viz., access to water wells and access to temples, would eventually find their way into the text of the Constitution through Articles 15(2) and 25(2)(b).

The governing principle behind what eventually became Articles 15(2) and 17 of the Constitution, therefore, was something that we can now define as the *anti-exclusion* principle:[78] the Constitution limits the power of groups and communities to *exclude* their constituents in a manner that would interfere with their freedom to participate in normal economic, social and cultural life, and thereby 'disrupt secured access to basic goods',[79] such as basic freedom, an adequate range of valuable opportunities, and self-respect.[80] CJI Sinha's important innovation in his dissenting opinion in *Saifuddin* was to *extend* the anti-exclusion principle from the specific logic of anti-discrimination under Articles 15(2) and 17 to the relations between religious communities and their members under Articles 25 and 26.

We can immediately see an important benefit of invoking the anti-exclusion principle over the essential religious practices test. The Court's use of essential religious practices is external, static, and acontextual, and thereby fails to be true to how the practitioners of religion make sense of conduct and doctrine in evolving social contexts. However, even if the Court was to change tack and attempt to faithfully track the dynamism of evolving religious practices, as many scholars have pointed out, this is an enquiry it is institutionally unsuited to undertake, and it raises legitimacy concerns. The anti-exclusion principle spares the Court from this impossible choice by shifting the analysis from the *content* of religious conduct and practice to its *discriminatory effect*. Of course, discrimination itself is a contextual enquiry, depending upon an investigation both of evolving social meaning (in cases of symbolic discrimination) as well as what goods count as 'basic goods' at any given time. However, it is an enquiry that has always been within the judicial domain and, indeed, is *constitutionally* placed within the judicial domain.

Furthermore, as I have developed it here, the anti-exclusion principle is substantially stronger than the principles proposed by other scholars of secularism and the interface between individual and group rights in the Indian polity. Partha Chatterjee, for instance, argues that balancing liberalism and multiculturalism requires allowing a 'group [to] insist on its right not to give reasons for doing things differently, provided it explains itself adequately in its own chosen forum'.[81] Akeel Bilgrami, on the other hand, advocates a 'negotiated and emergent secularism', which imagines the State as providing 'internal reasons addressing different communitarian perspectives from within their own internal substantive commitments ... so as to eventually provide for a common secular outcome, each on different internal grounds'.[82] Both Chatterjee and Bilgrami privilege the internal norms and reasons of the group (subject to certain conditions) over the external norms that might be imposed by the State. Rajeev Bhargava's slightly stronger concept of 'contextual secularism' allows for differentiated group rights subject to 'a dignified life for all',[83] without fleshing out what a dignified life might entail in practice. By contrast, the anti-exclusion principle holds that the external norm of constitutional anti-discrimination be applied to limit the autonomy of religious groups in situations where these groups are blocking access to basic goods.

V. Two Objections Considered

However, it is the strong nature of the anti-exclusion claim that gives rise to an obvious objection—that the logic of anti-discrimination law is not typically extended to religious groupings precisely because religion is deemed to be a private (even intimate) activity.[84] Furthermore, and partly for this reason, the actions of religious groups are unlikely to interfere with individuals' ability to access basic public goods. However, as Amy Gutmann points out, there are instances where even private or voluntary associations can act as 'source[s] of public goods' and thereby, through exclusion, can 'block' access to such goods.[85] In this context, the reader will recall how the argument of this chapter has been that religion and religious groupings play a much *thicker* role in Indian life (as the Constitution itself acknowledges) than they do elsewhere.[86]

This brings us to the third strand of CJI Sinha's dissenting opinion. As he observed, the effect of excommunication was not simply 'religious'. It extended to barring the individual from exercising her civil rights and, furthermore, by forbidding social or economic contact, effectively turned her into a 'pariah'. While this may not be constitutionally significant in jurisdictions where the influence of groups is significantly less, and where exit and entry barriers are easier to surmount,[87] it is precisely the thick nature of religious groupings in India that ensures that there is a closer relationship between the acts of religious communities and individuals' basic rights: 'you can never separate social life from religious life,' as Alladi Krishnaswamy Ayyar had pointed out in the Constituent Assembly.[88]

To put the issue another way: as Michael Walzer argues and the South African scholar Stuart Woolman contends in the precise context of imposing egalitarian requirements upon groups,[89] a regime of equality must ensure that 'no citizen's standing in one sphere or with regard to one social good can be undercut by his standing in some other social sphere, with regard to some other social good'.[90] In jurisdictions where religion plays a thin, i.e., relatively autonomous role, equality has little to say to the relationships between members of a religious community, since there is little chance of inegalitarianism within the community being translated into burdens in other spheres. However, in the words of Anupama Rao, in a society where 'ritual, economic and social domination'[91] were inextricably bound up with each other, and where 'practices of ... segregation [took place] across sites of exclusion',[92] Chief Justice Sinha's important insight in *Dawoodi Bohra* was that excommunication had impacts that went beyond the 'essentially' religious, and affected the excommunicated individual's access to basic public goods.

Articles 25(1) and 25(2), I would suggest, form the third limb of the anti-exclusion principle, in addition to Articles 15(2) (non-discriminatory horizontal access) and 17 (prohibition of untouchability). Understanding CJI Sinha's opinion through the lens of the anti-exclusion principle allows us to contrast it sharply with the majority opinion. The core of the majority's reasoning was that, since excommunication was based only on *religious* grounds, and was aimed at ensuring the integrity of the group, it was constitutionally protected under Article 25(1) and 26(b). The Act was thus not saved by the 'social reform' clause, notwithstanding excommunication's impact upon the individual's civil rights. Effectively, the majority opinion held the group's *religious identity* and *integrity* (subject to judicial determination) to be sacrosanct, ignoring the insight that it is possible that an individual's standing in one sphere (in this case, the religious sphere) can impact her standing in other spheres.

On the other hand, CJI Sinha's opinion gave primacy to the anti-exclusion principle, holding that group integrity would have to be *subject* to that.

It is at this point, however, that we must deal with another important objection. The above argument, so this objection goes, unduly subordinates the rights to associative freedom and cultural integrity to the claims of equality. As many scholars have argued, values of pluralism and diversity—to which the Constitution is unquestionably committed—require us to tolerate violations of equality and certain other non-basic rights within groups so as to protect the continued existence of groups.[93]

In fact, the thick nature of religious groups might actually provide an argument in favour of non-interference: given the diverse ways in which thick groups provide people their contexts of choice, group autonomy and preservation are even more important goals than they otherwise would be. To this, a textual point may be added: unlike other Constitutions[94] or international legal instruments[95] which guarantee the rights of individuals to exercise religious freedoms singly or *in community* with others, and refrain from vesting rights in groups *qua* groups,[96] the Indian Constitution, through Article 26(b), expressly makes groups the *bearers* of rights. This would suggest that textually the balance between individual and group claims must tilt towards the group.

While it is true that Article 26(b) makes groups the bearers of rights, the Constitution does not state the *basis* of doing so. It does not clarify whether groups are granted rights for the instrumental reason that individuals can only achieve self-determination and fulfilment within the 'context of choice'[97] provided by communities, or whether the Constitution treats groups, along with individuals, as *constitutive units* worthy of equal concern and respect.[98] The distinction is crucial, because the weight that must be accorded to group integrity, even at the cost of blocking individual access to important public goods, can only be determined by deciding which vision the Constitution subscribes to.

The answer to this question must be grounded in the specifics of Indian constitutional history.[99] Let us briefly consider that history. During colonial times, the British largely followed a policy of non-regulation of 'personal law', leaving 'communities' free to manage their own internal affairs[100] (something akin to the Ottoman 'millet' system).[101] The fundamental normative unit was the *group*, evidenced through a number of legal measures such as separate electorates, and penal provisions criminalizing insulting the religious feelings of any 'class'.[102] For this reason, when the legality of Dawoodi Bohra excommunication was brought before the colonial courts, the only enquiry made was as to whether, historically, the Dai had the power that he claimed to exercise.[103]

The absence of legal regulation, however, did not impede strong social movements within religious and other communities, focused upon two principles: individual freedom and choice *within* community spaces, and the right to social and political inclusion and participation. In an earlier chapter, we discussed Tanika Sarkar's important argument that the conception and vocabulary of women's rights first evolved in direct opposition to community control, in the debates surrounding the abolition of forced widow immolation[104] and the age of consent.[105] Crucially, these movements found expression in the Constitution.

Thus, as we have seen, despite a strong cultural consensus at the end of the nineteenth century, which purported to divide society into something approximating a public/political and private/community domain, consigning women to the latter as embodiments of the 'community'[106] and depriving them of participation in the public sphere, the early twentieth century saw a strong woman suffrage movement, which culminated in that most public of rights—universal adult franchise—during the framing of the Constitution.[107] Universal adult franchise under the Constitution marked a transformation not only in ascribing public citizenship to women, but in *expressly* doing away with the colonial-era separate voting electorates for religious communities, and marked a categorical turn away from a vision of society that treated groups as *constitutive* to one that understood their value to be *instrumental* in guaranteeing effective individual autonomy.

In addition, we have already discussed how the horizontal non-discrimination (Article 15[2]) and temple-entry (Article 25[2][b]) provisions were the results of movements that were expressly framed in the language of civil rights for individuals *against* their communities, even at the cost of the 'integrity' of the community, understood as the continuation of strongly held beliefs and practices.[108]

Indeed, it is these legacies that led Ambedkar to clarify, in the Constituent Assembly Debates, that notwithstanding the existence of minority and group rights in the Constitution, its basic unit was the individual;[109] and, more specifically, to remark, during the debates on the religious freedom clauses: 'What are we having this liberty for? We are having this liberty in order to reform our social system, which is so full of inequities, so full of inequalities, discriminations and other things, which conflict with our fundamental rights.'[110]

Crucially, Ambedkar was responding to repeated attempts in the Constituent Assembly to insulate personal laws from State interference by making them a part of the right to freedom of religion. Unlike the freedom of religion, a quintessentially individual right, this move would have established group supremacy over the individual in certain crucial matters, such as marriage, divorce, inheritance, and even property transfers.[111]

The Constituent Assembly's decisive rejection of these proposals indicates clearly that the attempt to establish groups as constitutive normative units in the Constitution failed. And it failed because the Constituent Assembly agreed with Ambedkar when he specifically argued (just as Chief Justice Sinha would argue a decade and a half later) that it wasn't merely the State, but the *social system*, i.e., the community, whose actions conflicted with individual rights and would accordingly have to be 'reformed'. The specific sites of reform, of course, have to be historically understood, and, as we have seen, defined by the manner of discrimination, which primarily took the form of economic, social, and cultural *exclusion*.

VI. Conclusion

The 'thick' role played by religion and religious groupings in Indian public life rules out a traditional 'liberal' approach to the right to freedom of religion. The Constitution itself eschews this approach, its very text abandoning liberal neutrality for explicitly 'reformist' intentions. The key questions are what, precisely, does the Constitution aim to reform, and how ought the judiciary effectuate its reformist intentions? The Supreme Court has answered these questions by developing the three-step test, which allows it to separate 'essential' from 'inessential' religious practices, and accord protection only to the former.

Ever since CJI Gajendragadkar's time, this has become not only an empirical, but also a normative enquiry. The Court has simply withheld constitutional protection from practices that seem out of step with the Constitution's progressive outlook, by deeming them 'non-essential'. However, for a number of reasons, this approach is unsatisfactory. It also conflates two distinct questions by making them part of the same test: the distinction between the religious and the secular, which the Constitution itself draws; and the distinction between the essential and the inessential, which it doesn't.

In this chapter, drawing upon CJI Sinha's dissenting opinion in *Saifuddin*, and locating it within the comprehensive transformative character of the Indian Constitution, I have proposed the anti-exclusion principle as a replacement for the 'essential practices test'. This principle will obviously not apply to the first category of cases (State control over religious institutional property), which will continue to be subject to the religious/secular distinction drawn by the constitutional text. It will, however, apply to cases where constitutional protection is sought for religious customs or practices, and where there is a conflict *within* religious communities.

The anti-exclusion principle stipulates that the State and the Court must respect the integrity of religious groups (and thereby treat the internal point of view of religious adherents as determinative of the form and content of religious practices) *except where* the practices in question lead to the exclusion of individuals from economic, social, or cultural life in a manner that impairs their dignity, or hampers their access to basic goods. The form of analysis is similar to that of anti-discrimination law. Under this approach, the Ananda Margis have every right to dance the *tandava* on the streets of Calcutta if they consider it essential to their faith, but the Dawoodi Bohras can be legitimately stopped from excommunicating and ostracizing their members.

One final point remains. Does the anti-exclusion principle apply at the threshold stage of deciding whether or not to extend constitutional protection to impugned religious practices, or does it apply to judging the constitutional validity of ostensibly reformatory State laws? In my opinion, it ought to apply at both stages, depending upon the case at hand. In a case like *Saifuddin*, for instance, where the challenge is to a State *law*, then the Court can begin by asking what the law is aiming to achieve; and if the law is aiming at instantiating the anti-exclusion principle, then it is to be upheld, regardless of the status of the impugned practice.

On the other hand, in cases like the disputes over the access to the Haji Ali and Sabarimala shrines, with which we began this chapter, there was a direct *clash* between two claimed rights: the constitutional right of women to worship under Article 25(1), and the right of the religious denomination to manage its own affairs under Article 26(b). In such a situation, since the foundation of the denomination's claim is exclusion, and the treatment of women as second-class members of the community, the claim will be overridden by the stronger individual right under Article 25(1), subject, of course, to a demonstration that the religious belief is genuinely held—an issue that was controversial in the case of *Sabarimala*, which came to the court as a PIL. This, I would submit, is a solution that allows the Court to give effect to the Constitution's transformative purposes without getting entangled in knotty questions of religious and theological doctrine.

Postscript—The Sabarimala Judgement

The Sabarimala case, with which we began and ended this chapter, was decided by a Constitution bench of the Supreme Court on 28 September 2018. In *Indian Young Lawyers' Association v. State of Kerala*, by a 4-1 majority, the Supreme Court decided in favour of women's right to enter Sabarimala.[112] While the Chief Justice and Justice Nariman decided the case along traditional lines, using the essential religious practices test and also analysing whether Article 26 was applicable, the dissenting opinion of Justice Malhotra and the concurring opinion of Justice Chandrachud threw up some interesting ideas. Justice Malhotra, for instance, rejected the essential religious practices (ERP) test altogether, on lines similar to what has been advocated in this chapter, but saw the question of religious worship as raising no significant fundamental rights issue at all.[113] Fascinatingly, Justice Chandrachud agreed that the ERP, in its present form, was unsustainable. What he also did, however, was to undertake a detailed Article 17 analysis, on the lines suggested in this chapter, advocate for a broad reading of the provision, and link it up with the anti-exclusion principle.[114] Justice Chandrachud's judgement is a powerful articulation of a transformative interpretation of Articles 25 and 26, and provides a strong intellectual foundation for advancing such a reading in the times to come.

6

The Freedom to Work: *Peoples Union for Democratic Rights* and Forced Labour

The connection between individual liberty and the shape and form of the economic structure of society may not be apparent to everyone. Nonetheless the connection between the two is real.

B.R. Ambedkar, Memorandum and Draft Articles on the Rights of States and Minorities, 24 March 1947

Necessitous men are not free men.

K.T. Shah, Minute of Dissent to the Draft Report of the Sub-Committee on Fundamental Rights, 17–20 April 1947

IN THE STORY OF the freedom struggle, the contribution of organized labour is often relegated to an insignificant footnote. Sometimes partners to—but more often, antagonists of—the dominant Indian National Congress,[1] labour and labour movements are the invisible warps in the tapestry of our constitutional evolution. Their importance can be glimpsed for a moment in history in the

1931 Bill of Rights,[2] which, as we have seen, was the most sustained and comprehensive such effort at a bill of rights before the drafting of the Constitution. As part of the Congress's stated commitment to 'end … exploitation' and secure 'real economic freedom' for the people of India, the 1931 Bill of Rights contained a detailed set of provisions, such as guarantees of a living wage, limited working hours, healthy conditions of work, maternity leave, and a social safety net, on a par with classical civil and political rights. In the Constitution, however, the 'labour provisions' were relegated to the unenforceable Directive Principles chapter, with the observation that rights incapable of or unsuitable for enforcement could not be granted the status of fundamental rights.[3]

The placement of labour rights in Part IV of the Constitution would appear to signal a constitutional intent to leave questions of economic structure outside the domain of fundamental rights. Yet, the bifurcation is not entirely obvious. Tucked away between the 'right to freedom' (Articles 19 to 22) and the 'right to freedom of religion' (Articles 25 to 28) lies a forgotten, almost vestigial, section of the Fundamental Rights chapter. Titled 'Right against Exploitation', it has only two provisions. Article 24 prohibits child labour in factories, mines, and other hazardous forms of employment. But before that, there is Article 23, the first part of which reads, innocuously enough:

> Traffic in human beings and *begar* and other similar forms of forced labour are prohibited and any contravention of this provision shall be an offence punishable in accordance with law.

With *begar*—a system of inter-generational bonded labour unique to India—Article 23, at its heart, may, at first glance, seem only a narrow protection from debt slavery and its variants. And so it appeared to the Supreme Court, which for the first three decades after the Constitution saw no occasion to invoke or interpret it. That changed dramatically in 1982. Dealing with the exploitation of contract labour hired to work on the Asian Games Village building project in the national capital, the Supreme Court held in *PUDR v. Union of India*[4] that the right *against* forced labour included the right *to* a minimum wage. Remarkably, the Court framed this not as a positive right or as a socio-economic guarantee that it was importing from the directive principles, but in the pure language of freedom: freedom *from* economic compulsions that drove workers to accept employment at wages even lower than the minimum rates.

This chapter is a reconstruction and a defence of the transformative vision of freedom articulated by the Supreme Court in *PUDR v. Union of India*. I begin with an analysis of the Court's insistence that the term 'forced labour' was not simply limited to physical or legal force, but applied equally to the 'compulsion of economic circumstances'.[5] I argue that, in doing so, the Court had to, and did, answer the following question: what kind of freedom did the Constitution envision (I)? In answering the question, the *PUDR* Court articulated a vision of freedom that included not just protection from arbitrary interference from the State, or from other human beings, but also from the concentrated power wielded through *human institutions and practices*, such as the market (II).

I go on to argue that *PUDR*'s adoption of this vision was justified in view of both the text of Article 23, as well as our constitutional history. The Indian Constitution did not take the existing economic structure and economic arrangements as a 'natural', immutable state of affairs. Rather, the Constitution aimed at transforming the economic structure, but to a limited extent (III). I conclude by examining the consequences of *PUDR*, both in the domain of the workplace, and in other domains which are not usually thought to raise issues of constitutional freedom, such as the household (IV). While the promise of *PUDR* is yet to be followed through by the Courts, it remains an invitation for us to view the Fundamental Rights chapter as embodying not merely a charter of *political* freedom but, through Article 23, one for realizing 'labour's constitution of (economic) freedom'.[6]

I. *PUDR v. Union of India*

Surrounded by parks, leafy avenues, and a sports complex, the Asian Games Village is one of South Delhi's more recognizable landmarks, built for the Asian Games in 1982. As with most other large-scale infrastructure projects in India, the Asian Games construction works were completed on the backs of contract and migrant labour working under exploitative conditions. The Peoples Union for Democratic Rights (PUDR) commissioned three social scientists to document the working conditions. On finding that the contractors were engaging in serious labour law violations, the PUDR took the case to the Supreme Court.[7] Before the Court, the PUDR alleged that the labourers were not being paid minimum wages, that women and men were not being remunerated equally, that children were being employed in a hazardous environment, and that there was widespread exploitation of contract labour in contravention of the Contract Labour Act.

Apart from contesting the case on merits, the Union of India (along with the Delhi Development Authority and the Delhi administration) raised two preliminary objections. The PUDR, they argued, had no standing to bring this case to court on behalf of the labourers. And even if they did, the violations, if any, were violations of ordinary labour laws (such as the Equal Remuneration Act and the Minimum Wages Act), which had been committed by private contractors. The remedies would lie under those laws. To take the State to Court under Article 32 of the Constitution, as the PUDR had done, required showing that some fundamental right of the labourers was at stake.[8]

The Court swiftly disposed of the first objection. These were the early days of the PIL era, but it had already been established that where people whose rights were being violated lacked the means or the ability to seek legal redress, others could bring their case to Court on their behalf, and in 'the public interest'.[9] In *PUDR v. Union of India*, these conditions were clearly fulfilled.[10] On the second objection, the Court noted that denying equal pay for equal work not only violated the Equal Remuneration Act, but also Article 14 of the Constitution. Likewise, employing children violated Article 24, and contravening the Contract Labour Act violated Article 21's right to life (which, after *Maneka Gandhi v. Union of India*, included a life with dignity).[11]

That, however, left the non-payment of minimum wages still to be accounted for. Which fundamental right provided a guarantee of a minimum wage? Counter-intuitively, the Court located it within a never-used and almost-forgotten provision of the Constitution: Article 23, which prohibited 'traffic in human beings and *begar* and other similar forms of forced labour'. But what did minimum wages have to do with forced labour? Wasn't forced labour limited to debt-slavery, or inter-generational bonded labour, exacted from people without any payment? That, precisely, was the argument made by the State.[12]

The Court rejected this argument, noting that it sought 'to unduly restrict the amplitude of the prohibition against forced labour enacted in Article 23'.[13] Why? Because:

> It is difficult to imagine that the Constitution makers should have intended to strike only at certain forms of forced labour leaving it open to the socially or economically powerful sections of the community to exploit the poor and weaker sections by resorting to other forms of forced labour.[14]

In fact:

> Could there be any logic or reason in enacting that if a person is forced to give labour or service to another without receiving any remuneration at all it should be regarded as a pernicious practice sufficient to attract the condemnation of Article 23, but if some remuneration is paid for it, then it should be outside the inhibition of that Article? If this were the true interpretation, Article 23 would be reduced to a mere rope of sand, for it would then be the easiest

> thing in an exploitative society for a person belonging to a socially or economically dominant class to exact labour or service from a person belonging to the deprived and vulnerable section of the community ...[15]

The Court thus began by making a defensive argument, noting that the existence of remuneration was not what changed the character of 'forced' labour to free labour. That, however, left the positive case still to be made: how was the word 'forced' (and, by extension, words such as 'compulsion' and 'freedom') to be understood under Article 23? The Court answered thus:

> Any factor which deprives a person of a choice of alternatives and compels him to adopt one particular course of action may properly be regarded as 'force' and if labour or service is compelled as a result of such 'force', it would be 'forced labour'.[16]

While a tautology in some sense, this formulation is surely too broad. The phrase 'any factor' makes no distinction between factors that are caused by human action, 'natural' factors that are within the domain of human power to overcome, and factors that are neither caused by human beings, nor are subject to their control. While we may have a philosophical debate about the 'true' meaning of force and freedom, a constitutional provision that is unable to draw the distinctions outlined above would be meaningless. Perhaps aware of this, the Court went on to clarify its position:

> Where a person is suffering from hunger or starvation ... where utter grinding poverty has broken his back and reduced him to a state of helplessness and despair and where no other employment is available to alleviate the rigour of his poverty, he would have no choice but to accept any work that comes his way, even if the remuneration offered to him is less than the minimum wage ... And in doing so he would be acting not as a free agent with a choice between alternatives but under the compulsion of economic circumstances and the labour or

> service provided by him would be clearly forced labour … it is not unoften that in capitalist society economic circumstance exert much greater pressure on an individual in driving him to a particular course of action than physical compulsion or force of legislative provision. The word 'force' must therefore be constructed to include not only physical or legal force but also force arising from the compulsion of economic circumstance which leaves no choice of alternatives to a person in want and compels him to provide labour or service even though the remuneration received for it is less than the minimum wage of course.[17]

There is, however, an important internal shift within this formulation. While the Court began by pointing out the absence of choice available to a person suffering from hunger or starvation, it progressed towards classifying this as the 'compulsion of economic circumstances'. It then clarified that it was a problem arising in, and out of, 'capitalist society' (where economic circumstances would be driven by the requirements of a functioning market).[18] Or, in other words, the 'force' exerted by economic circumstances acquires normative salience in the context of a capitalist/market society. Consequently, it is not simply hunger or starvation (or 'any factor') that necessitates 'forced labour', but the economic arrangements in a capitalist society, where, presumably, the only way to alleviate hunger or starvation is to contract with a far more powerful employer, in a relationship with no bargaining parity, and accept employment at whatever rate the existing market dictates. Until the point at which the rate was below the legislatively prescribed minimum wage, the Court held, it remained 'forced labour'.[19]

It is important to understand what the *PUDR* argument was not about. The Court did not ground the right to minimum wage in some vision of socio-economic rights, positive liberties, or by making the familiar argument that civil and political rights are meaningless without basic material security. Rather, the Court's argument was purely about the meaning of freedom, in its classical sense. To be 'forced' was not simply to have a gun put to your head (physical force), or to be threatened with legal sanctions (legal force). The economic arrangements of society equally exercised 'force' upon an individual, forming, shaping, and constraining the range of options open to her. As the Court began its discussion by noting:

> The reason for enacting this provision in the chapter on fundamental rights is to be found in the socio-economic condition of the people at the time when the Constitution came to be enacted. The Constitution makers, when they set out to frame the Constitution, found that they had the enormous task before them of changing the socio-economic structure of the country ... with a view to reaching social and economic justice to the common man.[20]

The specific shape this guarantee took was that of a right to a minimum wage.

Was there any warrant for this (somewhat left-field) understanding of force and freedom? Was the Court's attribution of freedom (and its absence) to society's economic arrangements—and, consequently, its articulation of freedom as freedom *from* the compulsion of economic circumstances—justified by the text, structure, history, and philosophy of the Indian Constitution? I will argue that it was; but before that I will trace the conflicting genealogies of the word 'freedom' and ground *PUDR*'s articulation within a rich intellectual tradition that was also the tradition that formed and influenced the drafting of Article 23.

II. Three Views on the Meaning of Freedom

Let us begin with our unreflective linguistic intuitions about the word 'freedom'. If someone has imprisoned me, we could say with perfect propriety that my freedom of movement has been curtailed.[21] On the other hand, human physiology dictates that I cannot fly unaided. Yet, we do not normally say, 'My freedom to fly has been restricted,' or 'I am not free to fly'. It would sound more correct to say, 'I am *unable* to fly unaided'. In our ordinary language we draw a distinction between inability and unfreedom.[22]

The philosopher David Miller articulates this intuition by observing that 'when we describe a person as unfree to do something we imply that an obstacle exists which stands in need of justification, and we are in effect calling on the human race collectively to vindicate its behaviour in permitting the obstacle to exist'.[23] In other words, while we can all agree to define freedom in terms of the absence of an obstacle (or constraint),[24] that is only the beginning of the story. The key issue is how we understand the idea of 'constraint' (or, in our context, the idea of 'force'), and 'why certain kinds of constraint play a central role in debates about freedom, and other seemingly no less significant kinds of constraint do not'.[25]

A. Freedom and Non-Interference

According to a dominant view (that is broadly labelled the 'liberal view of freedom'),[26] I am 'unfree' to the extent that an identifiable individual, or group of individuals, intentionally interferes in what I could otherwise do. What matters, therefore, is not the range of possibilities that are *actually* open to me, but only the intentional actions of others that limit those possibilities. While this understanding of freedom in terms of intentional interference has a long lineage,[27] Isaiah Berlin provided its most popular articulation in a famous essay titled 'Two Concepts of Liberty'. Berlin wrote:

> If I say that I am unable to jump more than ten feet in the air or cannot read because I am blind, or cannot understand the darker pages of Hegel, it would be eccentric to say that I am to that degree enslaved or coerced. Coercion implies the deliberate interference of other human beings within the area in which I could otherwise act … Mere incapacity to attain a goal is not lack of political freedom.[28]

Therefore, in Berlin's view, our intuitive linguistic distinction between 'unfreedom' and 'inability' maps onto the distinction between intentional interference and all other manner of obstacles. Berlin's argument was taken forward in the economic realm by Friedrich Hayek, who defined freedom as the absence of coercion, and coercion, in turn, as being subject to the 'arbitrary will of another'.[29] Like Berlin, therefore, Hayek insisted that freedom is not concerned with 'the range of physical possibilities from which a person can choose at a given moment of time'[30], but whether 'somebody else [has] power so to manipulate the conditions as to make [her] act according to that person's will'.[31] In almost direct contradiction to the point of view expressed by the Court in *PUDR*, therefore, the logic of Hayek's argument led him to state that:

> Even if the threat of starvation to me and perhaps to my family impels me to accept a distasteful job at a very low wage, even if I am 'at the mercy' of the only man willing to employ me, I am not coerced by him or anybody else. So long as the act that has placed me in my predicament is not aimed at making me do or not do specific things … its effect on my freedom is not different from that of any natural calamity—a fire or a flood that destroys my house or an accident that harms my health.[32]

In Hayek's view, the market cannot, by definition, be coercive or freedom-infringing, because it is simply an aggregate of numerous individual actions, performed by self-interested actors, none of which are 'aimed' at making a particular individual do or refrain from doing anything. Hayek called this 'spontaneous order'.[33] *PUDR*'s articulation of 'force' arising from 'the compulsion of economic circumstances', on this view, was a category mistake, a confusion of concepts. This form of compulsion was akin to a 'natural calamity'. To go back to our original example, the (capitalist) economy is like our body structure, which does not allow us to fly unaided—a natural, given, background circumstance which might determine what we are or are not *capable* of doing, or the range of options open to us, but which cannot be understood as a *constraint* upon freedom.

This does not, of course, mean that the individual under 'threat of starvation' is placed in a position equal to the 'only man willing to employ [him]'. Both Berlin and later the philosopher John Rawls conceded that. However, the difference, they argued, is not that the former is less free than the latter, but that the two individuals *relate* to their freedom differently. For Berlin, material deprivation might render freedom meaningless, but does not take away from its existence:

> It is important to discriminate between liberty and the conditions of its exercise. If a man is too poor or too ignorant or too feeble to make use of his legal rights, the liberty that these rights confer upon him is nothing to him, but it is not thereby annihilated.[34]

Similarly, Rawls drew a distinction between 'liberty' and the 'worth of liberty', noting that:

> The inability to take advantage of one's rights and opportunities as a result of poverty and ignorance, and a lack of means generally, is sometimes counted among the constraints definitive of liberty. I shall not, however, say this, but rather I shall think of these things as affecting the worth of liberty ... the worth of liberty is not the same for everyone. Some have greater authority and wealth, and therefore greater means, to achieve their aims.[35]

The argument, therefore, can be summed up thus: not every obstacle or constraint is an infringement of my freedom. The key distinction is between intentional obstructions, traceable to an individual or a set of individuals (e.g., my imprisonment), and obstructions that occur as part of the natural, background arrangements within which we exist and act (e.g., my inability to fly because of my body structure, or the economy).[36] In some cases, the latter situation might be unjust, and might require State intervention to remedy, but is not a situation of unfreedom.[37]

B. Freedom, Non-Domination, and Arbitrary Power

For all its intellectual dominance, this understanding of freedom in terms of intentional non-interference has been challenged. Drawing from ancient Greek and Roman articulations of liberty, which were then taken up by English parliamentarians during the civil wars of the seventeenth century,[38] scholars in the republican tradition argue that what matters is not freedom from *interference*, but freedom from *dependence*,[39] or 'arbitrary power'.[40] To take an easy example: a slave might have a benevolent master, who never interferes with anything that he wants to do. For all that, however, the slave remains unfree, because he is in a position of dependence upon the master, and the master retains the *power* to interfere arbitrarily, even though it may never be used.[41] The crucial shift is from understanding freedom as *non-interference*, to understanding it as *non-domination*,[42] which no longer requires an 'identifiable act of hindrance' in order to constitute a condition of unfreedom.[43]

The republican theory of freedom marks a departure from the liberal view in three distinct ways. First, it seems truer to our intuitions, in not limiting the definition of freedom to the mere absence of 'force or the coercive threat of it'.[44] Second, under the republican theory of freedom, laws might be freedom-reducing, but they might *also* be freedom-enhancing. If freedom is limited to non-interference, then *by definition*, every law is a constraint or interference upon freedom, even though it might be justified on other grounds. On an understanding of freedom as non-domination, however, laws that reduce or mitigate states of affairs in which one set of persons can exercise arbitrary power and domination over others (e.g., laws abolishing slavery) are, in themselves, freedom-enhancing.[45] This, too, seems truer to our intuitions. And third, most importantly, republicanism understands freedom as *social*. That is, freedom is not simply limited to an equation between two individuals or groups of individuals (whether A is interfering with B), but concerns questions of 'institutional design'.[46] Social or republican freedom requires a set of legal and institutional arrangements that prevent the possibility of domination and curtail the possibility of the exercise of arbitrary power.[47] This, in a nutshell, is the meaning of the popular republican adage: 'It is possible to be free only in a free State.'[48]

In many other respects, however, the republican theory has substantial overlap with the understanding of freedom as non-interference. Since it takes the relationship between master and slave[49] as its paradigm case, republicanism too insists that domination and arbitrary power must be a function of intent, and traced back to identifiable individuals (or groups). In other words, while republicanism does not insist upon an identifiable *act* of interference (the mere existence of arbitrary power is enough), it does insist upon an identifiable *agent* who is vested with power or dominance. Republicanism is committed to maintaining liberalism's 'distinction between securing people against the natural effects of chance and incapacity and scarcity and securing them against the things that they may try to do to one another'.[50]

What is crucial to note about this formulation is the binary that it imposes: between 'intentional obstruction' and the 'natural effects of chance and incapacity and scarcity'. That is, whatever cannot be defined in terms of intentional obstruction (e.g., imprisoning or enslaving me) is to be treated as natural (e.g., my inability to fly), and not, therefore, an infringement of freedom. And consequently, just as Berlin and Rawls distinguished between 'freedom' and the 'worth of freedom' or my 'ability to use freedom', republican theorists draw a distinction between 'factors that compromise liberty and factors that [merely] condition it'.[51]

The conflation of the non-intentional (obstructions) and the natural (obstacles) that simply 'condition' freedom instead of 'compromising' it leads republican theorists to an obvious corollary, which is relevant for our discussion of *PUDR*: in a market society operating through contractual relationships between people in formally equal positions, an individual is not placed in a position of dependence vis-à-vis another *person*. Therefore, the question of unfreedom does not arise.[52] In a language that strikingly resembles that of Hayek, the republican theorist Philip Pettit argues that:

> ... the property system or distribution will not be inimical as such to freedom is that, assuming as we have done that it does not license or issue from any form of domination, it will not entail that anyone is in dominating charge of another. The property regime can have the aspect of an environment akin to the natural environment. Like the natural environment, it will certainly affect the range or the ease with which people enjoy their status as undominated agents, and it may warrant complaint on that account, but it will not itself be a source of domination. It will not be a source of domination as far as it is the cumulative, unintended effect of people's mutual adjustments.[53]

On this definition, therefore, within the republican definition of freedom as non-domination, 'market offers are noncoercive'.[54] This is because, if a market in capitalist society is a 'decentralized and largely anonymous mechanism for aggregating information about the economic decisions of an indefinite number of people',[55] as Eric MacGilvray defines it, then 'the influence I have on you when I make a market offer need be no more inimical to your status as an undominated agent than the influence I have on you in revealing a mistake in your deliberative assumptions'.[56] Once again—even on the expanded republican theory of freedom—*PUDR*'s argument that the 'compulsion of economic circumstances (in a capitalist society)' can be freedom-infringing is relegated to a conceptual error.

However, as William Clare Roberts points out, 'both Hayek's and Pettit's claims about the freedom-preserving character of market interactions treat them as one-on-one interactions between buyers and sellers ... The question, for them, is whether some identifiable person, either in making me an offer or in considering my offer, is a threat to my freedom.'[57] Both the non-interference and the non-domination views of freedom, therefore, are undergirded by this search for the 'identifiable person'. And because, in the market, both the employer and the employee are formally free to enter into contracts with each other, this search for an identifiable dominating agent is a non-starter. Neither argument would hold, however, if this premise itself was challenged; i.e., if it could be convincingly argued that 'dependence is no less dependence for the absence of an identifiable individual to be depended on'.[58]

On some reflection, the premise is, indeed, not quite as obvious as it might appear at first glance. To insist upon an identifiable agent who either interferes or is in a position to exercise arbitrary power in freedom-infringing ways, appears to ignore a crucial insight about the nature of power and domination in modern society, which was most clearly articulated by Foucault. The 'non-sovereign, socially distributed character of human agency' entails that power is rarely focused or concentrated in an identifiable centre, but operates through multiple nodes and at various levels: in other words, it is 'structural'.[59] As Sharon Krause argues, therefore, the 'master-slave dynamic', that is paradigmatic of the republican theory of freedom as non-domination, seems unable to grasp the form of domination implicit in structures of thought and behaviour such as racism or patriarchy, which create 'the informal social inequalities that remain outside the reach of non-domination because of their often unintentional character'.[60]

The examples of racism and patriarchy are important, because they drive a wedge between the republican binary of 'intentional' domination (that compromises freedom) and 'natural' obstacles (that only condition it). While the loss of liberty caused to Dalits in a casteist society cannot be attributed to any single intentional act or agent, it would be as preposterous to chalk it down to nature, as it is to say that my body structure prevents me from flying. However, once it is accepted that there exists a space between intent and nature it is not at all obvious that that space can be filled *only* by the impersonal domination of racism or patriarchy. What about, for example, 'the forms of domination a person might experience in the anonymous labour market?'[61]

C. Freedom, Institutions, and Structures

Arguments for the space between intent and nature—a space where domination, dependence, and power are constituted by 'an ensemble of social relations'[62]—have existed for a long time. In fact, they came on the scene far before the articulation of racism and patriarchy as impersonal systems or structures of dominance. For example, as Arthur Ripstein articulates the ideas of freedom and dependence in Karl Marx's critique of capitalism:

> It is true that no individual stands in a relation of dependence on any other, insofar as the options of all are limited by the market … [but] to have one's activities entirely shaped by forces that are the result of human practices is to be enslaved, not merely limited in one's options.[63]

This articulation, as we can see, takes direct issue with the Hayek-Pettit view that *because* in a market economy, 'no worker [is] dependent on any *particular* employer',[64]*therefore* 'economic compulsion' is not an infringement of freedom, but just a narrowing (or limitation) of one's options in the backdrop of natural economic arrangements or states of affairs. Subjugation, on this counter-view, is not individual, but social; or, in other words, it is 'personal independence founded on objective dependence'.[65] To put it another way, the key shift is from the idea of *intent* to the idea of *design*. Recall Miller's original formulation of unfreedom, which posited 'an obstacle … which stands in need of justification, and [which] we are in effect calling on the human race collectively to vindicate'.[66] This structural formulation of unfreedom argues that *impersonal* or *unintentional* constraint might still need to be *justified*, as long as it is the product of human *design*, if not simply human *intent*.

This, in fact, was the precise argument made during a sustained effort to constitutionalize this view of freedom. In the course of the late-nineteenth century, the American labour movement drew upon the US Constitution to argue against the system of economic exchanges that 'by direct operation of law, or by indirect operation of unwise social arrangements,'[67] resulted in exploitation and unfreedom. As Alex Gourevitch articulates the argument (which he calls labour-republicanism),[68] these 'unwise social arrangements' yielded:

> … a form of domination arising from the background structure of property ownership and because the compulsion they [i.e., the labourers] felt did not force them to work for a specific individual. It is not that the 'structure' was somehow an 'agent', nor that there were no dominating agents. There were, in this case, many dominating agents—all those who defended property distributions that left the majority propertyless. Through human design and institution, workers were left with no reasonable alternative but to sell their labour.[69]

It is important to stress the point that this argument is not about anthropomorphizing structures and institutions, and vesting them with human agency. Rather, the argument is that these structures are designed and instituted by individuals and, therefore, the moral responsibility for their working lies upon human shoulders (and is not simply an amoral 'natural' way of working, like my body structure that prevents me from flying). Or, if one were to use the language of intent, the intent may not be to coerce any specific individual, but to construct a system whose effect is to narrow the range of options available to those subject to its functioning. It is because of this that talking about the 'compulsion of economic circumstances' in a capitalist economy, that is based upon individual market exchanges and contracts, albeit between persons of unequal bargaining power, begins to make sense.

The task before the American labour-republicans was to expand the scope of freedom by minimizing the scope of domination and also the power enjoyed (collectively) by employers. This, in turn, was to be achieved through labour regulations and unionization:

> A major argument not just for unionization and collective action, but for labor regulations – such as banning payment in script, abolishing convict and child labor, and instituting maximum hours laws – was that they reduced the kinds of terms that employers were able to impose at their own discretion. Although these regulations could not abolish the dependence of the wage-laborer on the employer, they could at least limit the kinds of arbitrary power he could exercise over the terms of contract. More generally, this analysis of the contract helped explain why employers sought dependence. Insofar as structural domination translated into personal domination in the setting of terms, employers enjoyed an arbitrary superiority in the ability to extract concessions from the workers.[70]

While at its most radical, the argument called for abolishing the system of wage-labour altogether (labelling it 'wage-slavery'),[71] in its more moderate form (as we see above), it made the impeccably republican argument about constraining and curtailing domination and arbitrary power *through* laws. Perhaps most crucially, however, American labour republicans consciously grounded their argument in the Thirteenth Amendment to the US Constitution,[72] which provided that:

> Neither slavery nor involuntary servitude, except as a punishment for crime whereof the party shall have been duly convicted, shall exist within the United States, or any place subject to their jurisdiction.[73]

The key phrase here is 'involuntary servitude', in particular the word 'involuntary'. Like 'forced', it is the word 'involuntary' that creates the bridge between ideas of freedom on the one hand and the manner in which economic arrangements constrain options on the other.

While this interpretation of the US Constitution was strenuously opposed—notably by invoking the 'natural and necessary laws' of market economics[74]—and, ultimately, rejected by the US courts,[75] as we have seen, it found fertile ground in *PUDR v. Union of India*.

Here, for the first time in Indian constitutional history, the Court drew a clear link between 'the compulsion of economic circumstances' and the constitutional guarantee of freedom expressed through the prohibition of 'forced labour'.[76]

D. Conclusion: A Moral Issue

> *... water is said to descend freely, or to have liberty to descend by the channel of the river, because there is no impediment that way, but not across, because the banks are impediments. And though the water cannot ascend, yet men never say it wants the liberty to ascend, but the faculty or power, because the impediment is in the nature of the water, and intrinsical.*
>
> Thomas Hobbes

We have discussed three different views about the meaning of 'freedom', 'constraint', and 'force', along with the meanings of a constellation of associated words such as 'ability', 'capacity', 'power', 'dependence', 'domination' and 'servitude'. Over time, these views have attracted their defenders as well as their detractors. In *PUDR*, the Supreme Court nailed its colours to the mast of the third view, what we have called labour-republicanism. The question is whether it was correct to do so. Yet before that, we must answer a more basic question: how do we judge whether it was correct to do so?

Let us go back for a moment to our initial example: the distinction between being imprisoned and being unable to fly. Let us complicate the situation somewhat. Imagine a world in which genetic modification is commonplace, and something that people regularly undergo in order to fly unaided. Suppose I am a political dissident and, as punishment, the government bars me from undergoing genetic modification. In this situation, I might be justified in saying, 'I am not free to fly,' rather than merely, 'I am not capable of flying.' A further twist: genetic modification is on the cusp of being perfected, and would be perfected with a little more investment, but the government refuses to accord it priority in its science budget, choosing to spend on space travel instead. Have I been deprived of my freedom to fly, or do I remain incapable of flying?

Futuristic and far-fetched as they may sound, such examples help us to see that even the seemingly clear-cut division between the 'intentional' and the 'natural' is not simply a neutral description of the world—as Thomas Hobbes' illustration about the flow of water would have us believe—but a matter of judgement.[77] As MacCallum admits:

> ... if one is concerned with social, political, and economic policies, and with how these policies can remove or increase human misery, it is quite irrelevant whether difficulties in the way of the policies are or are not due to arrangements made by human beings. The only question is whether the difficulties can be removed by human arrangements, and at what cost.[78]

While the example of flying may not directly speak to the question of freedom, it is easy to imagine other, non-futuristic examples that do. For example, does the government's failure to invest in disability-mitigating technologies impinge upon disabled persons' 'freedom of movement'? The answer would depend upon what we think is the 'normal baseline'—a world that disabled people must take as they find, or a world that must be consciously designed to facilitate the needs of disabled people. And that, in turn, depends upon our sense of moral commitment. As Benn and Weinstein discuss in a famous example:

> ... a man who lacks the physical means—whether muscular strength or ropes—to climb a cliff need not be unfree but only unable to climb it, though one way of depriving a man of his freedom to climb it is to take away his ropes.[79]

In other words, the distinction between being unfree and lacking the ability (or capacity) to *use* one's freedom is, again, not always simple or clear-cut. If I forcibly take away your ropes from you, then I am depriving you of your freedom to climb the cliff. But what if I was standing by with ropes in my hand and refused to give them to you (just like I could design cities to facilitate access for disabled people but choose not to)? Would I then be depriving you of your freedom? The answer, clearly, would turn not on taking apart the word 'freedom' semantically, but on the question of what my moral obligations to you are.

This leads us to an important insight: there is no a priori argument that will help us decide between the three (or more) theories of freedom discussed above, and no a priori argument that will help us draw clear lines between 'intention', 'design', and the 'natural world'. The question, rather, is inescapably moral. Our assumptions about what constitutes the 'natural order of things'; the background conditions that merely structure freedom instead of compromising it; our choice of seeing force and freedom through the prism of intentionality or the prism of design; and, indeed, *how* we understand intention and design are all moral judgements.

So, Benn and Weinstein are correct when they observe that:

> ... conditions formerly accepted as necessary may be called progressively into question; the frustrations to which they give rise come to be seen not merely as natural limitations on what is possible, but as restrictions on freedom ... the conditions of the market and the rights of property that governed the workers' bargaining power were generally taken to be no more alterable than the weather, the laws of supply and demand no more restrictive of freedom than the laws of gravity. The worker was free in negotiating with his employer because, in terms of all conceivably controllable conditions, there was no restriction on his ability and opportunity to make the best possible bargain. Trade unionism and socialist economic theory combined to break down these presuppositions. The workers came to protest not merely against low wages or inequality, but against economic unfreedom to do and enjoy many things they now saw as denied to them because the employing class was either unwilling

> or unable to change economic conditions that were none the less capable of change.[80]

Now, if this debate was being conducted in the abstract, its resolution would depend upon which theory, ultimately, seemed truest to our reflective moral commitments. Different persons would justifiably give different answers. And even if we accepted some of the premises of republicanism, it would also depend on what economic arrangement we think would, at the end of the day, advance freedom the most: a market republican would argue, for example, that even on republican terms, a market/capitalist society, compared to all others, represents the state of affairs that minimizes domination and dependence.

In the context of *PUDR*, however, the matter must be decided not by advancing the most persuasive moral or economic theory, but by excavating what *constitutional morality* would have to say about this question. In other words, the correctness of *PUDR* depends upon which theory of freedom is more consistent with the constitutional text, structure, and history. And to answer this, we must investigate how the Constitution envisions the relationship between freedom and economic structure.

Does the Constitution view the market-oriented economic structure and economic arrangements as part of the 'natural background', and its social relations as 'natural relations',[81] simply conditioning and structuring freedom rather than compromising it (in our original, uncomplicated example, akin to my body structure, or to the weather)? Or does the Constitution understand economic arrangements to be the product of human design, and in a morally salient way, so that the constraints they impose are to be treated as constraints on freedom, and overcome through the fashioning of constitutional remedies?[82] The text of Article 23 does not answer the question. Something more is needed.

III. Economic Structure and the Transformative Constitution

In this section, I argue that the Indian Constitution did not treat economic structure as part of the background, natural environment, which only conditioned the exercise of fundamental rights instead of compromising them. Rather, the founding philosophy of the Constitution understood economic arrangements (especially in the context of a capitalist economy) as potential infringements upon freedom and, consistent with labour-republicanism, understood State power as one method of protecting freedom *from* the market.

However, the story does not end here. While the Constitution recognized that economic arrangements and employers, leveraging economic arrangements, could exercise 'force' and 'coercion' over individuals, the primary task of overhauling the economic structure to nullify market coercion entirely was not left to the Constitution, but to Parliament, guided by the Directive Principles of State Policy. The Constitution's task was a more modest one—not to overhaul, but only to *mitigate* the harm caused by the market economy to freedom. Articles 23 and 24, within the rubric of the 'right against exploitation', were the constitutional shields for protecting freedom, and the importance of *PUDR* lay in recognizing and giving life to the guarantee of Article 23.

A. The Framing of Article 23

We see the first indications of this philosophy in the Karachi Resolution, discussed above. This document contained Clause 4, a predecessor clause of Article 23, which stated that 'labour [is] to be freed from serfdom or conditions bordering on serfdom'.[83] The structure of this clause is similar to Article 23, with 'serfdom' playing the role of *begar*, and 'conditions bordering on serfdom' playing the role of 'other similar forms of forced labour'. 'Serfdom', a word borrowed from the conventions of the International Labour Organization,[84] was, of course, at the heart of the republican conception of freedom, which located unfreedom in the idea of 'servitude'. Right from the beginning, therefore, the constitutional understanding of freedom had a republican slant, going beyond the simple understanding of freedom as non-interference.

While 'serfdom' itself remained a narrow word with a defined range of meaning, it is also important to note that this clause was nested within a much broader and more radical set of guarantees. Just before Clause 4 were guarantees of '[a] living wage for industrial workers, limited hours of labour, healthy conditions of work, protection against the economic consequences of old age, sickness, and unemployment',[85] and following it immediately was, '[the] protection of women workers, and specially adequate provisions for leave during maternity period'.[86] Together, these clauses made up 'Labour's Constitution of Freedom',[87] and would have required fundamental structural changes to implement. Crucially, these clauses were further nested within a set of classic civil and political rights, bookended on one side by freedom of speech and the press,[88] equal protection of laws,[89] and religious neutrality,[90] and, on the other, by adult suffrage.[91] From the perspective of liberty, therefore, the Karachi Resolution drew no ironclad distinction between civil/political rights and labour rights.

In fact, the Preamble to the Resolution categorically stated, 'This Congress is of the opinion that in order to end the exploitation of the masses, political freedom must include real economic freedom of the starving millions.'[92] While the use of the word 'exploitation' creates the bridge between the 1931 Resolution and Articles 23/24 of the Constitution, the use of the word 'include' to define the relationship between 'political freedom' and 'economic freedom' suggests that the two were not treated as separate but, rather, economic freedom was viewed as being a part of (classic) political freedom. The 1931 Resolution's Labour Code, then, was not about providing material benefits or socio-economic rights, but fundamentally about the idea of *freedom*. Indeed, the Preamble's stress on real economic freedom recalls the American labour republicans' insistence on effective freedom, which 'encompassed the ability not only to influence the conditions of working life, but to do so consciously, in combination with one's co-workers, using forms of action that yield immediate, unambiguous evidence of personal and collective potency … [and] was embedded in narratives of slavery, emancipation, and freedom.'[93]

This vision was carried forward into the Constitution-making process. For example, K.T. Shah, one of the few members of the Constituent Assembly who proposed a comprehensive model fundamental rights code, made explicit mention of Franklin Roosevelt's Second Bill of Rights and its focus on 'freedom from necessity'. In fact, in Shah's draft Bill of Rights, a guarantee of a minimum wage and the prohibition of forced labour were part of a single, compendious provision, viz., Article 40.[94]

Most tellingly, however, it was Ambedkar who provided the intellectual foundation for the relationship between constitutional liberty and economic structure. After proposing a draft fundamental rights code that included a prohibition upon 'forced labour or … involuntary servitude',[95] in his accompanying notes Ambedkar made an impeccably labour-republican argument that deserves to be quoted in full:

> … what is the purpose of prescribing by law the shape and form of the economic structure of society? The purpose is to protect the liberty of the individual from invasion by other individuals which is the object of enacting fundamental rights. The connection between individual liberty and the shape and form of the economic structure of society may not be apparent to everyone. Nonetheless, the connection between the two is real. It will be apparent if the following considerations are borne in mind.
>
> Political democracy rests on four premises which may be set out in the following terms:
>
> *The individual is an end in himself.*
>
> *That the individual has certain inalienable rights which must be guaranteed to him by the Constitution.*

That the individual shall not be required to relinquish any of his constitutional rights as a condition precedent to the receipt of a privilege.

That the State shall not delegate powers to private persons to govern others.

Anyone who studies the working of the system of social economy based on private enterprise and pursuit of personal gain will realize how it undermines, if it does not actually violate, the last two premises on which democracy rests. How many have to relinquish their constitutional rights in order to gain their living? How many have to subject themselves to be governed by private employers?[96]

According to Ambedkar, the market economy, based on 'private enterprise and pursuit of personal gain', created a situation where 'private employers' had the power to violate the liberty of the individual.[97] The task of constitutional law was to regulate the 'shape and form of the economic structure of society' in order to protect individual liberty. In this way, Ambedkar linked individual liberty and economic structure through the mode of constitutional law.

In what manner was individual liberty under threat by economic structure? Ambedkar went on to elaborate:

Constitutional lawyers assume that the enactment of fundamental rights is enough to safeguard their liberty and that nothing more is called for. They argue that where the State refrains from intervention in private affairs—economic and the social—the residue is liberty. What is necessary is to make the residue as large as possible and State intervention as small as possible. It is true that where the State refrains from intervention what remains is liberty. But this does not dispose of the matter. One more question remains to be answered. To whom and for whom is this liberty? Obviously, this liberty is liberty to landlords to increase rents, for capitalists to increase hours of work and reduce rate of wages. This must be so. It cannot be otherwise. For in an economic system employing armies of workers, producing goods *en masse* at regular intervals someone must make rules so that workers will work and the wheels of industry run on. If the State does not do it the private employer will ... In other words

> what is called liberty from the control of the State is another name for the dictatorship of the private employer.
>
> How to prevent such a thing happening? How to protect the unemployed as well as the employed from being cheated out of their fundamental rights to life, liberty, and pursuit of happiness? The useful remedy adopted by democratic countries is to *limit* the power of Government to impose arbitrary restraints in political domain and to *invoke* the ordinary power of the legislature to restrain the more powerful individual from imposing arbitrary restraints on the less powerful in the economic field. The inadequacy nay the futility of the plan has been well-established … [this] plan follows quite a different method. It seeks to limit not only the power of Government to impose arbitrary restraints but also of the more powerful individuals or to be more precise to eliminate the possibility of the more powerful having the power to impose arbitrary restraints on the less powerful by withdrawing from the control he has over the economic life of the people. There cannot be the slightest doubt that of the two remedies against the invasion by the more powerful of the rights and liberties of the less powerful the one contained in the proposal is undoubtedly more effective. Considered in the light of these observations the proposal is essentially a proposal for safeguarding the liberty of the individual.[98]

Ambedkar's argument speaks for itself, and needs no explanation. It would be worthwhile, however, to restate it within the framework developed above. Ambedkar was providing a direct riposte to the theory of freedom as non-interference and the absence of intentional coercion, by making the point that in a market economy, employers' power to set rules vested in them the 'control … over the economic life of the people'. Following republican thought, it was the *existence* of this control, and not any overt act of interference, that constituted the threat to freedom. Where Ambedkar departed from traditional republican thought and embraced labour republicanism was in his insistence that 'arbitrary power' need not be exercised intentionally, but was simply a *function* of existing economic arrangements.

It is of particular importance that throughout the argument, Ambedkar consistently used the language of liberty, and repeatedly stated that the Constitution existed to protect individual liberty by regulating the unequal relations of power that existed between employers and employees in a market economy. Moreover, Ambedkar was acutely conscious that his argument marked a departure from traditional ways of thinking about liberty and freedom in *not* treating economic structure as part of the natural background that only conditioned freedom. In fact, he specifically acknowledged this:

> The proposal marks a departure from the existing constitutions whose aim is merely to prescribe the form of the political structure of society leaving the economic structure untouched. The result is that the political structure is completely set at nought by the forces which emerge from the economic structure which is at variance with the political structure ... the soul of democracy is the doctrine of one man, one value. Unfortunately, democracy has attempted to give effect to this doctrine only so far as the political structure is concerned by adopting the rule of one man one vote which is supposed to translate into fact the doctrine of one man one value. It has left the economic structure to take the shape given to it by those who are in a position to mould it.[99]

Admittedly, Ambedkar's draft notes were written in the context of incorporating State socialism into the Constitution, a position that was not accepted by the Constituent Assembly, and from which Ambedkar himself subsequently resiled.[100] However, as I shall show, the vision of freedom, and the link between freedom and the economic structure, remained an underlying foundation of the Constitution as it emerged in its final form, and found expression in what eventually became Article 23.

Indications of this emerge from the Fundamental Rights Sub-Committee's first set of discussions on the draft fundamental rights, where it was proposed that 'every form of slavery or traffic in human beings is abolished and contravention of this prohibition shall be an offence'.[101] After some debate, it was decided to incorporate the US Constitution's prohibition on involuntary servitude[102] into the clause. Ultimately, in the Sub-Committee's Draft Report, the redrafted Clause 15 now prohibited 'slavery, traffic in human beings, the form of forced labour known as *begar*, any form of involuntary servitude except as a punishment for crime …'[103]

While the draft clause borrowed from the US Constitution, there was a crucial difference. The Thirteenth Amendment to the US Constitution provided that 'neither slavery nor involuntary servitude, except as a punishment for crime whereof the party shall have been duly convicted, shall exist within the United States'.[104] The US Courts had interpreted this provision narrowly, restricting its scope to actual slavery, or to relationships possessing the badges or incidents of slavery, such as the peonage system.[105] But despite having this model before them, and expressly borrowing the term 'involuntary servitude', the Sub-Committee chose to preface it with the words 'any form …'—words absent from the Thirteenth Amendment. Combined with the words 'every form' in its previous iteration, we can clearly see the conscious intention of the drafters *not* to restrict the operation of the draft clause only to relationships that bore a formal resemblance to slavery and *begar*.

The Fundamental Rights Sub-Committee finally split up Draft Article 15 into two parts, the first prohibiting trafficking in human beings, and the second retaining the broad preface to *begar* and prohibiting 'forced labour in any form including *begar*, and involuntary servitude'. When this clause came up for debate in the Constituent Assembly on 1 May 1947, K.M. Munshi proposed redrafting it to read: 'Traffic in human beings and begar and other similar forms of forced labour are prohibited, and any contravention of this prohibition shall be an offence.'[106] (This is—in relevant part—the language of the final constitutional guarantee, as it stands today.) Importantly, however, Munshi also provided the rationale for this restructuring. It was not to curtail the scope of the provision by replacing 'any form' with 'similar forms', but rather, it was simply 'to deal in one sentence with both subjects',[107] and do away with a specific exception for military service that was present at the time. Munshi then went on to note:

> The object of this is that if there is any sort of *forced labour like begar*, it will be prohibited. Traffic in human beings will be prohibited. But the other forms of labour e.g., labour, for educational purposes or for any other purpose of public service, will be regulated by legislation.[108]

Munshi's explanation is crucial, because it has a direct bearing on the debate in *PUDR v. Union of India*. In *PUDR*, the State had argued that the phrase 'similar forms' after *begar* qualified 'forced labour', and indicated that only those relationships which, like *begar*, resulted in the extraction of work *without compensation* could amount to 'forced labour'. The Court rejected this argument, noting that the 'similarity' was not based on the payment of compensation, but on the element of 'force'. Here, Munshi was making it clear that the purpose of 'similar forms' was to distinguish *unjustified* forced labour (exemplified by *begar*) from labour that was compelled (and therefore, in the descriptive sense, forced), but was *justified* (by virtue of being for educational purposes, or public service). Consequently, Munshi was effectively arguing that the word 'forced' in the Draft Article was *normative* in character. It retained its wide amplitude (as provided for in earlier drafts, which used the phrases 'any form' and 'every form'), but by adding the word 'similar' it would be ensured that compelled labour that could be justified under a larger public purpose would escape the prohibition of the section.

Munshi's proposed amendment was accepted by Ambedkar, who promptly responded that 'I have no objection to the redrafting of subclause (a) and (b) in order that they may run in a compact manner',[109] thus making it doubly clear that the substitution of 'any form' with 'similar forms' was not intended to lop off the width of the term 'forced labour'. The debate that then followed focused on the merits of retaining a specific exception for military service, where, arguing against Munshi, Ambedkar insisted that a specific exception be retained, otherwise 'it is perfectly possible for anybody to argue that even compulsory military service is *begar*'.[110]

The fact that Ambedkar deemed a specific exception necessary further strengthens the argument about the width of the term 'forced labour': there would be no need of carving out specific exceptions if the main clause was itself to be interpreted narrowly. After all, as P.K. Sen specifically pointed out, the word 'similar' 'is a vague word',[111] incapable of possessing specific boundaries. In fact, that the breadth of the core clause was settled was made most clear by Damodar Swarup Seth's attempt, in the December 1948 Debates regarding the Draft Constitution, to bring back the phrase 'servitude and slavery in all forms'[112] into the clause, and Ambedkar's rejection of it on the basis that it was 'unnecessary'[113] (i.e., that the Article already had a sweep wide enough to include 'all forms').

In addition, there were two important events that are relevant for our argument. The first was a proposal that, as part of its prohibition of human trafficking, the draft Article also prohibit prostitution. This proposal, vigorously argued for by several members, was voted down by the Assembly, with Renuka Ray protesting against the dual standards of morality that existed for men and women.[114] This suggests that Article 23 draws a clear distinction between *exploitation* and bare 'public immorality'.

Secondly, the meaning and purpose of Article 23 (Draft Article 11) was articulated by many members of the Assembly in clear and lucid terms. Perhaps the most eloquent among them was Dakshayani Velayudhan, the only Dalit woman in the Assembly, who pointed out that:

> ... even nowadays we find traffic in human beings in some parts of India and this clause will have a great effect on the underdogs of this land who will have a voice when India gets her independence. This clause will bring about an economic revolution in the fascist social structure existing in India. All the disabilities of the underdogs

> of this land are mainly due to the economic backwardness of the unfortunate brethren of the neglected community … Even if there is not the system of '*begar*' in other parts of India, almost a similar sort of compulsion exists throughout India and the majority of the people are subjected to exploitation economical and in all sorts of ways. The underdogs of this land are deprived of the facilities that make life happy … so, this clause when it comes into existence will give great relief to a great number of people who are subjected to economic exploitation.[115]

What stands out in this remarkable speech is that, just like Ambedkar, Dakshayani Velayudhan drew a clear link between economic structure, exploitation, and freedom. In particular, she noted that, while the paradigm case of *begar* was work without remuneration, 'a similar sort of compulsion' existed, marked by 'exploitation economical and in all sorts of ways'. For Velayudhan, therefore—like it had been for Ambedkar, K.T. Shah and K.M. Munshi, and like it would be for the *PUDR* Court in 1982—the point of placing *begar* front and centre in Article 23 was not its elements of physical force or absence of compensation, but that it was the paradigm case of *exploitation*. And when the prevention of exploitation became the heart of Article 23, the interpretation of force and freedom as inextricably linked with economic structure became inevitable.

The debates in the Constituent Assembly, therefore, reveal two crucial points. The first is that Article 23(1) was drafted in broad terms, intending to outlaw all forms of forced labour, and specifically those that were similar to *begar* in their exploitative capacity. Secondly, this exploitation was a function not merely of physical or legal force, but of the *economic structure* of society, which had a direct relationship with individual freedom. This was affirmed by members of the Constituent Assembly even after Ambedkar had abandoned his initial plan to incorporate State socialism into the Constitution.[116] In fact, they used Ambedkar's own language from his initial Notes on Fundamental Rights, that the Constitution was committed to the principles of economic democracy and 'one man, one value'.[117] As we have seen above, the chosen vehicle of the one-man-one-value principle was Article 23, and the prohibition of forced labour. So, while the Constitution did not, ultimately, impose an economic theory, it did impose a 'social vision'[118]—a vision in which economic arrangements were not part of the natural order of things, but had to be measured and judged according to their impact on freedom.

B. The Departure from International Conventions

The amplitude of Article 23 can also be deduced from the fact that, while it was inspired by international conventions, it departed in important respects from the language used by them. The first of these documents was the League of Nations' 1926 Slavery Convention (contemporaneous with the Indian debates on the subject), which aimed to prohibit the institution of slavery and the slave trade. The 1926 Convention specifically noted the continuum between slavery and forced labour, observing that 'it is necessary to prevent forced labour from developing into conditions analogous to slavery'.[119] While the phrase 'conditions analogous to slavery' is reminiscent of 'other similar forms of forced labour', the 1926 Convention was, nonetheless, clear that 'slavery is the status or condition of a person over whom any or all of the powers attaching to the right of ownership are exercised'.[120] The core of the Convention, therefore, was not actual exploitation, but legal control (right of ownership). As we can see, therefore, the Convention treated forced labour as existing within and on the fringes of the master-slave paradigm,[121] in line with republican thought.

Four years later, in 1930, the International Labour Organization passed a separate convention dealing specifically with forced labour, where, unlike the Indian Constitution, it defined the term thus: 'all work or service which is exacted from any person under the menace of any penalty and for which the said person has not offered himself voluntarily'.[122] One can see here glimpses of the freedom-as-non-interference view, where to 'be forced' assumes the existence of a specific penalty or threat of it.

Both the 1926 and 1930 conventions were referred to and clarified in the Economic and Social Council's 'Supplementary Convention on the Abolition of Slavery, the Slave Trade, and Institutions and Practices Similar to Slavery'. While the Supplementary Convention came into force after the passage of the Indian Constitution, it is relevant because it lay on a continuum with the 1926 and 1930 conventions, and added two further prohibitions that were viewed to be 'institutions or practices similar to slavery': debt-bondage (close to *begar*) and serfdom. Serfdom was defined as 'the condition or status of a tenant who is by law, custom or agreement bound to live and labour on land belonging to another person and to render some determinate service to such other person, whether for reward or not, and is not free to change his status'.[123]

The upshot of these international instruments is that while they used phrases such as 'voluntarily' and 'not free', which are consistent with the labour-republican argument that we have advanced above, these words were used in addition to, and not as substitutes for, the requirement of *legal subjection*.[124] Again, following republican thought, 'forced labour' within the international framework was expressed in the language of slavery, servitude, and serfdom. It is here that the Indian Constitution's conscious departure from this framework assumes relevance. The 1931 Resolution did use the phrase 'serfdom or conditions bordering on serfdom', and the Fundamental Rights Sub-Committee experimented with including the word 'servitude', before abandoning that as well. But the paradigm that the framers finally chose was neither slavery nor serfdom, but the uniquely Indian problem of *begar*. It was *begar* that anchored Article 23(1), necessitating an autonomous interpretation, independent of the intellectual baggage carried by words such as 'slavery' and 'serfdom'.

The autonomous character of Article 23 is more sharply visible when we compare it to similar provisions in other constitutions.

Forced labour has been a vexing problem for postcolonial nations in particular. For example, the Constitutions of Malaysia,[125] Kenya,[126] Botswana,[127] Uganda,[128] and Lesotho,[129] among many others, all have provisions outlawing it, and which have been interpreted by the courts. Notably, all these provisions are framed within the slavery/servitude paradigm, i.e., the prohibition of forced labour occurs as an adjunct to the prohibition of slavery and servitude.[130] The Indian Constitution's departure from this classic republican framework and its nod towards labour-republicanism in the Constituent Assembly Debates provide a powerful argument in defence of *PUDR*'s interpretation of 'forced labour', and of 'other similar forms', under Article 23.

C. The Directive Principles of State Policy and Constitutional Structure

We have seen that the bulk of 'Labour's Constitution of Freedom' from the 1931 Karachi Resolution ended up in the unenforceable Part IV of the Constitution, as Directive Principles of State Policy. Part IV contains the right to work, guarantees of equal pay for equal work, a social security net, a living wage, and industrial democracy and participation for workers (inserted later). While no law can be invalidated for not conforming to the DPSPs, this does not, as discussed in Chapter 3, make them irrelevant to constitutional interpretation.

The DPSPs are best understood as structuring principles, which help us to interpret and clarify the scope of the Fundamental Rights chapter. In other words, all other things being equal, out of two or more possible interpretations of a fundamental right, the one that advances the values set out in Part IV is to be preferred. As we have argued above, while the text of Article 23 is almost Delphic in its austerity, there is enough historical evidence to make a strong case for interpreting it in line with the labour-republican view of freedom. Reading it in the context of Part IV of the Constitution (which clearly envisages a transformation of the economic structure) further strengthens the interpretation of the word 'freedom' that I have advanced above.

Evidence that supports the argument can be found in Part III as well. Recall that Articles 23 and 24 are two of the few fundamental rights that regulate not only the relationship between individual and State, but also apply *horizontally*, i.e., between private parties. The other two horizontal fundamental rights in the Constitution are found in Articles 15(2) and 17, which we have discussed in the previous two chapters. Like Article 23, Articles 15(2) and 17 prohibit specific acts of denial of access, or of untouchability.

However, it is crucial to note that the *reason* they do so is not because of what the act, taken in isolation, does. After all, I should be free to refuse to touch whom I want, and decide for myself who I do business with. Consequently, what is prohibited is not the act itself, but what it *signifies*; and what it signifies is a *social practice* of exclusion and denial—the practice of religion and caste-based social and economic boycotts (Article 15[2]), and the practice of subordination through social doctrines of purity and pollution, expressed through untouchability (Article 17).

What Articles 15(2) and 17 challenge, therefore, is *impersonal domination*, i.e., institutions, which are the result of human design, but which cannot be pinned onto a specific human act or omission.[131] Our reading of Article 23(1) binds the Constitution's horizontal rights into a single, unified moral conviction: the conviction that freedom and equality are threatened not merely by the State, but by the exercise of power and domination through non-State structures, and that the task of the Constitution is to expand constitutional values by curtailing this power. Together, these three articles represent the constitutional ideal of *fraternity*: that is, an ideal that aims at the elimination of hierarchies and relations of power in social and economic relations, so that liberty and equality exist not only in terms of State action or inaction, but as constituent elements of everyday social and economic life.

In fact, soon after *PUDR*, the Andhra Pradesh High Court grasped this fundamental insight when, in *Poola Bhaskar Vijaykumar v. State of AP*, it noted:

> Article 17 which abolishes untouchability is not in the main a limitation on the power of the State power as an admonition to the society. So is Article 23 … thus understood Art. 23 should be held to be more a prohibition directed against the social practices of one member of the society against another rather than a prohibition against the State.[132]

What is important is how the High Court characterizes Articles 23 and 17. The *agent* that these Articles are directed against is the private individual (naturally), but the *act* that they seek to protect from is a 'social practice'. In other words, the *source* of domination is the social practice (or the social order), and it is *carried out* by private individuals. Indeed, this, precisely, is the argument of labour-republicanism, which Ambedkar expressed in such detail in his Notes on Fundamental Rights. The social and economic institutions of a market economy *create* an asymmetry of power between employers and employees, putting them in positions of dominance and dependence, respectively, and threatening the freedom of the latter.

One last point: the Supreme Court has defined 'minimum wage', broadly, as an evolving concept that must include, at the very least, enough for subsistence and basic social needs, such as education and healthcare.[133] Notably, the directive principles go further, and require the State to move towards securing a *living* wage—pegged at a degree higher than the minimum wage, and broadly defined as the normal needs of a human being in a civilized community including a fair and average level of comfort.[134] Historically, it was the concept of a living wage that the older constitutional documents, including the 1931 Resolution, highlighted. And indeed, all our arguments about force, freedom, and the coercive character of markets in the context of interpreting Article 23 apply equally to 'reading in' a constitutional right to a living wage. *PUDR* did not address the question, because it was dealing specifically with a case involving non-compliance with minimum wage provisions. However, there is no reason future courts need be constrained by the limits of *PUDR*.

Needless to say, the actual *fixing* of a minimum or living wage is a task beyond the competence of the courts. If the logic of *PUDR* were to be extended, therefore, the primary obligation would lie upon the State to affirmatively determine the actual wage. The State's obligation would flow from the Constitution, and therefore apply to every form of employment (including domestic work), instead of being limited by the contours of the Minimum Wages Act (or any other statute that the Parliament may choose to enact). The Court's task would be to ensure that the State is complying with the obligation, and in accordance with the manner in which *PUDR* interpreted Article 23.[135]

IV. Conclusion: The Roads Not (Yet) Taken

PUDR v. Union of India was the first judgement to articulate the transformative character of Article 23 of the Constitution. It was also a disciplined judgement. It remained aware of the limited extent to which Article 23 could be pressed into the service of transformative goals. After all, the framers *had* made a conscious decision to place 'Labour's Constitution of Freedom' in Part IV, excepting only the right against forced labour, and the prohibition of child labour in hazardous employment. Indeed, Ambedkar had been explicit about not imposing a full-blown economic theory upon future generations.[136] Had the Court then smuggled in the complete labour charter from Part IV into the meanings of 'force' and 'freedom', it would have been tantamount to rewriting the Constitution. *PUDR*'s solution was to implicitly acknowledge that, while the task of *overhauling* the economic structure in order to guarantee effective freedom remained with the Parliament, it was open to the courts to *mitigate* some of the market's more freedom-infringing outcomes.

A. An Unformed Legacy

This does not mean, however, that a minimum wage is the *only* guarantee that could be read into Article 23. *PUDR*'s transformative analysis of force and freedom could apply to other situations, depending upon context. Furthermore, the range of a constitutional provision, and its underlying philosophy, is not limited to testing and invalidating State action. Constitutional philosophy 'radiates' into the broader legal system as well, influencing how laws are interpreted and applied.

From this perspective, the judgement in *PUDR* is a signpost to a road not yet taken. Apart from one other judgement delivered the same year, striking down a Rajasthan law that exempted the government from paying a minimum wage for famine relief work,[137] *PUDR* marked both the beginning and the end of Article 23 as a potent fundamental right. Although it has never been overruled or doubted, subsequent judgements have refused to advance its underlying principles into other domains.

In particular, the Court has invoked formal doctrines of labour law to forestall Article 23 claims. For example, in *Lingegowd Detective and Security Chamber (P) Ltd. v. Mysore Kirloskar Ltd.*, the Supreme Court rejected a claim to minimum wages on the basis that the employment in question (detective services) was not a 'Scheduled Employment' under the Minimum Wages Act.[138] The Schedule to the Minimum Wages Act, however, could surely not override a fundamental right under Article 23. The Court's response to this was to say that *PUDR* was a judgement rendered 'in a totally different context'. The Court declined to explain what, exactly, the different context was, and how it was relevant to the judgement.[139]

Similarly, *State of Karnataka v. Uma Devi* involved the issue of the State's power to regularize employees who had been appointed through the 'back-channel'. The situation that existed, and which continues to exist, is that the State or its instrumentalities would recruit employees through ad hoc procedures, and then keep them on daily wages (an irregular, precarious, and low-paid status) for many years. In *Uma Devi*, the Supreme Court held that it would be illegal to regularize such workers, on the grounds that it would invade the Article 14 rights of regular recruits. Before the Court, it was specifically argued that the irregular recruits and the State were in an entirely unequal bargaining position; consequently, the State's conduct in keeping these recruits on daily wages with no security violated Article 23.

Uma Devi was thus an ideal case for an application of *PUDR*'s logic: the State's use of a depressed labour market to 'offer' exploitative terms to individuals who had no genuine 'choice' in the matter was a textbook case of what labour-republicanism would conceptualize as an infringement of freedom. Like in *Mysore Kirloskar*, however, the Court skirted around the argument, noting, 'After all, the employees accepted the employment at their own volition and with eyes open as to the nature of their employment ... it appears to us that importing these theories to defeat the basic requirement of public employment would defeat the constitutional scheme and the constitutional goal of equality.'[140]

The Court's casual dismissal of *PUDR*'s careful analyses as 'imported theories' is both unsatisfactory and, simply, incorrect. As we have seen, the use of unequal economic power to compel individuals to give up their constitutional rights in return for basic material security was precisely what Ambedkar warned against, and precisely what the Constituent Assembly wanted Article 23 to guard against. Far from being an imported theory, therefore, the Article 23 claim in *Uma Devi* was rooted in Indian constitutional law.

In fact, a few years before *Uma Devi*, the Allahabad High Court had indeed come to a radically different conclusion by applying the logic of *PUDR*. Dealing with the payment of lower wages and, subsequently, the termination of an ad hoc employee, the Court asked itself 'whether the State or its instrumentality under its unequal bargaining power can exploit youths and citizens of this country and take advantage of their poverty by exploiting them, knowing that they were being appointed against the rules, and, therefore, no right would accrue to them'.[141] Invoking *PUDR*, the Court answered in the negative, and held that a petitioner could not be deprived of her fundamental right under Article 23 even if she had 'voluntarily' taken up the job on offer. 'It is not the acceptance of the service voluntarily but the effect of it that results in exploitation.'[142] And the effect demonstrated that 'exploitation was writ large'.[143] It further said:

> [in India] there is no social security or unemployment allowance. The result is that the educated youth is willing to work on any terms. Like a drowning man, he clutches at any straw … for survival for the time being and hope of settlement in future … every day petitions have come before me of teachers who claim to be working for years without any salary in the hope that they may be regularized.[144]

This paragraph, in particular the telling phrase 'willing to work on any terms', illustrates the illusory nature of 'freedom' in the labour market, and the true scope of Article 23. What is of particular significance is how *Uma Devi* and the Allahabad High Court framed exactly the same set of circumstances in radically different normative language. For *Uma Devi*, it was about employees who accepted the terms of their employment 'on their own volition', and could not, therefore, complain afterwards. Formal consent, therefore, was the foundation of Article 23. For the Allahabad High Court, on the other hand, Article 23 was designed to prevent *exploitation*; and the question of formal voluntariness was insufficient at best to the question of whether, in context, exploitation existed. *Uma Devi* marked a retreat from the transformative logic of *PUDR*; the Allahabad High Court—which eventually ordered the petitioner's reinstatement and retrospective payment on the salary of a regular employee, until formal recruitment was undertaken—demonstrated what that transformative logic would look like in a more complex situation, and how it might be used across domains of labour law.

It is, of course, the Supreme Court's verdict in *Uma Devi*, albeit limited to the issue of regularization, that is the law of the land. So, for now, *PUDR* is a reminder of the road not quite taken.[145] That does not, of course, mean that it can never be taken.[146] With the rapidly changing character of work, and the rise of the sharing or platform economy, where unequal relationships of power have taken on more scattered and distributed forms, the courts are likely to have many more opportunities in the near future to revisit ideas of force and freedom and, as Ambedkar observed, interrogate the relationship between civil rights and the economic structure. It remains to be seen whether the Court will take up *PUDR*'s invitation to answer these questions in the voice of labour-republicanism.[147]

B. Force and Freedom in the Domestic Space

PUDR's crucial insights—that power could be exercised through structures and institutions; that domination could be impersonal; and that freedom could be infringed even in the absence of force or the threat of it—have applications beyond the marketplace. In fact, one space where it seems even more directly and unquestionably relevant is a space which is not normally thought to be relevant to constitutional norms—the space of the household.

It is, by now, a familiar argument that the division of labour within the household is gendered. Women bear a disproportionate burden, in terms of both labour time and volume.[148] These tasks include 'cooking, cleaning, collecting water and firewood, and caring for the ill, elderly, and children ... [which are] essential to maintaining the household ... [and] the fundamental support for the family's economic development'.[149] And, of course, this division of labour is rarely *voluntary* in the true sense of the term, but is constituted by a number of factors, viz., social customs and structures of thought, women's economic vulnerability and marginalization within the family, and often enough coercion in its classical sense.[150]

PUDR's arguments, therefore, apply squarely to housework, which, like *begar* in its original sense, remains unpaid and unremunerated labour: that is, individuals (predominantly women) engaging in housework have (at least) the fundamental, enforceable right to a minimum wage. In the global context, this is not a novel argument. Various arguments have been proposed for factoring in housework as an economic contribution that merits remuneration.[151] Another model, broadly known as 'community of property', contemplates giving women an enforceable right in the matrimonial property, even though it might *legally* belong to the husband.[152] The logic is a logic of redressal: while the property may be registered in the husband's name, because it has been bought by 'his' money, the very reason for such an asymmetrical situation is that the wife's labour in the household remains unpaid. Consequently, community of property regimes *recognize* the woman's economic contribution to the household by *stipulating* an equal legal interest on property that is purchased during the marriage.[153]

A community of property law has been debated in India, both at the central level and in the state of Maharashtra.[154] In the absence of specific legislation, however, the Supreme Court, so far, has elected to read relevant statutes such as the Domestic Violence Act narrowly, so as to exclude any claims that spouses might have to the matrimonial property.[155] Recognizing that *PUDR*'s arguments about force and freedom apply with equal strength to the household might be an important first step in remedying this. Article 23 then becomes the principled basis for *constitutionalizing* a right to remuneration for household work, which can be realized by crafting an appropriate judicial remedy.

This is not as outlandish as it may sound. In an interesting judgement, the Court of Appeal in Kenya interpreted Article 45(3) of the Kenyan constitution (which guarantees 'equal rights and responsibilities' in marriage) to require a 50 per cent division of property at the time of divorce.[156] The Court observed that the principle of equal rights and responsibilities in marriage amounted to a 'constitutional statement of the principle that marital property is shared 50-50 in the event that a marriage ends.'[157] Although the Kenyan courts subsequently resiled from this position,[158] it is clear from this that courts *need not* wait for the their legislatures to establish community of property regimes through legislation. In India, a transformative reading of Article 23 allows the courts to do just that.

All it needs is a constitutional vision, some judicial creativity, a progressive reading of existing laws such as the Domestic Violence Act, and a sprinkling of empathy.

Part Three
Liberty

Article 19

All citizens shall have the right–(a) to freedom of speech and expression.

(2) Nothing in sub-clause (a) of clause (1) shall affect the operation of any existing law, or prevent the State from making any law, insofar as such law imposes reasonable restrictions on the exercise of the right conferred by the said sub-clause in the interests of the sovereignty and integrity of India, the security of the State, friendly relations with foreign States, public order, decency or morality, or in relation to contempt of court, defamation or incitement to an offence.

Article 20

(1) No person shall be convicted of any offence except for violation of a law in force at the time of the commission of the Act charged as an offence, nor be subjected to a penalty greater than that which might have been inflicted under the law in force at the time of the commission of the offence.

(2) No person shall be prosecuted and punished for the same offence more than once.

(3) No person accused of any offence shall be compelled to be a witness against himself.

Article 21

No person shall be deprived of his life or personal liberty except according to procedure established by law.

Article 22

(1) No person who is arrested shall be detained in custody without being informed, as soon as may be, of the grounds for such arrest nor

shall he be denied the right to consult, and to be defended by, a legal practitioner of his choice.

(2) Every person who is arrested and detained in custody shall be produced before the nearest magistrate within a period of twenty-four hours of such arrest excluding the time necessary for the journey from the place of arrest to the court of the magistrate and no such person shall be detained in custody beyond the said period without the authority of a magistrate.

(3) Nothing in clauses (1) and (2) shall apply–

(a) to any person who for the time being is an enemy alien; or

(b) to any person who is arrested or detained under any law providing for preventive detention.

...

7

Privacy beyond the Public/Private Divide: *Sareetha* and Freedom within the Family

We are told that the practice of slavery has now been universally abolished, but does that mean that we, women, have gained freedom? No, we have not, but why? There are good reasons.

Rokeya Sakhawat Hossain, *Streejatir Abanati* (1904)

[S]elf-determination begins at home—and that is with every I, and the We whom the I chooses ... Exploitation in all its forms must have disappeared ... from ... individual relationships.

Herbert Marcuse, *An Essay on Liberation* (1971)

IN DECEMBER 1975, SIXTEEN-YEAR-OLD Sareetha, then a high-school student, married Venkatasubbaiah. After living together for a little more than six months, they separated. Sareetha soon became a popular actress, across South Indian languages. More than five years later, her husband decided that he wanted to live with her again. He moved court under Section 9 of the Hindu Marriage Act, arguing that Sareetha had withdrawn herself from his society 'without reasonable excuse', and that, therefore, he was entitled to a decree for the 'restitution of conjugal rights'[1] against her, i.e., a court order requiring Sareetha to return and live with him once more.

After losing before the subordinate court, Sareetha came before the Andhra Pradesh High Court, and advanced a claim that was made for the first time in Indian constitutional history.[2] She argued that Section 9 of the Hindu Marriage Act was unconstitutional, because it contravened her fundamental rights to equality, personal liberty, dignity, and privacy. The single-judge bench of the High Court agreed. Justice P.A. Choudary observed that the effect of a decree for the restitution of conjugal rights was to 'transfer the choice to have or not to have marital intercourse to the State from the concerned individual and ... to surrender the choice of the individual to allow or not to allow one's body to be used as a vehicle for another human being's creation to the State.'[3] This, he held, was an unacceptable intrusion into personal privacy, bodily integrity, and individual dignity, apart from having an unequal effect upon the lives of men and women. He struck down the Section.

Interestingly, the judgement of the Andhra Pradesh High Court came almost exactly one century after another case about the restitution of conjugal rights had been brought before the colonial courts, and whose judgements had sparked off a divisive debate about the public/private divide, the relationship between the colonial state and Indian society, and the rights that women had in and outside their marriage, their family, and their community. In *Dadaji Bhikaji v. Rukhmabai*, the High Court of Bombay was called upon to decide whether Dadaji, who had been married to Rukhmabai when he was nineteen, and she eleven, could enforce a decree for the restitution of conjugal rights eleven years after the marriage, even though they had never cohabited. Sitting as the Court of first instance, Justice Pinhey held that he could not. Correctly noting that the remedy of restitution of conjugal rights had 'no foundation in Hindu law', and had been 'transplanted from England into India', he decided to read existing precedent narrowly, and refused to 'compel this young lady of twenty-two to go to the house of the plaintiff in order that he may consummate the marriage arranged for her during her helpless infancy'.[4]

Justice Pinhey's brief, page-and-a-half-long opinion, delivered in 1885, generated a storm of controversy in British India and was swiftly reversed by a division bench of the Bombay High Court.[5] While the case ultimately ended in a settlement,[6] it was left to Justice Choudary, nearly a century, a freedom struggle, and a Constitution later, to tease out Justice Pinhey's tantalizing, opening foray into ideas of compulsion and consent within marriage, and transform it into a full-blown constitutional argument that placed individual privacy and decisional autonomy *within* the 'private' space of the family upon the pedestal of fundamental rights.

In this chapter, I argue that *Sareetha*'s exposition of the right to privacy represents a uniquely transformative moment in Indian constitutional history for two reasons: first, because of the manner in which it dismantled the conceptual iron cage of the public/private binary; and second, because of its insistence that the Constitution requires a *democratization* of what were considered 'private spaces' (the home), 'private relations' (marriage), and 'private functions' (sex and 'procreation').

I begin by tracing the genealogy of the right to privacy under Indian constitutional law, culminating with the Supreme Court's ambiguous formulation in *Gobind v. State of MP* (I); I argue that *Gobind's* abstract statement was compatible with at least three historic traditions of privacy. The first, borrowed from Enlightenment liberalism, is a tradition that visualizes privacy as a *spatial* concept, applicable to 'spaces' or, relatedly, to certain functions performed within those spaces (II). The second, that evolved in colonial India, and saw its high watermark during the Rukhmabai case, is a tradition that defends a right to privacy in terms of *relationships*, *communities*, or *social institutions* (III). However, in contradistinction to both the spatial and the institutional-relational view of privacy, there is a third tradition, which defines privacy in terms of an individual's right to exercise her autonomy in the taking of *private decisions*, including, especially, decisions about the use of her body.

In *Sareetha*, Justice Choudary held that it was this third vision of privacy that the Constitution was committed to, and, most importantly of all, that this vision would *prevail* in cases of a conflict with the spatial and functional-relational views of privacy (IV). After demonstrating the transformative character of the judgement, I provide a brief account of the legal aftermath of *Sareetha*, its failure to leave a lasting imprint upon Indian constitutional history and its possible revival, after the 2017 judgement of the Supreme Court in the famous right to privacy case (V).

I conclude by considering the implications of *Sareetha* for other areas of law, such as the constitutionality of the marital rape exception (VI). Even though it is no longer good law, *Sareetha* remains important because of how, in terms of transformative constitutionalism, it 'open[ed] out several worlds in which radical possibilities flicker[ed], exist[ed], and … [were ultimately] extinguished'.[7]

I. Privacy under the Indian Constitution

There is no expressly guaranteed right to privacy under the Indian Constitution. During the Constituent Assembly Debates, Somnath Lahiri's proposed constitutional provision safeguarding the privacy of correspondence was rejected.[8] Subsequent attempts by Kazi Syed Karimuddin and Pandit Thakur Das Bhargava to reinsert it into the constitutional text were rebuffed, despite Ambedkar's endorsement. This happened through a controversial voting procedure where the Vice-President of the Assembly twice said that 'the ayes have it', was twice contradicted by T.T. Krishnamachari, and the matter was hurriedly postponed after the Division Bell was rung for a vote.[9] The clause was quietly dropped, leading to bitter condemnation during the third reading of the Constitution.[10] But the Constitution came into being without an express fundamental right to privacy.

A few years later, an eight-judge bench of the Supreme Court, in *M.P. Sharma v. Satish Chandra*,[11] used this piece of constitutional history, and refused to 'read in' a right to privacy under the Constitution. This refusal continued in *Kharak Singh v. State of UP*,[12] where a six-judge bench of the Supreme Court (partially) upheld police surveillance of a 'history-sheeter'. However, *Kharak Singh* was delivered over a strong dissent by Justice Subba Rao, who insisted that 'it is true our Constitution does not expressly declare a right to privacy as a fundamental right, but the said right is an essential ingredient of personal liberty'.[13] And even the majority opinion was nowhere near as unequivocal as the eight judges in *M.P. Sharma*. The majority, in fact, held that nightly 'domiciliary visits' by the police were illegal, on the basis that the phrase 'personal liberty', under Article 21, was not limited simply to 'freedom from physical restraint or freedom from confinement within the bounds of a prison',[14] but included protection from 'unauthorised intrusion into a person's home and the disturbance caused to him thereby ... [which is] an ultimate essential of ordered liberty'.[15]

Consequently, it is hardly surprising that in 1975, the Supreme Court finally took the step that it could not bring itself to take in *Kharak Singh*. In *Gobind v. State of MP*,[16] a very similar case involving police surveillance, a three-judge bench of the Supreme Court drew upon both the majority and dissenting opinions in *Kharak Singh*, and 'read in' a fundamental right to privacy into Part III of the Constitution, which, it held, flowed from other, expressly guaranteed fundamental rights such as the right to personal liberty, the right to freedom of speech and expression, and the right to free movement. The Court's actual *statement* of what the right to privacy concretely meant, however, was almost Delphic:

> Any right to privacy must encompass and protect the personal intimacies of the home, the family, marriage, motherhood, procreation, and child rearing.[17]

As a statement of the constitutional right to privacy, this sentence is ambiguous.[18] It carries at least three meanings. First, the word 'home', right at the beginning, suggests a *spatial concept* of privacy. This is supported by the words that follow, all of which refer to activities that are normally carried out within the *physical space* that is the 'home'. Slightly distinctly, the terms in question might also be read referring to *functions* (especially 'motherhood', 'procreation', and 'child-rearing'), which are typically performed within the space of the home. Privacy, in its functional sense, provides a sanctuary to these (domestic-oriented activities). Note that the use of the term 'motherhood' (and not 'parenthood', or the additional 'fatherhood') suggests that, at the very stage of conceptualization, this is a gendered division.

Second, the word 'home' might be read to mean not a physical space, but the 'household'. Read this way, what unites 'home', 'family', 'marriage', 'motherhood', 'procreation' and 'child-rearing' is that they are all *social institutions* centred around the idea of the private, or domestic, sphere. Privacy, then, is to be understood in an 'institutional' or 'relational' sense, insulating certain social institutions or relations from State interference.

Third, 'marriage', 'motherhood', 'procreation' and 'child-rearing' are not merely institutions and relations, but they are also the result of *decisions*—decisions about how an individual uses her body, decisions that lie at the core of individual autonomy. Privacy, in this sense, protects the individual's bodily integrity and decisional autonomy.

For the sake of convenience, let us label these three conceptions of privacy as 'spatial-functional', 'relational-institutional' and 'decisional'. The failure of the Supreme Court in *Gobind* was a failure to clarify which understanding (or understandings) of privacy the Constitution was committed to. As we shall see, while there are overlaps between these different conceptions of privacy, there are also instances where they come into direct conflict. One such instance was *Sareetha*, which, I argue, was an instance of transformative constitutionalism because the Andhra Pradesh High Court consciously adopted a transformative understanding of privacy as the constitutional basis of the right, and equally consciously rejected the others. Any assessment of *Sareetha*, therefore, must read its conceptualization of privacy *in light* of the ambiguity that the Supreme Court created in *Gobind*.

However, in order to understand precisely what was so transformative about the idea of privacy advanced in *Sareetha*, we must first briefly consider the development of privacy in all the senses in which the word occurs in *Gobind*, viz., spatial, relational-functional, and decisional.

II. Historical Pathways—I: The Privacy of Space

The division of space into 'public' and 'private' has a long and contested lineage in Western political thought. Its importance is matched only by its complex protean and non-unitary character.[19] Broadly, the birth of political thought in ancient Greece was accompanied by a distinction between the *polis* (the city) and the *oikos* (the house).[20] The *polis* was the realm of 'freedom'—'free association between free citizens'[21] (who were necessarily male). By contrast, the *oikos* was the domain of 'necessity'—the performance of all the functions (such as production, reproduction, etc.) that made political life in the *polis* possible.[22] In other words, while the structuring principle of the *polis* was (political) equality, where no person ruled another,[23] the structuring principle of the *oikos* was inequality, or hierarchy (between master and slave, husband and wife, father and children).[24] The threshold of the house was where the norms of freedom and equality, that governed public life, gave way to the norms of hierarchy and inequality, which were deemed to track the *natural* differences between the inhabitants of the household.[25]

While the distinction between 'public' and 'private' largely disappeared during feudal times, with the manorial household coming to encompass both spheres,[26] the two concepts were resurrected with the onset of the Enlightenment and the revolutionary era. As scholars point out, the defining characteristic of the eighteenth-century revolutions that overthrew absolute monarchies was that they pitted an ascendant bourgeoisie class against the remnants of concentrated monarchical power.[27] To safeguard its interests from State meddling, the bourgeoisie carved out zones of inviolability, free from State interference. This included economic interests (defined in terms of the free market) as well as personal interests (the household).

As Seyla Benhabib notes, drawing from the work of Lawrence Stone:

> … from the beginning there were tensions between the continuing patriarchal authority of the father in the bourgeois family and developing conceptions of equality and consent in the political world. As the male bourgeois citizen was battling for his rights to autonomy in the religious and economic spheres against the absolutist state, his relations in the household were defined by non-consensual, nonegalitarian assumptions. Questions of justice were from the beginning restricted to the 'public sphere', whereas the private sphere was considered outside the realm of justice.[28]

It is important to note the shift in emphasis: unlike ancient thought, which accepted that hierarchy was the natural order of things in the private sphere, modern thought held that issues of equality were simply irrelevant to the private sphere: 'power relations in the "intimate sphere" have been treated as though they did not even exist'.[29]

As Ann Hughes puts it:

> … the attack on a monarch whose rule was legitimated partly through patriarchalism had implications for gender hierarchies within the household, although most parliamentarians and republicans were very careful to limit these implications, most often through various versions of a separation between public or civil authority from the private world of the household.[30]

This political conceptualization of the private domain found its way into legal thought towards the end of the nineteenth century. In the path-breaking 1890 article, 'The Right to Privacy', the American scholars Warren and Brandeis defended a 'right to seclusion' or a 'right to be left alone', which they linked with the space of the home ('a man's home is his castle').[31] After a few abortive attempts,[32] the US Supreme Court accepted something akin to a constitutional right to privacy against State surveillance, in the case of *Katz v. United States*.[33]

In *Katz*, FBI agents eavesdropped on an individual's phone conversation by attaching a recording device to the outside of a phone booth. The question was whether this constituted an 'unlawful search and seizure', in contravention of the Fourth Amendment of the US Constitution.[34] Reversing precedent that had limited the prohibition of State intrusion only to trespass upon pre-defined 'constitutionally protected areas',[35] the Supreme Court held that it did, noting, 'the Fourth Amendment protects people, not places'.[36] However, the fact that the conceptualization of privacy was not untethered from space, and the performance of certain kinds of actions within that space, was made clear in the concurring opinion of Justice Harlan, who understood the majority opinion as merely stating that:

> … an enclosed telephone booth is an area where, like a home … and unlike a field … a person has a constitutionally protected reasonable expectation of privacy … as the Court's opinion states, 'the Fourth Amendment protects people, not places. The question, however, is what protection it affords to those people. Generally, as here, the answer to that question requires reference to a 'place'.[37]

In other words, the right to privacy protected certain kinds of activities, whose character was based on the spaces within which they were conducted. In the years after, and, indeed, before *Katz*, this spatial-functional view has had to contend with other conceptualizations of privacy,[38] but it still remains a predominant view. For instance, in *Kyllo v. United States*,[39] while examining the question of whether the use of a thermal-imaging device, aimed from a public street into a private home to detect heat levels, violated the Fourth Amendment, the Supreme Court reiterated the proposition that the Fourth Amendment 'draws a firm line at the entrance to the house',[40] and 'in the home … *all* details are intimate details, because the entire area is held safe from prying government eyes'.[41]

The spatial-functional conception of privacy is not limited to the US, although it has perhaps received its most detailed treatment in that jurisdiction. Reference to the sanctity of the 'home' is found in multiple constitutional instruments.[42] In *Bernstein v. Bester*,[43] an early judgement of the South African Constitutional Court, Justice Ackermann summarized the argument:

> … it is only the inner sanctum of a person, such as his/her family life, sexual preference and home environment, which is shielded from erosion by conflicting rights of the community … privacy is acknowledged in the truly personal realm, but as a person moves into communal relations and activities such as business and social interaction, the scope of personal space shrinks accordingly.[44]

The basis of privacy, then, is the protection of a 'personal realm', and this 'realm' (as in *Gobind*) carries multiple valences: relations and institutions (family life), decisions (sexual preferences), and space (home environment). In Justice Ackermann's formulation, these multiple valences—one of which is space—co-exist and together constitute the 'personal realm' that a right to privacy exists to defend.

The centrality of space and function to privacy, however, has been subjected to serious criticism.[45] As Martha Nussbaum argues, 'appeals to the alleged privacy of the home have been used to defend the exemption of marital rape from sexual assault laws, and to discourage state interference with domestic violence or child abuse'.[46] Nussbaum's basic argument is that inequalities of power within the space of the home (what scholars have called 'private government'),[47] and the relations of dominance and oppression that these inequalities generate, are preserved and perpetuated by a conception of privacy that takes the space of the home as its basic unit. Similar arguments have been made by many different scholars, in different and nuanced ways.[48] As John Gardner sums up, 'Liberal law erects what we might call "privacy barriers" in its own path.'[49] What it suggests to us here is that there might be situations where thinking about privacy as composed of complementary conceptions involving space-function, relations, and decisions might not always be possible. Instead, there might be situations of conflict between these conceptions.[50]

III. Historical Pathways—II: The Privacy of Community

Katz was not the first US case that enunciated a constitutional right to privacy. Two years before, in *Griswold v. Connecticut*,[51] the US Supreme Court struck down a law penalizing the use of contraceptive devices, on the basis that it violated marital privacy. The Court located this right within the 'penumbra' of different constitutional provisions, such as the right against unreasonable searches, the right against self-incrimination, etc., which, it held, created 'zones of privacy'.[52] One of which was marital relationship.

Importantly, *Griswold* was not about the right of two consenting adults to use contraceptives while having sex, but about prohibiting the State from interfering with the marital relationship. In the previous section, we discussed cases where the units of privacy were spaces and functions; in *Griswold*, the unit of privacy was the 'social institution of marriage'.[53] In other words, since an institution cannot be a right-bearer, persons had the right to privacy to the extent that they participated in, and were part of, the social institution of marriage, and the scope of their right was limited by the bounds of that social institution.

A few years later, the Supreme Court of Ireland, while adjudicating a very similar claim for access to contraceptives, brought by a married couple, formulated the proposition in even starker terms (*McGee v. Attorney-General*). One judge invoked the 'privacy of the matrimonial bedroom',[54] and the other held that the offending statute 'violated [the woman's] right to privacy in regard to her matrimonial relations'.[55] The second statement is particularly instructive, because it specifically frames the individual right (to privacy) within the context of the social institution of marriage. In other words, an otherwise abstract and amorphous right to privacy becomes concrete and enforceable when it is exercised through a social institution.

I shall now argue that this institutional-relational view of privacy constituted the dominant tradition of privacy in colonial India, in the years leading up to Independence (although the issue was never framed in the vocabulary of privacy). The fundamental unit that claimed a right to privacy and to non-interference against the State was not the family, or the marital union, but the religious community, in its limited interior domain of 'personal laws' (laws governing the family, gender relations, marriage, divorce, inheritance, and so on).[56]

The genesis of this lay in the 1772 Regulations announced by Warren Hastings, India's first colonial Governor-General, which provided that 'in all suits regarding inheritance, marriage, caste, and other religious usages or institutions, the law of the Koran with respect to Mahometans, and those of the Shaster with respect to Gentoos shall be invariably be adhered to'.[57] This injunction was faithfully implemented by the colonial courts for the next century and a half, and more.[58]

The colonial government's motivations for adopting this policy of apparent partial 'non-interference' have been studied extensively.[59] What is important to note here is that personal laws were to be interpreted and enforced in colonial courts, by colonial judges. Therefore, it was the State, through its courts, that 'took on the role of defining and adjudicating that religious law'.[60] In the view of the colonial state, 'India [w]as an agglomeration of communities, with religion and caste forming the primary building blocks of Indian society … [which] rendered religious community rather than the individual the unit of legal and political recognition.'[61]

In the initial years, during the administration of the East India Company, this kind of adjudication respected the pluralism of diverse communities, as well as their capacity for self-government and evolution. For instance, caste disputes in Bombay were often resolved by taking the majority view of the members of that particular caste.[62] However, after the 1857 Revolution, the colony's legal and judicial system was entirely overhauled. The period now saw a shift to a more rigid model of community,[63] defined and characterized by canonical texts for both Hindus and Muslims.[64] Influenced by nineteenth-century social theory, which divided the world into a public sphere and a domestic, private sphere, the colonial state came to view caste, custom, and family as 'private and changeless matters that were outside the normal purview of the state'.[65] As Amrita Shodhan puts the point, 'The colonial judiciary's denial of the polities' ability to govern and their simultaneous exclusive governance by the colonial state led to the establishment of an individual as a member of a pre-legal original community, defined by birth and status.'[66] Importantly, this view of communities left no room for the possibility of cultural dissent.[67] The 'laws' of the community, drawn from the courts' interpretation of ancient texts and 'custom', were applicable to every individual deemed to be a 'member' of that community. For obvious reasons, the colonial government's conscious effort to maintain the 'structures of authority within the household'[68] had a specific impact on women who, in particular, were visualized as the embodiment of home and of community.[69]

The rhetoric of colonial administrators was soon imitated by their Indian counterparts. As Rosalind O'Hanlon points out in her introduction to Tarabai Shinde's *Stree Purush Tulna* (A Comparison Between Men and Women)—a text we shall return to later in this chapter—'ideas of a realm of custom and family beyond the reach of the state quickly entered the rhetoric of Indian politicians and reformers themselves ... [such] changes subordinated women more firmly to caste and family authority, and consigned them to a domain of "private life" supposedly outside politics'.[70] The community, through the institution of the family, came to be viewed as 'an exclusive sovereign domain where the nation was acting on its own, resisting colonial penetration'.[71]

This was seen in debates over a proposed Age of Consent Law in the late-nineteenth century,[72] but it was also seen most vividly in the fallout over the *Rukhmabai* case, where Justice Pinhey's first-instance judgement in favour of Rukhmabai was severely criticized as 'an interference in the sacrosanct arena of Hindu conjugality'.[73] By 1885, therefore, the community, *expressed through its personal laws*, had become a fundamental unity of Indian society, that could claim for itself an autonomous existence, free from legal intervention by the (secular) State. In modern terms, we would understand this as the right to privacy expressed *through* the community and the family, much like *Griswold* and *McGee* accorded a right to privacy to individuals *through* their participation in the marital union.

The colonial government's views were mirrored in another way by the nascent nationalist movement, which relegated questions of women's rights to the social background, to be resolved by the community in due course, and subordinated to the struggle for political independence from colonial rule.[74] For example, the Indian Social Conference—founded specifically to deal with issues of social reform, and which had always held joint annual sittings with the Indian National Congress since its inception—was eased out by the INC in 1895.[75] The effect of this was a *depoliticization* of issues relating to the family, which were no longer deemed to be of normative concern within the political movement for independence, but as issues that could only be subjected to internal reform by communities themselves.[76]

The colonial doctrine of 'non-interference' with 'personal laws' and the nationalist movement's separation of the political and the social complemented each other. The former established communities as autonomous units of self-governance, whose laws were determined by ancient texts, filtered through the colonial interpretive mirror (and texts which, of course, had never been composed through a democratic or egalitarian process). The latter denied the possibility of applying political argument and political norms of equality, autonomy, and self-determination to the 'personal' domain (which, in turn, was defined as the regime of community personal laws). Welded together, they formed an iron cage where members of communities found themselves subjected to 'personal laws' to which they had never consented, which violated those exact principles that the nationalist movement was demanding from the colonial state in the 'public domain', and against whose injustices there was no tribunal they could appeal to.[77]

IV. *Sareetha* and the Transformative Constitution

When *Sareetha* came to be decided, therefore, Justice Choudary had before him *Gobind's* oracular pronouncement about 'the home, the family, marriage, motherhood, procreation and child rearing'. This pronouncement was consistent with either or both of two long-standing intellectual traditions of privacy.

There was, however, a third tradition as well, of comparatively recent vintage. In *Eisenstadt v. Baird*, decided in 1972, the US Supreme Court had extended its *Griswold* ruling on the right to contraception to unmarried couples as well. By definition, this extension could not be justified on the grounds of the sanctity of the 'marital union'. However, in his majority opinion, Justice Brennan noted,'The marital couple is not an independent entity with a mind and heart of its own, but an association of two individuals each with a separate intellectual and emotional makeup. If the right of privacy means anything, it is the right of the individual, married or single, to be free from unwarranted governmental intrusion into matters so fundamentally affecting a person as the decision whether to bear or beget a child.'[78]

This conception of privacy, which we called decisional privacy at the beginning of this chapter, is focused on the individual's freedom to make fundamental choices for herself. It was affirmed by the US Supreme Court the next year in its famous *Roe v. Wade* decision, where a woman's (qualified) right to abort her foetus was justified on the basis that her *decision* whether or not to terminate her pregnancy fell within the right to privacy.[79] In *Gobind*, the Supreme Court drew upon American case law, citing both *Griswold* and *Roe,* although not *Eisenstadt,* to fashion the contours of an Indian right to privacy, thus suggesting inspiration from both the decisional and the relational conceptions.

There need be nothing wrong with this. The decisional and relational views of privacy could, in most cases, complement each other. *Sareetha* was a case, however, where they clashed directly. Because if privacy was to be understood relationally, and if the marital union was one of the *units* through which privacy was to be exercised, then the argument that Sareetha had a right to (decisional) privacy *within* the marriage and *against* her husband was simply incoherent. Sareetha's right to decisional privacy also clashed with the spatial conception of privacy, although in a different, and more indirect, way. As we have seen, the basis of a spatial right to privacy—closely connected to the distinction between public and private spheres—was the understanding that the writ of the State stopped at the threshold of the home. The extension of this argument was that within the space of the home (subject to certain exceptions), constitutional norms such as equality, privacy, and so on simply didn't apply. Consequently, on the spatial view of privacy, Sareetha's argument was a category mistake, i.e., she was relying upon rights in a space where they simply weren't available to her.

Sareetha, therefore, was not an easy case. Justice Choudary could not simply interpret *Gobind* in the manner that he wished, and apply it. He had to *choose* between contesting visions of privacy, all of which could persuasively be argued to flow from *Gobind*, and decide which of those visions was truest to the Constitution's transformative purpose.

A. Sareetha: *The Formulation of Privacy*

In considering the constitutional question, Justice Choudary noted that the concept of 'conjugal rights' was two-pronged: 'the right which husband and wife have to each other's society ... [and the right to] marital intercourse'.[80] This meant that the 'consequences of the enforcement of such a decree [of restitution of conjugal rights]'[81]—normally achieved through financial sanctions under the Code of Civil Procedure—'are firstly to transfer the choice to have or not to have marital intercourse to the State from the concerned individual and secondly, to surrender the choice of the individual to allow or not to allow one's body to be used as a vehicle for another human being's creation to the State'.[82] This 'transfer of choice', Justice Choudary held, 'offends the inviolability of the body and the mind'.[83]

It is important to note, however, that the *law* itself did not compel sexual intercourse. It only authorized a decree for *cohabitation*, which, in turn, could only be enforced through financial sanctions and not through physical force. That is why Justice Choudary wrote specifically of the *consequences* of enforcing the decree, and it is here that we see the first important break with the traditional conceptions of privacy. Justice Choudary was not content to simply end his enquiry at the point of cohabitation. Instead he went further, to find also that given the deeply unequal structure of the family, and given the myriad pressures, viz., physical, mental, emotional, and social, that could be brought to bear upon women within the family, compelled cohabitation would, in all likelihood, lead to compelled intercourse (exacerbated by the fact that under the Indian Penal Code, marital rape does not qualify as 'rape'). Taking the example of a Madhya Pradesh High Court decision where a woman called Tarabai was required by decree to go back to her husband, Justice Choudary observed, '*what could have happened to Tarabai thereafter may well be left to the reader's imagination*'.[84] This, for him, was completely unacceptable, because, 'it is impossible to conceive of sexuality on any basis except on the basis of consensual participation'.[85] And if a decree for restitution of conjugal rights effectively denied the possibility of mutual consent to sex, it went even further and denied choice in the matter of conception: '[in what] so intimately concerns her body and which is so vital for her life, a decree of restitution of conjugal rights totally excludes her'.[86]

We can pause here a moment and notice that marriage and procreation—two of the constituent elements in *Gobind*—were at the forefront of Justice Choudary's formulation of privacy. However, in his view, the basis for protection was neither spatial nor institutional, but rather that both activities involved fundamental choices that 'intimately concern[ed]' the body. This was made clear when Justice Choudary went on to locate his conception of privacy within the contours of *Gobind*. After citing *Gobind*'s formulation of privacy, he also quoted another paragraph from that case, where Justice Mathew had noted, 'there can be no doubt that privacy-dignity claims deserve to be examined with care'.[87] Seizing upon *Gobind*'s offhand invocation of dignity, Justice Choudary held that 'Gobind's *case* thus firmly laid it down that Article 21 protects the right to privacy and promotes the individual dignity mentioned in the [P]reamble to our Constitution'.[88] By framing privacy as a right that was inextricably connected with the concept of individual dignity, Justice Choudary was then able to decisively reformulate the right to privacy in its decisional sense:

> … any plausible definition of right to privacy is bound to take [the] human body as its first and most basic reference for control over personal identity.[89]

This was a clear repudiation of the philosophies that located privacy within spaces, or within institutions or relationships. Instead, it upheld a vision of privacy focused on the body, and individual control over the body. The subordination of institutional privacy to decisional privacy was then completed in the next line, when Justice Choudary effectively reversed the reasoning of *Griswold* and *McGee*, holding that '[the] definition [of privacy] is bound to include [the] body's inviolability and integrity and intimacy of personal identity, including marital privacy'.[90] Instead of a vision of privacy where the right could only be exercised *through* the marital institution, Justice Choudary articulated a vision where marriage was a protected institution *because* it was the result of an exercise of individual choice. In fact, to avoid any doubt whatsoever, he took note of the American line of cases from *Griswold* to *Roe*, and concluded with the observation that the 'right to privacy belongs to a person as an individual and is not lost by marital association'.[91]

It is important to understand that while the challenge in *Sareetha* was a challenge to a law (Section 9 of the Hindu Marriage Act), and was, therefore, a contest between the individual and the State, the right that was being claimed was a right to privacy *against* the marital spouse *within* the family. While the Court's judgement was the invalidation of the law, its reasoning went beyond that. This was particularly evident in Justice Choudary's invocation of the dissenting opinion of Justice Brandeis in the US Supreme Court judgement of *Olmstead v. New York*.[92] *Olmstead* was a 1928 case concerning the admissibility of evidence obtained through a wiretap. The majority held that the wiretap did not offend the Fourth Amendment, which was limited to prohibiting illegal searches of *'persons, houses, papers, and effects'*. Justice Brandeis, however, refused to read the Fourth Amendment in such a literal way. He observed:

> When the Fourth and Fifth Amendments were adopted, 'the form that evil had theretofore taken' had been necessarily simple. Force and violence were then the only means known to man by which a Government could directly effect self-incrimination ... But 'time works changes, brings into existence new conditions and purposes'. Subtler and more far-reaching means of invading privacy have become available to the Government.[93]

Justice Brandeis's basic point was that as invasive State technologies increase in scope and reach, the law must correspondingly evolve to continue effectively protecting the individual. Underlying this is the idea that there must, at all times, remain a *balance of power between State and individual.* The more power the State acquires, the further must the law reach to constrain its use, to prevent the evolution of a totalitarian society in which State power has completely overwhelmed the individual.

In *Sareetha*, Justice Choudary took Justice Brandeis's idea of a parity of power between individual and State, and *extended it to apply horizontally, in the private realm.* His link between cohabitation and compelled intercourse was based upon the difference in power within the marital relationship, and *Sareetha*'s striking down of Section 9 was a Brandeisian way to restore the balance. In a truly radical fashion, therefore, Justice Choudary's attempt was to bring about, in the smallest of ways possible, a democratization of the private sphere, by extending ideas of privacy and freedom to the marital relationship.[94] It is in this manner that *Sareetha* was a truly transformative decision.

B. Sareetha: *The Formulation of Equality*

Justice Choudary's last argument was with respect to Article 14, which guaranteed the equal protection of laws. Section 9 of the Hindu Marriage Act, of course, was *facially* neutral, because the remedy of restitution of conjugal rights was open to both husbands and wives. Theoretical neutrality, however, was not enough for Justice Choudary. He held:

> Bare equality of treatment, regardless of the inequality of realities, is neither justice nor homage to the constitutional principle … the question is how this remedy works in life terms. In our social reality, this matrimonial remedy is found used almost exclusively by the husband and is rarely resorted to by the wife … the reason for this mainly lies in the fact of the differences between the man and the woman. By enforcing a decree for restitution of conjugal rights, the life pattern of the wife is likely to be altered irretrievably whereas the

> husband's can remain almost as it was before … this is so because it is the wife who has to beget and bear a child … As a result, this remedy works in practice only as an engine of oppression to be operated by the husband for the benefit of the husband against the wife.[95]

Consequently, in addition to norms of decisional privacy, Justice Choudary also held the norms of equality to be applicable to the private sphere. Section 9 was held unconstitutional because it worked a relative injustice upon the wife *in the context* of her position within the marriage, and because of the greater disruption that compelled cohabitation would cause to her life than it would cause the husband.[96] The infusion of egalitarian norms into familial relationships was, once again, a repudiation of the relational and spatial conceptions of privacy that mandated that norms of public law were irrelevant to private relationships, or stopped at the threshold of the home. It was a further step towards democratizing the private sphere.[97]

C. **Sareetha** *and the Transformative Constitution*

What, however, was the *constitutional* basis of the judgement in *Sareetha v. Venkatasubbaiah*? In this section, I argue that even as the conception of privacy of community took root, there also flourished in India an oppositional intellectual and political tradition, which actively contested the public/private divide, and sought to introduce norms of liberty and equality into the precincts of the home. And a close reading of the Constitution reveals that it was this 'hidden transcript'[98] that ultimately became the basis of the Fundamental Rights chapter.

Despite some indications to the contrary, the Constitution does not recognize the 'community' (or any other institution, such as the family) as being the primary unit, or even *a* unit, of constitutional concern, or as an entity that can claim rights independent of its constituent individuals. As we have discussed in previous chapters, it does not do so because the framers were aware that, in a country where non-State institutions habitually exercised power akin to sovereign power over individuals,[99] an individual's rights were as much at risk from the private sphere as they were from the State.

For a start, in Section III above, we saw how the colonial state and the nascent nationalist movement mirrored each other in treating laws governing domestic relations, broadly defined as personal laws—deemed to be expressive of the community ethos—as off-limits to State intervention. These personal laws, which covered the family, marriage, succession, and so on, directly concerned the position and the rights of women within the community. As evidenced by public reaction to Justice Pinhey's first instance judgement in *Rukhmabai*, the dominant discourse opposed the application of external, non-community norms into the domestic space. However, this was not the only discourse; as Anupama Roy points out, 'at any given historical moment, the (anticolonial) national movement in this case, there may exist a plurality of discourses on women, which get constituted and reconstituted in an unequal yet dialogic relationship with each other'.[100]

Unsurprisingly, this oppositional discourse is found in the writings of women, in texts that, because of their unconventional form, have traditionally been excluded from the domain of political thought. Directly influenced by works such as Mary Wollstonecraft's *A Vindication of the Rights of Woman* and John Stuart Mill's *The Subjection of Women*,[101] which put forward radical proposals for levelling gender relations within the private sphere,[102], these writers critiqued family relations *in the language* of the public law norms of rights, liberty, equality, and anti-servitude,[103] through letters, memoirs, and epistles. In the writings of Soonderbai Pawar, for instance, we find an express reference to 'the liberty of the subject'[104] in her discussion of women's rights within the family, and a comparison of women's position to 'slavery'.[105]

Similar vocabulary was used by Masuda Rahman, writing in the context of Muslim women in colonial Bengal.[106] Krupabai Satthianadhan specifically called for 'giving [women] their own rights, not only in the family, but also in the society'.[107] In his defence of Tarabai Shinde's *Stree Purush Tulna* against a hostile reception from traditionalist thinkers, the prominent social reformer Jyotirao Phule framed his arguments in terms of an 'equalitarian husband-wife relationship ... [and] the breakdown of the old authority structures within the family'.[108] And in a hugely influential, very controversial, and fiercely contested text called *The High Caste Hindu Woman*, Pandita Ramabai critiqued the marital union, which required the subsumption of the wife's personality into the personality of the husband[109] (a proto-critique of a legal regime that strongly resembled coverture).[110] The most focused response to the sanctity of personal laws as expressions of filial privacy, however, came from Rukhmabai herself, soon after Justice Pinhey's judgement, when the *Rukhmabai v. Dadaji* controversy was raging with particular intensity. In two anonymous letters to the *Times of India*, Rukhmabai advanced arguments that bore striking similarities to Justice Choudary's excavation of inequalities within the family:

> ... marriage does not interpose any insuperable obstacle in the course of their [men's] studies. They can marry not only a second wife, on the death of the first, but have the right of marrying any number of wives at one and the same time, or any time they please. If married early they are not called upon to go to the house and submit to the tender mercies of a mother-in-law; nor is any restraint put upon their action because of their marriage.[111]

The social reformer Behramji Malabari described Rukhmabai's achievement as her rejection of the idea that a woman had a 'duty to be everything to everybody—to father, brother and husband ...'[112] Here, I suggest that what was crucial about Rukhmabai's opposition was not merely its *content*, but also its *framing*. Rukhmabai did not possess the specific vocabulary of rights that would find its culmination in the Indian Constitution, sixty-five years later. However, her articulation of the status of women under personal laws and within the family anticipated core ideas of liberty (restraint upon action) and equality (the different character of the obstacles faced by men and women in marriage), which would be at the heart of the nationalist movement for *political* independence from colonial rule. A few years before the nationalist movement articulated these demands in the public sphere, Rukhmabai had framed them in the private sphere. More importantly, this framing took place *in the context* of an ongoing litigation. This suggests that her attempt to infuse public norms into domestic life was not simply a call for internal reform, but an invitation to the *State* to intervene and protect women's rights *against* their husbands and *within* the family.[113]

I do not suggest, of course, that these arguments achieved mainstream consensus, or even popularity. More often than not, the authors of these texts were ignored, marginalized, ridiculed, or fiercely opposed,[114] although, notably, opposition was also framed in the language of rights, suggesting at least a common terrain of contestation.[115] The nationalist movement very consciously relegated the entire issue to the background, as a question that communities would have to deal with for themselves. This was also clear from the passage of the 1937 Muslim Personal Law (Shariat) Application Act, which sought to codify the application of *sharia* law to all Indian Muslims. What I do want to suggest, however, is that there *existed* a vocabulary of rights that transcended the public/private divide, and articulated a powerful vision of substantive equality, decisional freedom, and choice within ostensibly timeless and sacrosanct institutions such as marriage and the family. And I want to further suggest that the text and structure of the Indian Constitution makes sense only within the framework of this second, often marginalized vision of privacy within the private sphere.

Despite the existence of provisions such as Articles 26 (rights of religious denominations), 29 (right of any 'section' of citizens to preserve language, script, and culture) and 30 (rights of 'minorities' to education), which make specific mention of groups, the Fundamental Rights chapter, as a whole, clearly departs from according special sanctity to group autonomy. Previously in this book, we have discussed this in the context of religious groups as a whole, and I have argued that the Constitution is committed to the 'anti-exclusion principle': groups are accorded autonomy to the extent, and only to the extent, that their collective actions do not block individuals' access to those essential goods that are required to live a life of dignity. I want to suggest that the same logic applies, by extension, to the family, because the family is another non-State body that exercises coercive power over individuals (especially women), in a manner that is very similar to the power exercised by religious communities over their adherents. Parallels include an absence of choice when it comes to membership, no feasible exit option, and an overarching level of control.

That the family (or the marital institution) bears no normative priority under the constitutional scheme is buttressed by the fact that other constitutions that have wished to protect the family have done so in express terms. One such is the 1937 Constitution of Ireland, from which the framers of the Indian Constitution borrowed heavily. Article 41(1) of the Irish Constitution states:

> The State recognises the Family as the natural primary and fundamental unit group of Society, and as a moral institution possessing inalienable and imprescriptible rights, antecedent and superior to all positive law.[116]

The Indian Constitution contains nothing of the sort, suggesting the framers' reluctance to borrow the concept of the family—which, we may recall, is the terrain on which personal laws exist—as a rights-bearing entity. This is, of course, a negative argument, showing only that the Constitution does not indicate the superiority of the familial institution or the marital union on the question of rights. The *positive* argument defending *Sareetha*—that, actually, the right to individual decisional privacy should *prevail* over privacy arguments that take the family or the house as their bases—remains to be made. It can be made, I suggest, by examining the constitutional provisions from which the dissenting opinion of Justice Subba Rao in *Kharak Singh* and the judgement of the Supreme Court in *Gobind* drew out an implied right to privacy.

At issue in *Kharak Singh* was the constitutional validity of a police regulation that authorized extensive surveillance of history-sheeters (persons with a prior criminal record). These included secret picketing of the suspect's house, domiciliary visits at night, enquiries and reporting about his habits and movements, and the compilation of a comprehensive dossier relating to all of the above. The petitioner argued that this menu of police action violated his fundamental rights under Article 19(1)(a) (the freedom of speech and expression), Article 19(1)(d) (the freedom of movement), and Article 21 (right to life and personal liberty).

Justice Subba Rao (dissenting) agreed. Beginning with Article 21, he argued that the expression 'personal liberty' 'extended to the full range of conduct which the individual was free to pursue'.[117] He then made a very Brandeisian argument: that, in the modern age, 'conduct' was not limited to physical conduct, and personal liberty was not restricted to liberty of the physical body:

> … as civilization advances the psychological restraints are more effective than physical ones. The scientific methods used to condition a man's mind are in a real sense physical restraints, for they engender physical fear channelling one's actions through anticipated and expected groves.[118]

Writing in 1962, Justice Subba Rao had anticipated an argument that would be developed and invoked decades later, in other jurisdictions:[119] that the guarantee of personal liberty included a guarantee against *forced conformism* of thought and action, a conformism that could be psychologically compelled by constant, relentless State surveillance of an individual's private life. This was the connection between Article 21's right to personal liberty, and a right to privacy.

Justice Subba Rao then went on to argue that 'the right of personal liberty ... [is] a right of an individual to be free from restrictions or encroachments on his person, whether those restrictions ... are directly imposed or indirectly brought about by calculated measures'.[120] The very concept of 'indirect restrictions' imagines a right that has broken free of spatial boundaries. This was clarified further in his examination of Article 19(1)(d), where he noted, 'If a man is shadowed, his movements are obviously constricted. He can move physically, but it can only be a movement of an automaton.'[121] And even if, for the purposes of argument, Article 19(1)(d) *only* protected physical movement, that article read with Article 19(1)(a) (freedom of speech and expression) encompassed a broader liberty of conduct in a 'free country', where a man 'can do whatever he likes, speak to whomsoever he wants, meet people of his own choice without any apprehension, subject of course to the law of social control. The petitioner under the shadow of surveillance is certainly deprived of this freedom.'[122] Life under the shadow of surveillance was like a prisoner speaking to his wife, son, or friend in the presence of a jailor, in an atmosphere in which 'it is impossible for him to express his real and intimate thoughts to the visitor as fully as he would like'.[123]

It was this understanding of privacy—an implicit right flowing from the rights to freedom of expression, freedom of movement, and personal liberty—that was conditionally accepted by the Supreme Court in *Gobind*, with the Court noting that the right would have to be developed on a case-to-case basis.[124] And it was this understanding that was unconditionally accepted by a nine-judge bench of the Supreme Court in 2017. While declaring that the Indian Constitution guaranteed a fundamental right to privacy, the Supreme Court in *K.S. Puttaswamy v. Union of India* not only resurrected Justice Subba Rao's dissenting opinion in *Kharak Singh*, but also affirmed the argument advanced above, in its operative order:

> The right to privacy is protected as an intrinsic part of the right to life and personal liberty under Article 21 and as a part of the freedoms guaranteed by Part III of the Constitution.[125]

A combination of Justice Subba Rao's dissent in *Kharak Singh*, the majority opinion in *Gobind*, and the judgement of the Court in *Puttaswamy* demonstrates that the foundation of the right to privacy under the Indian Constitution—whatever its ultimate framing and substantive content—lies in a combined reading of Articles 19(1)(a), (d), and Article 21. And here is the crucial point: each of these rights protects aspects of decisional autonomy, viz., to speak with freedom, to move with freedom, and to be free of direct and indirect constraints upon personal conduct. Justice Subba Rao's insight in *Kharak Singh* was that none of these three rights could be *effectively* enforced unless there was an accompanying underlying right to privacy. The guarantee of privacy, thus, was a necessary constitutional implication, flowing from the guarantees of speech, movement, and personal liberty.

This derivation of the right to privacy under the Constitution demonstrates why *Sareetha*'s reading of *Gobind*'s ambiguous formulation was the correct reading. In other constitutions, the right to privacy was derived from provisions that explicitly indicated, or suggested, a spatial or institutional vision. This included the US Constitution's Fourth Amendment, which protected 'the right of the people to be secure in their persons, houses, papers, and effects',[126] or the Irish Constitution, which acknowledged the 'family' as a basic unit of society.[127] As we have seen, formulations of this kind were consistent with different understandings of privacy, viz., the home as space, the home as an institution, or the home as a place where private decisions are typically made. For this reason, the jurisprudence of these jurisdictions has veered between these different understandings of privacy, moulded according to the nature of the case before the Court.

Under the Indian Constitution, however, there is no such ambiguity. As we have seen, a provision akin to the US Fourth Amendment was rejected during the Constituent Assembly Debates.[128] However, contrary to what the Supreme Court suggested in *M.P. Sharma*, this did not mean that the very concept of privacy was rejected in the Constitution. What *was* rejected was a specific formulation, which the US Constitution drew from common law, targeted against the State tyranny of carrying out general warrants and searches against political opponents, and was, therefore, focused on the physical space of the home, and what it contained, viz., 'effects' and 'papers'.[129] The judgements in *Puttaswamy* recognized this, with more than one opinion acknowledging that the record of the Constituent Assembly *only* demonstrated that the framers did not wish to import that specific logic of the US Fourth Amendment into the Constitution. But the concept of privacy was not simply reducible to the prohibition of arbitrary searches and seizures, which was what the Fourth Amendment was limited to.[130]

Meanwhile, however, the presence of Articles 19(1)(a), (d) and 21 suggested an alternative view of privacy, freed from the constraints of spaces and institutions. Located within the contours of decisional autonomy, it was this view that *Sareetha* articulated via *Gobind*, and *Puttaswamy* affirmed three decades later.

Now, it may be objected that Articles 19(1)(a), (d), and 21 are directed against the State. And both *Kharak Singh* and *Gobind* were cases of State surveillance, not oppressive power relations within the family. In that sense, these cases remained solidly within the conventional public sphere, instead of dealing with private relations.

It is here that we must introduce another idea: categories of public and private do not come to us as a timeless, changeless, pre-existing binary. Rather, the binary is actively constructed *by* the State, *through* its laws, regulations, practices, and omissions. Section 9 of the Hindu Marriage Act is an excellent example of this: it is a State-made *law* that constructs the marital union as an entity within which constitutional norms of equality and decisional privacy do not apply.

The challenge in *Sareetha*, therefore, was not a challenge against the private conduct of Sareetha's husband. Rather, it was a challenge against a *law* that denied Sareetha the possibility of exercising her constitutional rights *by* constructing a private domain within which these rights were not applicable. And in striking down the law, Justice Choudary denied the State permission to do exactly that: to divide up the world into public and private domains in this facile manner, and to restrict the application of rights within the latter domain. What I have tried to argue is that there is no constitutional sanction for such action. Rather, the very logic of decisional privacy, as opposed to its spatial and institutional versions, militates against the construction of the public/private divide.

This, then, was the connecting thread between the dissident intellectual tradition of the late-nineteenth century, the constitutional text, and the judgement in *Sareetha*. Together, they advanced a transformative vision of constitutional justice that was based on democratizing what was traditionally thought of as the private sphere by introducing norms of equality and decisional privacy within the home, the family, and the community, and by holding the State to account for failing to respect this.

V. *Sareetha*: The Aftermath

A few months after Justice Choudary's decision in *Sareetha*, the High Court of Delhi decided the case of *Harvinder Kaur v. Harmander Singh Choudhry*,[131] which also involved a challenge to the constitutionality of Section 9. Disagreeing with Justice Choudary, Justice A.B. Rohatgi of the Delhi High Court observed that the purpose of the decree for restitution of conjugal rights was not to compel sex, but to bring about *cohabitation*, which meant 'living together as husband and wife'.[132] A Court did not, he held, have 'the means … [or] the capacity to enforce its decree in the marriage bed'.[133] Section 9 was constitutional, because 'a spouse is entitled to the other's society and if the law enforces this conjugal duty there is nothing wrong'.[134]

At the heart of the disagreement between Justices Choudary and Rohatgi, therefore, was the question of what exactly a decree of cohabitation implied. While Justice Choudary factored into his judgement the imbalanced and gendered power relationships that existed within the family, Justice Rohatgi refused to do so. And the reason for this becomes clear in the shape of a 'general observation' which he made after upholding the Section:

> Introduction of constitutional law in the home is most inappropriate. It is like introducing a bull in a china shop. It will prove to be a ruthless destroyer of the marriage institution and all that it stands for. In the privacy of the home and the married life, neither Article 21 nor Article 14 have any place. In a sensitive sphere which is at once most intimate and delicate, the introduction of the cold principles of constitutional law will have the effect of weakening the marriage bond.[135]

Here, we have the spatial and institutional visions of privacy, expressed to the full. And more than that, we have a direct repudiation of Justice Choudary's project of democratizing the conventional private sphere. Referring to both the home and to the marriage institution, Justice Rohatgi made it clear that constitutional norms could not be applied to the relationships that existed within these 'sensitive spheres'. Effectively, he treated the private sphere as sovereign unto itself, noting that 'constitutional principles find no place in the domestic code'.[136] That he considered the basic unit of privacy to be the marital *union*, and not the individuals within it, was then made clear by his observation that 'the spouses can claim a kind of sacred protection behind the door of the family home'.[137] What the spouses did to each other behind that door was not, apparently, the law's concern.

The year after this, the Supreme Court was called upon to resolve the disagreement between the Delhi and the Andhra Pradesh High Courts. It sided with the Delhi High Court, and held that Section 9 was constitutional. The Supreme Court held that 'conjugal rights, i.e., the right of the husband or the wife to the society of the other spouse is not merely creature of the statute. Such a right is inherent in the very institution of marriage itself'.[138] And Section 9, by enforcing this right, served 'a social purpose as an aid to the prevention of break-up of marriage'.[139]

While the Supreme Court's reasoning was not as categorical as the Delhi High Court's, its reference to a right 'inherent ... in the very institution of marriage itself' was a continuation of the same reasoning: that the rights-bearer was not the individual, but the institution. And the extent to which individuals had rights (in this case, the 'right' of the husband or the wife to each other's company) was exercised because of, and through, their membership of the institution.

Sareetha, thus, was overruled. And, along with that, its transformative critique of the public/private divide, its focus on power structures and imbalances within the family, and, most of all, its incipient attempt to democratize the conventional private sphere and subject it to public law and constitutional norms also passed into history. There it awaits a long-overdue resurrection.

But it is a resurrection that, after three decades, suddenly appears possible. Not only does the reasoning of the nine-judge bench of the Supreme Court in *Puttaswamy* stand as a vindication of *Sareetha's* transformative approach, but there are observations in that judgement that pointedly suggest that the time may have come for a rethink. In his concurring opinion, Justice Chelameswar observed that the relationship between privacy, State intrusion, and personal association 'is still a doubtful area'.[140] He followed this up with a footnote noting that 'the High Court of AP held that Article 19(1)(c) would take within its sweep the matrimonial association in T. Sareetha Vs. T. Venkata Subbaiah, AIR 1983 AP 356'. However, this case was later overruled by this Court ...'[141]

Overruled but, as Justice Chelameswar himself took pains to point out, now it is a doubtful area. And how would that doubt be resolved after *Puttaswamy*? The plurality opinion, authored by Justice Chandrachud, offered a resounding answer. After acknowledging, for the first time in judicial history, the feminist critique of privacy that has been at the heart of this chapter, Justice Chandrachud stated that 'the challenge … is to enable the state to take the violation of the dignity of women in the domestic sphere seriously while … protecting the privacy entitlements of women grounded in the identity of gender and liberty'.[142]

It would be difficult to imagine a clearer or more emphatic endorsement of Justice Choudary's transformative vision of the Constitution.

VI. Conclusion: The Implications of *Sareetha*'s Transformative Vision

Sareetha was a controversial decision. Critics pointed out that, over the years, Section 9 had been watered down so much that it was virtually toothless.[143] It could not be enforced by jailing the defendant, and even attachment of property was rare. At best, non-compliance with a decree for restitution of conjugal rights for a period of one year could itself become grounds for divorce under the Hindu Marriage Act, but nothing more.[144] So, far from compelling sexual intercourse, it didn't even effectively compel cohabitation. Other critics have taken issue with Justice Choudary's assumption that the remedy was biased against women, pointing out that it is often deserted wives who use Section 9 for legal redress[145] (both these points were discussed, to varying degrees, in the Delhi High Court's judgement).

There is merit in these criticisms, and it is certainly open to question whether, even if it had stood, *Sareetha* would have had any significant impact upon the rights of women in the family. However, what was ultimately crucial about *Sareetha* was not so much its outcome, but its reasoning and the implications that the reasoning, if applied consistently, would have for other areas of law. For example, through a specific exception under the Indian Penal Code, non-consensual sexual intercourse between a man and his wife is not 'rape'. The 'marital rape exception', as is well known, bases itself in the old common-law belief that marriage entails a one-time, permanent, and irrevocable consent to sex,[146] as well as the common-law legal regime of coverture, where the legal personality of the wife was subsumed within that of her husband, and who, therefore, *conceptually*, could not rape her.[147]

Those defences cannot now be invoked. What can, and has been, invoked, however, is the concept of marital privacy,[148] and the need to keep the family together while keeping the State out of the bedroom. These are defences grounded in the institutional and spatial conceptions of privacy. Under *Sareetha*'s two-pronged reasoning—where, first, decisional privacy was given normative priority over spatial and institutional privacy, and, second, the reality of unequal power structures within the family was taken into account when determining the constitutionality of a law—it is clear that the marital rape exception can no longer stand.[149]

Along with the marital rape exception, an entire branch of law would also not be able to stand. In 1952, the High Court of Bombay held that uncodified personal laws were not subject to the Constitution. In *State of Bombay v. Narasu Appa Mali*, the Court held that 'personal laws' did not constitute 'law' under Article 13 of the Constitution and for the purposes of the Fundamental Rights chapter.[150] This was because, among other things, they were derived from scripture, and not the result of any conscious act of legislation.

However, as Justice A.M. Bhattacharjee points out in his critique of the judgement,[151] what the Court failed to note is that whatever the source of personal laws, the State was deeply implicated in their existence by *actively enforcing them*[152] (indeed, the authority that personal laws enjoyed in colonial India stemmed from conscious State action, such as the Regulations of 1772 and 1793).[153] This, of course, was precisely the point made in *Sareetha*: the private sphere does not exist autonomously, but is defined and constructed by the State through its laws and practices.[154]

Furthermore, as a piece of history, the Court's analysis was entirely inaccurate. What had come to be known as personal law by 1952 was a motley blend of scripture and custom, sieved through a century and a half of colonial legal interpretation and even, at times, invention.[155] More importantly, however, the decision in *Narasu Appa Mali* replicated the colonial logic of treating the community, as expressed through its personal law, as the autonomous site, or unit, of privacy (with the exception that the State could now, under the Constitution, *legislate* on personal law with a view to social reform), regardless of the rights that it extended or denied to its members.

In denying the community or, for that matter, any institution normative priority over individuals when it came to the *fundamental individual right to privacy*, *Sareetha* fatally undermined the logic that underlay *Narasu Appa Mali*. The result, inevitably, would be that personal laws governing the private sphere would be subject to fundamental rights in the same manner that statutes and ordinary legislation are.

Lastly, *Sareetha*'s logic would also impact one of the most crucial, and legally under-examined, issues of the private sphere: that of unpaid housework overwhelmingly performed by women in households,[156] as discussed in the last chapter. As Don Slater points out, the public/private divide arose, at least in part, as a gendered division in the kinds of productive processes: '… the public world of work, production, and enterprise on the one hand, and the private world of domestic life and reproduction on the other'.[157] While the labour movement has been somewhat successful in introducing public law norms into the relationship of employment, the household and the productive processes within the household remain off-limits, under a continuing spatial/institutional vision of privacy. Therefore, 'the rules governing the sexual division of labour in the family have been placed beyond the scope of justice'.[158]

It was this vision that, as we saw, *Sareetha* undermined, by introducing the 'cold principles' of constitutional law into the home. In the previous chapter, we examined how the constitutionalization of remuneration for housework flows from *PUDR*'s transformative reading of the Constitution. *Sareetha* shows us how, at an even deeper level, the Constitution is committed to this manner of transformation.[159]

8

Speech, Association, Personal Liberty, and the State of Exception: *Jyoti Chorge v. State of Maharashtra*

Freedom of opinion and freedom of association ... [are] the two lungs that are absolutely necessary for a man to breathe the oxygen of liberty.

M.K. Gandhi, speech at the 36th Congress Session (1921)

I do not think that it was ever intended that Parliament could, at its will, treat the normal as the abnormal or the rule as the exception.

Justice Fazl Ali (dissenting), *A.K. Gopalan v. State of Madras*

ON 24 MARCH 2015, in *Shreya Singhal v. Union of India*,[1] the Supreme Court struck down Section 66A of the Information Technology Act. This provision, which criminalized 'grossly offensive', 'annoying', and 'inconvenient' online speech, had been regularly used to target political opposition. In a soaring judgement that dwelt upon the foundational importance of free speech in a pluralist democracy, Justice Rohinton Nariman marshalled half a century of legal precedent to hold that the Constitution's free speech guarantee allowed advocacy of repugnant or even revolutionary views, and only permitted the State to penalize speech that constituted 'incitement to violence'.

The Unlawful Activities Prevention Act (UAPA) is India's umbrella anti-terrorism legislation. Section 2(o)(ii) of the UAPA defines an 'unlawful activity' to include anything that 'disclaims, questions, disrupts or is intended to disrupt the sovereignty and territorial integrity of India'.[2] Associations with 'unlawful activity' as their object can be banned by the government,[3] and members of these associations imprisoned for up to two years.[4] There are parallel and more stringent punishments associated with membership of 'terrorist gangs'.[5]

How could the jurisprudence of the Supreme Court in *Shreya Singhal* coexist with a law that criminalizes 'questioning ... the sovereignty of India', and punishes a concept as fluid as 'membership'? In *Jyoti Chorge v. State of Maharashtra*,[6] the Bombay High Court held that it could not. Dealing with the bail applications of a group of individuals accused of being members of the banned Communist Party of India (Maoist)—popularly known as Naxals—Justice Abhay Thipsay held that the prosecution's evidence—that the accused had attended meetings, and were found in possession of literature supporting Naxalism—was insufficient to establish even a prima facie case under the UAPA. The concept of 'membership' of unlawful groups and terror gangs did not include passive membership (such as attending meetings, expressing sympathy, and so on), but only active membership, which was limited to incitement to lawless action.

In this manner, Justice Thipsay reconciled the Supreme Court's free speech jurisprudence with the text of India's anti-terror legislation. However, just a few months later, another judge of the Bombay High Court rejected the bail applications of individuals who were part of the very same group.[7] And Justice Thipsay's judgement remains an outlier. Not rejected by the Supreme Court, but not endorsed either, it enjoys a curious life in limbo.

In this chapter, I argue that *Jyoti Chorge v. State of Maharashtra* was a transformative judgement, because it was the clearest and most coherent act of judicial resistance to an almost overwhelming trend in Indian constitutional jurisprudence: the courts' willingness to uphold and endorse laws that severely curtail civil liberties by citing exceptional situations. I begin by outlining the gradual evolution of the Supreme Court's jurisprudence on the freedom of speech and association, which is meant to apply to times of normalcy (I); the Court's pro-liberty standards, however, have never been applied to two legal regimes that are specified under the Constitution: preventive detention under Article 22 (II), and the state of 'Emergency' (III).

In the context of the relationship between individual rights and State power, both these situations have seen the Court invert its normal legal and constitutional standards. However, while preventive detention and Emergencies are defined within the Constitution itself, over time, the Court has allowed its approach to these exceptional situations to become a norm, especially in the context of 'anti-terror' laws. Effectively, in assessing such laws, the Court has replicated its state of exception jurisprudence, and endorsed the creation of 'a permanent state of emergency'.[8]

In this context, I argue (V) that Justice Thipsay's judgement in *Jyoti Chorge* repudiated every element of this 'permanent state of exception jurisprudence'. Furthermore, this approach was the correct one: the framing of the Constitution marked a decisive break from the colonial culture of authority to a rule-bound regime, where exceptions were to be strictly and narrowly defined (VI). I conclude by examining the impact of Justice Thipsay's approach upon other restrictive legal regimes that continue to exist in various states, and how we might examine their constitutionality afresh (VII).

I. States of Normalcy: Freedom of Speech and Association under the Constitution

Article 19(1)(a) of the Constitution guarantees the freedom of speech and expression.[9] Article 19(2) permits the State to impose 'reasonable restrictions', 'in the interests of' eight specified grounds. Three of these grounds, viz., the sovereignty and integrity of India, the security of the State, and public order, suggest that the regulation of subversive or revolutionary speech is an important constitutional concern.[10] Of course, Article 19(2) does not interpret itself: the question of what constitutes a reasonable restriction in the interests of public order (for example) has to be decided by the courts.[11]

In interpreting reasonableness, the Court began its journey by adopting a highly deferential approach towards the State. It upheld a colonial blasphemy law (S. 295A of the IPC) as well as a colonial-inspired press censorship law, holding that the State's assessment of the dangers of subversive speech must be trusted. In 1960, however, this began to change. In striking down a law that criminalized advocating for tax evasion, the Court began to hold that the State must establish a relationship of 'proximity' between the speech that it wished to control or censor, and the public disorder that it feared. While the Court backslid a mere two years later in upholding the hated colonial law of sedition, its jurisprudence since then has been largely progressive. In 1989, it held that the connection between speech and public disorder must be as proximate as that of a 'spark in a powder keg'. And this finally culminated in *Shreya Singhal v. Union of India*, where the requirement of proximity and imminence was recast in the language of advocacy and incitement.

The history of the Court's free speech jurisprudence and, by extension, its jurisprudence on the freedom of association and assembly is thus an arc that gradually bends towards greater freedom. After *Shreya Singhal*, not only is incitement to imminent lawless action the only situation in which speech is punishable, but the burden of *proving* that there exists such a situation is placed upon the State, and is always subject to judicial scrutiny.[12] However, as the succeeding sections show, when it comes to 'exceptional situations', the Court has honoured its own civil rights jurisprudence far more in breach than in observance.

II. States of Exception—A: Preventive Detention

On 8 June 2017, in the aftermath of caste violence in the district of Saharanpur, the Government of Uttar Pradesh arrested Chandrashekhar Azad, a rising Dalit leader, on charges of rioting, attempt to murder, and looting. Azad was granted bail in November of that year, with the judge observing that the charges appeared to be 'politically motivated'. Even before he could walk free, however, the government issued an order of preventive detention against him under the 1980 National Security Act, on the basis that his release 'could' threaten public order and security.[13] Azad spent more than a year in jail without bail or trial before being released.

Azad's detention was not unique. In 1982, Professor Upendra Baxi wrote that the Indian legal system was constituted by two parallel regimes: while the criminal justice system (CJS) was characterized by elements of due process, personal rights, and rigorous judicial review of State power, these features were absent in a parallel 'preventive detention system' (PDS). According to Baxi, the PDS was an institution 'authorized by the Constitution itself'.[14] By this, Baxi presumably meant Article 22, which mandates that every arrested person be produced before a judicial authority within twenty-four hours, but, at the same time, allows Parliament to override this safeguard through legislation.[15] Further safeguards—in the form of periodic review of detention by an Advisory Board[16]—can also be overridden by Parliament.[17]

Of course, the preventive detention regime is not self-interpreting. Its 'parallel' operation, therefore, flows not so much from the constitutional text, as it does from the jurisprudence of the Supreme Court. This jurisprudence is marked by two glaring features: first, the Court has *insulated* the preventive detention regime from the rest of the Fundamental Rights chapter; and *then*, within the now self-contained regime of preventive detention, it has upheld executive supremacy and judicial deference.

The insulation of the preventive detention regime began in 1950 with *A.K. Gopalan v. State of Madras.*[18] *Gopalan* challenged the first (of many) preventive detention laws passed by the newly independent republic, and saw the first (of many) judicial verdicts in favour of the State.

In *Gopalan*, the Supreme Court rejected a constitutional challenge to the Preventive Detention Act of 1950. The case saw six separate opinions written by the six Justices on the bench (one of whom, Fazl Ali, dissented), and its exact ratio has always been controversial. It is *broadly* accepted, however, that *Gopalan* advanced the 'silos theory'[19] of fundamental rights: that is, separate fundamental rights (such as Articles 14, 19, 21, etc.) were to be read separately. An individual detained under a preventive detention law, authorized by Article 22, could not argue that because his detention violated his freedom of speech, it should *also* be tested under Article 19(1)(a) of the Constitution. If the preventive detention law fulfilled the procedural requirements of Article 22, it was constitutionally valid.

The silos theory was famously overruled in *R.C. Cooper v. Union of India*,[20] which held that fundamental rights formed an integrated whole and had to be read together. Now, had this approach been followed faithfully, a preventive detention law—which, undoubtedly, violated a detainee's right to freedom of speech and expression—would have had to be tested on the proximity requirement of Article 19(2). In other words, the *mere* fulfilment of the safeguards under Article 22 (the constitution of the advisory board or the legislative overruling of it) would no longer be enough to sustain the constitutional validity of a preventive detention law. However, somebody forgot to inform the Supreme Court.

In *Haradhan Saha v. State of West Bengal*,[21] the Court somehow managed to hold, 'even if Article 19 be examined in regard to preventive detention, it does not increase the content of reasonableness required to be observed in respect of orders of preventive detention'.[22] This reasoning, however, is deeply flawed. Article 22 merely lays down some procedural formalities that preventive detention has to comply with (such as the existence of parliamentary legislation), and it has nothing to say about *substantive* reasonableness. So, despite *R.C. Cooper*, and despite the fact that the Supreme Court would go on to hand down a host of judgements over the years in which it 'read together' Articles 14, 19 and 21,[23] in the very domain of law that originally gave rise to the silos theory, i.e., preventive detention, the Court continued to pretend that Article 22 existed in splendid isolation.[24]

The effect of this was simple and devastating. A number of provisions that simply wouldn't have withstood scrutiny had the Court applied its evolving civil rights jurisprudence (that would eventually culminate in *Shreya Singhal*) were upheld *simply* because they were part of a preventive detention law. So, for example, in *State of Punjab v. Sukhpal Singh*,[25] while interpreting preventive detention under the anti-terror Terrorist and Disruptive Activities (Prevention) Act (TADA), the Court held that:

> The power of preventive detention is precautionary power exercised reasonably in anticipation and may or may not relate to an offence … the anticipated behaviour of a person based on his past conduct in the light of surrounding circumstances may provide sufficient ground for detention.[26]

Readers will notice the striking similarity of the judgement with the Supreme Court's early free speech jurisprudence. For example, in *Virendra v. State of Punjab*, pre-censorship of a magazine had been justified on the grounds that a language agitation in Punjab 'might at any time' take a violent turn. Similarly, here the 'anticipated behaviour' of an individual, though based on 'adequate materials', was held to be sufficient justification for preventive detention.[27] And like *Virendra*, *Sukhpal Singh* decided that this judgement was best left to the executive, because 'those who are responsible for the national security or for the maintenance of public order must be the judges of what the national security or public order requires'.[28] Both cases, therefore, justified the infringement of civil liberties for *preventive reasons*, without any substantive check on how these reasons were invoked by the State. The only distinction is that while this position was entirely reversed by *Ram Manohar Lohia* in the domain of free speech and civil liberties, it continued to hold the field in the domain of preventive detention.

This exceptional character of the preventive detention regime was highlighted even more starkly in *A.K. Roy*, where the constitutionality of Indira Gandhi's National Security Act (the law under which Chandrashekar Azad was detained) was challenged. In *A.K. Roy*, the Court held adequate a chain of authority and accountability that *solely* involved executive action (the commissioner of police as the detaining authority, subject to review powers by the central government).[29] Furthermore, the *trigger* for the government exercising its powers of preventive detention was its subjective satisfaction that a person needed to be prevented from 'acting in any manner prejudicial to the defence of India, the relations of India with foreign powers, or the security of India'.[30] Notably, the latter two categories simply replicated two of the sub-clauses of Article 19(2), and it was argued in *A.K. Roy* that their very elasticity and vagueness effectively vested unbridled power in the hands of the executive. The Court's answer to this, in effect, was, 'that's too bad':

> ... there are expressions which inherently comprehend such an infinite variety of situations that definitions, instead of lending them a definite meaning, can only succeed either in robbing them of their intended amplitude ... if it is permissible to the legislature to enact laws of preventive detention, a certain amount of minimal latitude has to be conceded to it in order to make those laws effective. That we consider to be a realistic approach to the situation ... though an expression may appear in cold print to be vague and uncertain, it may not be difficult to apply it to life's practical realities.[31]

There are two remarkable features about this passage. The first is that the Court ran together three very different concepts: one, that an expression, by its very nature, had infinitely wide amplitude; two, that the legislature was being given 'minimal' latitude; and three, that the legislature was acting 'realistically'. In running them together, the Court effectively stated the realistic approach simply was to allow the legislature minimal latitude by permitting the use of words with an infinite amplitude. However, if *infinite amplitude* was both *minimal* and *realistic*, then it is difficult to see *what*, if anything, would violate either of those two conditions, and when, if ever, a law could be held unconstitutional (in other words, judicial scrutiny became essentially meaningless).

And secondly, while accepting that the words 'in print' *may appear* vague and uncertain, the Court held that they *may not* prove difficult in application (by the executive). This was a striking reversal of the doctrine of vagueness as applied to ordinary statutes. A few decades later in *Shreya Singhal*, as the Court would explain, vague statutes were unconstitutional precisely because they allowed the executive too great a discretion to infringe upon people's rights. In *A.K. Roy*, however, the Court held that a vague statute was *constitutional* because, presumably, the executive would apply it in a straightforward and predictable way. Almost four decades of the NSA's operation, culminating in the detention of Chandrashekhar Azad, show that, not for the first or the last time, the Court's faith in allowing vast discretionary powers to be vested in the executive was misplaced.

This Janus-faced approach of the Court—rhetorically repudiating the silos theory, while continuing to quietly apply it, and effectively insulating Article 22 from the rest of the Fundamental Rights chapter—continues till date, and was evident as recently as 2012. In *Dropti Devi v. Union of India*,[32] the Supreme Court upheld the constitutional validity of the Conservation of Foreign Exchange and Prevention of Smuggling Activities Act (COFEPOSA), whose stated justification for authorizing preventive detention was 'the conservation and augmentation of foreign exchange and prevention of smuggling activities'.[33]

After reciting the now-familiar development of law that made preventive detention laws subject to Articles 14, 19, and 21, the Court's legal analysis of whether the requirements of these Articles were satisfied occupied precisely zero paragraphs. After noting, 'the menace of smuggling and foreign exchange violations has to be curbed',[34] the Court simply stated, like an incantation, that 'on the touchstone of constitutional jurisprudence, as reflected by Article 22 read with Articles 14, 19 and 21, we do not think that the impugned provision is rendered unconstitutional'.[35]

Why? The Court did not—or could not—answer.

We are now in a position to understand Baxi's insight, with which we began this section: that the preventive detention regime exists parallel to the criminal justice regime. This has happened through a two-step process: first, the preventive detention regime has been effectively *insulated* from the rest of the Fundamental Rights chapter, by allowing the ghost of *Gopalan* to live on within the shadow of Article 22. And then, the foundational principles that govern the interpretation of other fundamental rights have been inverted under the preventive detention regime. At the heart of this inversion is the fact that the enabling legislation establishes a regime of *executive supremacy*. As the Nazi legal theorist Carl Schmitt famously wrote, 'Sovereign is he who decides the state of exception.'[36] The preventive detention regime is our first indigenous, judicially sanctioned state of exception.

III. States of Exception—B: Emergency

The Indian Constitution also enshrines a more familiar state of exception. The President is authorized to declare a state of Emergency if she is satisfied that 'the security of India or of any part of the territory thereof is threatened, whether by war or external aggression or armed rebellion'.[37] During an Emergency, Article 19 of the Constitution stands suspended, and the President is also authorized to pass an order effectively suspending other fundamental rights (except Articles 20 and 21).[38] The Emergency regime, which mirrors, in large part, the regime imposed by the British in colonial India,[39] therefore, constitutes what Giorgio Agamben calls 'a suspension of the juridical order'.[40]

Between 1962 and 1975, India was governed under multiple, successive emergency regimes, precipitated by the 1962 war with China, and the 1965 and 1971 wars with Pakistan. This culminated in the last, and most infamous, Emergency, imposed by Prime Minister Indira Gandhi after a series of political setbacks. Indira Gandhi justified the Emergency by arguing that the escalating protests against her rule constituted a grave internal disturbance.[41] It is now widely accepted that the justification was specious, and was advanced only to provide legal cover for the consolidation of political power and the systematic (and often violent) persecution of dissent. The infamy of Gandhi's political conduct, however, was matched by the infamy of the Supreme Court's judicial conduct. In *ADM Jabalpur v. Shivakant Shukla*,[42] the Court held that under the prevailing Emergency regime, the judiciary was barred from reviewing the habeas corpus petitions of the individuals who had been detained by the State. As a result, thousands of political opponents were subjected to unreviewed administrative detention. Many of them were tortured, and some were killed.[43]

ADM Jabalpur was a discredited decision at the moment of its birth. After the end of the Emergency and Indira Gandhi's electoral defeat, the incoming Parliament undid some of its worst effects through the Forty-Fourth Amendment. And after forty years, the Supreme Court held that it had, indeed, been tragically mistaken in 1976.[44]

However, the importance of *ADM Jabalpur* lies in how the four judges in the majority visualized the relationship between the Court and the executive during a state of exception. A close reading of their reasoning reveals that, far from being an outlier, as it is often proclaimed to be, *ADM Jabalpur* marked a *continuity* in the judiciary's approach to the state of exception: a continuity both with the preventive detention regime that we have discussed above, and a continuity with the Court's own emergency powers jurisprudence. This continuity is marked by four features.

A. Executive Supremacy

At the heart of our constitutional order is the requirement that the State *justify* a restriction upon civil rights before a court of law, and that the court *scrutinize* the State's legal arguments as well as the factual foundations upon which those arguments are based, in light of established constitutional standards. The Emergency regime, however, marks a complete inversion of this principle. It is the executive that defines both *when* an Emergency regime may come into existence, and *what* rights citizens may enjoy under that regime.[45] In *ADM Jabalpur*, this position was articulated most lucidly in the concurring opinion of Justice Beg, where he observed:

> Conditions may supervene, in the life of a nation, in which the basic values we have stood for and struggled to attain, the security, integrity, and independence of the country ... may be imperilled by forces operating from within or from outside the country. What these forces are, how they are operating, what information exists for the involvement of various individuals ... could not possibly be disclosed publicly or become matters suitable for inquiry into or discussion in a Court of Law.[46]

A similar logic was at play in the Court upholding Section 16(9A) of the Maintenance of Internal Security Act (MISA), which effectively barred a detainee from being informed of the grounds of his detention. Chief Justice Ray upheld the provision on the basis that the grounds of detention were 'confidential and deemed to refer to matters of State and to be against public interest to disclose',[47] and that 'the provision for periodical review entrusted to the Government under Section 16A(4) of the Act in the context of emergency provides a sufficient safeguard against the misuse of power …'[48] And to the fear that the vesting of unreviewable Roman era-style dictatorial powers with the executive (to be used at a time of its own choosing) was simply creating an architecture of abuse, the Court's response was: 'It simply can't happen.' For example, Justice Chandrachud noted:

> … above all the lofty faith in democracy which ushered the birth of the Nation will, I hope, eliminate all fear that great powers are capable of the greatest abuse.[49]

The regime of executive supremacy under the State of Emergency, therefore, boiled down to this: it was the executive's decision when to trigger an Emergency, what rights to allow citizens to exercise during an Emergency, and to set up a self-referential regime of accountability where the executive would sit in judgement over complaints against abuse of power by the executive. The constitutional concerns about the vesting of such concentrated and unaccountable power were rejected through incantations of good faith and trust in the benevolent motives of the government, and a recitation of the formula that the *possibility* of abuse could not be grounds to strike down a law.

B. Denial of Remedies

The Presidential Order under the State of Emergency barred individuals from approaching courts to enforce their rights under Article 21 of the Constitution, including the right to habeas corpus. It was argued before the Supreme Court that this effectively amounted to effacing Article 21 itself, because a right without a remedy, or a mechanism for enforcing it, was illusory. The Court rejected this argument, noting that the *right* under Article 21 continued to exist; it was simply that, during the period of the Emergency, nobody could move the courts to enforce it.

C. The Jurisdiction of Suspicion

Thirdly, *ADM Jabalpur* endorsed and authorized what Justice Beg referred to as the 'jurisdiction of suspicion':

> [P]reventive detention, in itself, is a departure from ordinary norms … It has been aptly described as a 'jurisdiction of suspicion' … it enables executive authorities to proceed on bare suspicion which has to give rise to a 'satisfaction' …[50]

Notice, however, that the 'satisfaction' involved was nothing more than the *subjective belief* of the executive that a person *might* be a threat in the future. Here again, therefore, we see an inversion of norms. Not only did the jurisdiction of suspicion eschew any requirement of proximity between the perceived threat and an actual instance of lawbreaking, but the executive's own assessment of the nature of the threat, and the factual foundations upon which its suspicion existed, were beyond the purview of judicial scrutiny.

D. Salus populi suprema lex

Such a complete inversion required a powerful justification to legitimize it. The Court found it in the incantation that extraordinary times require extraordinary measures. Justice Beg wrote, 'Even parents have to take appropriate preventive action against those children who may threaten to burn down the house they live in.'[51] Apart from infantilizing citizens as unruly children, this image of the burning house at the cusp of destruction and needing drastic preventive action to be saved animated much of the four judgements.[52] The majority judges drew upon the constitutional traditions regarding Emergency powers in the United Kingdom[53] to hold that the ultimate, overarching value was that of *salus populi suprema lex*, i.e.,'the people's welfare is the supreme law'. Without the conditions of security under which people's welfare could be pursued, the concept of individual rights was meaningless. For this reason, the Court rejected 'a too liberal application of the principle that courts must lean in favour of the liberty of the citizen ...'[54]

It was this combination of precepts—the State's responsibility to preserve the basic framework within which rights remained meaningful, and the State's paternal power to pre-empt and punish in order to do so—that finally drove the majority into perhaps its most notorious holding in *ADM Jabalpur*, i.e., that fundamental rights were a 'gift' to individuals from the State, and that could be taken away by the State, based on its determination of what *salus populi* demanded in a particular situation.[55] And the determination of what constituted the people's welfare was essentially a matter of 'high State policy', circling back to the first proposition of *ADM Jabalpur*: that of unreviewable executive supremacy.

E. Conclusion: ADM Jabalpur and the Culture of Authority

The Supreme Court in *ADM Jabalpur* endorsed a series of interlocking, interpretive propositions. First, that under the constitutional order, there exists a state of normalcy and a state of exception, the paradigmatic example of which is an Emergency. Second, that the executive has the sole prerogative of determining when the state of exception ought to replace the default state of normalcy, and what is to happen with respect to citizens' rights during an Emergency. Third, that the executive is guided by the principle of *salus populi suprema lex*. It is not for the courts to ask either whether the conditions requiring the state of exception to be called really exist or whether the executive's actions actually serve public welfare or not. *Fourth*, that during the state of exception, the executive can suspend rights, suspend remedies, and be the sole arbiter both for the content of the right and for the remedy. And lastly, that the fact that such a power is vested in the executive and is *capable* of abuse is no ground for the power not existing. The executive is always presumed to act in good faith. In sum, *salus populi suprema lex* operated like a blank cheque for State impunity, or, in terms more familiar to constitutional law, like the 'Ninth Schedule' of constitutional interpretation.[56]

These propositions can be subsumed under a single phrase: *ADM Jabalpur* endorsed a 'culture of authority'. It authorized a state of affairs where the political executive could act without giving *reasons* or *justifications* for its actions, either to citizens, or to courts. In such situations, whose initiation and continuation itself was left to the executive, individuals lost their status as rights-bearing citizens, and became—for the duration of the Emergency—colonial-era subjects once again.

IV. States of Exception—C: *Salus populi suprema lex*

The depravity of Indira Gandhi's Emergency, its decisive electoral repudiation, the starkness of the verdict in *ADM Jabalpur*, and some particularly ill-advised remarks by the majority judges have all combined to create a perfect storm, and assign to the case a special and unique place in constitutional hell. According to popular narrative, *ADM Jabalpur* marks the lowest point in the history of the Supreme Court, from whose shadow the Court redeemed itself by developing public interest litigation in the 1980s.[57]

This is a mistake. On a careful reading of the majority opinions in *ADM Jabalpur*, one is immediately struck by the number and range of precedents invoked by the Court. These included judgements both from the UK, and from colonial Indian courts, but they *also* included post-Independence judgements of the Supreme Court. As Kalyani Ramanth correctly points out, *ADM Jabalpur* had its antecedents.[58] For example, in *Makhan Singh v. State of Punjab*,[59] a 1964 judgement involving the Emergency proclamation arising out of the war with China, the Supreme Court had held that the proclamation barred the right to move the courts for *any* remedy, including those under specific statutes such as the Code of Criminal Procedure. In language that was virtually identical to that of *ADM Jabalpur*, the Court observed:

> How long the Proclamation of Emergency should continue and what restrictions should be imposed on the fundamental rights …

> are matters which must inevitably be left to the executive because the executive knows the requirements of the situation and the effect of compulsive factors which operate during periods of grave crisis, such as our country is facing today ... in a democratic State, the effective safeguard against abuse of executive powers whether in peace or in emergency, is ultimately to be found in the existence of enlightened, vigilant, and vocal public opinion.[60]

In this distilled paragraph, the many aspects of *ADM Jabalpur* are present: executive supremacy, the denial of remedies, an unquestioning faith in the executive, the abdication of the courts as the protectors of rights, and in favour of the political process, *when the very rights that are suspended* (such as personal liberty) *constitute the prerequisites of any meaningful political process*.[61]

Examples of similar cases could be multiplied,[62] but it is sufficient to say that before *ADM Jabalpur*, the Supreme Court had a consistent tradition of upholding absolute executive supremacy in the context of Emergency powers. Much more importantly, however, this tradition would continue even after *ADM Jabalpur*, after its repudiation by Parliament through the Forty-Fourth Amendment, and even after public recantation by some of the judges involved.

But it would continue informally: although an Emergency has never been declared after Indira Gandhi's defeat, the *elements* of the Emergency that we have discussed in the previous section have been repeated in a slew of 'anti-terrorism laws', and have been upheld by the Court. In the words of Ujjwal Kumar Singh, what this has done is to create a regime of 'interlocking legal systems',[63] where the state of exception and the state of normalcy become so enmeshed with each other, and what was meant to be a temporary and defined situation (under the Constitution) has been converted into a permanent and undefined one.[64]

To understand this better, let us go back to the four factors that defined the judicial approach in *ADM Jabalpur*, viz., executive supremacy, denial of remedies, the jurisdiction of suspicion, and *salus populi suprema lex* as the overarching principle, and examine what role they have played in the Supreme Court's adjudication in the years after *ADM Jabalpur*.

A. Executive Supremacy

In *Kartar Singh v. State of Punjab*, the constitutional validity of the Terrorist and Disruptive Activities (Prevention) Act (TADA) was challenged. TADA, a temporary law that was originally enacted to contain insurgency in Punjab, was eventually extended to all of India. To strengthen the hand of law-enforcement agencies, TADA made a number of departures from accepted principles of criminal procedure, such as allowing confessions made to police officers, authorizing detention for up to one year during the pendency of the investigation, and so on. The petitioners argued that these 'extraordinary provisions' violated the rights of the accused under Articles 14, 19, and 21 of the Constitution.

In *Kartar Singh*, the Supreme Court began by painting a picture of India as a nation at war, observing that many cities had been engulfed with 'blood bath, firing, looting, mad killing ... and reducing those areas into a graveyard'.[65] After spending around ten paragraphs in this vein, the Court set the stage for the constitutional analysis that was to follow, noting, 'to redress all the multiple dimensions of crimes ... is ... of course a very difficult task because the crimes and the criminals do not respect frontiers and the field of operation of the activities of the criminals know no territorial limits'.[66] However, the question of whether terrorism required *special laws* that loosened procedural safeguards, or whether it could be dealt with under the existing legislative framework, was actually at the heart of the controversy before the Court. In other words, purporting to state an uncontroversial factual position, the Court smuggled in its conclusion into the very premises of the argument.[67]

The factual narrative that the Court presented as a set of undisputable axioms was soon transmuted into constitutional argument. So, while considering the validity of the provisions establishing special courts, the Court observed that the 'harsh and drastic' provisions of the Act, 'departing from the procedures prescribed under the ordinary procedural law, are evidently for the reasons that the prevalent ordinary procedural law was found to be inadequate'.[68] The same justification was applied a few paragraphs later to uphold the validity of making police confessions admissible, with the Court noting 'the gravity of terrorism unleashed by the terrorists and disruptionists endangering not only the sovereignty and integrity of the country but also the normal life of the citizens, and the reluctance of even the victims as well as the public in coming forward, at the risk of their life'.[69] In both paragraphs, what was conspicuous by its absence was the Constitution: the constitutional justification of TADA occurred by invoking the *state of exception*, and not by invoking the Constitution.

The Court engaged in an almost identical act of context setting ten years later, while considering the constitutional validity of the Prevention of Terrorism Act (POTA), which was the successor to TADA (TADA had been allowed to lapse after public outcry). POTA was challenged on similar grounds. Like in *Kartar Singh*, the Court in *People's Union for Civil Liberties* (*PUCL*) *v. Union of India*, began by setting out a series of factual propositions that were treated as axioms, and which would go on to shape its legal analysis. Terrorism, it held, was 'the most worrying feature of contemporary life',[70] which needed 'new approaches … and new laws',[71] because what was at stake was 'a kind of war'.[72] Here again, contested factual propositions were treated as a background to the judgement, even before the Court identified, addressed, and dealt with the constitutional arguments.

The corollary to treating the state of exception as the established, normative background within which the Act was to be examined was, as we have seen, vesting concentrated powers in the hands of the executive, including the power to be a judge in its own cause. In the anti-terror cases, this aspect of executive supremacy was upheld by the Court in three separate contexts: at the stage of the triggering of the legal regime of the state of exception, at the stage of implementation, and finally, at the stage of accountability.

At the stage of triggering, in *Kartar Singh*, the Court upheld the power granted to the government to 'declare' an entire area as an 'affected area', to which the provisions of the Act would apply. It upheld a similar provision (with minimal judicial scrutiny for exceptional situations) in *Naga People's Movement for Human Rights v. Union of India*, which challenged the constitutional validity of the Armed Forces Special Powers Act.[73] Then, at the stage of implementation, in *Kartar Singh*, the Court upheld a provision that allowed confessional statements to be taken by 'executive magistrates', who were nominees of the central government, instead of 'judicial magistrates' (trained judges).[74] The Court made the highly circular argument that because executive magistrates were given judicial functions to perform, they were 'holding judicial office'.

Similarly, in *Naga People's Movement for Human Rights*, the Court adopted the army's own 'List of Dos and Don'ts' for soldiers exercising force under the Armed Forces (Special Powers) Acts (AFSPA) as 'binding', and went one step further—not only allowing executive supremacy under the regime of the state of exception, but effectively endorsing *military* supremacy. And *finally*, at the stage of accountability, in response to documented evidence of police abuses that were enabled by the legal regime established by the TADA, the Court's response in *Kartar Singh* was that it was 'heart-rending to note' all of this, and it advised the enforcing authorities to 'keep in view' the considerations of dignity and equal rights, lest the Court be forced to exercise its 'majestic judicial authority'.[75] Similarly, while examining and upholding the impunity granted to the military by the AFSPA, the Court observed that a complaint about misuse or abuse of power 'should be thoroughly enquired into … and the victim should be compensated by the State … and sanction should be granted to prosecute'.[76] Here, the Court's role was reduced to that of a concerned bystander doling out gratuitous and unenforceable advice.

It should now be clear how the judgements of the Supreme Court in *Kartar Sigh* (TADA), *PUCL* (POTA) and *Naga People's*

Movement (AFSPA) replicated the core logic of *ADM Jabalpur*: the executive remained supreme not only with respect to the decision to trigger a state of exception, but also with respect to what rights were permitted or prohibited to individuals living under that legal regime. And this executive supremacy, in turn, was justified not by turning to the Constitution, but to the unique, *exceptional* characteristics of the state of exception itself, characteristics that could only be truly understood and assessed by … the executive.

B. Denial of Remedies

At the heart of the Emergency regime was the suspension of the right to approach the courts to seek remedy for abusive State action. In the post-Emergency terrorism legislation, this defining feature was replicated in a slightly different form. Under the TADA and its successors, the POTA and the amended Unlawful Activities Prevention Act (UAPA), and a host of other 'special laws' dealing with organized crime and drug-peddling (among other things),[77] a Court is not permitted to release an accused on bail unless it feels that there are reasonable grounds for believing that he has *not* committed the offence (and will not commit an offence if released on bail).[78] In *Kartar Singh*, it was argued that this provision (a holdover from the Defence of India Rules of 1971) effectively made the grant of bail impossible, because it required criminal defence lawyers to disprove the prosecution's case without the chance to put it to critical scrutiny in a trial, i.e., without the benefit of leading evidence and cross-examining opposing witnesses. The only way in which bail could be won was if the prosecution's own case was riddled with tangible contradictions and infirmities even before it went to trial. It was, therefore, argued in *Kartar Singh* that the bail provision of TADA effectively reversed the foundational criminal law principle of 'innocent until proven guilty'.[79] However, the Court upheld the provision by employing the 'larger public interest' rhetoric of *ADM Jabalpur*:

> … the courts while dispensing justice in cases … under the TADA Act, should keep in mind not only the liberty of the accused but also the interest of the victim … and above all the collective interest of the community and the safety of the nation so that the public may not lose faith in the system of judicial administration …[80]

The upshot of this interpretation has been devastating. It is now a standard feature of terror trials that the accused remain in prison for over a decade, unable to get bail, while the trial progresses. In at least three high-profile cases between 2015 and 2017, the accused were acquitted after periods of seven, twelve, and fourteen years in prison. These statutes' bail provisions, therefore, accomplish through the back door what preventive detention laws and Emergency provisions accomplished directly—long-term deprivation of personal liberty without a finding of guilt, by choking off the remedies ordinarily available under criminal law.

C. The Jurisdiction of Suspicion

In at least three distinct ways, the post-Emergency terror statutes replicate the jurisdiction of suspicion. The first is the power of the State to ban 'terrorist organizations'. In *PUCL v. Union of India*, it was argued that the absence of a pre-decisional hearing before banning organizations under the POTA was unconstitutional, since it violated Article 19(1)(c)'s guarantee of the freedom of association. The Court's response to this was curious:

> Under Article 19(4) of the Constitution the State can impose reasonable restrictions, *inter alia*, in the interest of sovereignty and integrity of the country. POTA is enacted to protect sovereignty and integrity of India from the menace of terrorism. Imposing restrictions under Article 19(4) of the Constitution also includes declaring an organization as a terrorist organization as provided under POTA. Hence Section 18 is not unconstitutional.[81]

But somewhere between the first sentence and the last, the Court appeared to have forgotten about the existence of the word 'reasonable' in Article 19(4). The omission is crucial, because the requirement of proximity and rigorous judicial review—the heart of the Court's civil rights jurisprudence—flows from the requirement that restrictions must be 'reasonable'. By omitting the word, the Court was able to do away with both sets of constraints on State power, which it further justified (for good measure) by subsequently referring to the 'peculiar background of terrorism'.[82]

The second way in which the Court internalized the jurisdiction of suspicion was *by taking the perspective of guilt*. This perspective is visible in the Court upholding witness anonymity provisions in *Kartar Singh* (that severely curtailed the ability of defence counsel to conduct cross-examination). This was on the grounds that witnesses who gave evidence in *terror cases* exposed themselves to the possibility of severe reprisal. Similarly, in upholding the denial of anticipatory bail, where the Court observed:

> Can it be said with certainty that terrorists and disruptionists who create terrorism and disruption and inject sense of insecurity, are not likely to abscond or misuse their liberty if released on anticipatory bail.[83]

The strange thing about this observation, of course, is that it assumes that the person who applies for anticipatory bail *is* a terrorist or a disruptionist—labels that are only meant to be applied to people *after* they are convicted in a full-blown trial. In other words, the Court upheld the denial of basic procedural safeguards on the basis that terrorists would take advantage of them, while discounting the possibility that they would unjustly prejudice *innocent people who had been unjustly accused of terrorism* (and who, therefore, could neither intimidate witnesses, nor 'misuse' their liberty).

Thirdly, terror statutes embody a particularly crude and unreconstructed vision of guilt by association. Under the AFSPA, an entire area or region could be declared subject to the provisions of the Act and its regime of military impunity. TADA, POTA, and UAPA all criminalized (and criminalize) membership of terrorist or unlawful organizations. The concept of membership is a boundlessly vague one, that takes within its ambit a whole range of potential activities (such as tacit support, ideological agreement, or even presence at meetings) that fall well short of actual commission of terrorist acts, or even of conspiracy to commit those acts. This effectively criminalizes association *itself*, once again eschewing the basic elements of reasonableness under Article 19.

D. Salus populi suprema lex

This is a legal regime, therefore, that is indistinguishable in effect from the regimes sanctioned by the courts under Article 22 (preventive detention) and Part XVIII (Emergency Provisions). It is a regime that is defined, characterized, and constituted by vesting in the State the power to deprive individuals of their personal liberty for long periods without trial and without proof of guilt. And the overall justification for the regime remains identical: the existence of exceptional background circumstances, which compel the State to take such action *for the greater good*.

A corollary of the *salus populi suprema lex* principle is an argument that, through repetition, has achieved the force of incantation: that the *possibility of abuse of power* does not render a statutory provision unconstitutional. This was the view the Court took in *Kartar Singh*. This was also the view that it took in *PUCL*, when it was pointed out that the 'possibility' of abuse was no longer a possibility, but that TADA (POTA's precursor) actually *had* been misused, as demonstrated by the overwhelming number of acquittals under the Act.[84] This was, yet again, the view it took in *Naga People's Movement for Human Rights*, while rejecting the argument that the shoot-at-sight powers under the AFSPA were unconstitutional.[85]

But ultimately, this is yet another argument where the conclusion is smuggled into the premise. The Court divides up the constitutional objection into two discrete parts, viz., the nature of the provision, which is innocuous and inoffensive; and then its subsequent 'abuse' by mala fide actors, which is somehow detached from the provision itself. This, however, is a strained and artificial way of approaching the issue. The argument has never been that the provision and its abuse are two separate events. Rather, the argument is that the vesting of concentrated, unaccountable power in the executive, in a manner that fundamentally alters the relationship between the individual and the State, is precisely what constitutes abuse, and renders a statute unconstitutional.

The Constitution envisages a certain set of constraints upon State power. These constraints are exemplified by the insistence that State coercion, when it is justified on preventive grounds, must meet the standard of proximity, and its factual foundations be rigorously scrutinized by an independent judiciary. The unconstitutionality of the terror statutes, therefore, lies not in how the political executive might misuse them, but in how they *remove* these basic constraints that are designed to check the power of the State, and to prevent it from becoming abusive. In *ADM Jabalpur*, Justice Khanna recognized this clearly and sharply:

> … experience should teach us to be most on our guard to protect liberty when the Government's purposes are beneficent … [the] greatest danger to liberty lies in insidious encroachment by men of zeal, well-meaning but lacking in due deference for the rule of few … whether such things [i.e., abuses] actually come to pass is not the question before us; it is enough to state that all these are permissible consequences from the acceptance of the contention that Article 21 is the sole repository of the right to life and personal liberty and that consequent upon the issue of the Presidential order, no one can approach any court and seek relief during the period of emergency against deprivation of life or personal liberty. In other words, the position would be that so far as executive officers are concerned, in matters relating to life and personal liberty of citizens, they would

> not be governed by any law, they would not be answerable to any court and they would be wielding more or less despotic powers.[86]

ADM Jabalpur is now discredited, and Justice Khanna's dissent is celebrated. But while *Jabalpur* lives on in the Supreme Court's judgements in *Kartar Singh*, *PUCL*, and *Naga People's Movement for Human Rights*, Justice Khanna's dissent remains that ineffectual angel vainly beating its luminous wings in the void.[87]

E. Conclusion

The Supreme Court's upholding of terror statutes has followed a specific pattern. At the beginning of its judgement, the Court constructs an uncontested factual narrative that makes the case for the state of exception. This narrative is flat, linear, and consists of a series of spectacularly violent events, without any further enquiry into causes or consequences.[88] The terror statutes' vesting of concentrated power in the hands of the executive, through clear departures from established rules of criminal law and criminal procedure, is then justified by referring back to the state of exception. To put it another way, instead of subjecting the state of exception to the Constitution and to constitutional standards, the Court effectively requires that *the Constitution* be moulded and modified so that *it* fits with the demands and requirements of the state of exception.

Effectively, therefore, the Court has *read into the Constitution* a third state of exception. Unlike the other two, viz., the preventive detention regime and the Emergency regime, this third state of exception is not contemplated by the Constitution. For this reason, it is not a discrete event that is bounded in time and space, and whose parameters are clearly spelt out. It is, rather, a self-reproducing 'generalization of the security paradigm',[89] a state of exception that has woven itself so intimately into the fabric of the constitutional cloth that it is no longer clear what is normal and what is the exception.

V. *Jyoti Chorge* and the Transformative Constitution

In 2002, a group of young men and women formed a troupe called the Kabir Kala Manch, dedicated to using music and poetry to fight social injustices. A few years later they were in prison, detained under the provisions of the UAPA. The State argued that the Kabir Kala Manch was a cultural front for the banned Communist Party of India (Maoist), and its performers were members of the CPI-Maoist or 'Naxalites'. According to the charge sheet, Naxalite literature had been found in their possession, as well as publicity material for the organization, and phone numbers and contact lists of other (alleged) CPI-Maoist operatives. They had, further, been performing plays that were 'full of communist ideology' and 'instigative' against the government.[90] Witnesses (themselves 'surrendered Naxalites') claimed that they had seen some of the members of the troupe in the company of senior CPI-Maoist figures and carrying weapons at Naxalite training camps. Dhavala Rama Dhengale, one of the accused, confessed to having provided his house as a meeting place for CPI-Maoist leaders (he subsequently retracted this).

After spending a year and a half in jail, the bail applications of Jyoti Chorge and Sushma Ramtekke came up before the Bombay High Court. Recall that under the UAPA, a Court is statutorily barred from granting bail unless there are reasonable grounds to hold that the accused has *not* committed the offence. The question before the Bombay High Court, therefore, was a simple one: did the factual materials in the prosecution's charge sheet, which the accused had not rebutted (indeed, they could not rebut, because the trial had not even started), make out an offence under the UAPA?

The prosecution argued that the accused were members of the CPI-Maoist, fully aware of its activities, and 'had knowingly associated with persons indulging into such activities'.[91] Even though there was no evidence to show that the accused had themselves *committed* acts of terrorism, it was argued that 'the entire ideology and philosophy of the [CPI-Maoist] was dangerous, and was destroying the nation'.[92] Here, therefore, we see the four elements of the state of exception: the supremacy of the executive in deciding *who* was a threat to the nation, the denial of legal remedies against the deprivation of personal liberty (in this case, bail), the jurisdiction of suspicion (guilt by association), and an overarching justification grounded in *salus populi suprema lex*. Under the continuing logic of *ADM Jabalpur*, this should have been an easy case.

It was not. Justice Abhay Thipsay began by noting that, on the basis of the State's evidence, it was clear that in some sense the accused were 'members' of the CPI-Maoist. And membership had been defined very widely, and with drastic penal consequences (denial of bail and imprisonment for life). But at this point, Justice Thipsay parted company with the logic of the state of exception. His first observation, after noting the provisions of the UAPA, was:

> Because of these drastic provisions, the concept of 'membership' that has been contemplated in section 20 and incidentally, in section 38 needs to be carefully considered, and properly interpreted in the light of Article 19 of the Constitution of India.[93]

Here, then, was a starting point that was the polar opposite of the approach of the Court in *Kartar Singh* and *PUCL*. While those cases had looked to the state of exception to justify 'drastic provisions', here the Court looked to the Constitution to draw a boundary around them. In this way, Justice Thipsay rejected the first limb of the state of exception, emphasizing constitutional supremacy over executive supremacy. The prosecution then changed tack and invoked the jurisdiction of suspicion, arguing that:

> ... there was a great danger to the whole nation from the [CPI-Maoist], and that the unity and integrity of the nation was already in danger because of their activities ... section 20 of the UAP Act has been deliberately worded very widely by keeping these aspects in mind ... mere association with such type of people, and sharing their ideology would make a person a member of their organization.[94]

That is, Naxalism was like 'contagion': anyone brought into contact with it must be deemed to have been infected, and requiring quarantine.[95] However, Justice Thipsay rejected this argument in short order, relying upon three recent judgements of the Supreme Court. In *Arup Bhuyan*,[96] *Indra Das*,[97] and *Raneef*,[98] a bench of the Supreme Court led by Justice Markandey Katju had held that there was a distinction between 'passive' and 'active' membership of banned organizations. Active membership, which alone could be criminalized, entailed *actual* incitement to violence or to lawless action. Citing these judgements, Justice Thipsay noted that:

> ... passive membership is not what is contemplated by section 20 of the UAP Act. It is very clear from the observations made by the Supreme Court that if section 20 were to be interpreted in that manner, it would at once be considered as violative of the provisions of section 19 of the Constitution of India ...[99]

Consequently, Section 20 of the UAPA was read down *in order* to make it compatible with the Court's civil rights jurisprudence (and, in particular, the requirement of proximity).

In sum, therefore, as Justice Thipsay correctly observed, the foundation of the allegations against the accused was no more than 'they are sympathizers of Maoist philosophy, and that they are intending to, or likely to, play an active role in the organization in future'.[100] Echoing the judgement of the Supreme Court in *Ram Manohar Lohia*, more than half a century ago, he then held that under the Constitution, this could not be grounds for denial of liberty. Bail was granted.

The judgement in *Jyoti Chorge*—and its companion case, *Dhavala Rama Dhengale v. State of Maharashtra*, in which Justice Thipsay granted bail to four more members of the Kabir Kala Manch in January 2013—provides a clean and stark counterpoint to the judgements in *Kartar Singh*, *PUCL*, and the other progeny of *ADM Jabalpur*. The distinction lies not so much in the outcome; after all,

Kartar Singh and *PUCL* involved constitutional challenges, and consequently were far more likely to invite judicial caution than a bail judgement. The distinction lies in something deeper: as a matter of *constitutional interpretation*, *Jyoti Chorge* systematically repudiated the logic of the state of exception. And Justice Thipsay was able to do so because he remained unmoved by the incantation of *salus populi suprema lex*, instead countering it with the following words from *Arup Bhuyan*:

> We are living in a democracy, and the above observations apply to all democracies.[101]

This was delivered almost as a rebuke to the logic of the state of exception. It put forth the view, instead, that what it meant to be democratic was to *not* allow the state of exception to come to dominate all other values. What it meant to be democratic was to test the state of exception and the extraordinary powers claimed by the State against the standards of the Constitution, *and not the other way around*. So, if the State wished to criminalize membership of banned organizations, then it was the Constitution that would impose constraints on how broadly the concept of membership could be stretched, and what manner of actions could be criminalized consistently with the guaranteed rights to freedom of expression, assembly, and association. These were rights that lost neither their valence nor their amplitude simply through the invocation of *salus populi suprema lex*.

Unsurprisingly, therefore, Justice Thipsay's factual narrative was radically different from the factual narrative advanced in *Kartar Singh* or *PUCL*. In those cases, the Court framed TADA and POTA as responding to consistent, organized, and faceless acts of violence, which seemed to exist in a political and social vacuum.[102] By contrast, Justice Thipsay, in examining the past conduct of the accused, observed:

> A number of persons are influenced, and get attracted towards the Maoist Philosophy because of the oppression of the weaker section which they might have experienced in the social set up … it is impossible to hold that all such persons are to be treated as members of a terrorist organization, or that they are liable to be punished for having some faith in such philosophy, or for having sympathy for those who propagate such philosophy.[103]

What, for the *Kartar Singh* and *PUCL* courts, was a 'scourge' and therefore needed extraordinarily harsh measures (a state of exception) to contain, for Justice Thipsay was essentially a political and social problem that called for an equivalent solution, but required the *court* to apply its normal, liberty-protecting jurisprudence. The reasoning in *Jyoti Chorge*, therefore, was not simply a matter of legal doctrine, but also a matter of underlying constitutional foundations, as it must be. It challenged the very legitimacy of the permanent normalizing of the state of exception, with its attendant erosion of foundational civil rights.

VI. The Constitution and the Culture of Justification

The judgements in *Jyoti Chorge* and *Dhavala Rama Dhengale* were not born in isolation. In both cases, Justice Thipsay relied on the Supreme Court trio of *Raneef*, *Arup Bhuyan,* and *Indra Das* to apply the 'active membership' standard to interpreting the UAPA. These judgements themselves were part of an older judicial tradition. In *Kartar Singh*, while dissenting on the issue of the admissibility of police confessions, Justice Ramaswamy had observed 'such an erosion [of constitutional safeguards] is anathema to the rule of law … and a clear negation of Article 50 of the Constitution'.[104] Justice Sahai joined him in dissent on this point, and also held that Section 5 of the TADA, which automatically criminalized possession of arms and ammunition in a 'Notified Area', would have to be read down to apply only to those cases where there was some material to show that the person intended to use those arms for terrorist or disruptionist purposes.[105] This interpretive technique was similar to that used by Justice Thipsay in *Jyoti Chorge*, and was likewise an attempt to push back against the incorporation of the principles of guilt by association and the jurisdiction of suspicion into terror statutes.[106] And both dissenting opinions in *Kartar Singh* ultimately drew from Justice Khanna's conviction that the Constitution simply did not permit the concentration of unaccountable power under the guise of a state of exception.

As we have seen, however, this view has remained an outlier. It is not the view taken by judgements dealing with the preventive detention regime, by Emergency judgements pre-*ADM Jabalpur*, or by judgements under terror statutes after the Emergency. The question then arises: was Justice Thipsay's repudiation of logic of the state of exception correct?

I argue here that it was. And not only was it correct, but that it also exemplified and vindicated a crucial aspect of the Constitution's transformative character. The Indian Constitution was transformative in the sense that it marked a transition from a *permanent state of exception* under the colonial legal regime to a regime defined by the rule of law, where exceptions were to be clearly defined, narrowly construed, and subject to rigorous judicial oversight. It was never the Constitution's purpose that the executive be vested with virtually unreviewable powers of deciding both upon the existence of the state of exception *and* the scope of rights available to individuals for its duration. And the Constitution did not contemplate the existence of 'a no man's land between public law and political fact',[107] where the logics of the state of exception and the rule of law would become indistinguishable.

The argument is based on four prongs. First, that the colonial legal regime was characterized by a permanent state of exception, which was marked by executive supremacy, denial of remedies, and the jurisdiction of suspicion, under an overarching justification based on the *special character* of the colony. Second, political resistance against this state of exception, and the articulation of an alternative understanding of the relationship between the individual and the State, was an integral aspect of the freedom movement, which culminated in Independence and the drafting of the Constitution. Third, debates in the Constituent Assembly indicate that the insertion of Article 22 and the preventive detention regime was not to privilege a state of exception over the norm, but the reverse, i.e., to define and *create a regime of accountability* for situations where power might be concentrated in the hands of the State. Fourth, this reading makes sense if we understand the framing of the Constitution in two ways: as a transformation of Indians from subjects to citizens, and as a transformation from the culture of authority to the culture of justification.

A. The British Regime and the Permanent State of Exception

The permanent state of exception established by the colonial regime in India was anchored to the sweeping powers enjoyed by an unelected political executive, viz., the Governor-General. His office was vested with the power to issue 'ordinances' (having the force of law) in emergency situations, and this power was often used to authorize preventive detention.[108] Even after the incremental growth of representative institutions in India under the 1919 and 1935 Government of India Acts, the Governor-General continued to possess overriding powers of legislation, effectively making the (partially) elected legislative assemblies subservient to the executive. These powers were at the Governor-General's 'satisfaction', and therefore virtually unreviewable.[109]

While executive supremacy, exercised through ordinances, was most frequently in use during the two World Wars, there existed a parallel legislative and executive framework that replicated the features of the state of exception, even in peacetime. As early as 1818, a Bengal Regulation authorized preventive detention for the 'preservation of tranquillity' and security from either foreign intervention or 'internal commotion'.[110] In the inter-war years, the notorious Rowlatt Act, which became the flashpoint for nationalist protests, authorized preventive detention for up to two years. The Emergency Powers Ordinance of 1932 was used both to ban organizations and to impose a regime of preventive detention.[111]

Moreover, in a striking foreshadowing of the UAPA's targeting of associations and criminalization of membership, in 1871, the colonial regime enacted the Criminal Tribes Act, which embodied the jurisdiction of suspicion and guilt by association par excellence. The Criminal Tribes Act labelled entire tribes as *presumptively criminal*, and established a regime of surveillance, reporting to the police (subject to penal consequences), and forced relocation to labour camps. Actual commission of an offence was not required, as long as the official concerned formed a 'subjective satisfaction' that the individuals and groups in question had the 'potential' to commit crimes. Blood or kin relationships with designated 'criminals' was sufficient for the Act to apply, representing a complete inversion of the basic criminal law principle of individual responsibility.[112]

The justification for this repressive legal regime, a regime that established concentration camps and separated children from their parents, was located in the 'special character' of the colony. It was argued that as the natives were not yet ready for democratic self-government of the kind that existed in Britain, they could not yet be trusted to responsibly exercise the rights and freedoms available to British citizens.[113] Indeed, so ingrained was this jurisprudence of permanent exception, that when the colonial courts struck down sweeping surveillance measures, Lieutenant-Governor Sir Donald MacLeod complained that this was because the courts' experience was limited to 'dealing with the crime after it has been committed'.[114] In terms eerily similar to the prosecution's argument for interpreting membership under the UAPA broadly in order to criminalize entire groups subscribing to a particular ideology, it was argued by the colonial regime that for the criminal tribes, 'criminal behaviour was the defining characteristic of the group's social existence'.[115]

B. The Nationalist Response

As discussed above, the permanent state of exception established by the British regime was a point of focus for the nationalist movement. The critique of the regime was primarily political, of course, but it also had a *constitutional* form. Soon after the passage of the Rowlatt Act, in two annual sessions of the Indian National Congress separated only by three years from each other, the Presidential Address focused on the relationship between personal liberty and concentrated executive power. In his 1919 address, Motilal Nehru critiqued the Rowlatt Act specifically for its endorsement of executive supremacy and imposition of a jurisdiction of suspicion, arguing that '[just] because there are … some persons who endanger public safety, the whole nation must submit to the disgrace of allowing this terror to hang over it … the only justification pleaded is that the Act is not meant for the innocent and the law-abiding who need have no fear of its application to them. But … the sole judge of the innocence or guilt of any person … is the executive'.[116]

After pointing to various aspects of the Rowlatt Act that enshrined executive supremacy, Nehru noted, 'No executive in the world, however competent it may be, has any business to usurp the jurisdiction of duly constituted courts or deprive the people of the protection afforded by them.' He went on to specifically reject the doctrine of necessity, i.e., exceptional situation, that was invoked by the British to justify the law,[117]and articulated an alternative framework focused on the 'future inviolability of our civic rights', specifically with a view to precluding a 'reign of terror' that might be initiated by a 'panic-stricken executive'.[118] And of course, it was Gandhi who organized a sustained campaign against the Rowlatt Act, while also famously condemning the law of sedition at his own trial.

Three years later, in 1922, C.R. Das observed in *his* Presidential Address, 'The personal liberty of every Indian today depends to a great extent on the exercise by persons in authority of wide, arbitrary or discretionary powers. Where such powers are allowed the rule of law is denied.'[119] Das used this framework to critique the Bengal Regulation of 1818, as well as the Criminal Law Amendment Act of 1908 and the Prevention of Seditious Meetings Act of 1911. Anticipating Justice Khanna by fifty-five years, Das noted that the concentration of power in the hands of the political executive was objectionable 'not because it was never exercised for the safety of the nation, but because the existence of the power was inconsistent with the existence ... of individual liberty'.[120] And making an impeccable argument against the logic of the state of exception, Das concluded by arguing that '[only] if you have recourse to law and order to establish and defend the rule of law ... [is] your law and order entitled to claim the respect of all law-abiding citizens'.[121]

These critiques did not end with the lapse of the Rowlatt Act in 1922. The Criminal Tribes Act, with its sweeping jurisdiction of suspicion and tarring of entire communities as 'presumptively criminal', was criticized by leading nationalists, most prominently by Jawaharlal Nehru, as not only illegitimate, but contrary to the very basis of civilization.[122] More specifically, soon after the lapse of the Rowlatt Act, in an otherwise conservative set of lectures titled 'The Rights and Duties of the Indian Citizen', writer and legislator Srinivasa Sastri took specific aim at the 1818 Bengal Regulation and its progeny, noting, 'To arm the executive permanently with the power to take away a citizen, lock him up, and refuse even to bring him up for trial is nearly a direct repeal of the liberty which I have placed at the head of the list—the liberty of the person.'[123]

Immediately after the Government of India Act, 1935, another legislator, S. Satyamurti, unsuccessfully moved a private member's bill that specifically critiqued the law of sedition for failing to include a proximity requirement, and suggested an amendment that would limit its operation to the promotion of 'physical force or violence or public disorder'.[124] This pre-Independence civil liberties tradition culminated in Hansa Mehta's Presidential Address to the All India

Women's Conference in 1945, where she drew a specific comparison between Emergency powers in India and their counterpart in Britain.

While Mehta made the limited argument that the Indian Emergency powers ought to be liberalized to accord with the more rights-protective standard in wartime Britain, in one crucial aspect, she made a far more radical claim: that although the State was empowered to encroach upon liberties in times of emergency or crisis, 'such occurrences are, however, rare, and the State would have to prove the emergency before it can take any drastic measures'.[125] Here was a proto-version of the culture of justification: the triggering of an Emergency is not simply the prerogative or 'subjective satisfaction' of the State, *but must be justified*.

We can therefore see that the attainment of Independence in 1947 was preceded by an almost three-decade-long civil liberties tradition that had three salient features: first, it defined personal liberty in opposition to concentrated State power; second, it critiqued the different aspects of the state of exception, viz., executive supremacy, denial of remedies, the jurisdiction of suspicion, and public-good justifications, from the perspective of the right to personal liberty; and third, perhaps most importantly, its arguments were *universalistic* in cast. They were not couched against the British government as an alien, foreign power, but against the concentration of executive power *generally*. This is especially significant when we consider the fact that these arguments arose in the wider context of a movement for national self-determination, but as far as personal liberty was concerned, they transcended that immediate context. They would therefore remain applicable even after the government was no longer foreign or alien, but *of* the people. [126]

C. The Constituent Assembly

In his critique of the Supreme Court's preventive detention jurisprudence, the civil rights lawyer K.G. Kannabiran argued that the Court, guided by a sense of colonial continuity, ignored the impact of the freedom struggle upon constitutional interpretation. Kannabiran suggested that:

> Motilal Nehru's presidential address at Amritsar in the year 1919, the undelivered address of C.R. Das at the Gaya Congress, Satyamurti's speech in the Central Legislative Assembly in February 1936, or Gandhi's speech at his sedition trial before Judge Broomfield are excellent sources for working out a system of jurisprudence and a theory of rights even at the commencement of the Constitution.[127]

Kannabiran's argument was straightforward: there was an entire tradition of civil rights thought, closely associated with the freedom movement, that the Court could draw upon in adjudicating cases involving executive power and the rights of citizens. However, the argument misses a crucial link: what is it that makes *these* historical materials salient in interpreting the Constitution? It is important to remember that, while the thinking represented by Motilal Nehru, C.R. Das, Satyamurti, and others was an integral part of the freedom movement, it was by no means the only point of view. C.R. Das spent half his Presidential Address fulminating against the Moderate Wing of the Indian National Congress that had supported the colonial regime's 'law and order' legislation and ordinances. Immediately after criticizing the Bengal Regulation of 1818, Srinivasa Sastri expressed anguish that his colleagues in the legislative council had voted to *extend* it.[128] And after the 1935 Government of India Act, many of the *elected* provincial Congress governments passed preventive detention and public safety acts that closely resembled their colonial counterparts.

Therefore, if we are to successfully argue that it is the intellectual tradition of Motilal Nehru, C.R. Das, Gandhi, Satyamurti, Sastri and Hansa Mehta—let us call this the civil rights tradition—that should guide us in interpreting the Constitution, then there is one further link in the chain that must be included. That link is the Constituent Assembly. We have to show that underlying the text of Articles 21 and 22 was the civil rights tradition that we have outlined above, and not its restrictive counterpart. That argument depends upon a close reading of the Constituent Assembly Debates.

In doing so, we must first deal with a seemingly insurmountable argument. As members of the Constituent Assembly pointed out at the time, and as theorists and scholars have pointed out since, India is almost unique among the constitutions of the world in that it *specifically* authorizes a preventive detention regime.[129] Not only that, the insertion of Article 22 into the Constitution was strongly resisted by multiple members of the Constituent Assembly, precisely on the grounds of individual liberty and State overreach. However, not only did they fail in their attempt to have preventive detention removed, but many of their amendments aiming to soften it were also rejected.[130]

The defenders of preventive detention employed a broad set of arguments, ranging from the precarious communal situation existing at the time, to an expression of faith that the new government of independent India would not seek to abuse or exploit provisions that the colonial regime had freely invoked to stifle dissent. Ultimately, preventive detention remained. Consequently, the very existence of Article 22 in the Constitution—enacted after fierce disagreement, and as a conscious choice—surely represents the triumph of the logic of the state of exception.

On the contrary, however, a close reading of the Constituent Assembly Debates suggests that Article 22 was not an *authorizing* provision, but a *saving* provision.[131] To understand this, recall that the Constituent Assembly witnessed a stormy debate over whether Article 21, which guaranteed the right to life and personal liberty, should include a 'due process' clause on the lines of the US Constitution, i.e., in depriving a person of life or liberty, was the State required to follow *due process*, instead of merely '*procedure established by law*'?[132] Some members argued that due process would allow the Court far-reaching powers of interference in government policy (as the US experience had shown).[133] On the other hand, if due process was omitted in favour of procedure established by law, then the courts' role would be minimal. Life and personal liberty could be infringed by Parliament simply by enacting a law.[134] In the Constituent Assembly, Ambedkar observed that he saw merit in both arguments, and would leave it to the wisdom of the House to decide.[135] The House decided to drop the due process clause.

Then, in order to provide a degree of *constitutional protection* to individuals against arbitrary arrest, Ambedkar introduced what became Article 22 of the Constitution (one of the members of the Constituent Assembly specifically referred to it as 'compensation',[136] another said it was 'caution',[137] and a third called it a 'compromise').[138] Article 22(1) required that a person who was arrested had to be informed of the grounds of his arrest and to be defended by a lawyer, while Article 22(2) required that any arrested person be produced before a magistrate within twenty-four hours (essentially, habeas corpus).

The preventive detention regime followed, in Articles 22(3) to (7) (which we have discussed above). Article 22(3) began with the words 'nothing in clauses (1) and (2) shall apply ... to any person who is arrested or detained under any law providing for preventive detention'.[139] Notably, when Ambedkar rose to defend this Article after a fierce six-hour debate in September 1949, he did it in these words: 'I and my friends had been trying in some way to restore the content of due procedure in its fundamentals without using the words "due process".'[140]

This historical background should make the structure of Articles 21 and 22 clear. The phrase 'procedure established by law' under Article 21 allowed the State to deprive an individual of her life or liberty, as long as it was done under a valid law. Articles 22(1) and (2) were framed as an exception to Article 21, and required that a person deprived of their liberty be entitled to certain procedural rights, and be produced before a judicial authority (core due process requirements). And *then*, the preventive detention regime was framed *as an exception to the procedural safeguards under Articles 22(1) and (2).*

In other words, a person detained under a preventive detention law could not invoke Articles 22(1) and (2) and, for example, claim the right to be produced before a magistrate within twenty-four hours.

But that is all. Neither the drafting history nor the text of Articles 21 and 22 suggests that the preventive detention regime was meant to be a complete code, insulated from the rest of the Constitution. Also, neither suggests that a preventive detention law was immunized from challenge under Articles 14, and especially under Article 19's guarantees of speech, assembly, association, and movement. In fact, quite the contrary: the text suggests that the preventive detention regime was meant to operate as an exception *only* to the procedural safeguards from arrest under Articles 22(1) and (2).[141]

Why then did the courts interpret, and continue to interpret, the preventive detention regime isolated from the rest of the Constitution? The answer lies in *A.K. Gopalan v. State of Madras*, which is widely perceived to have done two things: declared that Article 22 was a complete code in itself, and advanced the silos theory of constitutional rights. The silos theory, however, has no support in the text of the Constitution or in the Constituent Assembly Debates, and was overruled in *R.C. Cooper v. Union of India*.[142] And, as H.M. Seervai points out, only one judge out of six in *Gopalan* actually held that Article 22 was a complete code.[143] Indeed, the Chief Justice specifically rejected this argument,[144] a point with which Justice Fazl Ali, in his now-resurrected dissenting opinion, agreed.[145] He then went on to point out that 'the article does provide for [only] some matters of procedure ... there is ample latitude still left to the Parliament, and if the Parliament makes use of that latitude unreasonably, Article 19(5) may enable the Court to see whether it has transgressed the limits of reasonableness'.[146]

This reading of the text and structure of the Constitution, its history, and the *Gopalan* opinion and its aftermath leads to the following conclusion: the Constitution does not, and did not, intend to create a preventive detention regime that is insulated from fundamental rights review. It only meant the preventive detention regime to be immune from two very specific procedural safeguards (production before a magistrate and immediate disclosure of grounds) that were constitutionally guaranteed to the accused at the time of arrest.

But this tells us something further: despite the pre-Independence history of provincial Congress governments making liberal use of preventive detention laws even as their leaders criticized them in the national sessions, despite the advocacy of strong law-and-order arguments in the Constituent Assembly, and despite frequent references to the violence of Partition that was engulfing the country, the Constituent Assembly finally voted to provide for a highly circumscribed and narrowly defined preventive detention regime. Further, this was to be interpreted in light of all other fundamental rights, apart from two sub-clauses that were specifically excepted. If anything, this was a *rejection* of the logic of the state of exception, and a victory for the civil rights tradition. As Ambedkar himself noted, preventive detention was required only because of the 'present circumstances in the country'.[147] In *A.K. Gopalan,* Justice Fazl Ali recognized this fundamental insight when he observed:

> I do not think that it was ever intended that Parliament could, at its will, treat the normal as the abnormal or the rule as the exception.[148]

The point here is a straightforward one, i.e., the concrete, specific and narrow framing of Article 22 indicated that states of exception were permitted to exist only insofar as, and to the extent that, they were expressly authorized by the Constitution, *and at no other time, and no further*. This is what Ambedkar meant when, responding to severe criticism from Pandit Thakur Das Bhargava, he retorted: 'What I am trying to do is to curtail that power (of preventive detention) and put a limitation upon it.'[149] And it is in this fashion that we must understand Kannabiran's argument that the Constitution marked a break with the colonial past, in that it substituted a permanent state of exception, that could be triggered at the will of the executive, with a regime of the rule of law, in which the exception was defined, temporary, and not intended to take over the entire legal regime.[150]

D. The Culture of Justification

There is a deeper argument for why this must be so. As discussed in the Prologue, the standard argument for colonial continuity is that much of the legal structure erected by the British was carried forward into independent India, including the entire preventive detention apparatus, and ordinance and emergency powers. Given that the legal structure remained the same, it is argued that the content of individual rights effectively remained unchanged.

What this argument ignores, however, is that a change in *political structure* must necessarily have an impact upon the *nature of rights*;[151] that is, when the structural assumptions underlying a right are transformed, that right can only properly be understood in the context of the new legal and political structure.[152] To argue that nothing changed at the moment of Independence because the legal *structure* was carried over ignores a fundamental point: that Independence and the framing of the Constitution marked a transformation in the existing *political structure*, which would necessarily impact how the existing legal structure was to be understood and interpreted.

What was this fundamental shift, beyond a mere transfer of power? Kannabiran argued that it was the transformation of the Indian people from *subjects* to *citizens*, embodied in the Preambular phrase, 'We the People … give to ourselves this Constitution'.[153] In a recent book, Ornit Shani took this argument further when she pointed out that independent India's first general election was not merely an 'evolutionary' moment that was the logical culmination of the partially representative institutions that had been set up by the British, but a revolutionary moment that transformed voting and participation in governance from a privilege accorded by the rulers at their will to a *right*.[154]

At the heart of this shift from subjecthood to citizenship, marked by the coming into being of universal suffrage as a *right*, was the transformation from a culture of authority to a culture of justification: that is, from a regime in which the exercise of authoritarian power was at the discretion of those who wielded it to a system in which every exercise of power by those placed in the temporary position of governance must be *justified* to citizens.[155] It was this point that Hansa Mehta stressed upon in her address on civil liberties, when she placed *accountability* at the heart of any democratic system.[156] It was also this insight that was at the heart of Justice Thipsay's opinion in *Jyoti Chorge*, when he rejected the State's arguments to endorse the culture of authority under the UAPA by making a specific and pointed reference to democracy.

In 2017, the Supreme Court affirmed an important element of this constitutional vision when it overruled *ADM Jabalpur* on the point that fundamental rights were not a gift of the State, but inhered in the People who had given Themselves the Constitution.[157] Visualizing rights as a gift, that can be taken away at will, is redolent of the culture of authority. The rejection of that view restores the original constitutional ideal of the culture of justification.

VII. Conclusion and Endnotes

We are now in a position to understand the flaws with the Court's state-of-exception jurisprudence. Starting with treating preventive detention as a 'complete code', and emergency powers as non-justiciable, the Court has incrementally extended constitutional insulation to anti-terror laws, by extending the logic of the state of exception. In doing so, the Court has, essentially, carried forward the interpretive approach that was a staple feature of the colonial regime, ostensibly on the basis that much of the legal structure continues to remain the same. Ultimately, this justifies carving out islands marked by executive supremacy, the denial of remedies, the jurisdiction of suspicion, and the overarching justification of *salus populi suprema lex*, to create a permanent state of exception.

This, however, is flawed because it ignores the creation of the Constitution as a transformative moment. Textually, the Constitution repudiated the state of exception by limiting *what* it could serve as an exception to. Structurally, it repudiated it through a Fundamental Rights chapter that would constrain the existence of the state of exception. And philosophically, it repudiated it through a shift from a culture of authority to a culture of justification. The upshot of this is straightforward: a state of exception is to apply only to the *express extent* that the Constitution authorizes, and at all times it is to be subject to a regime of justification, embodied by judicial review. At all *other* times, the Court's 'normal' civil rights tradition applies.

Jyoti Chorge vindicated this transformative constitutional vision by refusing to depart from the civil rights tradition in the teeth of the State's invocation of the state of exception, and by pegging the interpretation of an anti-terror statute not to the state of exception, but to the Constitution. *Jyoti Chorge*, therefore, was faithful to the vision expressed by the civil rights spokespersons of the freedom movement and the dissident judges of the Supreme Court. But, above all, it was faithful to the transformative vision of the Constitution.

What follows? One, of course, is a case for universalizing the interpretive approach in *Jyoti Chorge*, and rethinking the Supreme Court's jurisprudence on preventive detention (especially its judgements upholding 'special laws' such as the COFEPOSA, which extended preventive detention to cases involving 'the conservation of foreign exchange',[158] and placed it in the Ninth Schedule, to boot!) and on emergency powers. But there is more. It is important to note that in India, the state of exception is both centralized and federated. It endures not only in central security statutes such as the UAPA and the AFSPA, but also in a host of state laws. Most prominent among these are the 'Goonda Acts'. Originally legislated in the state of Bengal by the colonial regime in 1923, ostensibly to control petty crime (but with the underhand motive of persecuting political activity),[159] the Goonda Acts now exist in nine different states.

For example, Karnataka's Goonda Act authorizes the government to detain a person for up to one year (subject to confirmation by an advisory board within three weeks) in order to '*prevent* him from acting in any manner prejudicial to the maintenance of public order'.[160] Actions prejudicial to the maintenance of public order, in turn, are defined to include situations where a goonda (or a slum-grabber or video or audio pirate) is 'engaged *or is making preparations for engaging* in a set of defined activities. While some of these offences include drug peddling or human trafficking, others are pure speech offences under the IPC, such as sedition or subversive speech under S. 153A, and even copyright offences.[161] The Act then goes on to replicate features of the MISA that was upheld in *ADM Jabalpur*, including a provision that the requirement of disclosing the grounds of detention to the detainee is overridden by the power of the detaining authority not 'to disclose facts which it considers to be against the public interest to disclose.'[162]

The Goonda Acts are preventive detention statutes. However, to the extent that they permit the government to preventively detain persons whom it suspects *might* be making preparations for engaging in speech that *could* constitute an offence under the Indian Penal Code, the Information Technology Act, or copyright law,[163] it is evident that they fail all standards of proximity under Article 19.[164] They are contemporary exemplars of the jurisprudence espoused under the *Haradhan Saha–A.K. Roy* line of cases, where the Court paid lip service to *Cooper's* repudiation of the silos theory of fundamental rights, but nonetheless continued to insulate the preventive detention regime from Part III and 14-19-21 scrutiny. If, however, the *Cooper* standard was to be applied faithfully, and the state-of-exception immunity withdrawn from the Goonda Acts (as *Jyoti Chorge* withdrew it for the UAPA), there is little doubt that the Goonda Acts are at least partially unconstitutional.[165]

While the Goonda Acts test the extent to which the courts are prepared to let preventive detention statutes exist in an implicit Ninth Schedule, state Public Safety Acts raise constitutional questions of the second kind—the entrenchment of a permanent state of emergency. In proscribing and punishing 'unlawful' acts of association and organization, state Public Security Acts go significantly beyond the limits of even the UAPA. For example, the Chhattisgarh Vishesh Jan Suraksha Adhiniyam (Chhattisgarh Special Public Safety Act) of 2005 includes within the definition of unlawful activity 'encouraging or preaching disobedience to established law and its institutions',[166] an act that was *expressly* held to be protected under Article 19(1)(a) in *Ram Manohar Lohia*. Section 8 of the Act then specifically *delinks* membership of unlawful organizations with 'taking part in meetings or activities', and makes *both* punishable.[167]

There are further provisions that, in a manner similar to the UAPA, provide for forfeiture of funds of organizations declared unlawful, and so on. What sets apart many of these state public security laws is that they exist in states that are racked by militancy, whether it is separatism in Kashmir[168] or Naxalism in Chhattisgarh.[169] Their continued existence, therefore, is an indicator of the incremental subordination of the Constitution, and constitutional standards, to pervasive and permanent states of exception.

Furthermore, our legal system is riddled with legislation that has nothing to do with public or national security, but nonetheless incorporates elements of the state of exception. At the forefront stands the Bombay Prevention of Beggary Act, another brutal colonial holdover now existing in twenty Indian states. This law, as its name suggests, effectively criminalizes poverty and creates 'status offenders': that is, it punishes people not for what they have done, but for who they are.[170]

Quite apart from the constitutional problems with criminalizing the *act* of begging in the first place, the Act goes much further: it constructs a jurisdiction of suspicion by criminalizing individuals for 'having no visible means of subsistence and wandering about or remaining in any public place in such condition or manner as makes it likely that the person doing so exists [by] soliciting or receiving alms';[171] it authorizes detention for up to one year for 'crimes' of this kind;[172] and it endorses guilt by association by allowing courts to detain *dependants* of 'beggars'.[173] It is one thing to normalize the state of exception *in the context* of anti-terrorism. It is quite another to enshrine it as just another method of 'social control'.[174]

Justice Thipsay's judgement in *Jyoti Chorge*, consequently, is not simply about bail standards under the UAPA. Its transformative reach extends much further and much deeper. It has the potential to dismantle some of the most suffocating features of India's security-State legal apparatus, as well as its social control legal apparatus, and erect in its place a judicial philosophy that places personal liberty and the freedom of speech and association at the heart of the constitutional order. Its rejection of the permanent state of exception, and its unravelling of the complex web that has bound together normalcy and exception into a repressive mesh, is true to the Constitution's text, structure, and philosophy, and true to the civil liberties tradition that animated the framing of the Fundamental Rights chapter. But it is a lonely truth, not yet accepted or validated by the accumulated force of judicial opinions.

Whether the Court will choose to adopt the transformative constitutional vision of *Jyoti Chorge* in any significant manner, so that the world's largest democracy sees no more Chandrashekhar Azads condemned to jail without trial and without bail, is a question that only the future can answer.

9

Privacy and the Criminal Process: *Selvi v. State of Karnataka*

What happens after a person is arrested or detained? His troubles begin then. When he is detained or arrested and he is in the clutches of the police, he is alone in the world, and the forces of the Police, the forces of the Crown and all other forces combine against him and he is helpless.

Thakur Das Bhargava, Constituent Assembly Debates (September 1949)

IN THE EARLY 2000s, the Karnataka government's Forensic Science Laboratory (FSL) at Bengaluru unexpectedly shot to fame. Notorious counterfeiter Abdul Karim Telgi, accused terrorists, alleged Naxalites, and run-of-the-mill criminals were all subjected to a 'truth serum', under the influence of which they apparently 'sang like canaries',[1] condemning both themselves and their accomplices. Important leads were supposedly revealed and knotty crimes were cracked. The assistant director of the FSL even earned the sobriquet of Doctor Narco or Narco Queen (after 'narco-analysis', the technical term for the process of using this 'truth serum').[2]

By the end of the decade, fame had turned to infamy. In a letter written from Nagpur Central Jail, in December 2008, Arun Ferreira, an accused Naxalite, publicly accused Doctor Narco of fabricating his test results to achieve the outcome that the government wanted.[3] Dismissing his objections, an unnamed expert at the FSL confidently proclaimed, 'During narco-analysis the subject goes through phases of trance ... [when] he speaks the truth'.[4] An unnamed police officer proclaimed, with equal confidence, that Ferreira had confessed to his crimes, and provided the investigation with vital evidence of further terrorist activities.[5]

After five years in jail, Arun Ferreira was acquitted of all charges.[6]

In the meantime, doubts and concerns grew over narco-analysis, both for its unreliability, and for the near-third-degree manner in which it was administered. Constitutional challenges wound their way through multiple high courts, until finally *Selvi v. State of Karnataka* ended up before the Supreme Court. It was contended that three of the most prominent interrogation techniques, viz., narco-analysis, the lie-detector test, and brain-mapping, violated an accused person's right against self-incrimination under Article 20(3), and her right to life and personal liberty under Article 21 of the Constitution.

The case seemed to have scant chance of succeeding. The colonial logic that had privileged the maintenance of law and order over the rights of the accused, and that had seen no problem with conscripting the individual's body (and her private spaces) for the purposes of law enforcement and crime detection, had been largely endorsed by the post-Independence Supreme Court.[7] The Code of Criminal Procedure allowed general warrants and searches,[8] and recent amendments had expanded the extent to which the body could be requisitioned in a criminal investigation, bringing in DNA profiling, among other things.[9] In this context, the mere administration (even if forced) of a drug that sent the subject into a hypnotic trance (narco-analysis), or the measurement of physiological (lie-detector) or cognitive (brain-mapping) responses to questions, seemed relatively minor infractions, if at all.

In *Selvi*, the Supreme Court disagreed. It declared the forced application of all three interrogation techniques to be unconstitutional. In this chapter, I argue that *Selvi* was a transformative judgement because of the way in which it understood and articulated the relationship between the individual and the State in the context in which the imbalance of power between the two is at its highest: when the individual is accused and the State is the interrogator.

I begin by describing two possible competing philosophies that underlie criminal legal regimes: the crime control model, which views the accurate solving of crime to be the highest goal of the law, and the due process model, which holds that even for the detection of crime, there are lines that the State cannot cross (I); I then demonstrate how the Supreme Court's early judgements on Article 20(3) were delivered within the framework of the crime control model (II), and how *Selvi* departed from this understanding in its interpretation of the words 'voluntary' and 'compelled' (III). In conclusion I contend that *Selvi's* embrace of the due process model is correct in light of our pre-constitutional experience of an authoritarian State and the decision of the framers to elevate the guarantee of self-incrimination from a procedural safeguard to a constitutional right (IV). Furthermore, it has important implications for our understanding of the limits that the Constitution and the Code of Criminal Procedure impose upon the police and upon the criminal investigation process (V).

I. Two Models of the Criminal Process

According to the dominant understanding, the practices and procedures of criminal investigation, evidence, and trial are structured around determining truth. A crime scene is scoured for fingerprints. A suspect's call data records are accessed to know whom she might have conspired with. Witnesses are cross-examined in court to test the credibility of their narrative. It is, of course, understood that in a fallible world, even the best procedures will yield, at the highest, an approximation of the truth. For this reason, the standard for conviction in criminal cases is 'beyond all *reasonable* doubt', instead of 'beyond *all* doubt'. And whether in science fiction novels[10] or in the euphemistic dubbing of Doctor Narco's procedure as a 'truth serum', the effort has always been to reduce to a vanishing point the gap between the truth and the determination of truth by the criminal legal procedure.

But that is not all. We recognize, as well, that there are limits to what the State can do to individuals in the quest for truth. In the words of the US Supreme Court, 'too high a price may be paid even for the unhampered enforcement of the criminal law, and that, in its attainment, other social objects of a free society should not be sacrificed'.[11] This is reflected most starkly in the debates around torture. Some argue that torture should be outlawed because *it doesn't work*. It is unreliable, encourages shoddy investigations, and all other things being equal, a system with institutionalized torture will lead to worse outcomes in terms of controlling crime. Others argue that this framing is a mistake. Torture should be outlawed because it violates human dignity. It should be outlawed even if it could be demonstrated that *it worked perfectly*.[12] To test both positions, there exist a number of well-worn hypotheticals. Is torture permissible in a 'ticking time-bomb' scenario? Can you retrieve evidence from a person's body by subjecting him to stomach-pumping?[13] What about the forceful administration of a truth serum that actually worked perfectly, if such a thing was invented one day?

In 1964, in a famous but controversial article titled 'Two Models of the Criminal Process', the US jurist Herbert Packer argued that the answers to such questions would depend upon the values that underlay the criminal legal system. Packer proposed two possible models: the 'crime control model' and the 'due process model'. Under the crime control model, the ultimate goal of the criminal process is the 'repression of criminal conduct'.[14] He wrote, 'In order to achieve this high purpose the Crime Control Model requires that primary attention be paid to the efficiency with which the criminal process operates to screen suspects, determine guilt, and secure appropriate dispositions of persons convicted of crime.'[15] Simplifying greatly, therefore, 'the criminal process ... must put special weight on the quality of administrative fact-finding. It becomes important, then, to place as few restrictions as possible on the character of the administrative fact-finding processes and to limit restrictions to such as enhance reliability, excluding those designed for other purposes.'[16] Under the crime control model, the question of whether torture was to be allowed or not would have to be answered after conducting empirical studies to determine whether, on the whole, evidence obtained under torture is more or less reliable than evidence obtained without. In simpler language, whether torture *works*.

In contrast with the crime control model, the due process model holds that 'the combination of stigma and loss of liberty that is embodied in the end result of the criminal process is the heaviest deprivation that government can inflict on the individual'.[17] Therefore, 'because of its potency in subjecting the individual to the coercive power of the state, the criminal process must ... be subjected to controls that prevent it from operating with maximal efficiency'.[18] In other words, under the due process model, the coercive edge of the criminal process must be tempered in a manner that, on some occasions, will have the inevitable effect of *retarding* efficiency, in service of other values such as human dignity and individual freedom.[19]

Consider, for example, the notorious 'exclusionary rule' in evidence law. The exclusionary rule stipulates that evidence obtained through unconstitutional means (e.g., a warrantless search, or through torture) is inadmissible in court. Naturally, this includes situations in which the quality and relevance of evidence is entirely unrelated to the manner in which it was obtained. Consequently, the crime control model, which is concerned with accurate determination of guilt, will only judge evidence with regard to its relevance, and will see little reason to deny admitting illegally obtained evidence. On the other hand, the due process model, which is concerned with protecting citizens' rights (including against warrantless searches and torture) might well determine that an effective way of protecting these rights is to ensure that evidence obtained in their violation, cannot be used against the accused. Upon the spectrum, for example, the United Kingdom and India veer more towards considering evidence based primarily on its reliability, while the United States remains more sensitive to the manner in which it is collected.[20]

Criminal legal systems attempt to strike a balance between the two models, i.e., to allow the State enough power to detect and punish crime, but not so much power that the individual is entirely effaced before the State.[21] As is evident with the fate of the exclusionary rule, different countries strike the balance differently. Furthermore, the balance is a contested one, subject to constant battle between the proponents of crime control and the supporters of due process. This battle assumes particular salience in circumstances where an aspect of criminal procedure can be justified under both models, but the degree of protection it affords to individuals will change depending upon which model is endorsed.

For example, Article 20(3) of the Constitution stipulates that 'no person accused of an offence shall be compelled to be a witness against himself'. It codifies the long-standing common-law 'privilege against self-incrimination', which, on some reflection, can fit within both the crime control and the due process models. Compelled testimony—simply by virtue of being compelled—will often be flawed. Reasonable criminals are unlikely to willingly give evidence incriminating themselves, and history bears witness to the fact that coerced, false confessions have been the norm rather than the exception. Consequently, the crime control model, with its focus on accurate determination of guilt and innocence, has good reason to guarantee a right against self-incrimination.[22] The due process model, of course, is concerned with the rights violations that invariably accompany compelled, self-incriminatory testimony, and has equal, if different, reason to guarantee that right as well.[23] It is quite possible, therefore, that as the Canadian Supreme Court observed, a self-incrimination clause may be driven by *both* elements: 'to protect against unreliable confessions ... and ... to protect against the abuse of power by the state'.[24]

However, these two rationales are not always complementary. It is when they clash that the difference becomes particularly significant. To go back to our earlier example, if an infallible truth serum is invented, then its use under the crime control model would no longer be problematic, since the central objection to compelled testimony—the likelihood of inaccuracy—has been removed. However, a very different set of concerns would be articulated by the proponents of due process: in particular, concerns about the right to privacy.

Article 20(3), therefore, is not self-interpreting. Its protective scope, and the extent to which it can check the State's power as an interrogator, depends upon which philosophy it is underpinned by. The sparse wording of the text offers us no assistance to decide that question. We must therefore turn to how, over the years, the Indian Supreme Court has understood this right against self-incrimination.

II. Let the Body Speak: Self-Incrimination and the Early Supreme Court

Soon after Independence, the Supreme Court was called upon to decide its first case dealing with the scope of the right against self-incrimination. In *M.P. Sharma v. Satish Chandra*, certain persons were suspected of committing large-scale corporate fraud, through a network of companies. Under the Code of Criminal Procedure (as it then stood), the police applied to the district magistrate for a warrant to search the offices of the various companies. The magistrate issued the warrant. Searches were carried out at thirty-four places, and documents seized. The petitioners (who held various positions in the companies) came to Court and asked that the warrants be quashed. They argued that the search and seizure of their private documents violated their rights under Article 20(3) of the Constitution. In case the documents contained something incriminating, their forced seizure would amount to compelling the petitioners to be 'witnesses against themselves'.

The first question before the Court, therefore, was whether the words 'to be a witness' (as part of the phrase 'no person shall be compelled to be a witness against himself') included self-incrimination through documentary evidence. The Court held that it did. It defined a 'witness' as any person who furnished (or was required to furnish) evidence. 'To be a witness', therefore, meant 'any positive volitional act that furnishes evidence'.[25] There was no reason this could not include documents.

The next question, then, was whether a search and seizure amounted to compelling a person to be a witness against herself. Here, the Court held that it did not:

> ... there is no basis ... for the assumption that a search or seizure of a thing or document is in itself to be treated as compelled production of the same ... A notice to produce is addressed to the party, concerned and his production in compliance therewith constitutes a testimonial act by him within the meaning of Article 20(3) as above explained. But search warrant is addressed to an officer of the Government, generally a police officer. Neither the search nor the seizure are acts [sic] of the occupier of the searched premises. They are acts of another to which he is obliged to submit and are, therefore, not his testimonial acts in any sense.[26]

In other words, to be a witness indicated that the person in question was performing a testimonial act of some kind (being compelled to speak, or being compelled to produce documents). However, when the forces of law and order searched premises and seized documents, there need not be any involvement of the person herself. Article 20(3), therefore, was violated if a person was forced to produce incriminating documents (by the police, or by a court order), but not if those documents were recovered in a police raid.[27]

This distinction seems somewhat thin and formalistic.[28] How did the Court justify it? It employed two arguments. First, it made a direct reference to the crime control model, noting, '[The] power of search and seizure is in any system of jurisprudence an overriding power of the State for the protection of social security and that power is necessarily regulated by law'.[29] The scope of compulsion under the self-incrimination clause, therefore, was to be defined and limited within the framework of the crime control model. And second, the Court made extensive reference to the colonial legal landscape. First, it observed:

> Article 20(3) embodies the principle of protection against compulsion of self-incrimination which is one of the fundamental canons of the British system of criminal jurisprudence and which has been adopted by the American system and incorporated as an article of its Constitution. It has also, to a substantial extent, been recognized in the Anglo-Indian administration of criminal justice in this country by incorporation into various statutory provisions. In order, therefore, to arrive at a correct appraisal of the scope and content of the doctrine and to judge to what extent that was intended to be recognized by our Constitution-makers in article 20(3), it is necessary to have a cursory view of the origin and scope of this doctrine and the implications thereof as understood in English law and in American law and as recognized in the Indian law.[30]

Using this interpretive framework, the Court was able to hold that there was no warrant to read the self-incrimination clause broadly, because the principle had been repeatedly contested and criticized in English common law.[31] Furthermore, the Court observed that in successive criminal procedure codes, enacted in India in 1861, 1872, and 1882, there was a clear distinction between a search and seizure, and compelled production of documents. It then noted that because the framers of the Constitution had consciously declined to insert into the Constitution a right akin to the US Fourth Amendment (that prohibited unreasonable searches and seizures), they implicitly intended this position to remain unchanged.[32]

M.P. Sharma did two things. It accorded a broad reading to the phrase 'to be a witness' in Article 20(3), including both oral testimony and documentary evidence within its scope (and also expanding its scope beyond the courtroom, to include police interrogations). However, it then employed the crime control model and colonial law to accord a narrow reading to the word 'compelled', holding that it only applied to forced production of documents, and not to a search and seizure under the Criminal Procedure Code (even though, in most cases, the result would be the same).[33]

The breadth of the first part of the Court's holding—a radical departure from colonial practice in placing constraints upon police interrogation—caused significant churning in criminal legal proceedings across the country.[34] Unsurprisingly, therefore, the broad reading of witness came under serious challenge seven years later, in *State of Bombay v. Kathi Kalu Oghad*, when the Court set up an eleven-judge bench to reconsider the verdict of eight judges in *M.P. Sharma*.[35] If to be a witness meant to furnish evidence, it was argued, then compelled fingerprinting, or the taking of bodily measurements (as part of criminal investigations, under the Identification of Prisoners Act of 1920), was clearly unconstitutional. So were the compelled taking of handwriting samples for comparison[36] and the admissibility of (otherwise inadmissible) confessions to the police that led to the recovery of evidence.[37] High courts across the country returned conflicting findings on the issue, and the case came up to the Supreme Court for resolution.

In *Kathi Kalu*, the Court evidently felt that fidelity to *M.P. Sharma's* definition of witness would outlaw some important criminal investigation procedures, and invalidate long-standing provisions of the Evidence Act, as well as other colonial laws such as the Identification of Prisoners Act. Its response was to hastily backtrack. It did so, as we shall see, by extending to the rest of Article 20(3) the logic that *M.P. Sharma* had used to narrow the meaning of compelled.

The majority began by holding that *M.P. Sharma* had been incorrect to equate to be a witness with to furnish evidence. To be a witness meant something narrower. It meant to communicate *knowledge* of a relevant fact. Providing a fingerprint, or a handwriting sample, did not involve communicating knowledge, and therefore did not amount to being a witness.[38] Notice, however, that in comparison with how we use the word 'witness' in everyday language, this seems a strained and artificial interpretation. There is no invariable association of witness with conscious, testimonial act: the very existence of the colloquialism dumb witness (as noted by the Court in *M.P. Sharma*) is evidence of this. So, also, is our reflexive attribution of the role of witness to decidedly unconscious entities such as history, as well as the fact that the sentence 'your fingerprints at the scene of the crime speak of your guilt' sounds entirely natural.

The majority, therefore, had to dig deeper. It did so by taking from *M.P. Sharma* the phrase 'a positive, volitional act' (of furnishing evidence), and equating 'volition' with the *ability to alter a state of affairs*. In other words, the Court held that (unlike oral or written testimony), a person had no ability to *change* their fingerprints, or their bodily measurements, or (subject to certain exceptions) the character of their handwriting. The giving of fingerprints or a blood sample, therefore, did amount to furnishing evidence, but not to 'being a witness', because the *character* of the evidence was not within the 'volition' or control of the person.[39]

For this reason, the Court noted, fingerprints or handwriting samples did not themselves incriminate an accused. It was only when they were matched against, say, a fingerprint found at the scene of crime or a forged document with the accused person's signature that they became salient as evidence. But *taken by themselves*, they remained 'innocuous'[40] (once again, the Court equated innocuous with unchangeable). The concurring and partially dissenting opinion in *Kathi Kalu* deepened this argument by noting that even if it could be said that fingerprints or handwriting samples fell within the definition of being a witness, the individual was not being compelled to become a witness *against himself*. This was because, as reasoned above, it was not the sample that incriminated him, but the fact that the sample was successfully matched with another piece of evidence.[41]

At the heart of the judgement in *Kathi Kalu* was the understanding that one is a witness only about a fact, or a state of affairs, which one has the power to change or alter (volition). A moment's reflection should make clear that the foundation of this analysis is the crime control model. That which the accused cannot change has an independent character, a character that does not depend upon the will of the accused (which, presumably, can be undermined or overcome in interrogation). To put it simply, the evidentiary character of fingerprints, or bodily measurements, or handwriting samples (or even blood samples), is not affected by the nature of the interrogation that the accused was subjected to. Therefore, interpreting Article 20(3) as drawing a line between evidence that the accused can change and evidence that she can't demonstrates that the overriding concern is with the character of the evidence, its accuracy, and its reliability.[42]

Indeed, this concern was evident in both the majority and the concurrence. The majority noted that in protecting the right of the accused against self-incrimination, 'lawmakers could not have intended to put obstacles in the way of efficient investigation'.[43] The concurrence counselled that because they had no evidentiary value in themselves, allowing the taking of fingerprints or handwriting samples would not tempt law-enforcement officials to become lazy or to take short-cuts[44] (for example, like allowing police confessions would). To buttress this interpretation, the majority, in particular, relied extensively upon the colonial landscape, citing both 'English law on the subject'[45] and colonial statutory provisions. Taking note of the provisions of the Evidence Act (1872), the Code of Criminal Procedure (1898), and the Identification of Prisoners Act (1920), the majority observed that the 'framers were aware' of this legal landscape, and consequently the constitutional right under Article 20(3) was to be interpreted *within* this framework.[46]

At first glance, this seems decidedly odd. The natural method would be to subject existing laws to constitutional standards, instead of *deriving* constitutional standards from existing laws that preceded the Constitution itself. It is not so odd, however, if we understand that, in the view of the Court, the function of the Constitution was not so much as to *transform* the relationship between the State and the individual, but to *preserve* it. This is visible most starkly in a judgement (*Shyamlal Mohanlal Choksi*) delivered soon after, which also considered the issue of compelled production of documents under the Code of Criminal Procedure. The majority held that, in view of Article 20(3), the provisions requiring compelled production could not apply to a person accused of an offence. But in his dissenting opinion, Justice Shah observed that the Court's interpretation went against the previous 'eighty years' of jurisprudence.[47] The fact that sixty-three out of these eighty years were spent under a colonial regime was considered to be of no consequence. This interpretation could make sense only if the framing of the Constitution was seen as a moment of conservation and continuity, rather than a moment of transformation and change.[48]

Let us sum up. Article 20(3) guarantees the right against self-incrimination, stipulating that 'no person shall be compelled to be a witness against himself'. In *M.P. Sharma v. Satish Chandra*, the Supreme Court held that a search and seizure by the police did not amount to compulsion under Article 20(3), because the accused herself was not being forced to do anything. In *State of Bombay v. Kathi Kalu Oghad*, the Court held that to be a witness only included a conscious testimonial or communicative act (knowledge of a relevant fact), and was limited to furnishing only that type of evidence that a person had control over, or ability, to alter. The Court did this by taking the word 'volitional' from *M.P. Sharma*, and equating it with 'changeable'. In *M.P. Sharma*, the clauses on search warrants were upheld. In *Kathi Kalu*, the provisions of the Evidence Act and the Identification of Prisoners Act were upheld. Both judgements rested upon two conceptual premises: first, that Article 20(3) embodied the crime control model, and the *content* of the phrase 'no person shall be compelled to be a witness against himself' was to be determined by considering the impact upon efficient, accurate, and reliable criminal investigation; and second, that judicial interpretation of Article 20(3) must be such that the constitutional provision was brought in line with the existing legal framework of criminal investigation and procedure, a substantial part of which was of colonial origin.[49]

III. *Selvi* and the Due Process Model

The judgements in *M.P. Sharma* and *Kathi Kalu*—delivered by benches of eight and eleven judges, respectively—settled the issue for a few decades. In the meantime, however, with advances in technology and in interrogation techniques, the bright lines drawn in those cases began to blur, not just in India, but all over the world. In *Schmerber v. California*, the US Supreme Court maintained the difference between 'physical' and 'testimonial' evidence (on the lines of *Kathi Kalu*), but acknowledged that there existed a wide range of situations in which the distinction would break down.[50] And ten years later, in *Horvath v. The Queen*, the Canadian Supreme Court was compelled to reconsider the entire common law jurisprudence on the meaning of 'voluntariness'. *Horvath* involved a murder case in which the accused was subjected to a lengthy period of interrogation, during which he confessed to the murder, and provided the location of the murder weapon. It was later found that, as a result of the intensity of the interrogation, he had been in a 'light hypnotic state'[51] during this time. It was argued that this would have no bearing on the issue of compelled self-incrimination, because, as per the classic common law definition of voluntariness, laid down in Halsbury's Laws of England and by the 1914 case of *Ibrahim v. The Queen*, a statement was voluntary if 'it has not been obtained from [a person] by fear of prejudice or hope of advantage, exercised or held out by a person in authority, or by oppression'.[52] However, a closely divided Supreme Court discarded this definition, and held that what mattered was whether the individual was 'in full and voluntary control and possession of his faculties'[53] when making the statement. The Court grounded this definition within the right to privacy, noting that the individual's will was overborne,[54] and in the process 'a police officer has gained unconsented access to what in a human being is of the utmost privacy, the privacy of his own mind'.[55] Consequently, the statements were held to be inadmissible, notwithstanding a psychiatrist's testimony that the accused had been probably telling the truth 'as he saw it'.

It was in this transformed context—both technological and constitutional—that, almost fifty years after *Kathi Kalu*, the Supreme Court was called upon to re-examine the meaning of Article 20(3). *Selvi v. State of Karnataka* involved a constitutional challenge to the forcible use of three popular interrogation techniques. In narco-analysis, an individual was injected with sodium pentothal[56], 'a drug which lowers inhibitions … and induces the person to talk freely'.[57] She was then questioned while under the effect of the drug. Under the polygraph, or lie-detector, test, a person's physiological responses (such as 'respiration, blood pressure, blood flow, pulse and galvanic skin resistance'[58]) were measured to determine whether she was likely to be lying or telling the truth. The BEAP (brain electrical activation profile or brain-mapping) test was designed to detect 'whether an individual is familiar with certain information by way of measuring activity in the brain that is triggered by exposure to selected stimuli'.[59]

Selvi was a difficult case. While the judgements in *M.P. Sharma* and *Kathi Kalu* had dealt with very different issues, the analytical framework that they had employed remained controlling. In narco-analysis, the administration of sodium pentothal could be compared to the seizure of documents in *M.P. Sharma*: at the point of compulsion, there was no testimonial act, and, therefore, no violation of Article 20(3). Under *Ibrahim*'s definition of voluntary, the individual was not compelled to answer questions simply because she was under the influence of the truth serum. Lie-detector tests and brain mapping bore a family resemblance to *Kathi Kalu*. Like fingerprints, they involved *physiological* responses that were not *in themselves* incriminatory, but only of value when put alongside other pieces of substantive evidence.[60]

And yet, the analogies were not quite so clear-cut. Was it possible to draw a bright-line distinction between the administration of sodium pentothal (compelled) and the subsequent interrogation (voluntary)? Didn't the results of a lie-detector or a BEAP test determine what was in the individual's mind, and were, therefore, of a nature different from fingerprints or blood samples, or even DNA? *Selvi*, thus, gave the Court a chance to reconsider not just the meaning of Article 20(3), but also its underlying values.

However, the State argued that the case presented no trouble at all. Section 53 of the Code of Criminal Procedure already allowed for the examination of 'blood, bloodstains, semen, sputum, sweat' through the use of 'modern and scientific techniques including DNA profiling and other such tests'.[61] Consequently, it was contended that the three interrogation techniques at issue ought to simply be read into Section 53.

The Court rejected this argument, noting that Section 53 referred only to 'bodily substances' and not to 'testimonial responses'.[62] However, the facts in *Selvi* were precisely those in which the seemingly straightforward distinction between testimonial/communicative and physical/real evidence—as pointed out in *Schmerber v. California*—came undone. While an interview under the effects of sodium pentothal evidently involved a 'testimonial response', what was it about physiological reactions (in lie-detector tests and brain-mapping) that brought them within the category of testimony and not physical evidence?

The Court answered this question by going back to *Kathi Kalu*, and holding that a testimonial act involved 'the imparting of knowledge by a person who has personal knowledge of the facts that are in issue'.[63] It then applied this definition to the facts:

> Even though the actual process of undergoing a polygraph examination or a BEAP test is not the same as that of making an oral or written statement, the consequences are similar. By making inferences from the results of these tests, the examiner is

> able to derive knowledge from the subject's mind which otherwise would not have become available to the investigators. These two tests are different from medical examination and the analysis of bodily substances such as blood, semen, and hair samples, since the test subject's physiological responses are directly correlated to mental faculties. Through lie-detection or gauging a subject's familiarity with the stimuli, personal knowledge is conveyed in respect of a relevant fact.[64]

Therefore, the key distinction between the BEAP and lie-detector tests and the facts of *Kathi Kalu* and, by extension, the ingredients of Section 53 of the CrPC was the involvement of the mind: while both involved physiological responses, it was only in the former case that these responses were 'directly correlated to ... mental faculties'.

But that then raised the further question: what was it about the involvement of the mind (a *physical* part of the body, after all)[65] that made the distinction salient? The Court answered this by noting that:

> The compulsory administration of the impugned tests impedes the subject's right to choose between remaining silent and offering substantive information. The requirement of a 'positive volitional act' becomes irrelevant since the subject is compelled to convey personal knowledge irrespective of his/her own volition.[66]

In this paragraph, the Court made a fundamental interpretive shift from the foundations of *Kathi Kalu*. In *Kathi Kalu, M.P. Sharma's* articulation of the 'positive volitional act' had been understood in terms of reliability of the evidence. Volition had been interpreted to mean having the power to alter a piece of evidence (such as oral testimony), a definition that flowed from the imperatives of the crime control model. In *Selvi*, however, the Court understood volition (or voluntariness) not in the language of the changeable and the unchangeable, but in the language of choice, a choice whether or not to convey personal information.

Of course, in a trivial way, being forced to provide a blood sample or a fingerprint also involves conveying personal knowledge (of your blood group or your fingerprint pattern) irrespective of your volition.[67] In earlier cases, the Court had gotten around that by arguing that a blood sample or a fingerprint was innocuous *in itself*. Only when subsequently corroborated with another piece of evidence (fingerprints at the scene of the crime) did it become incriminatory. However, that reasoning was not open to the Court in *Selvi*, because physiological responses to stimuli are also innocuous *in themselves*. The responses to stimuli in a lie-detector test or a BEAP do not possess incriminatory content, like a confession or a signed document does. So, even though mental processes were involved, these mental processes lacked the essential attribute that set apart oral or documentary testimony, and indeed, appeared closer to physical evidence taken in the form of blood or DNA.

Essentially therefore, the Court was holding two sets of ideas, one legal and one factual: volition as defined as choice (legal), and the distinction between physiological and mental faculties as the factor that set apart BEAP and lie-detector tests from fingerprints, blood samples, and DNA (factual). To complete the argument, it would have to find a constitutional bridge between the two, an argument for why the issue of choice became particularly salient in cases where what was at stake was interference with mental processes per se.

The Court built this bridge upon *R.C. Cooper*'s theory of intersecting rights under the Constitution. Following *Cooper* and *Maneka Gandhi*, it held that the nature, scope, and interpretation of Article 20(3) could not be considered in isolation from Article 21, which guaranteed the right to life and personal liberty. One aspect of personal liberty was the right to privacy:

> In conceptualising the 'right to privacy' we must highlight the distinction between privacy in a physical sense and the privacy of one's mental processes ... We must recognise the importance of personal autonomy in aspects such as the choice between remaining

> silent and speaking. An individual's decision to make a statement is the product of a private choice and there should be no scope for any other individual to interfere with such autonomy, especially in circumstances where the person faces exposure to criminal charges or penalties. Therefore, it is our considered opinion that subjecting a person to the impugned techniques in an involuntary manner violates the prescribed boundaries of privacy.[68]

The constitutional bridge between volition and interference with mental processes, therefore, was Article 21's conception of mental privacy and the right to informational self-determination. As the Canadian Supreme Court had noted in *Horvath*, the right to remain silent 'includes not only the right to censor any information which is on [the] conscious mind but also the right to control the administration of artificial processes whereby unconsciously held information might emerge into consciousness'.[69] In other words, any individual, including an accused, had the right to informational self-determination, that is, the right to control information about herself.[70]

We are now in a position to understand the argument in *Selvi*, and the break that it made with the crime control logic of *M.P. Sharma* and *Kathi Kalu*. In *Kathi Kalu*, volition, defined in terms of changeability, had played a crucial role, and its definition was derived from the crime control model: information that you had no control over, or power to change, could not possibly be fabricated. In *Selvi*, on the other hand (although the Court did initially embark upon a discussion of the reliability of the investigative techniques), the Court framed volition in terms of choice. It then drew a distinction between physical privacy (blood samples, fingerprints, DNA) and mental privacy.[71] Linking the word 'witness' to testimony, and understanding testimony as the impartation of information present within the mind of a person, the Court placed the concept of mental privacy—understood as autonomous mental processes and informational self-determination—at the heart of the guarantee against self-incrimination. And with this, it was able to undermine *M.P. Sharma*'s formalistic view of compulsion as well: it was not simply about whether a person was being compelled, in the narrow sense, *at the time of the testimonial act*, but about the entire set of circumstances under which the testimonial act came to be.[72]

At the heart of this reading of Article 20(3) was the understanding that the sparse phrase 'no person shall be compelled to be a witness against himself' had to be interpreted in the context of the Fundamental Rights chapter as a whole, and especially Article 21 of the Constitution. Through this, the due process model—which placed strong emphasis on human dignity and individual rights as being non-negotiable in the criminal process—came to shape the scope and meaning of the self-incrimination clause. The distinction with *M.P. Sharma* and *Kathi Kalu* could not be starker: crime control and colonial law on the one hand, due process and the Constitution on the other.

The judgement in *Selvi*, ultimately, was a vindication of the ideals expressed, perhaps most eloquently, by Justice Claire L'Heureux-Dubé, of the Canadian Supreme Court:

> Although the search of an individual's home is an invasion of privacy, and although the taking of fingerprints, breath samples or bodily fluids are even more private, there is no doubt that the mind is the individual's most private sanctum. Although the state may legitimately invade many of these spheres for valid and justifiable investigatory purposes vis-à-vis the accused, it is fundamental to justice that the state not be able to invade the sanctum of the mind for the purpose of incriminating that individual. This fundamental tenet is preserved, in its entirety, by the principle against self-incrimination.[73]

IV. Due Process and the Transformative Constitution

Was *Selvi* correct in introducing the due process model as a constituent element of Article 20(3) of the Constitution? I argue here that it was. While elements of the guarantee against self-incrimination existed in the colonial era (as noticed by the Court in *M.P. Sharma*), they were partial in character, and subservient to the overall colonial imperative of law and order. This was not just in terms of their substantive content, but in the very structure of the criminal justice system in colonial India. This was a structure that vested concentrated power in the hands of the executive, regularly undermined the separation of powers, and intentionally denied to Indians the rights and liberties that were available to individuals in Britain. The clearest example of this was provided by the Lieutenant-Governor during the debates around the Criminal Procedure Code of 1873. While defending provisions that authorized sweeping police searches (of the kind that would never have been allowed in Britain), the Lieutenant-Governor noted that:

> [such rights] were especially out of place in a country where it was not pretended that the subject enjoyed that liberty which was the birthright of an Englishman, and it was not intended to introduce rules into the criminal law which were designed with the object of securing the liberties of the people. That being so, His Honour thought they might fairly get rid of some of the rules, the object of which was to secure for the people that jealous protection which the English law gave to the accused. It seemed to him that they were not bound to protect the criminal according to any Code of fair play, but that their object should be to get at the truth, and anything which would tend to elicit the truth was regarded by the Committee to be desirable for the interests of the accused if he was innocent, for those of the public if he was guilty … for instance, His Honour did not see why they should not get a man to criminate himself if they could; why they should not do all which they could to get the truth from him; why they should not cross-question him, and adopt every other means, short of absolute torture, to get at the truth. They had already done a good deal in the direction of clearing away English prejudices, and the Committee proposed to make further concessions to common sense in the present Bill.[74]

This 'colonial common sense' was partially quoted by Justice Shah in his dissenting opinion in *Shyamlal Mohanlal*, soon after he had pithily summarized the state of colonial law:

> The Evidence Act and the Code of Criminal Procedure were enacted at a time when the primary aim of the Government was to maintain law and order. The Legislature was merely a branch of the executive government, and was not in the very nature of things concerned with the liberty of the individual.[75]

Of course, for Justice Shah, this was a reason *not* to read in an expansive right against self-incrimination into Article 20(3). However, this was because he and, for that matter, the majorities in *M.P. Sharma* and *Kathi Kalu* continued to be in thrall to the unarticulated assumption that the Constitution changed nothing. This assumption, of course, is at entirely at odds with the argument of this section: that the framing of the Constitution was a transformative moment that *elevated* what had been a heavily diluted aspect of criminal procedure into a fundamental right, and one which was organized around ideas of freedom and autonomy.

To understand why this is so, we need to go beyond the text of the Article. In stipulating that no person shall be compelled to be a witness against himself, the framers were using words that had a long, almost ancient, vintage. While the most familiar predecessor was the Fifth Amendment of the US Constitution,[76] the framing of the self-incrimination clause in the language of being a 'witness' against oneself had its origins in common and canon law.[77] Over the years, it had been invoked to justify a number of competing rationales[78] (two of these being the crime control and due process models), without a decisive verdict in any direction. As the Canadian Supreme Court summed it up, 'The principle against self-incrimination may mean different things at different times and in different contexts.'[79]

The austere text of Article 20(3), therefore, tells us nothing about its underlying values. Nor do the Constituent Assembly

Debates help to answer the question. The guarantee against self-incrimination found its way into the Constitution almost absent-mindedly, without any debate.[80] That, however, does not exhaust the interpretive resources open to us. If the text of Article 20(3) does not speak, its *placement* in the Fundamental Rights chapter certainly does.

Alongside Articles 19, 21, 20(1), 20(2), and 22, Article 20(3) is located in the sub-section of Part III titled 'Rights to Freedom'. Neither the placement of Article 20(3) nor the company it keeps are accidental, and nor were they inevitable.[81] The first, a conscious move by the framers, tells us that liberty is, at least, *one* of the values that constitutes the Indian Constitution's guarantee against self-incrimination. The case for due process being at the foundation of the self-incrimination guarantee grows stronger if we fan out still further. The provisions that accompany Article 20(3) under the heading 'Rights to Freedom' include all the basic civil rights, viz., speech, assembly, association, movement, life, and personal liberty, that constitute the basis of human dignity and autonomy. And indeed, it was by reading Article 20(3) alongside 21 that the Court in *Selvi* gave the guarantee against self-incrimination its foundations in mental privacy and informational self-determination. In this family of rights that must be read together and in harmony (as *R.C. Cooper* correctly taught us), the crime control model strikes a discordant note.[82] Article 20(3), therefore, is illuminated by the constellation of freedoms that surround it, all of which point to due process being at the heart of the guarantee against self-incrimination.[83]

The difference is not merely formal, or linguistic. As Ian Dennis points out, it makes all the difference whether the guarantee against self-incrimination exists for utilitarian reasons (ensuring reliability), or whether it is treated as 'an adjectival right in the criminal process'.[84] The reason being:

> Once the privilege is granted the status of a procedural right, one which is an essential component of a fair trial, it acquires much

> greater force. It is then capable of applying broadly in a range of different contexts, and it becomes much more difficult to negotiate, in the sense that acute problems arise over the conditions, if any, under which it can be overridden by legislation or judicial decision.[85]

It is this distinction that the theorists of colonial continuity failed to grasp. And it is in understanding it that we are also now in a position to understand the fundamental error in *M.P. Sharma*'s case. In *M.P. Sharma*, the Court surveyed the pre-Independence legal landscape, found a number of legal provisions that chipped away at the scope of the self-incrimination guarantee, and concluded from this that the *constitutional* right against self-incrimination had, therefore, to be reconciled with the law as it stood. This was a mistake, because it ignored the transformative character of the Constitution. It ignored, in particular, the fact that whatever minimal procedural guarantees that existed in the colonial period existed within the framework of law and order. In stark contrast, on the other hand, the self-incrimination clause had been consciously articulated in the language of freedom, and nested within a group of rights that unambiguously spoke the vocabulary of civil liberties.[86]

It is important to note that this argument does not seek to prove too much. It is not my case that due process and individual freedom are the *only* values underlying Article 20(3).[87] The values of reliability and accuracy, under the crime control model, remain relevant and important. They are found, for example, in Section 27 of the Evidence Act, which—in specific cases of recovery of evidence pursuant to a statement—allows that statement to be admissible in evidence even if it is an otherwise barred confession to a police officer. The argument, however, is that in *interpreting* the scope of Article 20(3), and, in particular, the meanings of words such as 'compelled' and 'to be a witness', the individual freedom-oriented values of the due process model have to be given a central and framing role. *Selvi* was the first judgement under Article 20(3) that understood this, and, therefore, introduced the concept of mental privacy as a core organizing principle emerging out of a combined reading of Articles 20(3) and 21.[88] For this reason, it is a transformative judgement.

V. Conclusion

The relationship between the individual and the State is at its most unequal when an accused person is brought face to face with the machinery of official power. Constitutional rights are actualized only when they are applied meaningfully to such relationships. This requires infusing constitutional norms into the legal framework that structures the relationship between the accused and the forces of law and order at the point of greatest vulnerability: the interrogation room.

This legal framework is constituted in the first instance by the Code of Criminal Procedure and the Evidence Act and, secondly, by multiple special laws that lay down the procedure for dealing with specific categories of offences. *Selvi* reversed a decades-old logic that had come to be a staple feature of the Supreme Court's jurisprudence: that a system of law instituted by a colonial regime, with the expressed purpose of controlling a subject population, could be applied without alteration to the relationship between a constitutional democracy and its citizens. It did so by placing the individual, and individual rights, at the heart of its interpretation of the guarantee against self-incrimination, and making privacy the organizing principle to determine the interplay between the Constitution and the criminal process.

The actual impact of *Selvi*, however, depends on whether future judgements take its transformative logic forward. While the correctness of *Selvi* was affirmed by a nine-judge bench of the Supreme Court in *Puttaswamy*,[89] some of its insights remain untapped. For example, it is an accepted part of Indian law, driven by imperatives of crime control, that *illegally* obtained evidence remains admissible in Court, as long as it is relevant. *Selvi*, however, drew a distinction between *illegal* and *unconstitutional* evidence, and held that exclusionary principle would apply to the latter.[90] While this distinction was also made in previous cases such as *Kathi Kalu*, *Selvi's* clear reiteration—drawing from its own application of the due process model—placed the issue back in the spotlight, this time within the due process framework. For example, Section 27 of the Evidence Act stipulates that police confessions, otherwise inadmissible under Section 25, become admissible *to the extent that* they lead to recovery of material evidence. But to the extent that a police confession is *compelled*, it cannot be admitted in evidence, *even if it leads to recoveries*. This can, potentially, check some of the more abusive police practices that are presently staple features of investigations, such as disclosure and pointing out memos, the contents of which are the result of compulsion, but where the compulsion is of no relevance to their admissibility.[91]

Furthermore, the actual holding in *Selvi* is of only limited reach. While the Court made due process the foundation of interpreting the phrases 'compelled' and to be a 'witness against himself', Article 20(3) has a third, crucial element: it applies only to an accused person. In *M.P. Sharma*, the Court resisted an attempt to confine Article 20(3) to the courtroom, and observed that the ambit of the Article covered any 'person against whom a formal accusation relating to the commission of an offence has been levelled which in the normal course may result in prosecution'.[92] While the Court also clarified that it was not deciding whether or not the right would apply in other cases, subsequent judgements invoked 'formal accusation' as a *necessary* requirement to trigger Article 20(3).[93] The criminal legal scholar, Abhinav Sekhri, points out that this limitation became significant with the passage of a number of laws, dealing with socio-economic offences, that were enacted or modified in the 1960s. Laws such as the Sea Customs Act and, subsequently, the Foreign Exchange Management Act and the Narcotics, Drugs and Psychotropic Substances Act, institute a detailed *investigatory* regime before the stage of a formal accusation. Although the investigating officers have the same powers as police officers, including search, seizure and arrest, issuing summons to individuals, who are bound to answer on pain of perjury, and imposing detention, they are *deemed*, by legal fiction, not to be police officers.[94] However, the Supreme Court has held that because, under these investigatory regimes, there is no 'formal accusation', *Article 20(3) does not apply*.[95]

If the heart of the due process model is a concern for protecting the rights of individuals who are placed in a special position of vulnerability vis-à-vis the State, then the Court's exclusion of entire legal regimes from the ambit of Article 20(3), purely on the basis of formalistic reasoning, is indefensible. After *Selvi*, therefore, we have an anomalous situation, where Article 20(3) appears to have been partially interpreted from the perspective of the due process model, and partially from a restrictive perspective that can only be traced back to the imperatives of crime control. As we have argued, if *Selvi* is correctly decided, then the Court's judgements interpreting the word accused perhaps call for reconsideration. To extend the meaning of 'accused' to situations where an individual is subjected to 'detention in custody by any authority during an investigation',[96] as Sekhri suggests, would be a true vindication of *Selvi's* transformative potential.

And lastly, not only Article 20(3), but an overwhelming part of Indian criminal law remains dominated by the crime control model. As Chandra and Satish draw out in some detail, the remaining clauses of Article 20, the right to fair trial, the right to counsel, and the rights upon arrest and bail (which were also discussed in the previous chapter) have all been shaped by the imperatives of crime control, with due process being virtually obliterated. This is demonstrated, for example, by the Court's readiness to uphold reverse-onus clauses in special laws, dispense with the right to counsel for pre-trial proceedings, and *even* question the beyond-reasonable-doubt standard for guilt in criminal law.[97]

One *Selvi* can hardly shift the accumulated weight of a few decades. But it can, at least, remind us of one thing. Society despises those who are accused of crimes. It is the easiest thing in the world for a constitutional court to strip the despised, the hated, and the shunned of their rights, claiming that it is responding to the collective conscience or the collective cry of society. It is easy to say that the rights of the individual must give way to the greater good of society, especially when society has already decided that that individual is dispensable. That is the easy way to popular acclaim and public applause.

But our Constitution exists because the easy path is not always the right path, and the Courts exist because, unlike an individual accused, they have the institutional resilience to withstand popular opprobrium when they decide to forsake the easy path for the right path. Ambedkar's relief that the Draft Constitution had adopted the individual as its unit would end up as little more than a cruel joke if the individual has to leave behind her rights at the entrance of the police station. *Selvi's* radical insight is that it is the moral orphans among us—despised by society and at the mercy of the State—who, far from being dispensable, stand *most* in need of constitutional sanctuary. Until that insight percolates through the rest of our criminal law, our Constitution's transformative potential will remain unrealized.

Epilogue

'Something of Freedom Is Yet to Come': The Aadhaar Case, Technological Self-Determination and the Future of Transformative Constitutionalism

'Imagine a guy walking on the road at 2 a.m., who is looking suspicious. A police patrol can take the suspect's photograph with our app, and within a second receive details about his crime history.'

V. Gnanadesikan, CEO of FaceTagr, in an interview to *FactorDaily* (2018)

'The Constitution is not a charter of servitude.'

Shyam Divan, oral arguments in the Aadhaar case (2018)

ON THE AFTERNOON OF 10 May 2018, the Attorney-General for India rose and informed the courtroom that the second-longest hearing in the history of the Supreme Court had just concluded. Spanning thirty-eight days of argument, spread out over four months,[1] the 'Aadhaar case' had been historical in many ways. More than six years in the making (the first petition had been filed in 2012), it had generated an extraordinary amount of interest and passion both within and outside the courtroom.

Answers to parliamentary questions, World Bank reports, scientific diagrams, affidavits from rural India, and an unprecedented PowerPoint presentation had all formed part of the arguments[2] in the Court. And outside it, duelling newspaper columns had carried on an intense and often acrimonious debate, which occasionally spilt over into the courtroom. Accusations of fudged documents, and uncharacteristically fraught exchanges between counsel and the Bench, had raised the temperature to fever pitch. Overall, when the Constitution Bench reserved judgement on 10 May 2018, nobody was left in any doubt about the complexity, the global significance, and the constitutional importance of the issues that the five Supreme Court justices would have to grapple with.

What was the Aadhaar case about? Pared down to the essentials, Aadhaar is a numerical identifier issued to an individual by the government. Upon enrolling for an Aadhaar number, the individual must part with her biometrics (fingerprint and iris) and certain demographic details. The biometric information is stored in a centralized database. At the heart of the Aadhaar system is the principle of authentication: information (for example, fingerprints) submitted by individuals seeking to prove their identity in order to establish eligibility for a benefit or service is 'matched' with the information already stored in the database, which was given at the time of enrolment. If the centralized database sends back an affirmative response, the users are deemed to have successfully proven that they are, in the words of the Unique Identification Authority of India (UIDAI), 'who they claim they are'.[3]

When Aadhaar was first introduced at the turn of 2010, enrolment was advertised as voluntary, aimed at facilitating citizens' access to services by providing a swift and accurate method of authenticating one's identity. But by the time the Supreme Court came to hear the case in 2018, Aadhaar had become virtually indispensable for carrying on life in India. It had been made mandatory for opening a bank account, for obtaining a mobile SIM card, and for paying income tax.

Biometric authentication had also been made mandatory for availing a host of basic entitlements designed for the most vulnerable members of society, such as access to the public distribution system. Private corporations, too, had begun to use Aadhaar as a mandatory means of identification. And so, the Aadhaar challenge evolved from just another run-of-the-mill constitutional challenge into something far more urgent and significant. Eventually, when it was argued, the case had become about the legitimacy of a State-created nation-wide information database, the circumstances under which it had been built, the conditions under which it was maintained, and the situations in which it could be used.

'The Constitution is not a charter of servitude,' Shyam Divan, lead counsel for the petitioners, memorably proclaimed during the course of arguments. Indeed, as the Aadhaar case unfolded, it became increasingly clear that it was being fought upon the terrain of transformative constitutionalism, in all its diverse, layered, and bitterly contested dimensions. At its heart, the petitioners argued, the case was about the relationship between the individual and the State, under a democratic and republican Constitution. By building a nationwide centralized biometric database, and by giving itself the power to track people's daily transactions every time they were required to authenticate themselves, the State was distorting the balance of power that was at the heart of the constitutional order, and threatening freedom.

Elements of transformative constitutionalism were also present in the specific challenges mounted by the petitioners. By compulsorily fingerprinting almost the entire population just to prevent the possibility of identity fraud, was the Aadhaar programme not simply replicating the 'jurisdiction of suspicion' that had formed the basis of the repealed Criminal Tribes Act and the disgraced *ADM Jabalpur* judgement? Was not the forced taking of fingerprints and iris scans a severe and unjustified violation of personal privacy? Would not the very existence of a centralized database and the ability to profile individuals cast a chilling effect upon the exercise of fundamental freedoms?

Did not evidence show that the failure of biometric authentication (an inexact process at the best of times) had disproportionately impacted the most vulnerable? Had it not hit the labourer whose fingerprints had been erased by decades of manual work, the leprosy patient who didn't have fingerprints, and the bedridden widow who could not march to the ration shop to authenticate herself? Was not this perpetuation of existing disadvantage a negation of the constitutional promise of substantive equality? By vesting unaccountable power in the hands of a new class of middlemen—those who operate the authentication machines, and therefore control the fate of welfare recipients—did not this system create a new private regime of power, flying in the face of constitutional fraternity? Was it constitutional to allow private parties into the 'Aadhaar ecosystem' in the absence of a data protection law? All these issues, and more, were raised by the petitioners.

On the other side, the State invoked transformative constitutionalism as well. Rampant identity fraud, it argued, was impeding its welfare obligations under the Directive Principles of State Policy. As the most efficient and effective method of identification, biometric authentication would ensure that welfare benefits were only going to those entitled to them, and save the State substantial amounts of money by preventing 'leakage'. Aadhaar, therefore, was a vehicle for the State to achieve the transformative ambition of Part IV of the Constitution. It was a goal important enough to justify compulsion, and the statutory framework had enough safeguards to contain the possible abuses of power and system failures that the petitioners feared. Preventing identity fraud, and thereby tackling tax evasion, banking scams, and terrorism, was also invoked as the justification for making Aadhaar mandatory for income tax, bank accounts, and mobile phones.

By a 4-1 majority, the Supreme Court upheld the constitutionality of the Aadhaar programme, while limiting, in some important respects, its scope and use.[4] This is not the place for a detailed critique of the Aadhaar judgement(s) or of Justice Chandrachud's dissent, which accepted most of the arguments advanced above.[5] What is notable, however, is the Court's failure to engage with the real terms of the debate, and the stakes at issue. While in concrete terms, the Aadhaar case was about the constitutional validity of a centralized biometric database, what it *represented* was something far more fundamental. Aadhaar was the first time that the Supreme Court was asked to consider how the widespread and pervasive use of technology was resetting the relationship between the State, society, corporations, and the individual. And this was a relationship that, in many ways, was now defined and characterized by data and information. Aadhaar was the first case to raise these questions, but it will not be the last. And—apart from the necessary role of Parliament in framing laws and regulations—the future of transformative constitutionalism in the twenty-first century, I contend, will depend upon how our courts will, or will not, interpret and update the Constitution to address this inescapable reality.

Through the course of this book, I have attempted to articulate a transformative understanding of the Constitution, rooted in liberty, equality, and fraternity. These guiding principles establish the framework within which democracy can thrive and flourish. In different ways, they are each concerned with the question of *power*. Liberty guarantees individual freedom by constraining State power. Equality authorizes, and sometimes mandates, that State power be used to remedy historical and institutional disadvantage. And fraternity seeks to dismantle social hierarchies by equalizing private regimes of power. In the cases that we have discussed in this book, relations of power have been understood in tangible and material ways: access to public goods through reservation policies, social exclusion through the practice of excommunication, physical confinement through preventive detention, and so on. While these forms of power will, of course, remain salient, what the Aadhaar case made starkly clear was that information, power, and the Constitution are now inextricably linked. Power is being increasingly exercised through, and sometimes by, technology and, in particular, through regimes and systems of information. In the opening words of the scholar Virginia Eubanks' recent book, *Automating Inequality*:

> Since the dawn of the digital age, decision-making in finance, employment, politics, health, and human services has undergone revolutionary change. Forty years ago, nearly all of the major decisions that shape our lives—whether or not we are offered employment, a mortgage, insurance, credit, or a government service—were made by human beings ... Today, we have ceded much of that decision-making power to sophisticated machines. Automated eligibility systems, ranking algorithms, and predictive risk models control which neighborhoods get policed, which families attain needed resources, who is short-listed for employment, and who is investigated for fraud ... Digital security guards collect information about us, make inferences about our behavior, and control access to resources.[6]

The question that we must now urgently address is how the Constitution, through the trinity of liberty, equality, and fraternity, is supposed to constrain, shape, and use this power, in continued service of democracy.

I. Information, Power, and the Constitutional Trinity

> *'Constitutional guarantees cannot be subjected to the vicissitudes of technology.'*
>
> *Justice K.S. Puttaswamy v. Union of India*
> (Justice Chandrachud, dissenting)

Let us recall the foundational arguments of this book. In Part I, we discussed equality, the first pillar of the constitutional trinity.

Transformative equality is not merely about requiring impartial and even-handed treatment by the State. Nor does it limit itself to asking whether State action was *motivated* by malice or hostility towards an individual or a class. Rather, it recognizes that disadvantage is historical and enduring. It is the product of how social institutions are designed. Inequality manifests itself in the *effects* that these institutions, in their working, have upon individuals and groups. Transformative equality prohibits the State from perpetuating institutional discrimination, and, where necessary, commits it to overcoming structural disadvantage through special measures and affirmative action.

The constrained vision of formal equality would view technological intervention as an unvarnished solution for social problems. After all, technology cannot discriminate on grounds of caste or sex. An algorithm cannot be biased against minorities. Transferring decision-making powers from opaque and fallible human beings to transparent and automated information systems would ensure that the State cannot, by definition, violate Articles 14 and 15(1) of the Constitution.[7] Indeed, this is part of a broader narrative about the infallibility or, at least, neutrality of technology-driven decision-making, popularly known as 'automation bias'.[8]

But this narrative disintegrates upon the touchstone of transformative equality, in three distinct ways. First, it ignores the human bias that exists at the time of data collection. In August 2018, the tech magazine *FactorDaily* provided a chilling account of how the Chennai Police used a system called FaceTagr to surveil a busy marketplace and, by querying their existing criminal database, checked whether 'any criminals [were] identified in the area'.[9] The police had no reason to suspect any particular individual of committing any particular crime: they simply engaged in dragnet surveillance to check whether anybody who had committed a crime *before* (and was, therefore, in the database) happened to be in the area (effectively stigmatizing anyone who had been convicted *and* already served their time).

The CEO of FaceTagr proudly told *FactorDaily* that with their app, 'a guy walking on the road at 2 a.m., who is looking suspicious' could be photographed by the police, and his identity cross-checked with the criminal database. This, it should be obvious, is simply the Beggary Act updated for the information age. Apart from the obvious privacy concerns, it is abundantly clear that, in the eyes of the police, 'a guy' who 'looks suspicious' for walking on the road at 2 a.m. will invariably come from a certain socio-economic class, measured simply by his appearance. And in this way, the FaceTagr app will invariably facilitate targeting the homeless and the destitute.[10]

Second, and of more direct concern to transformative equality, techno-utopianism fails to assess technological systems as social institutions, where discrimination and bias occur not through individual actions, but assume an institutional *form*.[11] Even when there is no intentional bias at the time of collection, the process of collection will invariably imbibe *existing* patterns and structures of discrimination, which will then be fed into the model that constitutes the algorithmic system. This, by now, is a demonstrated problem and, as we can obviously see, it implicates transformative constitutionalism in its deepest sense.

Take, for example, DNA data banks, which exist in many countries, and will probably exist in India by the time this book is in your hands.[12] India's proposed DNA profiling bill provides for the storage and retention of the DNA profiles of 'suspects', 'undertrials', and 'offenders'. A suspect's profile must be expunged after the Police Report is filed. However, an undertrial's profile is retained until a court orders otherwise, and there are no provisions for expunging an offender's profile (no matter what the character or gravity of the offence).

Effectively, therefore, the DNA Bill creates an enduring data bank of undertrials, and a permanent data bank of all offenders, making no distinction between house trespassers and murderers. These criteria appear to be neutral. Consider, however, that, whether as undertrials or as convicts, Dalits and Muslims are disproportionately represented in India's prison population, a statistic that is linked to the fact that criminal justice regimes are inevitably skewed along socio-economic parameters.[13] Consequently, if the DNA data bank 'is primarily composed of those who have been touched by the criminal justice system and that system engages in practices that routinely and disproportionately target minority groups, there will be an obvious skew or bias in the database and the repositories'.[14] Further, the retention of DNA profiles perpetuates the disadvantage that would otherwise end with the completion of the prison sentence.[15]

The justification given by the framers of the Bill, of course, is that storing an offender's DNA profile will make it easier to identify him if he were to commit another crime. This logic implies, however, that once a convicted criminal, *always* a potential criminal. It goes far beyond even the stringent provisions of the Habitual Offenders Act, which require fingerprinting after the *third* conviction within a period of five years, and then require the deletion of records after a period of five more years. And its operation, as we have seen, not only tracks the institutional biases that are already constitutive of the criminal justice system, but also systematizes and perpetuates them.

It also perpetuates them in another manner. Contrary to popular perception, DNA identification, like any other form of probabilistic identification, is fallible, and the possibility of false positives only increases with the size of the database. So, as Sheldon Krimsky and Tania Simoncelli point out in their analysis of US DNA data banks:

> With all African American DNA on the database, it is reasonable to assume that false convictions in that population group will actually increase because DNA fallibility follows racial lines. In cases where individuals have been falsely convicted because of mishandled DNA, they have disproportionately been people of colour.[16]

Therefore, as Virginia Eubanks observes, 'when automated decision-making tools are not built to explicitly dismantle structural inequities, their speed and scale intensify them'.[17]

This speaks not only to the issue of intensifying pre-existing institutional bias through ignoring it, but also to the third way in which transformative equality is particularly concerned with issues of technology: their disproportionate effect upon the vulnerable and the marginalized. To those whose fingerprints did not match while attempting to open a bank account, or who temporarily found themselves shut out of the online income-tax portal because of a mismatch of names between Aadhaar and their PAN cards, biometric authentication was a source of harassment, nuisance, and bother. However, for those who depended upon the public distribution system for their monthly supply of food, an authentication failure meant death.[18]

Just like the 'false positives' in the DNA database would disproportionately hit the most vulnerable in the context of criminal trials, Aadhaar's technological regime, *by design*, impacted those most in need of their basic entitlements. Indeed, before even the stage of biometric authentication failure, the Aadhaar system shut out an entire class of people from accessing the benefits that it had been made the drawbridge to: homeless people, who had no address proof, and could therefore not even apply for an Aadhaar number.[19]

It is this manner of institutional disadvantage—in its diverse and myriad forms—that the Constitution—through its philosophy of transformative equality—was always meant to address, and will *need* to address in the years to come.

There is yet another way in which automated identification systems implicate questions of transformative equality: 'by freezing its targets in time, portraying them as aggregates of their most difficult choices'.[20] For example, one of the interveners in the Aadhaar challenge was the Safai Karmachari Aandolan (SKA), an organization that represents manual scavengers across the country. While responding to Aadhaar being made mandatory for accessing rehabilitation schemes for manual scavengers, Bezwada Wilson, as the head of SKA, observed:

> ... as manual scavengers we want to come out of the identity and destroy it forever. We don't want that identity again. Any marginalized community, any manual scavenging or vulnerable community wants to destroy its existing identity; that is our whole struggle. So, you are branding; even if I come out of this and get liberation also, but in your Aadhaar, my occupation, where I come from, everything will be there.[21]

While the government argued in Court that Aadhaar fulfilled the dream of 'One Nation, One Identity', for someone like Bezwada Wilson, a fixed identity was more a nightmare than a dream: because it would ensure the continued reification of a structurally inegalitarian society.

Technological systems, of course, are by no means limited to the State. They are now at the heart of the 'private regimes of power', which the constitutional value of *fraternity* is concerned with. In some ways, this was evident in the Aadhaar challenge itself. As far back as 1964, the journalist Vance Packard had presciently observed how, in the case of centralized data banks, 'we all fall under the control of the machine's managers, to some extent'.[22] In a situation where basic entitlements had been made subject to successful biometric authentication, that 'control' lay with the individuals who were tasked with manning the Point of Service (POS) machine on which biometric authentication was done as a precondition to distributing the monthly supply of grain.

The government argued that by replacing the middleman (who would manually check your identity) with the POS machine, a major source of bribery and corruption in the system had been eliminated through a simple, technological fix. As oral arguments in court revealed, however, the system had created a new class of middlemen, whose power lay in their control of the biometric drawbridge to something as basic as food.

The issues, however, go significantly beyond a national biometric authentication system. With the long retreat of the State from the economic life of the country, many decisions that directly impact fundamental rights are now made by private entities, which wield an increasing amount of power. Take, for example, the issue of healthcare in a nation that has failed to guarantee universal coverage to all its citizens. That role will come to be performed by private insurance companies whose business model depends upon excluding those at risk of sickness (i.e., those who need healthcare the most). As a reliable method of predicting the possibility of certain kinds of diseases, DNA information is thus an excellent proxy for insurers to shape their policies around, and exclude the most vulnerable constituencies of the population from coverage or charge them sky-high premiums. This is a recognized risk: in the US, for example, insurance companies *and* employers are barred by law from basing hiring or enrolment decisions upon genetic information.[23]

In early 2018, for the first time in India, a single judge of the Delhi High Court handed down a little-discussed but hugely important judgement that articulated a *right against genetic discrimination* under Article 14 of the Constitution.[24] Unsurprisingly, the judgement was delivered in the context of insurance contracts. In particular, it was considering a contract that excluded 'genetic disorders' from the scope of coverage. In its recognition of genetic heritage as protected grounds that would trigger heightened scrutiny under Article 14, Justice Pratibha Singh extended the transformative reasoning of *Naz Foundation*, which we have discussed in Chapter 2.

But she also did something even more important. She held that the right against genetic discrimination extended both to State *and* private insurance contracts. Why? Because there is inequality of bargaining power between the insurer and the citizen, which allowed the latter no real say in determining the scope or terms of the relationship. As a matter of constitutional law, this is probably not sufficient to attract Article 14. But it does serve as a crucial recognition that the intersection of private regimes of power, individual rights, and technology is something that transformative constitutionalism can no longer ignore. An articulation of constitutional fraternity that addresses this web of relationships, therefore, is increasingly urgent.

The most obvious and visible impact of the advance of technology, of course, is upon the third pillar of the trinity: liberty. In the Aadhaar challenge, for example, the petitioners led with an argument based on surveillance. They attempted to demonstrate how a centralized information database, tracking every individual transaction through the authentication requirement, would cast a chilling effect upon the exercise of fundamental freedoms. The State's response, interestingly, was not to justify surveillance, but to argue that the Aadhaar Act provided enough legal and technological safeguards that would make surveillance *impossible*. Across the Bar, therefore, the impact of centralized databases, of tracking and recording the daily transactions that constituted the web of an individual's life, and of aggregating information silos—basically, of the 'collection, storage and sharing about the behaviour and choices of ... people'[25]—was not in dispute. What was in dispute was whether the *design* of Aadhaar enabled or precluded surveillance.

In August 2018, however, Anand Venkatanarayanan reported that the National Crime Records Bureau was making an increasingly aggressive push for access to the Aadhaar database for law-enforcement purposes, which was barred by the Aadhaar Act as it then stood.[26] The importance of this is evident from the fact that during the Supreme Court hearing, the petitioners had argued that the fingerprinting of the entire population for the purposes of checking *future* identity fraud treated everyone as a potential suspect, and recreated the jurisdiction of suspicion that had been the hallmark of the Criminal Tribes Act.[27]

The government responded by arguing that fingerprinting under Aadhaar was merely for identification purposes, and not for criminal law. A 'merging' of the nationwide Aadhaar and restricted police fingerprint databases would, of course, dissolve this distinction, and ensure that now everyone *was* a potential criminal suspect. Venkatanarayanan went on to point out that notwithstanding the

UIDAI's denial, many Indian state governments, such as the state of Andhra Pradesh, had already 'created a vast fully interlinked resident database that has merged the crime and civilian aspects'.[28] The local 'state hub' had:

> ... information about all its residents, the GPS coordinates of their homes, medicines they use, food rations they eat, what they say about their chief minister on their social media accounts, their caste, bank accounts on which they receive their scholarships, pensions and their Aadhaar numbers.[29]

Meanwhile, in the neighbouring state of Telangana, 'not only [were] the Aadhaar numbers of drunken drivers ... seeded into the crime database, their family members' Aadhaar numbers were also seeded'.[30] In Telangana's capital, Hyderabad, the police would regularly demand the Aadhaar number of anyone arrested, regardless of whether they were eventually convicted or not. Therefore, Venkatanarayanan concluded, 'a vast database [i.e., Aadhaar] that allows other entities (including states to build their own parallel and bigger) databases with parallel biometrics, by design, is exactly the architecture that an all-encompassing surveillance state would need'.[31]

The Supreme Court's Aadhaar judgement was limited to the central Aadhaar database. It thus leaves open a host of issues pertaining to the constitutionality of the state data hubs and, indeed, to the function creep, i.e., the merging of the civilian and criminal databases. From the Chennai cop who uses FaceTagr to non-consensually take a photograph of a 'suspicious person' and upload it to a database (which might, one day, be the Aadhaar database[32]) to the 360-degree view of citizens that is offered by state databases, the dangers of surveillance are both real and present. Future courts have a heavy responsibility to adjudicate the fundamental rights claims that will inevitably come before them. But to do that, as Eubanks points out, it is crucial to understand the difference between old surveillance (individualized targeting) and new surveillance:

> ... in new data-based surveillance, the *target often emerges from the data*. The targeting comes after the data collection, not before. Massive amounts of information are collected on a wide variety of individuals and groups. Then, data is mined, analysed, and searched in order to identify possible targets for more thorough scrutiny ... If the old surveillance was an eye in the sky, the new surveillance is a spider in a digital web, testing each connected strand for suspicious vibrations.[33]

It was this argument—that rights are affected in the *design* of databases and not by their *potential abuse* in some imagined future—that the Supreme Court in the Aadhaar case failed to engage with. It was left to Justice Chandrachud, in dissent, to point out this simple fact. It remains to be seen whether a future court will engage with it.

That is because the issues will not go away. Let us briefly return to the question of DNA data banks. In the US, the police use DNA information to engage in familial searches. DNA from a crime scene can return a partial match with an existing profile in the database, which indicates that a family member of the profile-holder has the exact matching DNA. This becomes the basis of the police investigation. As is obvious, it brings in entire families within the scope of a criminal investigation (with all its attendant problems), purely on the basis of a possible relation with the accused.[34]

Would this be permitted by the Indian Constitution, in a nation with a long history of violent police abuse? Then, there is the issue of spatial privacy: we shed DNA everywhere we go, providing a detailed and accurate map of our movements. To what extent do we retain our privacy rights over this 'abandoned DNA' is a question that other jurisdictions have already begun to ask.[35] And finally, but perhaps most crucially, there is that deceptive-sounding phrase—predictive policing. Based upon the idea that a crime can be prevented *before* it happens, predictive policing, put simply, profiles people's past behaviour to predict how they are likely to behave in the future. Effectively, this is behind the Chennai Police's use of FaceTagr to ascertain whether any past criminals are in an area, and to start investigating before anything has happened. The constitutional problems with such an approach are manifold. As Eubanks points out, 'equity requires the ability to develop and evolve … [but] mathematical models, by their nature, are based on the past, and on the assumption that patterns will repeat'.[36]

And DNA has the potential to do predictive policing on steroids. It is already argued that DNA analysis can reveal genetic predispositions towards certain kinds of behaviour. On the one hand, this is halfway towards reviving the discredited nineteenth-century notions of criminals by birth, now with the added gloss of modern science. And the road from genetic predispositions to eugenics is shorter and easier to traverse than most people recognize. On the other hand, the temptation for law enforcement, and for a court that has always been extraordinarily sympathetic to the demands of law enforcement, to use it with 'appropriate safeguards' is immense.

It is here that transformative constitutionalism—as articulated in *Selvi*—is crucial. There are some things, some invasions of personal rights, some exercises of State power that the Constitution simply does not allow, no matter what benefits they may be scientifically proven to have. Indeed, as scholars note, the increasing accuracy of automated decision-making, especially statistical prediction, will make starker the 'trade-off between fairness and utility'.[37] The choices will become more controversial and more painful to make. *Selvi*, I suggest, lays down some excellent principles about where and how, under a transformative Constitution, we must hold the line.

Technological and information systems impact freedom in a second way: by serving as drawbridges (and often, as walls) between individuals and their basic entitlements. A large part of the arguments in the Aadhaar challenge turned upon the question of *exclusion*, i.e., cases of biometric authentication failure, where the machine's determination of who you are is given precedence over who *you* say that you are. The State argued that, through administrative orders, it would ensure that in cases of authentication failure, other forms of identification would be accepted, and that nobody would be deprived of their rights simply because their fingerprints (or iris scans) failed to match.

The constitutional correctness of that specific argument aside, there is a deeper debate to be had about the role of algorithmic decision-making in determining identity for the purpose of accessing welfare rights. There is now an emerging consensus that an individual has the right not to be subjected to a decision 'based solely on automated processing ... which produces legal effects [that] significantly affect him or her'.[38] In a famous 1970 judgement called *Goldberg v. Kelly*, the US Supreme Court held that a right to a full hearing existed before someone's welfare benefits were terminated. In an age where welfare benefits have now been made dependent upon biometric authentication, the right to a fair hearing (presently not mandated under the Aadhaar Regulations, and, in fairness, not argued before the Court) in this and other contexts may have to be judicially read in as a compulsory requirement into a statute that makes automated processing a precondition for access to any right or benefit.

Even with a right to a fair hearing, however, automated processing shifts the burden of identification upon the individual.[39] Having been rejected by the machine, the individual must now, using other means, demonstrate that she is who she claims to be, and not a ghost.[40] In its own way, this resets some of the fundamental axioms of our legal and constitutional system:

> '... it is better that ten guilty men go free than one innocent man goes to jail ... then modernization flipped that on its head.' Automated eligibility [is] based on the assumption that it is better

> for ten eligible applicants to be denied public benefits than for one ineligible person to receive them.[41]

This again impacts more than one pillar of the constitutional trinity. Critiquing a proposed Australian Bill introducing facial recognition technology (which will also probably be a feature of Aadhaar authentication by the time this book is in your hands), Cynthia Wong noted, 'errors shift the burden onto individuals to show they are not who the system says they are, undermining the presumption of innocence … and this may disproportionately impact already vulnerable communities if the system misidentifies them at higher rates'.[42]

When does this burden become too onerous to attract constitutional scrutiny? The majority did not believe that the threshold had been crossed in Aadhaar (refusing to even examine the evidence placed on record), while Justuce Chandrachud, on the other hand, observed, 'Basic entitlements in matters such as foodgrain can brook no error. To deny food is to lead a family to destitution, malnutrition and even death.'[43] Obviously, this too is a question that will occur and recur in the years to come.

There is also a deeper issue here. In Chapter 8 of this book, we discussed how the shift from a culture of authority to a culture of justification is integral to the project of transformative constitutionalism. When decision-making shifts to automated processes, this dichotomy becomes even sharper because 'decisions … are made not by humans or even human-legible rules, but by less scrutable mathematical techniques'.[44] In technical terms, this has been labelled as creating a black-box society.[45] At its root, it is simply a replication of the culture of authority, updated for the information age.

It, therefore, becomes crucial to subject automated decision-making to the culture of justification. One way, as we discussed above, is through a right to a fair hearing, *before* a person is deprived of any entitlements by an automated decision-making process,

Other mooted solutions include the EU General Data Protection Regulation's (GDPR) similar right to an explanation, as well as possible judicial remedies requiring disclosure of 'the source code for decision-making systems'.[46] Source-code disclosure is meant to indicate the precise manner in which the decision has been arrived at, and allow for the identification of possible biases that are baked into the system.[47]

Whether this will achieve the goal is, however, controversial, as source codes are 'illegible to non-experts and unpredictable to experts as well'.[48] In this context, however, recall our discussion of sex discrimination under Article 15(1) of the Constitution. Transformative constitutionalism seeks to address structural and institutional biases by going beyond interrogating the *reasons* for State action, and looking to their *effects*. Source-code disclosure, in turn, tells us only about the *method* of decision. In a somewhat inexact sense, it is the algorithmic equivalent of 'reasons for State action'. Transformative constitutionalism, therefore, may require the application of something like a disparate impact/ disproportionate effects approach to algorithmic decision-making, in order to substantially address issues of bias and discrimination sufficiently.[49]

The precise manner in which the culture of justification is to be legally encoded into the operation of technological systems, of course, is something that the courts must develop as the cases come before them. But what we can clearly see is this: much like the three pillars of transformative constitutionalism, viz., liberty, equality, and fraternity, take their shape and form from each other, the interface between technology, the information society, and the Constitution must be examined as a whole. Control over data impacts freedom, perpetuates institutional disadvantage, and also helps to consolidate private regimes of power. Automated processing excludes individuals from accessing their rights, disproportionately excludes the most vulnerable, and gives private parties unaccountable control over determining issues of access and exclusion. And so on.

For those who find the drawbridge pulled up against them, the constitutional promise has failed. There are far too many of those. It is now our task to dismantle the drawbridge, fill up the moat, and replace the castle walls with gateways. The proliferation of mirror databases and the CCTNS (Crime and Criminal Tracking Network and Systems) suggests that it may be almost too late to undertake this task, but the future of transformative constitutionalism depends upon it. The Constitution must, as Justice Chandrachud noted urgently in his dissenting judgement in Aadhaar, 'address the dialogue between technology and power'.[50]

Indeed, the future of republican democracy depends upon it.

II. Conclusion: Technological Self-Determination and the Transformative Constitution

At the time of Independence, India was a society characterized by authoritarian political power, legal and social inequalities, and unaccountable private regimes of domination. The Constitution acknowledged both this legacy and this reality, and sought to transform it. In this book, I have attempted to articulate that transformative constitutional vision through nine judgements.

But today, transformative constitutionalism is at risk in a world where the relationship between individuals, communities, corporations, and the State is mediated, and sometimes even defined, by technological systems. Like most other things, this is not a problem that can be *solved* in a courtroom; but it does require a constitutional and judicial *response*.

In early 2018, the Supreme Court took a first step towards articulating such a response. *Common Cause v. Union of India* concerned the legality of passive euthanasia. A Constitution Bench of the Supreme Court located the right to assisted dying within the contours of the fundamental right to life and personal liberty.[51] But there was something more that emerged from a close reading of the concurring opinions: a concern that the decision about whether to receive or to decline medical intervention or medical treatment is a choice for the individual to make. This concern was crystallized in a single sentence from the opinion of the Chief Justice: 'should [the individual] be [a] "guinea pig" for some kind of experiment?'[52]

What does this mean? It means that there exists a right to refusal. An individual has a choice to refuse being conscripted into a technological system, whatever its beneficial purpose might be. In *Common Cause*, the context was medical intervention, but the principle is broader. Medical intervention is only one example of a world in which technological systems are embedded in the fabric of our daily lives.

What is this broader principle? I call it the right to technological self-determination, and I define it as follows:

> Individuals have the right to engage with technological systems on their own terms, the right to opt into or opt out of such systems without suffering for it, and the right not to be subjected to technological intervention without being given meaningful choice. Technological self-determination is the right of every individual to determine how, on what terms, and to what extent, she will engage with technological systems.[53]

This is, of course, an abstract principle. But I would argue that technological self-determination must form the basis of how we understand the relationship between technological systems and the constitutional trinity of liberty, equality, and fraternity. Technological self-determination must be at the heart of the transformative constitutional order of the twenty-first century.

In his dissenting judgement in the Aadhaar case, Justice Chandrachud grasped the beginnings of this principle, when he observed:

> Identity includes the right to determine the forms through which identity is expressed and the right not to be identified. [With Aadhaar] ... that concept is now 'flipped' so that identification

> through identifiers becomes the only form of identity in the time of database governance. This involves a radical transformation in the position of the individual.

And he, therefore, held that the right to a choice in establishing one's identity—including by refusing to submit to a biometric-based identification system—was now a constitutionally protected right.

There is little doubt that the Aadhaar case represents a setback to a full-blooded articulation of technological self-determination as a guiding constitutional principle. But in the *Common Cause* judgement, and in Justice Chandrachud's dissenting opinion in Aadhaar, we have the ideal in its incipient form, almost a chrysalis, awaiting metamorphosis. It has already become a part of the contrapuntal narrative, the contemporary story of the Supreme Court read against the grain, the alternative canon reassuring us that, in the waiting-room of history, to 'set alight the sparks of hope in the past'[54] is always a possible dream.

Perhaps the history of transformative constitutionalism in India tells us that it has ever been thus.

Notes

Prologue: The Past Is a Foreign Country

1. The term 'jagirdar' refers to a type of feudal landholder in India, dating back to medieval times.
2. *State of Gujarat v. Vora Fiddali Badruddin Mithibarwala* (1964) 6 SCR 461.
3. Id., ¶114 (concurring opinion of Justice Shah).
4. Id. (concurring opinion of Justice Shah).
5. Id., ¶136 (concurring opinion of Justice Shah).
6. Id., ¶14 (dissenting opinion of Justice Ayyangar).
7. *Virendra Singh v. State of UP* (1955) 1 SCR 415, ¶28.
8. *State of Gujarat v. Mithibarwala*, supra, ¶136.
9. Id., ¶134.
10. Id.
11. Id.
12. *Krishna Kumar Singh v. State of Bihar* (2017) 3 SCC 1 (majority opinion of Justice Chandrachud); *Kalpana Mehta v. Union of India* 2018 SCCOnline SC 512 (concurring opinion of Justice Chandrachud); *Government* of *NCT of Delhi v. Union of India*, C.A. No. 2357/2017.

13. For a nuanced assessment of the 'colonial continuity' line of thought, see Arudra Burra, 'The Cobwebs of Imperial Rule', (2010) 615 *Seminar: We the People*, available at http://www.india-seminar.com/2010/615/615_arudra_burra.htm, visited on 25 May 2018.
14. B.N. Rau, *India's Constitution in the Making* 1 (Calcutta: Orient Longman 1960).
15. See, e.g., Granville Austin, *The Indian Constitution: Cornerstone of a Nation*, Ch. 1(New Delhi: OUP 1996). Uday Mehta calls it, therefore, a 'succession of personnel'. Uday S. Mehta, 'Constitutionalism' in *The Oxford Companion to Politics in India* 15, 19 (Jayal & Mehta eds., New Delhi: OUP 2010). As Klug points out, however, ultimately, the Constituent Assembly 'emerged as a fully sovereign, unrestricted, constitution-making body', not something that you could say for many of India's counterparts in other parts of the world, where the transition was far more 'managed', and 'the Westminster Parliament enacted each post-Independence Constitution'. Heinz Klug, *Constituting Democracy: Law, Globalism, and South Africa's Political Reconstruction* 94 (Cambridge: Cambridge University Press 2000). See Javed Majeed, 'A Nation on the Move': The Indian Constitution, Life Writing and Cosmopolitanism' (2016) 13(2) *Life Writing* 237, who makes the same point. See also Sarbani Sen, *The Constitution of India: Popular Sovereignty and Democratic Transitions* (New Delhi: OUP 2011). For a comparative discussion, see *Hinds v. The Queen* [1977] AC 195. For a contrary view, arguing that the work of the Assembly must be characterized in light of the political vicissitudes that led to its formation, see Arvind Elangovan, '"We the People?" Politics and the conundrum of framing a constitution on the eve of decolonisation' in *The Indian Constituent Assembly: Deliberations on Democracy* 10–35 (Udit Bhatia ed., London: Routledge 2018). Interestingly, the membership of the Constituent Assembly was cited by some members as a reason for dissolving it, and redrafting the Constitution afresh by a different Assembly, elected on the basis of universal adult franchise. See e.g., Parliament of India, *Constituent Assembly Debates, Vol. VII*, 5 November 1948 (speech of Damodar Swarup Seth), available at http://164.100.47.194/Loksabha/Debates/cadebatefiles/C05111948.html.

16. See generally, Subhash C. Kashyap, *Our Constitution: An Introduction to India's Constitution and Constitutional Law* (2nd ed., New Delhi: National Book Trust 2011). B.N. Rau himself was a key figure in the drafting of both documents.
17. *M.P.V. Sundararamier v. State of AP*, 1958 SCR 1422. This objection was made repeatedly in the Constituent Assembly as well.
18. Ruti Teitel, 'Transitional Jurisprudence: The Role of Law in Political Transformation', (1997) 106 *Yale Law Journal* 2009, 2057. But see Arvind Elangovan, 'Provincial Autonomy, Sir Benegal Narsing Rau, and an Improbable Imagination of Constitutionalism in India, 1935–38', (2016) 36(1) *Comparative Studies of South Asia, Africa and the Middle East* 66, for a more complex relationship between the 1935 Act and the 1950 Constitution.
19. Subhash Kashyap, *Our Constitution*, supra. The immediate trigger for this was the large-scale political violence that accompanied the birth-pangs of the new nation. For background context, see Austin, *The Indian Constitution: Cornerstone of a Nation*, Ch. 3, supra.
20. Sandipto Dasgupta, '"A Language Which is Foreign to Us": Continuities and Anxieties in the Making of the Indian Constitution' (2014) 34(2) *Comparative Studies of South Asia, Africa and the Middle East* 228, 237. See, e.g., *M.P. Sharma v. Satish Chandra*, 1954 SCR 1077, using this history to hold against a fundamental right to privacy under the Constitution (but overruled on this point in *Justice K.S. Puttaswamy (Retd.) v. Union of India*, (2017) 6 SCC 1).
21. Uday S. Mehta, 'Constitutionalism', supra, 16; Rochana Bajpai, *Debating Difference* (New Delhi: OUP 2011); see also, Dasgupta, 'A Language That is Foreign to Us', supra, 231, discussing how the Constituent Assembly was often required to adopt the register of an administrator (rather than a sovereign).
22. *Madras Bar Association v. Union of India*, (2014) 10 SCC 1.
23. Uday S. Mehta, 'Constitutionalism', supra, 19 (*emphasis* mine); but see, contra, Dasgupta, 'A Language That is Foreign to Us', supra, 230, using the word 'absolutist' to describe the colonial regime.
24. Government of India Act, 1935.
25. In the words of Rohit De, a 'whiggish narrative.' See Rohit De, 'Constitutional Antecedents' in *The Oxford Handbook of the Indian Constitution* 17, 17 (Sujit Chaudhry et al eds., New Delhi: OUP 2016).

26. As Dr B. Pattabhi Sitaramayya, the President of the Congress Party, observed during the third and final reading of the draft Constitution in the Constituent Assembly, 'it was by an imperceptible transition from the stage of bureaucracy and dependence to the stage of a *republic* and *cooperative commonwealth* that we have wrought these transformations.' Notice the seemingly contradictory juxtaposition of 'imperceptible transition' and 'transformation'. Parliament of India, *Constituent Assembly Debates, Vol. XI*, 25 November 1949 (speech of Dr B. Pattabhi Sitaramayya), available at http://164.100.47.194/Loksabha/Debates/cadebatefiles/C25111949.html. This issue split the Constituent Assembly, and was the subject of bitter criticism in the Third Reading.
27. Among the various scholarly works that make this argument, see, e.g., Shahid Amin, *Event, Metaphor, Memory: Chauri Chaura 1922–1992* (Berkeley: University of California Press 1995); Gyanendra Pandey, 'A Rural Base for Congress: The United Provinces 1920–1940' in *Congress and the Raj: Facets of the Indian Struggle 1917–1947* (D.A. Low ed., London: Arnold Heinemann, 1997).
28. Partha Chatterjee, *Nationalist Thought and the Colonial World: A Derivative Discourse* (2nd ed., Minneapolis: University of Minnesota Press 1993).
29. Mithi Mukherjee, *India in the Shadows of Empire: A Legal and Political History (1774–1950)* (New Delhi: OUP India 2009); Partha Chatterjee, *Nation and Its Fragments: Colonial and Postcolonial Histories* (Princeton: Princeton University Press 2004).
30. Nivedita Menon, 'Citizenship and the Passive Revolution: Interpreting the First Amendment' in *Politics and Ethics of the Indian Constitution* 189–211 (Rajeev Bhargava ed., New Delhi: OUP 2008). In the 'third [i.e., final] reading' of the Constitution in the Constituent Assembly, Mahboob Ali Baig labelled it 'disappointing, conservative, and reactionary'. Parliament of India, *Constituent Assembly Debates, Vol. XI*, 21 November 1949 (speech of Mahboob Ali Baig Sahib), available at http://164.100.47.194/Loksabha/Debates/cadebatefiles/C21111949.html. Dr P.S. Deshmukh argued that the Constitution was about 'maintaining the *status quo*'. Parliament of India, *Constituent Assembly Debates, Vol. XI*, 22 November 1949 (speech of Dr P.S. Deshmukh),

available at http://164.100.47.194/Loksabha/Debates/cadebatefiles/C22111949.html.

31. Arvind Elangovan, 'The Making of the Indian Constitution: A Case for a Non-Nationalist Approach', (2014) 12(1) *History Compass* 1.
32. K.G. Kannabiran, *The Wages of Impunity: Power, Justice and Human Rights* 21–22 (New Delhi: Orient BlackSwan 2004). See also Rohit De, 'Constitutional Antecedents', supra, 31–32.
33. See, for example, Nehru's speech introducing the Objectives Resolution. *The Framing of India's Constitution: Select Documents* 4–11 (B. Shiva Rao ed., Gurgaon: Universal Law Publishing 1967).
34. Parliament of India, *Constituent Assembly Debates, Vol. VII*, 4 November 1948 (Speech of Dr B.R. Ambedkar), available at http://164.100.47.132/LssNew/cadebatefiles/C04111948.pdf, visited on 25 May 2018. See also Uday Mehta, 'Indian Constitutionalism' in *The Oxford Handbook of the Indian Constitution*, supra, 38, 48: ('… the dominant temper of mind in the assembly was revolutionary'; and Hanna Lerner, 'The Indian Founding', ibid., 54, 58.
35. For the limited and constrained nature of the 1935 Government of India Act, see Arvind Elangovan, 'Provincial Autonomy, Sir Benegal Narsing Rau, and an Improbable Imagination of Constitutionalism in India, 1935–38', (2016) 36(1) *Comparative Studies of South Asia, Africa and the Middle East* 66; see also Andrew Muldoon, *Empire, Politics, and the Creation of the 1935 India Act: Last Act of the Raj* (Farnham: Ashgate 2009).
36. In the speech cited above, as Dr Sitaramayya pointed out, 'We have extended the franchise which gave us three and a half crores of voters at the time when the British left this country, to seventeen crores of voters who will adorn the electoral rolls immediately next year.' Parliament of India, *Constituent Assembly Debates,* supra. A five-fold increase in the franchise is probably more of a transformative change than an 'extension' of the franchise. See also, Ornit Shani, *How India Became Democratic* (New Delhi: Penguin 2018).
37. Uday S. Mehta, 'Constitutionalism', supra, 20.
38. The term 'transformative constitutionalism' is borrowed from South African scholarship. While I place myself firmly in the tradition of constitutional scholarship that began with Karl Klare's famous article,

'Legal Culture and Transformative Constitutionalism', (1998) 14 *South African Journal on Human Rights* 146 (1998), my exploration of the concept will not necessarily subscribe to all the valences that it has acquired in South Africa. The articulation of transformative constitutionalism in this book, in its focus on constitutionalism's impact on 'institutional life and social practice', also owes a debt to the founding texts of the US critical legal studies movement. See, e.g., Roberto Unger, *The Critical Legal Studies Movement* 53 (Cambridge: Harvard University Press 1983); and especially Robin West, 'Progressive and Conservative Constitutionalism', (1989–1990) 88 *Michigan Law Review* 641.

39. Teitel, 'Transitional Jurisprudence', supra, 2014. As Terry Eagleton interpreted Walter Benjamin, 'what drives men and women to revolt against injustice is not the dream of liberated grandchildren, but memories of enslaved ancestors'. Terry Eagleton, 'Walking the Dead', *The New Statesman*, 12 November 2009, available at https://www.newstatesman.com/ideas/2009/11/past-benjamin-future-obama. Justice Albie Sachs put a more poetic gloss upon the same sentiment: the purpose of a Constitution is to transform 'misfortune to be endured into injustice to be remedied'. *Volks v. Robinson*, 2005 (5) BCLR 446, ¶222 (Constitutional Court of South Africa) (dissenting opinion of Justice Sachs).
40. And, as in the case of the great legal codification projects, of experimenting upon them. See, e.g., Elizabeth Kolsky, 'Codification and the Rule of Colonial Difference' (2005) 23(3) *Law and History Review* 631.
41. For an understanding of how these individual rights exist in a 'co-equal' relationship with democratic participation, see Jurgen Habermas, *Between Facts and Norms* (Cambridge: MIT Press 1996). For recent monographs highlighting the place of rights in the Indian constitutional scheme, see Madhav Khosla, *The Indian Constitution: A Short Introduction* (New Delhi: OUP 2012); Arun Thiruvengadam, *The Constitution of India: A Contextual Analysis* (New Delhi: Hart Publishing India 2017).
42. Ananth Padmanabhan, 'Rights' in *The Oxford Handbook of the Indian Constitution*, supra, 581, 582.

43. Cathi Albertyn and Beth Goldblatt, 'Facing the Challenge of Transformation: Difficulties in the Development of an Indigenous Jurisprudence of Equality' (1998) 14 *South African Journal on Human Rights* 248, 249; Dikgang Moseneke, 'Transformative Adjudication: The Fourth Bram Fischer Memorial Lecture' (2002) 18 *South African Journal on Human Rights* 309.
44. See e.g., Nick Dirks, *Castes of Mind: Colonialism and the Making of Modern India* (New Jersey: Princeton University Press 2001); Sudipta Kaviraj, *Trajectories of the Indian State: Politics and Ideas* (Ranikhet: Permanent Black 2010); Radhika Singha, *A Despotism of Law* (New Delhi: OUP 1998), and the work of Christopher Bayly; Mark Juergensmeyer, *Religious Rebels in the Punjab: The Ad Dharm Challenge to Caste* 143 (New Delhi: Navayana 2009), noting the absence of centralized authority and the prevalence of political competition between different groupings; see also, Partha Chatterjee, describing the thought of Rabindranath Tagore—'the laws of the state had limited jurisdiction and were subordinated to the rules of right conduct prescribed by community practices'—in 'Nationalism, Internationalism, and Cosmopolitanism: Some Observations from Modern Indian History', (2016) 36(2) *Comparative Studies of South Asia, Africa and the Middle East* 320, 331.
45. Sudipta Kaviraj, *The Imaginary Institution of India* 12 (Ranikhet: Permanent Black 2010).
46. Christopher Bayly, *Recovering Liberties: Indian Thought in the Age of Liberalism and Empire* 35–36 (Cambridge: Cambridge University Press 2011).
47. Anupama Roy, *Gendered Citizenship: Historical and Conceptual Explorations* ix (Revised ed., Hyderabad: Orient BlackSwan 2013).
48. Sudipta Kaviraj, 'Ideas of Freedom in Modern India' in *The Idea of Freedom in Asia and Africa* 97, 108 (Stanford: Stanford University Press 2002).
49. Article 19(1)(a), Constitution of India. While Gandhi's own vision of a decentralized India founded upon independent village-republics was never seriously considered by the Constituent Assembly, his impact upon the thinking of the Congress Party that he led for three decades—and which constituted a bulk of the Assembly—cannot be underestimated. Gandhi's public commitment to the freedom of

speech and association as foundational values of the new order is evident from his speech at his sedition trial, his address at the 36th Congress Session in 1921, and from his writings in *Young India*. See, e.g., B. Pattabhi Sitaramayya, *The History of the Congress* 380 (Madras: Law Printing House 1935).

50. These three words, of course, bring with them two centuries of contestation, and are not in themselves determinative of a transformative purpose. It is how a particular Constitution chooses to understand them that determines whether, and to what extent, it is transformative.
51. Parliament of India, *Constituent Assembly Debates, Vol. XI*, 25 November 1949 (speech of Dr B.R. Ambedkar), available at http://164.100.47.194/loksabha/writereaddata/cadebatefiles/C25111949.html, visited on 25 May 2018.
52. It is a common misconception that the colonial regime did not enforce caste distinctions and gave to India 'the rule of law'. The most notorious example was the Bombay Government's refusal to enrol a Mahar student (who had converted to Christianity) in school, because other students refused to share the same physical space. Anupama Rao, *Caste Question: Dalits and the Politics of Modern India* 71 (Ranikhet: Permanent Black 2010). See also, the injunction granted by the Office of the Legal Remembrancer in Bombay, prohibiting Dalits from taking water from the Chavdar tank, until the main suit on the issue was decided. Ibid., 83. Some of these issues are discussed in greater detail in Chapter 5.
53. Parliament of India, *Constituent Assembly Debates, Vol. XI*, 25 November 1949 (Speech of Dr B.R. Ambedkar), supra.
54. See, e.g., Roberto Unger, *False Necessity* 164 (London: Verso 2001): 'Society becomes denaturalized to the extent that its formative practices and preconceptions are open to effective challenge in the midst of ordinary social activity.'
55. Cathi Albertyn and Beth Goldblatt, 'Facing the Challenge of Transformation: Difficulties in the Development of an Indigenous Jurisprudence of Equality', (1998) 14 *South African Journal on Human Rights* 248, 249.
56. These are the words of a former Deputy Chief Justice of the South African Constitutional Court. See Dikgang Moseneke, 'Transformative Adjudication', supra, 318–19.

57. See e.g., B.R. Ambedkar, 'Castes in India: Their Mechanism, Genesis and Development', (1917) XLI *Indian Antiquary*, available at http://www.columbia.edu/itc/mealac/pritchett/00ambedkar/txt_ambedkar_castes.html. This was originally a paper presented by Ambedkar at an anthropology seminar at Columbia University. See also Eleanor Zelliott, *Ambedkar's World: The Making of Babasaheb and the Dalit Movement* 70 (New Delhi: Navayana 2012). See also Ian Shapiro, 'On Non-Domination' (2012) 62 *University of Toronto Law Journal* 293.
58. *The Framing of the Constitution: Select Documents*, supra, 11, 12.
59. See, e.g., *Lal Zenda Coal Mines Mazdoor Union (CITU) v. Western Coalfields Ltd.* (2015) 3 Bom CR 413, where the Bombay High Court invoked fraternity to override the express terms of a statute, and compel the members of a trade union to contribute to the Prime Minister's National Relief Fund. See also, *Subramanian Swamy v. Union of India* (2015) 13 SCC 356, where the Supreme Court invoked fraternity (!) to uphold the constitutionality of criminal defamation.
60. Michael W. Dowdle and Michael A. Wilkinson, 'Introduction and Overview' in *Constitutionalism Beyond Liberalism* 1, 12 (Michael W. Dowdle and Michael A. Wilkinson eds., Cambridge: Cambridge University Press 2017).
61. 'Comments and Suggestions on the Draft Constitution', *The Framing of India's Constitution: Select Documents, Vol. 4*, p. 3, 5 (Gurgaon: LexisNexis 2015).
62. See e.g., Charles Taylor, *Sources of the Self: The Making of the Modern Identity* (Cambridge: Harvard University Press 1989); Will Kymlicka, *Multicultural Citizenship: A Liberal theory of Minority Rights* (Oxford: Clarendon Press 1995).
63. As a young Ambedkar trenchantly remarked, 'The atomistic conception of individuals in a Society so greatly popularised—I was about to say vulgarised—in political orations is the greatest humbug.' B.R. Ambedkar, 'Castes in India', supra.
64. Parliament of India, *Constituent Assembly Debates, Vol. VII*, 4 November 1948, supra (speech of Dr B.R. Ambedkar). Attempts to introduce a provision affirming the sacredness of the family into the Constitution, on the lines of the Irish Constitution, did not succeed. Attempts to make the 'village republic' the basic unit of the Constitution failed likewise. See, e.g., Parliament of India, *Constituent Assembly Debates*,

Vol. VII, 22 November 1948, available at http://164.100.47.194/Loksabha/Debates/cadebatefiles/C22111948.html.

65. *S. Krishnan v. State of Madras*, 1951 SCR 621, ¶43 (dissenting opinion of Justice Vivian Bose)
66. Admittedly, 'citizenship' is itself a limited, and often exclusionary, prism.
67. Dowdle & Wilkinson, 'Introduction and Overview', supra.
68. Dowdle & Wilkinson, 'Introduction and Overview', supra, 17; see also Dieter Grimm, *Constitutionalism: Past, Present, and Future* (Oxford: Oxford University Press 2016); Seyla Benhabib, *The Claims of Culture: Equality and Diversity in the Global Era* (New Jersey: Princeton University Press 2002).
69. Dowdle & Wilkinson, 'Introduction and Overview', supra, 17. Hailbronner argues that it was also the default position in German pre-war constitutionalism. See Hailbronner, *Traditions and Transformations: The Rise of German Constitutionalism* 46 (Oxford: Oxford University Press 2015).
70. The phrase is Corey Robin's. See Corey Robin, *The Reactionary Mind* 15 (2nd ed., New York: Oxford University Press 2017).
71. See, also, Karl Klare, 'Legal Culture and Transformative Constitutionalism', supra, 151, arguing that one of the purposes of the post-liberal, transformative Constitution is the 'extension of democratic ideals into the "private sphere"'. Here again, the Indian Constitution anticipated future developments in the West. See e.g., David Sciulli, *Theory of Societal Constitutionalism: Foundations of a non-Marxist critical theory* (Cambridge: Cambridge University Press 1992), developing the concept of 'social authoritarianism'; Elizabeth Anderson, *Private Government: How Employers Rule Our Lies (and Why We Don't Talk About It)* (New Jersey: Princeton University Press 2017).
72. Austin, *The Indian Constitution*, supra.
73. Article 37, Constitution of India.
74. Pratap Bhanu Mehta, 'What is Constitutional Morality', (2010) 615 *Seminar: We the People*, available at http://www.india-seminar.com/2010/615/615_pratap_bhanu_mehta.htm, visited on 25 May 2018.

75. Parliament of India, *Constituent Assembly Debates, Vol. VII*, 15 November 1948 (speech of Dr B.R. Ambedkar). This point was emphasized by many of the framers during the Third Reading of the Draft Constitution.
76. As B.M. Gupte, in one of the last interventions before the Constituent Assembly, pointed out: 'The Constitution is certainly not socialistic but there are unmistakable leanings towards socialism.' Parliament of India, *Constituent Assembly Debates, Vol. XI*, 23 November 1949 (speech of B.M. Gupte), available at http://164.100.47.194/Loksabha/Debates/cadebatefiles/C23111949.html.
77. But see, Timothy Fish Hodgson, 'The Mysteriously Appearing and Disappearing Doctrine of the Separation of Powers: Toward a Distinctly South African Doctrine for a More Transformative Constitution' (2018) 34(1) *South African Journal on Human Rights* 57. Hodgson argues that, in the context of South Africa, a commitment to transformative constitutionalism requires rethinking the separation of powers that, in its traditional form, is inextricably linked with the structural-liberal paradigm.
78. Upendra Baxi, 'Taking Suffering Seriously: Social Action Litigation in the Supreme Court of India', (1985) 4(6) *Third World Legal Studies* 107.
79. See, infra, Ch. 3.
80. *Maneka Gandhi v. Union of India* (1978) 1 SCC 248.
81. See, e.g., the discussion in Hailbronner, *Traditions and Transformations*, supra, distinguishing between 'reactive' and 'activist' constitutionalism. The former is focused on limiting government power (e.g., the US), while the latter lays out a comprehensive vision for society (e.g., the South African). My point here is that the Indian *Constitution* is activist, but it does not contemplate an activist *judiciary*.
82. As the Chief Justice of South Africa (which first articulated the concept of transformative constitutionalism) noted, '... the Constitution itself entrenches the notion of different roles for the different arms of government'. Justice Pius Langa, 'Transformative Constitutionalism' (2006) 17 *Stellenbosch Law Review* 351, 357.
83. It is not within the scope of this book to go into the historical reasons for this, which include, among others, the fact that the Congress

party's composition made a thoroughgoing economic and social transformation impossible. The framers' refusal to constitutionalize socio-economic rights is attributable, in part, to this. Borrowing from Gramsci, scholars have, therefore, labelled the process a 'passive revolution'. See e.g., Sudipta Kaviraj, 'A Critique of the Passive Revolution', (1988) 23(45) *Economic and Political Weekly* 2429. See also, Pranab Bardhan, *The Political Economy of Development in India* (Oxford: Blackwell 1984).

84. The distinction is important. See, e.g., Pierre de Vos, 'Substantive Equality after Grootboom: The Emergence of Social and Economic Context as a Guiding Value in Equality Jurisprudence', (2001) 2001 *Acta Juridica* 52, 68–69. See also Michaela Hailbronner, *Traditions and Transformations: The Rise of German Constitutionalism*, supra, 3. It was also something that was recognized clearly by the framers of the Constitution, as is evident from many of the speeches at the third reading of the Draft Constitution. See, in particular, the speech of Shrimati Purnima Banerjee: '... this Constitution has provided us with the means for changing the structure of society'. Parliament of India, *Constituent Assembly Debates, Vol. XI*, 24 November 1949 (speech of Shrimati Purnima Banerjee), available at http://164.100.47.194/Loksabha/Debates/cadebatefiles/C24111949.html. As articulated in this book, therefore, the role of the courts in implementing the transformative Constitution is less ambitious than, for example, the role that many contemporary scholars assign to the South African courts. For a survey of relevant literature, see Hodgson, 'The Mysteriously Appearing and Disappearing Doctrine of Separation of Powers', supra.

85. And when the courts act in this manner, it brings with it its own pathologies. For a root-and-branch critique of the enterprise of PIL, see Anuj Bhuwania, *Courting the People: Public Interest Litigation in Post-Emergency India* (New Delhi: Cambridge University Press 2017). Although I do not have space to develop this view further in this book, it is my contention that PIL has actively harmed the development of a rigorous transformative constitutionalism. By making Article 21 the repository for all socio-economic rights and all aspects of good governance, and by undermining constraints such as the separation of powers, PIL has provided courts with an easy way out: any social

problem brought to the courts is shoehorned into Article 21 (and often with new-spun remedies), without active consideration of how a transformative Constitution would *actually* treat it. It is no surprise that, ever since the advent of PIL, there has been very little development in (for example) the substantive equality doctrine of the Court, or any rigorous understanding of fraternity.

86. Kannabiran, *The Wages of Impunity*, supra, 137. For a nuanced critique of the PIL enterprise, see S.P. Sathe, *Judicial Activism in India* (New Delhi: Oxford 2003). Defenders of PIL do not deny that it departs from the constitutional scheme, but argue that is justified on consequentialist grounds (in particular, legislative and executive inaction). For an essay that acknowledges the criticisms but concludes that *on balance* PIL is justified until 'governance deficit shrinks', see Shyam Divan, 'Public Interest Litigation' in *The Oxford Handbook of the Indian Constitution*, supra, 662.
87. See e.g., David Singh Grewal and Jedediah Purdy, 'The Original Theory of Constitutionalism', (2018) 127 *Yale Law Journal* 664.
88. For an articulation of precisely this point, see the speech of Shrimati G. Durgabai in the Constituent Assembly, at the third reading of the Constitution. Parliament of India, *Constituent Assembly Debates, Vol. XI*, 24 November 1949 (speech of Shrimati G. Durgabai), available at http://164.100.47.194/Loksabha/Debates/cadebatefiles/C24111949.html.
89. Etienne Mureinik, 'A Bridge to Where? Introducing the Interim Bill of Rights', (1994) 10 *South African Journal on Human Rights* 31.
90. The classic book on the subject of courts remains Gerald N. Rosenberg's *The Hollow Hope: Can Courts Bring About Social Change?* (2nd ed., Chicago: University of Chicago Press 2008). For a more normative critique and for a useful survey of literature, again in a comparative perspective, see e.g., Eoin Daly, 'Reappraising judicial supremacy in the Irish constitutional tradition' in *Judges, Politics, and the Irish Constitution* 29–49 (Laura Cahillane et al. eds., Manchester: Manchester University Press 2017). See also Richard Bellamy, *Political Constitutionalism: A Republican Defence of the Constitutionality of Democracy* (Cambridge: Cambridge University Press 2007). The most famous critique of the rights framework, on the other hand, remains Karl Marx, *On the Jewish*

Question (1844), available at https://www.marxists.org/archive/marx/works/1844/jewish-question/index.htm. For a more modern critique, see the references in Gunther Frankenberg, *Comparative Constitutional Studies: Between Magic and Deceit* 57, ff. 115 & 116 (Cheltenham: Elgar 2018). As Frankenberg writes: 'Notwithstanding their indeterminate nature, ideological content, possessive-individualist connotations and negative side-effects, rights have been historically and still are the centrepiece of most constitutions.' Ibid.

91. See Rohit De, *The People's Constitution: Litigious Citizens and the Making of Indian Democracy* (forthcoming 2018). See also Sanford Levinson, *Constitutional Faith* (Revised ed., New Jersey: Princeton University Press 2011). Or see Laurence Tribe's trenchant 'I do not regard the rulings of the Supreme Court as synonymous with constitutional truth.' Laurence Tribe, *American Constitutional Law* iii (New York: The Foundation Press 1978). For a summary of the major American writing on 'popular constitutionalism', see Hailbronner, *Traditions and Transformations*, supra, 37.
92. Robert Cover, 'The Supreme Court, 1982 Term – Foreword: Nomos and Narrative', (1983–1984) 97 *Harvard Law Review* 1, 19. One of the more famous books about the Supreme Court in recent times is titled *Supreme but not Infallible* (New Delhi: OUP 2001). See also the section titled 'Multitudinous Constitutionalism' in Upendra Baxi, 'Preliminary Notes on Transformative Constitutionalism' in *Transformative Constitutionalism: Comparing the apex courts of Brazil, India and South Africa* 19, 26–28 (Oscar Vilhena et al eds., Pretoria: Pretoria University Law Press 2013, available at http://nludelhi.ac.in/download/publication/2015/Transformative%20Constitutionalism.pdf). As the succeeding pages should make clear, however, this book does not share Baxi's understanding of transformative constitutionalism; nor does it share his interpretive commitments.
93. Alessandro Portelli, 'The Oral Shape of the Law' in *The Death of Luigi Trastulli and Other Stories: Form and Meaning in Oral History* 241, 269 (Albany: State University of New York 1991). See also Robert Cover, 'The Supreme Court', supra.
94. Radhika Singha, *A Despotism of Law: Crime and Justice in Early Colonial India* 162 (New Delhi: Oxford University Press 1998).

95. See, e.g., *Supreme Court Advocates-on-Record Assn. v. Union of India*, (1993) 4 SCC 441; *I.R. Coelho v. Union of India*, (2007) 2 SCC 1. In the famous 'right to privacy judgement' (*Justice K.S. Puttaswamy v. Union of India*, (2017) 10 SCC 1, the concurring opinion of Justice S.K. Kaul had a full section titled 'The Constitution of India—A Living Document.'
96. See, e.g., the proliferating use of Article 142 of the Constitution.
97. As Justice Antonin Scalia of the United States Supreme Court pointed out in his critique of the Supreme Court's application of the 'evolving standards of decency' test to interpret the Eighth Amendment's prohibition of 'cruel and unusual punishment', if you peg the scope of rights to such a subjective standard, there is no warrant for believing that the rights will always be ratcheted up in an expansive direction, rather than ratcheted down to become more restrictive. The same considerations apply to judicial interpretation. In recent times, the 'ratcheting down of rights' *purely* on the touchstone of judicial ideology has been most clearly visible in the judgements of Supreme Court Justice Dipak Misra, in the domain of freedom of speech: the Supreme Court has taken upon itself broad censorial powers that cannot be justified under any respectable interpretation of the constitutional text. See, e.g., Gautam Bhatia, 'The Illegality of the National Anthem Order', *Indian Constitutional Law and Philosophy*, 30 November 2016, available at https://indconlawphil.wordpress.com/2016/11/30/the-illegality-of-the-supreme-courts-national-anthem-order/, visited on 27 May 2018. The 'living document', therefore, is a sword that cuts both ways, and cuts deep.
98. See, e.g., *Krishna Kumar Singh v. State of Bihar*, (2017) 3 SCC 1, where Justice D.Y. Chandrachud advanced a lucid account of how the interpretation of the Constitution's Ordinance-making powers was dependant on understanding how the constitutional structure in India evolved historically.
99. Named after the Supreme Court judgement in *A.K. Gopalan*, this phrase is used to (derisively) refer to the initial period of the Supreme Court's existence, when it was perceived to be excessively formalist and conservative. And derision was broadly the reaction of the nine-judge bench of the Supreme Court during oral arguments in the Puttaswamy case (2017), when some of the counsel arguing for the Union of India

attempted to invoke the original intention of the framers to make the point that the Indian Constitution did not guarantee any right to privacy.

100. This debate is not unique to India. See, e.g., Grewal and Purdy, 'The Original Theory of Constitutionalism', supra, 668: 'Both originalism and living constitutionalism ultimately fail to reconcile constitutional authority with popular sovereignty.'

101. There is, of course, no bright line standard to determine this, and is a matter of argument.

102. The concept itself is virtually incoherent when applied to the polyvocal Constituent Assembly.

103. See, e.g., Ronald Dworkin's defence of the US Supreme Court judgement in *Brown v. Board of Education*, that interpreted the US Constitution's Fourteenth Amendment to outlaw segregation. Ronald Dworkin, 'Constitutional Cases' in *Taking Rights Seriously* 131–150 (Cambridge: Harvard University Press 1977). Unlike the US Constitution, the Fundamental Rights chapter of the Indian Constitution is not *merely* a statement of principles. For example, to name just three, Articles 16(4) (reservations), 17 (prohibition of 'untouchability'), and 24 (prohibition of child labour in hazardous industries) represent very concrete commitments that were responding to tangible legacies of injustice. However, as I shall argue through the course of this book, these specific commitments are concrete manifestations of the principles already contained in the Constitution, and can serve as interpretive aids to provide those principles with flesh.

104. This approach comes closest to Jack Balkin's 'framework originalism'. See Jack M. Balkin, *Living Originalism* (Cambridge: Belknap Press 2014).

105. K.G. Kannabiran, *The Wages of Impunity*, supra, 18.

106. Michael R. Anderson and Sumit Guha, 'Introduction' in *Changing Conceptions of Rights and Justice in South Asia* 1, 4 (Michael Anderson and Sumit Guha eds., New Delhi: OUP 1998).

107. See, for example, the debates surrounding the Indian Civil Liberties Union (ICLU), which was established by Jawaharlal Nehru in the 1930s. Nilanjan Dutta, 'From Subject to Citizen: Towards a History of the Civil Rights Movement' in *Changing Conceptions of Rights and Justice in South Asia*, supra, 275, 278–9. See, also, the debates

surrounding the famous Karachi Fundamental Rights Resolution. Kama MacLean, 'The Fundamental Rights Resolution: Nationalism, Internationalism, and Cosmopolitanism in an Interwar Moment', (2017) 37(2) *Comparative Studies of South Asia, Africa and the Middle-East* 213.

108. Tanika Sarkar, 'Something Like Rights? Faith, Law and Widow Immolation Debates in Colonial Bengal', (2012) 49(3) *The Indian Economic and Social History Review* 295.
109. Eleanor Zelliott, *Ambedkar's World* 56, supra.
110. For example, the first articulations of civil rights in the colonial era arose out of the regime's deportation of editors and press censorship. See, e.g., C.A. Bayly, 'Rammohan Roy and the Advent of Constitutional Liberalism in India, 1800-30', (2007) 4(1) *Modern Intellectual History* 25.
111. On this point, see the extended discussion in Kaviraj, 'Ideas of Freedom in Modern India', supra, pp. 97–143. As Mark Juergensmeyer puts the point while discussing the discourse of Punjab's Ad-Dharm movement, 'the major factors that moulded the movement as a whole were largely Indian: the example of Arya Samaj, the *qaum* models of Sikhs and Indian Muslims, the traditional religious identity of the lower castes, and the communal egalitarianism of the *panthik* movements'. Mark Juergensmeyer, *Religious Rebels in the Punjab: The Ad Dharm Challenge to Caste* (New Delhi: Navayana 2009). In his critique of Edward Said, Sumit Sarkar warns us against the trap of essentializations when writing Indian history. See Sumit Sarkar, 'Orientalism Revisited: Saidian Frameworks in the Writing of Modern Indian History', (1994) 16(1–2) *Oxford Literary Review* 205.
112. Portelli, 'The Oral Shape of the Law', supra, 247.
113. For a critical discussion of the uses and misuses of history in 'contextual interpretation', see Pierre de Vos, 'A Bridge Too Far? History as Context in the Interpretation of the South African Constitution' (2001) 17 *South African Journal on Human Rights* 1.
114. Aditya Nigam, 'A Text Without Author: Locating the Constituent Assembly as Event', (2004) 39(21) *Economic and Political Weekly* 2107, 2108.
115. Johann van der Waal, *The Horizontal Effect Revolution and the Question of Sovereignty* (Berlin: Walter de Gruyter 2014).

116. De Vos, 'A Bridge Too Far?', supra, 1.
117. For readings of the Constitution that doubt its transformative character and attribute to it a more conservative hue, see the essays in *The Indian Constituent Assembly: Deliberations on Democracy*, supra.
118. Robert Cover, 'The Supreme Court', supra, 4.
119. Ibid., 39.
120. Edward Said, *Culture and Imperialism* 78–79 (New York: Knopf 1994).
121. Walter Benjamin, 'On the Concept of History', available at http://members.efn.org/~dredmond/ThesesonHistory.html.
122. For a similar account, see Robert Cover's idea of 'redemptive constitutionalism'. Robert Cover, 'The Supreme Court', supra, 34.

1: Sex Discrimination: *Anuj Garg* and the Anti-Stereotyping Principle

1. Section 30, Punjab Excise Act, 1914.
2. *Anuj Garg v. Hotel Association of India* (2008) 3 SCC 1.
3. Ibid., ¶55.
4. For the purposes of this chapter, the words 'sex' and 'gender' are used interchangeably. Readers interested in following up on the debate can refer to Joan Scott, 'Gender: A Useful Category of Historical Analysis' (1986) 91(5) *The American Historical Review* 1053–75; Mari Mikkola, 'Feminist Perspectives on Sex and Gender', *Stanford Encyclopedia of Philosophy*, available at https://plato.stanford.edu/entries/feminism-gender/, visited on 23 July 2017. For a judicial elaboration drawing the distinction between (biological) sex and (socially constructed) gender, see *G v. B*, MAHGB-000291014 (High Court of Botswana).
5. It is important to acknowledge that the judgements analysed in this chapter, the historical trajectory that is charted, and the theory of equality that I advance do not take into account the intersection of sex and caste and, therefore, the experience of discrimination that is faced by Dalit women. It also operates under a gender-binary framework which is insensitive to the discrimination faced by gender fluidity. These are shortcomings that are shaped partly by the historical record, and partly by the constraints of my own subject position, and my ability (or lack thereof) to transcend it. I attempt to address some of these issues elsewhere in this book. Thanks to Shreya Atrey for bringing this point to my attention.

6. Catherine Albertyn, 'Substantive Equality and Transformation in South Africa' (2007) 23 *South African Journal on Human Rights* 253, 255.
7. See, e.g., Jimena Suarez Ibarrola and Gautam Bhatia, 'Gender Discrimination' in *The Max Planck Encyclopedia of Comparative Constitutional Law*, available at http://oxcon.ouplaw.com/view/10.1093/law-mpeccol/law-mpeccol-e127, visited on 23 July 2017. See also, observations by Justice Patanjali Shastri, in *Kathi Raning Rawat v. State of Saurashtra*, AIR 1952 SC 123: '[Discrimination means] to make an adverse distinction with regard to; to distinguish unfavourably from others.' For a more detailed consideration of this, see, infra, Chapter 3.
8. On the issue of separate schools for boys and girls, see Anindita Pattanayak, 'Guest Post: Same-Sex Schools and Gender Discrimination under the Constitution—I', *Indian Constitutional Law and Philosophy*, available at https://indconlawphil.wordpress.com/2015/05/18/guest-post-same-sex-schools-and-gender-discrimination-under-the-constitution-i/, visited on 23 June 2017.
9. For a discussion of this issue in a comparative context, see *Andrews v. Law Society of British Columbia* (1989) 1 SCR 143 (dissenting opinion of Justice McIntyre) (Supreme Court of Canada); see also *Mmusi v. Presiding Officer* (2012)] MAHLB-000836–10 (High Court of Botswana), holding that the act of differentiation must impair human dignity in order to qualify as constitutionally prohibited discrimination. Under the South African Constitution, Section 8(3), discrimination must be 'unfair', and if it is on the basis of the grounds listed under the Constitution, there is a preliminary presumption that it is unfair. See, e.g., *Gumede v. The President* (2009) (3) BCLR 243 (Constitutional Court of South Africa).
10. In addition, there might, on occasion, be disagreement over whether a particular distribution of benefits and burdens is *unequal*. See, for example, the collection of judgements known as the 'Air Hostess Cases', where (female) air hostesses were required to retire at a younger age than (male) air flight pursers, but were granted accelerated avenues of promotion as compensation. *Air India v. Nargesh Mirza*, AIR 1981 SC 1829; *Air India Cabin Crew Association v. Yeshaswinee Merchant* (2003) 6 SCC 277.

11. For an extended discussion, see Tarunabh Khaitan, *A Theory of Discrimination Law* (Oxford: Oxford University Press 2015). For a few judicial pronouncements on this vexed issue, see *Brooks v. Canada Safeway Ltd.* (1989) 1 S.C.R. 1219 (Supreme Court of Canada); *Geduldig v.* Aiello, 417 U.S. 484 (1974) (Supreme Court of the United States); *Wimberly v. Labour and Industrial Relations Commission*, 479 U.S. 511 (1987) (Supreme Court of the United States), and its critique in Martha Minnow, 'Justice Engendered' (1987) 101 *Harvard Law Review* 1, 25. For a broader discussion, see *British Columbia Public Service Employees Relations Commission v. BCGSEU* (1999) 3 S.C.R. 3.
12. *CN v. Canada*, 1987 1 SCR 1114, 1134–1135 (Supreme Court of Canada).
13. Shreya Atrey, 'Guest Post: Article 15(1) Through the Lens of Intersectionality', *Indian Constitutional Law and Philosophy*, https://indconlawphil.wordpress.com/2015/06/10/904/, visited on 23 July 2017.
14. See, e.g., Minnow, 'Justice Engendered', supra.
15. See, e.g., Joan Williams, 'Deconstructing Gender' (1989) 87 *Michigan Law Review* 797. To understand that physical differences are not intrinsically salient, consider an alternative, hypothetical workplace where, for some reason, all doorways are exceedingly low; in this workplace, physical differences in height would acquire the salience that pregnancy has in the real world.
16. Article 15(3), Constitution of India.
17. But see *State of Kerala v. N.M. Thomas*, AIR 1976 SC 940, infra, Chapter 3.
18. Under the Constitution, Articles 14 to 18 are collectively grouped under the heading 'Rights to Equality'. See also *Indra Sawhney v. Union of India*, AIR 1993 SC 477.
19. Other constitutions are more categorical about this. See, e.g., Section 15(2), Canadian Charter of Rights and Freedoms; Section 9(2), Constitution of South Africa. For an analysis, see Ratna Kapur, 'Gender Equality' in *The Oxford Handbook of the Indian Constitution* (Sujit Choudhry et al. eds., New Delhi: OUP 2016), 742, 746.
20. See, e.g., the split verdict of the South African Constitutional Court in President of the Republic of *South Africa v. Hugo*, 1997 (6) BCLR 708,

on the question of whether a presidential pardon to all imprisoned single mothers with children under the age of twelve violated the guarantee against sex discrimination, given that it was based upon both the reality as well as the stereotypes about mothers being the predominant care-givers in the family. See also *Stec v. The United Kingdom* (2006) ECHR 393 (European Court of Human Rights), for a discussion of the blurred line between taking into account 'factual inequalities' and perpetuating stereotypes.

21. *Mahadeb Jiew v. B.B. Sen*, AIR 1951 Cal 563.
22. See also *Sucha Singh Bajwa v. State of Punjab*, AIR 1974 P&H 162; *Nalini Ranjan Singh v. State of Bihar*, AIR 1977 Pat 171; for cases where this logic was applied to uphold educational segregation, see *Anjali Roy v. State of West Bengal*, AIR 1952 Cal 825; for similar reasoning in a case with similar facts from another jurisdiction, see *Magaya v. Magaya* (1998) SC 210/98 (Supreme Court of Zimbabwe); the reasoning is also somewhat similar to an interesting case argued before the High Court of Zambia, where the denial of entry to an unaccompanied woman to a bar was argued to not discriminate on grounds of sex alone, but on the grounds that the woman did not have male company. The high court rejected the argument. *Longwe v. International Hotels*, 1992/HP/765.
23. In effect, the Court was saying that Article 15(1) was violated only when the discrimination was against *all* men, or all women. In technical terms, this mode of reasoning is known as the 'comparator analysis'. See, e.g., Khaitan, *A Theory of Discrimination Law*, supra. See also, *Hassam v. Jacobs* (2009) (11) BCLR 1148 (Constitutional Court of South Africa).
24. Legislatively, it would be ridiculously easy to achieve an end run around this. For example, a hypothetical legislature that wished to discriminate against women within the bounds of the law could simply exclude 'all women below ten feet' from accessing certain benefits. This would, in effect, include all women, but formally, the classification would still be drawn on the 'grounds' of sex and height, and not 'only' sex. A similar example is discussed by Lord Pannick and cited by the Supreme Court of Canada in *Brooks v. Safeway Ltd.*, supra.
25. *R.S. Singh v. State of Punjab*, AIR 1972 P&H 117.

26. Ibid., ¶9, citing the 1908 United States Supreme Court judgement in *Muller v. Oregon*.
27. Ibid., ¶17. See also *Weatherall v. Canada*, [1993] 2 S.C.R. 872 (Supreme Court of Canada). For a similar case from the United States, see *Dothard v. Rawlinson*, 433 U.S. 321 (1977), and Catherine MacKinnon's critique of it in 'Reflections on Sex Equality under Law' (1991) 100(5) *The Yale Law Journal* 1281, 1305–06.
28. Kapur, 'Gender Equality', supra, 742, 748. See also Kalpana Kannabiran, *Tools of Justice: Non-Discrimination and the Indian Constitution* (New Delhi: Routledge India 2012).
29. A judgement that is broadly in line with such reasoning is *Ambika Prasad Mishra v. State of UP*, AIR 1980 SC 1762, where a blatantly discriminatory land ceiling law which, among other things, did not count women as holders of land if their husbands were tenure holders, and counted only 'adult sons' for the purposes of extending the land ceiling, was upheld by the Court. This is a judgement of the Constitution Bench of the Supreme Court, and would therefore, in the ordinary course of things, require detailed analysis. The reason I have not included it in the body of the chapter, however, is that its 'reasoning' is so opaque and incoherent, it simply isn't susceptible to constitutional critique. The judgement was authored by Justice Krishna Iyer who, not for the only time, uses language that does everything but make a point. What, for instance, is the meaning of the following lines, which constitute the core of the judgement? 'But this legal sentiment and jural value must not run riot and destroy provisions which do not discriminate between man and woman qua man and woman but merely organise a scheme where life's realism is legislatively pragmatized. Such a scheme may marginally affect gender justice but does not abridge, even a wee-bit, the rights of women.' (Ibid.) What does it mean to say that 'if land-holding and ceiling thereon are organised with the paramount purpose of maximising surpluses without maiming woman's ownership no submission to destroy this measure can be permitted using sex discrimination as a means to sabotage what is socially desirable ...'? (Ibid.) Or that 'Some of us may not be happy with the masculine flavour of this law but it is difficult to hold that rights of women are unequally treated, and so, the war for equal gender status has to be waged elsewhere ...'?

(Ibid.) For an assessment of this judgement, see Gautam Bhatia, 'Jural Values Running Riot: The Strange Case of *Ambika Prasad Mishra v. State of UP*', *Indian Constitutional Law and Philosophy Blog*, https://indconlawphil.wordpress.com/2016/06/02/jural-values-running-riot-the-strange-case-of-ambika-prasad-mishra-vs-state-of-up/ visited on 29 July 2017.

30. *Air India v. Nargesh Meerza* (1981) 4 SCC 335.
31. Ibid. The Court relied upon its prior judgement in *C.B. Muthamma v. Union of India*, AIR 1979 SC 1868, where Justice Krishna Iyer had used the phrase 'handicaps of either sex'.
32. Nargesh Meerza, supra, ¶80.
33. Ibid., ¶101.
34. As the Canadian Supreme Court correctly explained in a pregnancy discrimination case, 'an unfair disadvantage may result when the costs of an activity from which all of society benefits are placed upon a single group of persons'. See *Brooks v. Canada Safeway*, supra.
35. For a more detailed argument about how pregnancy-based discrimination replicates the separate spheres theory, see Wendy Williams, 'The Equality Riddle: Pregnancy and the Equal Treatment/Special Treatment Debate' (1985) 13 *New York University Review of Law and Social Change*, 325, 352–53.
36. For judgements after *Nargesh Meerza* that have broadly followed this approach, see *A.M. Shaila v. Chairman, Cochin Port Trust* (1995) IILLJ 1193 (High Court of Kerala) (upholding the exclusion of women from employment as shed clerks on the basis of their 'physical structure and special susceptibilities', and 'the need to protect them'); *Leela v. State of Kerala*, 204 (102) FLR 107 ('the very nature of ... [women's] commitment to the family and the social environment require that they cannot be entrusted with all those duties which men may be asked to perform').
37. *Yusuf Abdul Aziz v. State of Bombay*, 1954 SCR 930.
38. Article 15(3), Constitution of India.
39. See also, *Girdhar Gopal v. State*, 1953 CriLJ 964 (MP), where the MP High Court upheld the constitutionality of Section 354 ('outraging the modesty of woman') by invoking 'propriety, public morals, decency, decorum and rectitude' as additional grounds that took the law outside the purview of Article 15(1). For a more recent judgement, see *Ramesh*

Gajnan Rege v. Gauri Ramesh Rege, WP No. 10312/2014, where the Bombay High Court upheld a provision of the Hindu Marriage Act that obligated a father to maintain his unmarried daughters even after the age of majority, but not unmarried sons. Ratna Kapur and Brenda Cossman define this as the 'protective approach' to sex discrimination. Ratna Kapur and Brenda Cossman, 'On Women, Equality and the Constitution: Through the Looking Glass of Feminism' (1993) 1 *National Law School Journal*.

40. Smt. *Sowmithri Vishnu v. Union of India*, AIR 1985 SC 1618.
41. *Rani Raj Rajeshwari Devi v. State of UP*, AIR 1954 All 608.
42. Ibid., ¶73.
43. Ibid., ¶96. See also *Pritam Kaur v. State of PEPSU,* AIR 1963 P&H 19, a somewhat similar case, endorsing the proposition that 'a classification that the Constitution forbids cannot possibly be said to be reasonable'. And, *Mrs A. Cracknell v. State of UP*, AIR 1952 All 746.
44. *Radha Charan Patnaik v. State of Orissa*, AIR 1969 Ori 237.
45. Ibid., ¶17.
46. Ibid.
47. Ibid., ¶18.
48. *Walter Alfred Baid v. Union of India*, AIR 1976 Del 302.
49. Ibid., ¶10.
50. *A.N. Rajamma v. State of Kerala*, W.A. No. 682 of 1982 (High Court of Kerala). See also *Vijayamma v. State of Kerala* (1978) IILLJ 323 Ker., decided four years earlier.
51. Ibid., ¶14.
52. Ibid., ¶1. Later, the High Court made the sharp observation that the basis of stereotypes was the fact that it was men who had the power to make rules: 'If the work of say, a Duffadar, a Cleaner-cum-Conductor, Court Keeper, Chairman, Housekeeper or a Field Worker does not suit a woman or she would feel humiliated by such work it is for her to decide whether she should apply for the concerned job and not for the male dominated legislature or the male dominated bureaucratic machinery which may be functioning as a delegated legislative body to decide whether women should be permitted to do such work or not.' Ibid.
53. For judgements after *Rajamma* that endorsed this reasoning, see, e.g., *Vasantha v. Union of India* (2001) IILLJ 843 (High Court of Madras),

striking down a provision of the Factories Act that prohibited evening work for women, and directing the State to take measures to ensure their safety; *Triveni v. Union of India*, 2002 (5) ALT 223, saying much the same thing.

54. For an alternative typology, which overlaps with this one without being identical, see Kapur and Cossman, 'On Women, Equality and the Constitution', supra.
55. Anuj Garg, supra, ¶46. The language is somewhat similar to that used by the High Court of Botswana a few years later which, in striking down discriminatory customary inheritance laws, observed that their effect was to 'subject women to a status of perpetual minority, placing them automatically under the control of male heirs, simply by virtue of their sex'. *Mmusi v. Presiding Officer*, supra.
56. Anuj Garg, supra, ¶47.
57. *Rajbala v. State of Haryana*, (2016) 1 SCC 463.
58. See, e.g., Bertha Wilson, 'Women, the Family, and the Constitutional Protection of Privacy' (1992) 17 *Queen's Law Journal* 5, 13. For judgements dealing with facially neutral laws that were shown to have a disparate impact upon women, see, e.g., *Zarb Adami v. Malta*, 44 EHRR 3 (European Court of Human Rights) (jury service); for an excellent exposition of the argument, albeit ultimately rejected, see the judgement of the High Court of Zimbabwe in *Madzara v. StanbicBank Zimbabwe Ltd* (2015) ZWHHC 546; see also *S v. Jordan* (2002) 11 BCLR 1117 (Constitutional Court of South Africa), where the Court, over a dissenting opinion by Justices Sachs and O'Regan, rejected the argument that a penal provision treating a sex worker as a primary offender and a client as a secondary offender was gender discriminatory, because sex workers were overwhelmingly female.
59. Rosalind O'Hanlon, *A Comparison Between Women and Men: Tarabai Shinde and the Critique of Gender Relations in Colonial India* 15 (Madras: Oxford University Press 1994).
60. Anupama Rao, *Gendered Citizenship: Historical and Conceptual Explorations* (New Delhi: Orient BlackSwan 2013).
61. Partha Chatterjee, 'Colonialism, Nationalism and Colonised Women: The Contest in India' (1989) 16(4) *American Ethnologist* 622, 624.
62. Roy, *Gendered Citizenship*, supra, 74.

63. Padma Anagol, *The Emergence of Feminism in India* 208 (London: Routledge 2006).
64. Roy, *Gendered Citizenship*, supra, 116.
65. Anagol, *The Emergence of Feminism in India*, supra, 116.
66. M.K. Gandhi, 'The Role of Woman', cf. Reba Som, 'Jawaharlal Nehru and the Hindu Code: A Victory of Symbol over Substance?' in *Women and Social Reform in Modern India: A Reader* 243 (Sumit Sarkar and Tanika Sarkar eds., Bloomington: Indiana University Press).
67. Maitrayee Chaudhury, 'The Indian Women's Movement' in *Feminism in India* 118–19 (Maitrayee Chaudhury ed., London: Zed Books 2005); an amendment to add 'ideals of fatherhood' in addition to 'ideals of motherhood' was rejected.
68. Ibid., pp. 121–24.
69. Bankim Chandra Chattopadhyay, *Samya* 55 (Bibek Debroy trans., New Delhi: Liberty Institute 2002).
70. Ibid., Ch. 5.
71. Ibid., 58.
72. Tanika Sarkar, *Hindu Wife, Hindu Nation* 94 (Indiana University Press 2010), writing about the work of Ishwar Chandra Vidyasagar.
73. 'Letters from a Hindu Lady', *Times of India* (1885), cf. Padma Anagol, 'Rebellious Wives and Dysfunctional Marriages: Indian Women's Discourses and Participation in the Debates over Restitution of Conjugal Rights and Child Marriage Controversy in the 1880s and 1890s' in *Women and Social Reform in Modern India*, supra. A few decades later, B.R. Ambedkar would echo Rukhmabai's language when he noted that 'woman … has been an easy prey to all kinds of iniquitous injunctions, religious, social or economic. But man as a maker of injunctions is most often above them all.' B.R. Ambedkar, 'Castes in India: Their Mechanism, Genesis and Development', (1917) XLI *Indian Antiquary*, available at http://www.columbia.edu/itc/mealac/pritchett/00ambedkar/txt_ambedkar_castes.html. There is also a striking similarity between her language and that of the 1848 Seneca Falls Declaration kickstarting the US suffrage movement, which noted that man has attempted to 'destroy her [i.e., woman's] confidence in her own powers, to lessen her self-respect, and to make her willing to lead a dependent and abject life'.

74. Rokeya Sakhawat Hossain, 'Woman's Downfall' (Mohammad A. Quayum trans.), available at https://ziladoc.com/download/womens-downfall-rokeya-sakhawat-hossein_pdf (visited on 25 June 2018).
75. Anagol, *The Emergence of Feminism in India*, supra, 30.
76. Krupabai Satthianadhan, *Miscellaneous Writings* (Madras: Srinivasa Varadachariar & Co. 1896).
77. Anagol, *The Emergence of Feminism in India*, supra, 44.
78. 'Maharashtrian women resorted to a rich vocabulary in the Marathi language to express ideas that are now considered feminist terms and enrich the Indian feminist lexicon with concepts and terms such as the following: *bhaginvarg* (sisterhood); *strihak* (women's rights); *strivarg* (womankind or womanhood); *strianubhav* (women's experience); *bandhivasan* (bondage); *dasyatva* (slavery); *mokaleek* (independence or freedom); *strijati* (female sex); *purushjati* (male sex); *purusharth* (manliness and masculinity). These phrases occur regularly in the colloquial and formal texts written by Maharashtrian women and the most significant of the magazines within the broader women's press of the time, *Arya Bhagini*, literally uses the concept of *bhagini* (sisters) in its title—a telling sign of the times.' Anagol, 'Rebellious Wives and Dysfunctional Marriages', supra, 427.
79. V. Geetha, 'Periyar, Women and an Ethic of Citizenship' (1998) 33(17) *Economic and Political Weekly* WS9–WS15; S. Anandhi, 'Women's Question in the Dravidian Movement c. 1925–1948' (1991) 19(5/6) *Social Scientist* 24.
80. See Leela Kasturi, 'Report of the Sub-Committee, *Women's Role in the Planned Economy*, National Planning Committee Series (1947)' in *Feminism in India*, supra, 136–55.
81. Ibid., 139.
82. Ibid., 144.
83. Ibid., 149.
84. Geraldine H. Forbes, 'Votes for Women: The Demand for Women's Franchise in India: 1917–1937' in *Symbols of Power: The Political Status of Women in India* 3, 6 (Vina Mazumdar ed., Bombay: Allied Publishers 1979).
85. Gail Pearson, 'Reserved Seats—Women and the Vote in Bombay' (1983) 20(1) *The Indian Economic and Social History Review* 47, 51.

86. Forbes, 'Votes for Women', supra, p. 6.
87. Cf. Roy, *Gendered Citizenship*, supra, 169. For an account of how this argument was consistently deployed by Sarojini Naidu, perhaps the most prominent woman in Indian public life, see Sumita Mukherjee, *Indian Suffragettes: Female Identities and Transnational Networks* (New Delhi: OUP 2018).
88. Forbes, 'Votes for Women', supra, 5.
89. Ibid., 8.
90. Ibid., 7.
91. For example, WIA representatives argued for the vote on the basis of women's roles as mothers and educators; Rameshwari Nehru argued for it based on the need for women to control the environment of the home. Chaudhury, 'The Indian Women's Movement', supra, 117, 125.
92. Forbes, 'Votes for Women', supra, 9.
93. Sarojini Naidu, *Speeches and Writings* (1925), cited in Roy, *Gendered Citizenship*, supra, 164.
94. See, e.g., B.R. Ambedkar, *The Annihilation of Caste,* available at http://ccnmtl.columbia.edu/projects/mmt/ambedkar/web/readings/aoc_print_2004.pdf, visited on 26 August 2017.
95. Wendy Singers, *A Constituency Suitable for Ladies* 25 (New Delhi: Oxford University Press 2007).
96. The WIA had boycotted the Conference at the behest of the Congress. See Mukherjee, *Indian Suffragettes*, supra.
97. Roy, *Gendered Citizenship*, supra, 163; they also made the argument that reservations were required for 'real equality of opportunity in the political arena,' Pearson, 'Reserved Seats', supra, 53; this, of course, is an entirely separate argument that, conspicuously, does not rely upon or endorse the separate spheres theory. In the Indian Franchise Committee's Report of 1932, much of which was incorporated into the 1935 Government of India Act, both arguments—constituency representation and genuine equality of opportunity—were invoked to justify special representation. Indian Franchise Committee, *Report of the Indian Franchise Committee, Volume 1*, 78–87 (2nd ed., Calcutta: Government of India Central Publication Branch 1932), available at http://eci.nic.in/eci_main/eci_publications/books/miscell/Indian%20Franchise%20Committee-Vol-I.pdf, visited on 26 July 2017.
98. Government of India Act, 1935.

99. Forbes, 'Votes for Women', supra, 14.
100. Aparna Basu, 'Women's Struggle for the Vote: 1917–1937' (2008) 35(1) *The Indian Historical Review* 128, 130. The similarities with Abigail Adam's famous 'Remember the Ladies' letter to John Adams are obvious.
101. Mrinalini Sinha, *Specters of Mother India: The Global Restructuring of an Empire* 51 (Durham: Duke University Press 2006).
102. Ibid., 132.
103. Ibid. For other examples of resistance to the dominant cultural-nationalist argument during the debates over the Sarda Act, see ibid., 181.
104. Ibid. In fact, it was in seconding this very resolution that Sarojini Naidu stressed on the 'separate destinies' of men and women, thus laying bare the schism at the heart of the women's demand for the vote.
105. Sinha, *Specters of Mother India*, supra, 222.
106. Ibid., 223.
107. Karachi Resolution of the Indian National Congress, 1931.
108. As noted above, it is important to parse the language in which the argument for reservation and special representation was made. As Subbarayan and Shahnawaz did argue, special representation was required to achieve genuine parity and equality. This classic argument for affirmative action—framing it as a tool to overcome entrenched institutional barriers—does not, of course, rely on social feminism or separate spheres. In fact, it acknowledges the subordination created by the prevalence of theories such as separate spheres, and seeks to overcome it. As we have seen, however, to a large extent, the argument for special representation *was* made, and opposed, on the terrain of social feminism.
109. Pearson, 'Reserved Seats', supra, 54.
110. Ibid., 61.
111. Chaudhury, 'The Indian Women's Movement', supra, 127.
112. Indian Franchise Committee, *Report, Volume 1*, supra, ¶216.
113. Subbarayan, for example, went from advocating special representation to opposing it.
114. Sarojini Naidu was the most prominent example. See, e.g., Pearson, 'Reserved Seats', supra, 49.
115. See, e.g., ibid., 65; Mukherjee, *Indian Suffragettes*, supra.

116. See, e.g., Sinha, *Specters of Mother India*, supra, Ch. 5.

117. Anupama Roy highlights 'the difficulty of weaving together a single thread of events or debates that can be labelled *the* suffrage debate or *the* suffrage movement'. Roy, *Gendered Citizenship*, supra, 127. This is also true for the broader feminist movement in colonial India. As Padma Anagol points out, many early feminists believed that the only route to progress was through a 'strategy of accommodation'. Accordingly, they focused on countering opposition by arguing that female emancipation would *not* threaten domestic life. Anagol, *The Emergence of Feminism in India*, supra, 62, 81, 101.

118. For instance, one of the main goals of the suffrage movement was an expansion of the women's electorate, and principled positions often took a backseat towards achieving this goal. See, e.g., Sinha, *Specters of Mother India*, supra; Roy, *Gendered Citizenship*, supra. Additionally, for the tricky and often paradoxical positions some of the leaders of the women's movement had to take because of the imperatives of staying on the side of the Congress-led nationalist movement, see, e.g., Geraldine Forbes, 'Caged Tigers: First Wave Feminists in India' (1982) 5(6) *Women's Studies International Forum* 525, 534.

119. For a similarly structured argument linking American sex equality jurisprudence with the suffrage movement, see Reva Siegel, 'She the People: The Nineteenth Amendment, Sex Equality, Federalism and the Family' (2002) 115(4) *Harvard Law Review* 947. See also Ellen DuBois, *Feminism and Suffrage: The Emergence of an Independent Women's Movement in America, 1848–1869* (Ithaca: Cornell University Press 1978); Ellen DuBois, 'The Radicalism of the Woman Suffrage Movement: Towards a Reconstruction of Nineteenth Century Feminism' (1976) 3 *Feminist Studies* 63; W. William Hodes, 'Women and the Constitution: Some Legal History and a New Approach to the Nineteenth Amendment' (1971) 25 *Rutgers Law Review* 26. For a bibliography of the spectrum of arguments, see Gautam Bhatia, 'Comprehensive Transformative Amendments: Theory and Practice' (2015) 13 *Dartmouth Law Journal* 1.

120. In the Constituent Assembly Debates, there was no extensive discussion on the prospect of separate electorates for women. The idea was comprehensively rejected by Renuka Ray (one of the few women in the Constituent Assembly). See Parliament of India, *Constituent*

Assembly Debates – Volume IV, Friday, 18 July 1947 (speech of Renuka Ray), available at http://parliamentofindia.nic.in/ls/debates/vol4p5.htm. For a broader discussion, see Shefali Jha, 'Rights versus Representation: Defending Minority Interests in the Constituent Assembly' (2003) 38(16) *Economic and Political Weekly* 1579–83.

121. For the link between the two, and the proposition that the 1931 Resolution advocated 'complete equality', see the statements of Ilina Sen, 'Women's Politics in India' in *Feminism in India* supra, 187, 190.

122. Article 326, Constitution of India. An additional amendment, specifying that nobody could be excluded from electoral rolls on the grounds of religion, race, caste, or sex was initially incorporated into the Constitution, but ultimately removed on grounds of redundancy. Parliament of India, *Constituent Assembly Debates, Vol. VIII*, 16 June 1949.

123. For example, in responding to a demand for women's representation in the Constituent Assembly, H.V. Kamath argued that 'woman is ruled more by the heart … and where the affairs of Government are concerned, we have to be cold and calculating'. Parliament of India, *Constituent Assembly Debates, Vol. X*, 11 October 1949 (Speech of H.V. Kamath).

124. Article 39(e), Constitution of India.

125. Parliament of India, *Constituent Assembly Debates*, *Vol. VII*, Monday, 22 September 1948 (speech of H.V. Kamath).

126. Ibid. (speech of Lakshminarayan Sahu).

127. Article 15(1), Constitution of India.

128. See, e.g., *Andrews v. Law Society of British Columbia*, supra, discussing the non-discrimination clause of the Canadian Charter of Rights and Freedoms: 'The enumerated grounds do, however, reflect the most common and probably the most socially destructive and historically practised bases of discrimination' (dissenting opinion of Justice McIntyre). See also *Law v. Canada* (1999) 1 S.C.R. 497.

129. For an account of the debates around the drafting of Article 15(1), which suggested, on more than one occasion, the preoccupation of the drafters with various strands of social feminism, see Sanjay Jain, 'Guest Post: Women and the Constituent Assembly – II: The Framing of the Non-Discrimination Clause', *Indian Constitutional Law and Philosophy*, https://indconlawphil.wordpress.com/2015/09/04/

guest-post-women-and-the-constituent-assembly-ii-the-framing-of-the-non-discrimination-clause/, visited on 29 August 2017. The point remains, however, that whatever the *intentions* of the framers, ultimately it is their choice of *words* that matters. For example, when Jayaprakash Narayan proposed an additional non-discrimination clause dealing with possession of property and occupation, it was rejected with a note that restrictions on property could be imposed in the interests of the general public (with specific reference to gender-unequal personal laws), and that it might be important to prohibit women from pursuing certain occupations such as that of rickshaw-puller or labourer in the mines. See B. Shiva Rao, *The Framing of India's Constitution: Select Documents, Vol. IV* 29–30 (New Delhi: Universal Law Publishing 2015). This is a classic example of what Dworkin calls 'application intentions', i.e., how the framers intended their words to be *applied*; however, as he points out, in the structure of constitutional interpretation, application intentions can well be at odds with the words that are *actually* used, when understood in their comprehensive textual, historical, and structural contexts. Ronald Dworkin, *Freedom's Law: The Moral Reading of the American Constitution* (Cambridge: Harvard University Press 1996). My argument here is that the framers' application intentions, driven by their understanding of social feminism, were not, finally, reflected in the text of Articles 15(1) and 326.

130. For a detailed list, see Kirti Singh, 'Laws and Son Preference in India: A Reality Check', *United Nations Population Fund* (2012), available at https://www.unfpa.org/sites/default/files/jahia-news/documents/publications/2013/LawsandSonPreferenceinIndia.pdf, visited on 25 June 2018.

131. Sharanya Gopinathan, 'Why Are Women Banned from Open Jail Benefits in India', *The Ladies Finger*, 8 October 2017, available at http://theladiesfinger.com/open-prisons-india-women/.

132. For another list of such discriminatory laws, and how challenges to them have failed in the courts, see Kapur and Cossman, 'On Equality, Women and the Constitution', supra.

133. See, e.g., Nishita Gupta, 'This Campaign Is Asking the Govt to Make Sanitary Napkins Tax-Free and We Say It's About Time', *ScoopWhoop*, https://www.scoopwhoop.com/this-campaign-is-asking-the-govt-to-

make-sanitary-napkins-taxfree/#.0qelxk6em, visited on 30 August 2017. There is an argument, in this specific case, that the removal of the tax would not bring the price down. In any event, the tax was withdrawn in July 2018.

134. A similar set of arguments would apply to the issue of menstrual leave, which was also in the news in the summer of 2017.

135. Section 56, Code of Civil Procedure, 1908.

136. *Shrikrishna Eknath Godbole v. Union of India*, 2016 SCC OnLine Bom 9559, ¶5.

137. *Inspector (Mahila) Ravina v. Union of India*, W.P. (C) 4525/2014 (High Court of Delhi), ¶12.

138. See, for example, the fascinating discussion by the Supreme Court of Canada in *Symes v. Canada* (1993) 4 S.C.R. 695, on whether the refusal to allow childcare expenses to be deducted as 'business expenses' for income tax purposes was gender discriminatory, since childcare expenses were predominantly borne by women. See also the discussion in British Columbia Public Service Employee Relations Commission, supra: *British Columbia Public Service Employees Relations Commission v. BCGSEU* (1999) 3 S.C.R. 3: 'Under the conventional analysis, if a standard is classified as being 'neutral' at the threshold stage of the inquiry, its legitimacy is never questioned. The focus shifts to whether the individual claimant can be accommodated, and the formal standard itself always remains intact ... [this] bars courts and tribunals from assessing the legitimacy of the standard itself... '

139. As the Canadian Supreme Court put it in *Brooks v. Safeway Ltd*, supra, the inequality is not created by nature, but by legislation (which, in the context under discussion, denied unemployment benefits for pregnancy). Justice Albie Sachs, dissenting in the South African case of *Volks v. Robinson* (2005) 5 BCLR 446, put the point even more clearly when he recommended that 'patterns of gender inequality reinforced by the law be not viewed simply as part of an unfortunate yet legally neutral background'.

140. In *P. Vasantha v. Union of India* (2001) IILLJ 843 (Mad), the High Court of Madras observed that 'benign' measures under Article 15(3) would have to be tested on the basis of whether they were designed to remedy the effects of past discrimination, and did not in themselves perpetuate stereotypes; in *Government of Andhra Pradesh v. P.B.*

Vijaykumar, AIR 1996 SC 1648, the Supreme Court upheld gender quotas in recruitment on the basis that Article 15(3) was designed to improve women's 'participation'; similar reasoning was employed by the Kerala High Court in *K.R. Gopinath Nair v. The Senior Inspector*, AIR 1987 Ker 167, in upholding quotas in cooperative society committees ('… prejudices, strong prejudices, existed against women for long periods of history …'); see also *Dattatraya Motiram More v. State of Bombay*, AIR 1953 Bom 311. From other jurisdictions, see the judgement of the Lesotho Court of Appeal in *Ts'epe v. Independent Electoral Commission and ors.* (2005) LSHC 93 (Lesotho), where affirmative action in the form of election quotas was upheld on the basis of remedying past and existing institutional disadvantage, on the basis of statistics regarding representation. In a useful typology, Kapur and Cossman ('On Equality, Women and the Constitution', supra) distinguish between the 'protective approach' and the 'corrective approach' to Article 15(3).

141. *Joseph Shine v. Union of India*, W.P. (Crl.) 194/2017. For an analysis, see Gautam Bhatia, 'The Supreme Court Decriminalises Adultery', *The Indian Constitutional Law and Philosophy Blog* (27 September 2018), available at https://indconlawphil.wordpress.com/2018/09/27/the-supreme-court-decriminalises-adultery/.
142. Id., ¶62 (concurring opinion of Justice Chandrchud).
143. Id., ¶12.2 (concurring opinion of Justice Malhotra).
144. Id., ¶14 (concurring opinion of Justice Malhotra).

2: Equality Before Law: *Naz Foundation* and Equal Moral Membership

1. Parliament of India, *Constituent Assembly Debates*, 13 December 1946 (Speech of Pt. Jawaharlal Nehru), available at http://parliamentofindia.nic.in/ls/debates/vol7p10.htm; see also Tarunabh Khaitan, 'Reading *Swaraj* into Article 15: A New Deal for the Minorities', (2009) 2 *NUJS Law Review* 419.
2. *Naz Foundation v. NCT of Delhi*, 160 DLT 277 (2009) (High Court of Delhi).
3. S. 377, Indian Penal Code, 1860.
4. Naz Foundation, supra, ¶130–31.

5. Article 14, Constitution of India.
6. Tarunabh Khaitan, 'Equality: Legislative Review under Article 14' in *The Oxford Handbook of the Indian Constitution*, supra, 699.
7. Douglas Sanders, 'Section 377 and the Unnatural Afterlife of British Colonialism in Asia' (2009) 4(1) *Asian Journal of Comparative Law* 1, 7.
8. Alok Gupta, 'Section 377 and the Dignity of Indian Homosexuals' (November 18, 2006) 41(46) *Economic and Political Weekly* 4817.
9. *Khandu v. Emperor*, AIR 1925 Sind 286, ¶2; *Khandu*'s proposition that oral sex was an offence under S. 377 was affirmed in *Khandu v. Emperor*, AIR 1934 Lah. 261, although that case involved an individual having oral sex with a bullock; around the same time, the Judicial Committee of Sind held that penetrative anal sex amounted to an offence under S. 377 (*Nowshirwan Irani v. Emperor*, AIR 1934 Sind 206). In *Naz Foundation*, the petitioner argued that S. 377 was based on 'Judeo-Christian moral and ethical standards which conceive of sex in purely functional terms'. Naz Foundation, supra, Petition, p. 8 (on file with the author).
10. *Lohana Vasantlal Devchand v. The State* (1968) 9 CLR 1052, affirmed in *Brother John Anthony v. State* (1992) CrilLJ 818, which also held manual sex to fall within the scope of S. 377. Fellatio (albeit in a case of child sexual exploitation) was also held to constitute an offence in *Childline India Foundation v. Allan John Waters*, (2011) 2 SCC (Cri) 900.
11. Ibid., ¶12.
12. Ibid., ¶14.
13. *Fazal Rab Choudhary v. State of Bihar* (1982) 3 SCC 9.
14. The Malaysian Penal Code, which, like the Indian Penal Code, originated from the colonial British, also prohibits 'carnal intercourse against the order of nature', which it defines as 'the introduction of the penis into the anus or mouth'. S. 377A, Malaysian Penal Code, 1976.
15. Naz Foundation, supra, Petition, p. 30 (on file with the author).
16. In the words of the High Court of Fiji, which struck down a nearly identically worded section, a sodomy law defined as 'criminal ... conduct essential to the sexual expression of the homosexual relationship'. *Dhirendra Nadan v. State*, Criminal Appeal Case Nos. HAA 85 & 86 of 2005 (High Court of Fiji).

17. How this distinction could ever be enforced, or subjected to judicially manageable standards in a court of law, is of course another question.
18. For example, in *State of Kerala v. Kundumkara Govindan* (1969) CriLJ 818), the High Court of Kerala held that the (forcible) insertion of a man's penis between a woman's thighs (i.e., anal rape) constituted an offence under S. 377; In *Calvin John Francis v. State of Orissa* (1992) I OLR 316, the High Court of Orissa held that oral rape was an offence under S. 377; see also *Brother John Anthony v. State*, supra (manual sex, which need not be between two men). These cases are not dispositive of the issue, since they are all cases of non-consensual sexual assault. Notably, however, courts in Singapore have found that consensual fellatio between men and women violates the (identically worded) S. 377 of their penal code. See, e.g., *Annis bin Abdullah v. PP* (2004) SCHC 52; *PP v. Kwan Kwong Weng* (1997) 1 SLR 697.
19. Naz Foundation, supra, counter-affidavit of Respondent No. 5, B.P. Singhal, p. 15 (on file with the author).
20. Article 14, Constitution of India.
21. Section I, Fourteenth Amendment to the Constitution of the United States.
22. See, e.g., *Chiranjit Lal Choudhry v. Union of India*, 1950 SCR 869.
23. See, e.g., *Tigner v. Texas*, 310 U.S. 141 (1940) (Supreme Court of the United States). H.M. Seervai, *Constitutional Law of India, Vol. 1*, 453 (4th ed., New Delhi: Universal Law Publishing 2015).
24. Ibid. The phrase 'class legislation' is directly borrowed from nineteenth-century US legal jurisprudence, and refers to laws that favour the interests of a particular class of people, rather than the public as a whole. See Melissa L. Saunders, 'Equal Protection, Class Legislation, and Colorblindness' (1997) 96 *Michigan Law Review* 245.
25. *State of West Bengal v. Anwar Ali Sarkar*, 1952 SCR 284. For a chronology of how the 'rational nexus' test as the concrete exposition of 'reasonable classification' came to be established in Indian law, see P.K. Tripathi, *Some Insights into Fundamental Rights* 52–58 (University of Bombay 1971).
26. Joseph Tussman and Jacobus tenBroek, 'The Equal Protection of Laws' (1949) 37(3) *The California Law Review* 341, cited in *State of Gujarat v. Shri Ambica Mills Ltd.*, 1974 SCR (3) 760.

27. For a more recent treatment of the kinds of questions that may arise in such situations (albeit in the context of the proportionality test applied by courts while reviewing legislation for compatibility with human rights), see Cora Chan, 'Proportionality and the Invariable Baseline Intensity of Review' (2013) 33(1) *Legal Studies* 1.
28. In the Indian context, this was pointed out by P.K. Tripathi, who framed it as a question of 'the quantum of disparity' that was consistent with equality. Tripathi, *Some Insights into Fundamental Rights*, supra, 67.
29. That is, if there were no arguments from either side, would the court uphold or invalidate a particular legislative classification?
30. Tussman and tenBroek, supra, 354.
31. Ibid., 356.
32. Ibid.
33. Ibid., 358. Tussman and tenBroek also proposed a fifth issue—whether the equal protection clause protected certain basic rights—which I do not deal with here.
34. Chiranjit Lal Chowdhury, 1950 SCR 869, ¶67 (majority opinion of Justice Mukherjea); see also, ¶18 (concurring opinion of Justice Fazl Ali).
35. State of *Gujarat v. Shri Ambica Mills* (1974) 4 SCC 656.
36. *Supdt. and Remembrancer of Legal Affairs v. Girish Kumar Navalakha* (1975) 4 SCC 754.
37. *State of Bombay v. F.N. Balsara*, 1951 SCR 682, holding that an exemption for armed forces from a prohibition law passed the scrutiny of Article 14 (and reversing the High Court judgement on this point), on the simple assumption that interfering with the armed forces' 'unique way of life' might impact their morale; *State of West Bengal v. Anwar Ali Sarkar*, 1952 SCR 284, striking down a law that set up special courts for the purpose of 'speedier trials of certain offences', without any further stipulation on which offences; *Kathi Raning Rawat v. State of Saurashtra*, 1952 SCR 435, upholding a similar law where the purpose of special courts was to try crimes that affected public tranquillity and public order; *Budhan Choudhry v. State of Bihar*, 1955 SCR (1) 1045, upholding S. 30 of the Code of Criminal Procedure; *Ram Krishna Dalmia v. S.R. Tendolkar*, 1959 SCR 279, upholding the

establishment of a Commission of Enquiry to investigate the affairs of certain companies.

38. For a restatement, see In re Special Courts Bill, (1979) 2 SCR 348. For a general defence of his approach in common law, grounded in institutional legitimacy and competence, see Julian Rivers, 'Proportionality and Variable Intensity of Review' (2006) 65(1) *Cambridge Law Journal* 174.
39. See, infra, Section II(C).
40. Article 15(1), Constitution of India.
41. Starting, of course, with the famous *Brown v. Board of Education*, 347 U.S. 483 (1954).
42. Kathi Raning Rawat, supra, ¶7.
43. In 2007, a two-judge bench of the Supreme Court appeared to incorporate the US principle of 'strict scrutiny' for certain kinds of classifications, into Article 14. Opposition to this is based on the premise that the Constitution had *already* codified two tiers of scrutiny, viz., 'rational review' under Article 14, and non-discrimination on six specific grounds, under Article 15. See, e.g., Vikram Raghavan, 'Navigating the Noteworthy and Nebulous in Naz Foundation' (2009) 2 *NUJS Law Review* 397, 414–15.
44. *Andrews v. Law Society of British Columbia* (1989) 1 S.C.R. 143 (Supreme Court of Canada).
45. See, e.g., Susanne Baer, 'Equality' in *The Oxford Handbook of Comparative Constitutional Law* 982, 986 (Michael Rosenfeld and András Sajó ed., OUP 2012): 'In the history of equality jurisprudence, the focus on rationality has however served to weaken the claims for equal treatment.'
46. This included 'strict scrutiny' for racial classifications (*Adarand Constructors v. Pena*, 515 U.S. 200 [1995]), and 'intermediate scrutiny' for sex-based classifications (*United States v. Virginia*, 518 U.S. 515 [1996]).
47. *Harksen v. Lane*, 1997 (11) BCLR 1489 (Constitutional Court of South Africa). But, see, Pierre de Vos, 'Substantive Equality after Grootboom: The Emergence of Social and Economic Context as a Guiding Value in Equality Jurisprudence', (2001) 2001 *Acta Juridica* 52, 61, for a critique.

48. Chiranjit Lal Choudhry, supra, ¶9 (concurring opinion of Justice Fazl Ali).
49. *State of West Bengal v. Anwar Ali Sarkar*, supra, ¶44 (majority opinion of Justice Mukherjea) and ¶87 (concurring opinion of Justice Aiyar).
50. *E.P. Royappa v. State of Tamil Nadu*, 1974 SCR (2) 348.
51. Catherine A. MacKinnon, 'Sex Equality under the Constitution of India: Problems, Prospects, and Personal Laws' (2006) 4(2) *International Journal of Constitutional Law* 181, 188.
52. Seervai, *Constitutional Law of India, Vol. 1*, supra,437.
    Ruma Pal, 'Judicial Oversight or Overreach' (2008) 7 *SCC Journal* 9.
53. See, e.g., *Maneka Gandhi v. Union of India* (1978) 2 S.C.R. 621; *Ajay Hasia v. Khalid Mujib* (1979) 3 S.C.R. 1014; *Air India v. Nargesh Meerza* (1982) SCR (1) 438.
54. See Khaitan, 'Equality', supra, 702; see also T.M. Andhyarujina, 'The Evolution of Due Process of Law by the Supreme Court' in *Supreme But Not Infallible* 193 (B.N. Kirpal et al. eds., OUP 2004); B.N. Srikrishna, 'Skinning a Cat' (2005) *SCC Journal* 3.
55. Shayara Bano, supra, articulating 'arbitrariness' in the language of proportionality.
56. *Dipak Sibal v. Punjab University*, 1989 (2) SCC 145.
57. Ibid., ¶20.
58. See, e.g., Seervai's critique of *Kathi Raning Rawat*: Seervai, *Constitutional Law of India*, supra, 516.
59. See e.g., *Dr Pradeep Jain v. Union of India* (1984) 3 SCC 654, where the Court examined affirmative action policies under Article 14 on the assumption that the default purpose of any admission policy was 'merit'.
60. See, e.g., *Nagpur Improvement Trust v. Vithal Rao*, 1973 SCR (3) 39.
61. In *Anwar Ali Sarkar*, Justice Das pointed out that 'the object by itself cannot be the basis of the classification'; *State of West Bengal v. Anwar Ali Sarkar*, supra, ¶62 (partially concurring and partially dissenting opinion of Justice Das). Seervai agrees (Seervai, *Constitutional Law of India*, supra, 495). However, there is no explanation for this; to simply say, as Seervai does, 'the object of the statute cannot furnish the differentia because the object and the differentia are distinct and separate' (ibid.) is tautological. Seervai's own analysis of the Supreme Court's judgement in *R.K. Garg v. Union of India* (1981) 4 SCC 675

faults the impugned classification as 'reeking with immorality', which seems to speaks to legislative purpose (ibid., 496).

62. See, for example, *Subramanian Swamy v. Director, CBI* (2014) 8 SCC 682, where the Court struck down a legal provision that prohibited corruption investigation against high-level government officials without prior sanction, ostensibly on the basis of illegitimate purpose, but gave no further explanation.
63. As the Court noted, a strange feature of the case was that two ministries, viz., the Ministry of Home Affairs and the Ministry of Health and Welfare, took opposite stands on the issue.
64. Naz Foundation, supra, ¶24. See also, Written Submissions of the Union of India, pp. 15–21 (on file with the author).
65. *Naz Foundation v. NCT*, supra, Written Submissions of the Union of India, pp. 81–86 (on file with the author).
66. Naz Foundation, supra, ¶¶61–74.
67. See, e.g., Counter-Affidavit of Respondent No. 8 (Voices Against 377), Annexure R6 (2006 Delhi Declaration), on file with the author.
68. Naz Foundation, supra, ¶¶62–66.
69. Ibid., ¶70.
70. Ibid., ¶71.
71. Ibid., ¶92.
72. The distinction between a relationship of rationality (that the classification cannot be unconnected or irrelevant to the object) and a relationship of reasonableness (which also examines the 'severity' of the restriction—a question of degree) is brought out by P.K. Tripathi. See Tripathi, *Some Insights into Fundamental Rights*, supra, 95.
73. See, e.g., Bernhard Schlink, 'Proportionality' in *The Oxford Handbook of Comparative Constitutional Law*, supra,718.
74. See, e.g., the equality doctrine of the Federal Constitutional Court of Germany, discussed in Susanne Baer, 'Equality: The Jurisprudence of the German Constitutional Court' (1998–99) 5 *Columbia Journal of European Law* 249, 263; see also *Alekseyev v. Russia*, Application Nos. 4916/07, 25924/08 and 14599/09, European Court of Human Rights.
75. *R v. Oakes* (1986) 1 S.C.R. 103 (Supreme Court of Canada).

76. *S v. Makwanyane*, 1995 (3) SA 391 (Constitutional Court of South Africa).
77. *Teri Oat Estates v. UT Chandigarh* (2004) 2 SCC 130; see also Tarunabh Khaitan, 'Beyond Reasonableness: A Rigorous Standard of Review for Article 15 Infringement' (2008) 50(2) *Journal of the Indian Law Institute* 180.
78. Aharon Barak, 'Proportionality (2)' in *The Oxford Handbook of Comparative Constitutional Law*, supra, 738–48.
79. See, e.g., ibid., 734. For a detailed, conceptual analysis of how the standard may be applied in human rights cases, see Cora Chan, 'Proportionality…', supra.
80. *Anuj Garg v. Hotel Association*, AIR 2008 SC 663.
81. Naz Foundation, supra, ¶107.
82. Following the same method, the Court of Appeal of Hong Kong said it would 'scrutinize with intensity whether the difference in treatment is justified'. *Secretary for Justice v. Yau Yuk Lung Zigo*, FACC No. 12 of 2006 (Court of Final Appeal of the Hong Kong Special Administrative Region).
83. Naz Foundation, supra, ¶111.
84. For a more detailed exploration of 'personal autonomy', see Khaitan, 'Reading *Swaraj* into Article 15', supra, 422–423.
85. Naz Foundation, supra, ¶113.
86. One year before *Naz*, and one year after *Anuj Garg*, a proto-version of this argument was made by Tarunabh Khaitan: '… it is an extremely plausible proposition that unspecified grounds that are analogous to those protected under article 15(1) … are similarly protected under article 14'. Khaitan, 'Beyond Reasonableness', supra, 203.
87. Naz Foundation, ¶13. See also Law Commission of India, *42nd Report*, ¶16.126 (1971); Subsequently, in its *172nd Report*, the Law Commission recommended the repeal of S. 377.
88. *Norris v. Ireland* (1988) ECHR 22 (26 October 1988).
89. *National Coalition for Gay and Lesbian Equality v. The Minister of Justice*, 1999 (1) SA 6 (CC).
90. *Lawrence v. Texas*, 539 U.S. 558 (2003); note, however, that *Lawrence* turned upon the fact that what was at stake was a 'fundamental liberty interest' of the petitioner.

91. Naz Foundation, supra, Additional Written Submissions on Behalf of Petitioner, p. 1 (on file with the author). The petitioner made this argument in the context of the right to privacy, but, as the Court's judgement shows, the form of the argument largely overlaps with Article 14.
92. Ibid., p. 2. The other judgements that the petitioner relied upon were all in the context of a broader proportionality enquiry.
93. In *Dudgeon v. The United Kingdom* (1982) 4 EHRR 149, the European Court of Human Rights held that giving effect to public morality *was* a legitimate State purpose, although in the circumstances of the case, it was overridden.
94. See, e.g., Naz Foundation, supra, Affidavit of the Union of India (on file with the author).
95. Naz Foundation, supra, ¶92.
96. Ibid., ¶80. The reasoning echoed that of the High Court of Fiji, which had struck down Fiji's anti-sodomy law as unconstitutional: *Dhirendra Nadan v. State*, HAA 85&86 of 2005.
97. The argument was made by Voices Against 377, relying upon the Constitutional Court of South Africa. Naz Foundation, supra, Outline of Arguments of Respondent No. 8, p. 9 (on file with the author).
98. Naz Foundation, supra, ¶80.
99. *R v. M* (C), 41 C.R. (4th) 134 (1995).
100. Naz Foundation, supra, ¶79. Although the Court's discussion of constitutional morality was located in the part of its judgement dealing with Article 21 (privacy) of the Constitution, its application to whether there existed a 'compelling State interest' that justified invading privacy suggests that it would apply equally to the question of whether there existed a 'legitimate State interest' under Article 14.
101. Article 25(1), Constitution of India.
102. Article 29, Constitution of India.
103. Articles 19(1)–19(3), Constitution of India.
104. See, e.g., Schlink, 'Proportionality', supra, 723: 'The legitimacy of a legislative measure … follows from the Constitution alone'. Importantly, while the parties before the Court had linked S. 377's class hostility with the arbitrariness test (see, e.g., Counter-Affidavit of Respondent No. 8, Voices Against 377, p. 23 [on file with the author]),

the Court drew a stronger, and more defensible, connection with illegitimate purpose.

105. *Lawrence v. Texas*, 539 U.S. 558 (2003).
106. *National Coalition for Gay and Lesbian Equality v. Minister of Justice*, 1998 (12) BCLR 1517, ¶108.
107. See, e.g., Edwin Cameron, 'Sexual Orientation and the Constitution: A Test Case for Human Rights' (1993) 110 *South African Law Journal* 450, 452.
108. Ryan Goodman, 'Beyond the Enforcement Principle: Sodomy Laws, Social Norms, and Social Panoptics' (2001) 89(3) *California Law Review* 643; cited in Naz Foundation, supra, ¶49.
109. Naz Foundation, supra, Affidavits placed before the High Court by Respondent No. 8 (on file with the author); discussed in ¶¶21–22 of the judgement. A clarification is necessary: Respondent No. 6, viz., Joint Action Council, Kannur, argued, 'wrongful use of a law does not invalidate it'. (Naz Foundation, supra, Counter-Affidavit of R6 (on file with the author). This is true: the *constitutionality* of a law will not be affected by executive abuse; the remedy lies *against* the specific instance of abuse. However, it was not the petitioner and Respondent No. 8's case that S. 377 was being *abused* by the police; rather, as the petitioner pointed out in its Rejoinder to R6, it was that the language of S. 377 (and its judicial interpretation) did not preclude or forbid the police from doing what they were doing to homosexuals and transgender people. Naz Foundation, supra, Petitioner's Rejoinder to Respondent No. 6's Counter-Affidavit, p. 459 (on file with the author). It was in *this* sense that the law's 'impact' was discussed.
110. Naz Foundation, supra, ¶94.
111. *Khandige Sham Bhat v. The Agricultural Income Tax Officer*, 1963 SCR (3) 809.
112. Susanne Baer, 'Equality: The Jurisprudence of the German Constitutional Court' (1998–99) 5 *Columbia Journal of European Law* 249, 253.
113. Naz Foundation, supra, Written Submissions of the Petitioner, ¶119 (on file with the author).
114. See, e.g., *State of Kerala v. N.M. Thomas*, 1976 SCR (1) 906.

115. For instance, in his landmark book, Professor P.K. Tripathi calls Articles 15 to 18 the 'supporting provisions' for Article 14. Tripathi, *Some Insights into Fundamental Rights*, supra, 50.
116. It is scarcely surprising that Articles 14 and 15 were considered together by the Court.
117. Section I, Fourteenth Amendment to the Constitution of the United States of America.
118. See, e.g., *Nebbia v. New York*, 291 U.S. 502 (1934): 'And the guaranty of due process, as has often been held, demands only that the law shall not be unreasonable, arbitrary or capricious, and that the means selected shall have a real and substantial relation to the object sought to be attained.' Ibid., p. 526. See also *United States v. Carolene Products*, 304 U.S. 144 (1938).
119. B. Shiva Rao, *The Framing of India's Constitution: Select Documents*, Vol. II 118 (New Delhi: Universal Law Publishing 2015).
120. Ibid., 171.
121. Ibid., 173.
122. Another indication of the shift can be gleaned from the fact that in the Commonwealth of India Bill, a proto-Constitution drafted in 1925 under the leadership of Annie Besant, the right to equality before law makes its first appearance as an *explicit* rule of law guarantee: 'All persons residing within the Commonwealth, whether permanently or temporarily, are equal before the Law, and *shall be tried for similar offences in Courts of the same order and by Judicial Officers of the same grade*.' (Commonwealth of India Bill, 1925, http://cadindia.clpr.org.in/historical-constitutions/AVsOrUsy7SXahIyw4igo--the-commonwealth-of-india-bill-national-convention-india-1925 visited on 12 June 2017). Notably, the part in italics is absent from the final version of Article 14, suggesting, once more, the decoupling of the equality guarantee from formal rule of law. Similarly, the Constitution of India Bill of 1895 stipulated 'the law shall be equal to all'. Shiva Rao, *The Framing of India's Constitution, Vol. 1*, supra, 7.
123. Ibid., 41.
124. Ibid., 89.
125. The Constituent Assembly itself did not discuss the divergent formulations. Consequently, the Debates do not provide us with an interpretive solution either way.

126. Article 17, Constitution of India. For an analysis, see G. Bhatia, 'Freedom from Community: Individual Rights, Group Life, State Authority, and Religious Freedom under the Indian Constitution' (2016) 5(3) *Global Constitutionalism* 351.
127. Parliament of India, *Constituent Assembly Debates*, Vol. III (30 April 1947); Vol. VII (30 November 1948).
128. For a more detailed discussion, see, infra, Chapter 5.
129. Bankim Chandra Chattopadhyay, *Samya* (Bibek Debroy trans., New Delhi: Liberty Institute 2002)
130. Ibid.
131. E.g., the Constitution of India Bill, 1895, supra; The Commonwealth of India Bill, 1925, supra. The Nehru Report, 1928, cf. Shiva Rao, *The Framing of India's Constitution, Vol. 1*, supra, p. 58.
132. The Karachi Resolution, 1931.
133. Ibid.
134. S. 298, Government of India Act 1935.
135. See, e.g., Gail Omvedt, *Seeking Begumpura: The Social Vision of Anticaste Intellectuals* (New Delhi: Navayana 2008); Jotirao Phule, 'Ghulamgiri' (Slavery) in *The Selected Writings of Jotirao Phule* (G.P. Deshpande ed., New Delhi: LeftWord Books 2002); Mukta Salve, 'About the Grief of the Mangs and the Mahars (1855)' in *A Forgotten Liberator: The Life and Struggle of Savitribhai Phule* (Braj Ranjan Mani ed., Mountain Peak 2008); B.R. Ambedkar, *The Annihilation of Caste* (New Delhi: Navayana 2014).
136. The story of sexual orientation is just such a story.
137. *Lawrence v. Texas*, 539 U.S. 558, 579–80 (2003).
138. Ronald Dworkin, 'Constitutional Cases' in *Taking Rights Seriously* 163–85 (Cambridge: Harvard University Press 1977).
139. S. 15, Canadian Charter of Rights and Freedoms, 1985.
140. For an account, see, e.g., Joshua Sealy-Harrington, 'Assessing Analogous Grounds: The Doctrinal and Normative Superiority of a Multi-Variable Approach' (2013) 10 *Journal of Law and Equality* 37.
141. S. 9(1), Constitution of South Africa, 1996.
142. S. 9(3), Constitution of South Africa.
143. See, e.g., Chris McConnachie, 'What is Unfair Discrimination? A Study of the South African Constitutional Court's Unfair

Discrimination Jurisprudence', D.Phil. Thesis, University of Oxford 2014 (on file with the author).

144. *R v. Kapp*, 2008 SCC 41 (Supreme Court of Canada); *Egan v. Canada* (1995) 2 S.C.R. 513: 'whether or not sexual orientation is based on biological or physiological factors, which may be a matter of some controversy, it is a deeply personal characteristic that is either unchangeable or changeable only at unacceptable personal costs, and so falls within the ambit of s. 15 protection as being analogous to enumerated grounds'; but see *Vriend v. Alberta* (1998) 1 S.C.R. 493 (concurring opinion of Justice L'Hereux-Dubé) holding that 'grounds' are merely illustrative of the real issue, which is the impact (in terms of disadvantage and indignity) upon groups; see also Khaitan, 'Reading *Swaraj* into Article 15', supra, 423, arguing that the concepts of 'immutability' and 'fundamental choice' underpin Article 15(1), and Khaitan, 'Beyond Reasonableness', supra, 200, arguing that 'group vulnerability' is merely an 'embellishment' to the personal autonomy grounding. I disagree.

145. Chris McConnachie, 'Human Dignity, "Unfair Discrimination" and Guidance' (2014) 34(3) *Oxford Journal of Legal Studies* 609.

146. For a version of this argument, see Jed Rubenfeld, 'The Right of Privacy' (1989) 102 *Harvard Law Review* 737; ironically, in *Naz Foundation*, it was Respondent No. 6—arguing for the retention of S. 377—who made this argument most clearly: '… very few people identify others in terms of their sexual orientation'. Naz Foundation, supra, counter-affidavit of R6, (on file with the author). Respondent No. 8, Voices Against 377, did hint at the immutability framework, arguing that same-sex intercourse was entirely natural for homosexuals. In my view, the Court correctly did not adopt this much-criticized 'born this way' framing of the issue.

147. McConnachie, 'Human Dignity', supra.

148. For a similar, though less detailed, analysis, see the judgement of the High Court of Fiji in *Dhirendra Nadan v. State*, supra.

149. The Court also found that S. 377 violated Article 15(1), because it perpetuated stereotypes about gender roles. I do not have the space here to examine that argument in full.

150. *Suresh Kumar Koushal v. Naz Foundation* (2014) 1 SCC 1.

151. See, e.g., Tarunabh Khaitan, 'Koushal v. Naz: Judges Vote to Recriminalise Homosexuality' (2015) 78(4) *The Modern Law Review* 672.
152. *Koushal v. Naz*, supra, ¶42.
153. See, e.g., *Baker v. Carr*, 369 U.S. 186 (1962).
154. *Rajbala v. State of Haryana* (2016) 1 SCC 463.
155. *Rajbala v. State of Haryana*, supra, ¶85.
156. *State of West Bengal v. Anwar Ali Sarkar*, supra, ¶92 (concurring opinion of Justice Bose).
157. Naz Foundation, supra, Written Submissions of the Union of India, p. 56 (on file with the author).
158. Although, in view of serious scholarship arguing for treating obesity as an 'analogous ground' under Section 15 of the Canadian Charter, perhaps no claim can be simply dismissed out of hand! See, e.g., Emily Luther, 'Justice for All Shapes and Sizes: Combating Weight Discrimination in Canada' (2010) 48(1) *Alberta Law Review* 167.
159. See Law Commission of India, *Report No. 256: Eliminating Discrimination against Persons Affected by Leprosy* (April 2015), http://lawcommissionofindia.nic.in/reports/Report256.pdf (visited on 13 June 2017). (An interesting aside: the author of this law commission report is A.P. Shah, who also wrote the High Court's opinion in *Naz Foundation*).
160. See, e.g., Susanne Baer's discussion of a German Federal Constitutional Court case involving legislative differentiation of compulsory notice period for blue-collar and white-collar workers. Susanne Baer, 'Equality', supra.
161. *State of Maharashtra v. Indian Hotel & Restaurants Association* (2013) 8 SCC 519.
162. Ibid., ¶¶112–13.
163. Ibid., cited in ¶121.
164. This line from Charles Evan Hughes was quoted by Justice Khanna in his dissenting opinion in *A.D.M. Jabalpur v. Shivakant Shukla*, AIR 1976 SC 1207.
165. *Navtej Johar v. Union of India*, W.P. (Crl.) No. 76/2016. For an analysis, see Gautam Bhatia, 'Civilisation has been brutal: Navtej Johar, Section 377, and the Supreme Court's Moment of Atonement', *Indian Constitutional Law and Philosophy Blog* (6 September 2018), available

at https://indconlawphil.wordpress.com/2018/09/06/civilization-has-been-brutal-navtej-johar-section-377-and-the-supreme-courts-moment-of-atonement/.

166. Id., ¶27 (concurring opinion of Justice Chandrachud).
167. Id., ¶14 (concurring opinion of Justice Malhotra).

3: Equality of Opportunity: *N.M. Thomas*, Group Subordination, and the Directive Principles

1. Marc Galanter, *Competing Equalities: Law and the Backward Classes in India* 1 (Berkeley: University of California Press 1984).
2. The phrase 'color-blind' belongs to Justice John Marshall Harlan of the Supreme Court of the United States, dissenting in the notorious *Plessey v. Ferguson*, 163 U.S. 537 (1896), on the issue of racial segregation in trains. For an account of the genealogy and meaning of the phrase, see, Reva Siegel, 'From Color-Blindness to Antibalkanization: An Emerging Ground of Decision in Race Equality Cases' (2010–11) 120 *Yale Law Journal* 1278–1366.
3. Writing in 1962, L.A. Sheridan identified a number of other constitutions having similarly structured provisions. L.A. Sheridan, 'Equal Opportunity of Public Employment: Non-discrimination in Public Services in India' (1962) 11 *International and Comparative Law Quarterly* 782. Examples included Nigeria and Malaya.
4. This chapter does not, however, present an essay on reservation jurisprudence, which is a vast and complex subject overlapping with questions of sociology and anthropology, and with many attendant facets, such as the identification of backward classes, judicial review, the use of subjective and objective tests to determine group membership, appointments and promotions and other aspects of employment, the interplay of Article 335 with Article 16, and so on. Nor does it join the debate on whether reservations have been successful, or are self-defeating, perpetuating the exact problems that they were originally designed to solve. On the subject as a whole, the classic, though now dated, text remains Marc Galanter's magisterial *Competing Equalities*, supra. In this chapter, I focus on reservation jurisprudence only for making a broader argument about the constitutional vision of equality.
5. *State of Kerala v. N.M. Thomas*, (1976) 2 SCC 310.

6. Galanter, *Competing Equalities*, supra.
7. Dr Jayasingrao Pawar, *Rajarshi Shahu Chatrapatinche Jahirname va Hukumname* (Pune: Mehta Publishing House 2018).
8. For example, Mysore, in 1921: see *Encyclopaedia of Dalits in India: Human Rights: Role of Police and Judiciary* 280 (Sanjay Paswan and Paramanshi Jaideva eds., New Delhi: Kalpaz Publications 2003).
9. See, e.g., the Government of India Act, 1919; and the Government of India Act, 1935.
10. For an analysis of the shift from group to the individual as the basic normative unit of society, and how nationalism was the driving force behind it, see Rochana Bajpai, *Debating Difference: Group Rights and Liberal Democracy in India* 89 (New Delhi: OUP 2011).
11. Article 29(2) of the Constitution states: 'No citizen shall be denied admission into any educational institution maintained by the State or receiving aid out of State funds on grounds only of religion, race, caste, language or any of them.'
12. *State of Madras v. Champakam Dorairajan*, 1951 SCR 525.
13. Ibid., ¶9.
14. Article 46, Constitution of India.
15. Champakam Dorairajan, supra, ¶10. Importantly, a factor that proved decisive for the Court was that when *Champakam Dorairajan* was decided, Article 15(4) did not exist.
16. Champakam Dorairajan, supra, ¶12.
17. *Missouri v. Jenkins*, 515 U.S. 70, 120 (concurring opinion of Justice Thomas); See also Baroness Hale in *R (European Roma Rights Centre) v. Immigration Officer at Prague Airport* (2004) UKHL 55, ¶82 (UK House of Lords): 'The object … is to ensure that each person is treated as an individual and not assumed to be like other members of the group'.
18. In *S.A. Partha v. State of Mysore*, AIR 1961 Kant 220, the High Court of Karnataka pointed this out. The permissive 'shall not prevent' language is also found in European legal instruments, and has also been treated as an exception to the rule. For examples, see Sandra Fredman, *Discrimination Law* 242–46 (2nd ed., New York: OUP 2011).
19. General Manager, *Southern Railways v. Rangachari*, 1962 SCR (2) 586.
20. Ibid., ¶20.

21. See also, *State of AP v. Sagar*, 1968 (3) SCR 595, ¶7: 'The Parliament has by enacting cl. (4) attempted to balance as against the right of equality of citizens the special necessities of the weaker sections of the people by allowing a provision to be made for their advancement.'
22. *M.R. Balaji v. State of Mysore*, 1963 Supp (1) SCR 439.
23. This framing of reservations being about individual equality *versus* social justice can be seen even in some of the most eloquent judicial defences of affirmative action. See, e.g., the discussion in *D.G. Viswanath v. Chief Secretary to the Government of Mysore*, AIR 1964 Kant 132 (High Court of Karnataka).
24. *T. Devadasan v. Union of India* (1964) 4 SCR 680.
25. *C.A. Rajendran v. Union of India* (1968) 1 SCR 271.
26. See, e.g., the discussion in *Sukhnandan Thakur v. State of Bihar*, AIR 1957 Pat 617. See also Sheridan, 'Equal Opportunity of Public Employment', supra, 785.
27. Rangachari, supra. For a number of examples of the use of Article 14's reasonable classification standard to test affirmative action schemes under Articles 16(1) and (4), see Galanter, *Competing Equalities*, supra.
28. *Sukhnandan Thakur v. State of Bihar*, supra, ¶17.
29. Article 335 of the Constitution, for example, states that 'the claims of the members of the Scheduled Castes and the Scheduled Tribes shall be taken into consideration, consistently with the maintenance of efficiency of administration'.
30. See e.g., Rangachari, supra.
31. The Patna High Court, in Sukhnandan Thakur, supra, ¶20, labelled it as 'personal differentiation'. See also the discussion in *Virendra Singh Varma v. Additional Director of Agriculture, U.P.*, AIR 1960 All. 647: 'For example, if his application had been rejected … on the ground that he had a particular colour, or was tall or short or fat or some other reason which was wholly irrelevant to the qualifications which a candidate should possess, then in that event it might have been said that article 16 had been infringed.'
32. Fredman, *Discrimination Law*, supra, 109, 234.
33. See, for instance, the reasoning of *Baroness Hale in Ghazdan v. Godin-Mendoza* (2004) UKHL 30, ¶130 (UK House of Lords): '… the sex or colour of the person [is] simply irrelevant to the choice that [is] being made … because it [is] based on an irrelevant characteristic which

the woman or the black did not choose and could do nothing about'. See also, *Corbierre v. Canada* (1999) 2 SCR 203 (Supreme Court of Canada), which used the phrase 'immutable'. Fredman, *Discrimination Law*, supra, 14. In the previous chapter, we criticized the immutability approach.

34. For a nuanced critique of the spectrum of choice and control, see the opinion of Lord Walker in *R (RJM) v. Secretary of State for Work and Pensions* (2008) UKHL 63 (UK House of Lords).
35. T. *Devadasan v. Union of India* (1964) 4 SCR 680.
36. Ibid., ¶26 (dissenting opinion of Justice Subba Rao).
37. Ibid. Legend has it that Shahuji Maharaja also used the example of horses to persuade an unconvinced critic of the merit of reservations.
38. Ibid.
39. Ibid.
40. *State of Kerala v. N.M. Thomas* (1976) 2 SCC 330, ¶31 (majority opinion of CJI Ray).
41. Ibid., ¶37.
42. Ibid., ¶37.
43. See, e.g., the observations of the Supreme Court in *Triloki Nath Tiku v. State of Jammu and Kashmir* (1969) 1 SCR 103.
44. Ibid., ¶208 (dissenting opinion of Justice Khanna).
45. Ibid.
46. Ibid., ¶95 (partially concurring and partially dissenting opinion of Justice Beg).
47. Sukhnandan Thakur, supra, ¶18.
48. Ibid., ¶54 (majority opinion of Justice Mathew).
49. Ibid., ¶55 (majority opinion of Justice Mathew).
50. Ibid., ¶58 (majority opinion of Justice Mathew).
51. Ibid., ¶59 (majority opinion of Justice Mathew).
52. Ibid., ¶60 (majority opinion of Justice Mathew).
53. Ibid., ¶62 (majority opinion of Justice Mathew).
54. See, e.g., Monique Wittig, 'One Is Not Born a Woman' in *The Lesbian and Gay Studies Reader* 103–09 (Henry Abelove et al. eds., London: Routledge 1993).
55. Ibid., ¶53 (majority opinion of Justice Mathew).
56. Ibid., ¶75 (majority opinion of Justice Mathew).
57. Ibid., ¶141 (majority opinion of Justice Krishna Iyer).

58. Interestingly, the formulation of attributing responsibility to 'society' was replicated three years later by Justice Brennan at the Supreme Court of the United States, dissenting in an affirmative action case called *Regents of University of California v. Bakke*, 483 U.S. 265, 369 (1978): '... government may adopt race-conscious programs if the purpose of such programs is to remove the disparate racial impact its actions might otherwise have, and if there is reason to believe that the disparate impact is itself the product of past discrimination, whether its own or that of society at large'. Justice Brennan's opinion was accepted by the Supreme Court in *Indra Sawhney v. Union of India*, 1992 Supp (3) SCC 217, making for a fascinating example of judicial dialogue across countries.
59. A point made by Galanter, *Competing Equalities*, supra, 391–95.
60. The most sustained effort to identify 'backward classes' along the markers of educational, political, and social barriers was made by the Mandal Commission, whose findings were challenged, and discussed in some detail, by the nine-judge bench of the Supreme Court in *Indra Sawhney v. Union of India*, 1992 Supp (3) SCC 217. For a historical chronology of various states' attempts to identify backward classes in terms of social and institutional subordination, see Galanter, *Competing Equalities*, supra.
61. For a detailed critique of this position, see H.M. Seervai, *Constitutional Law of India*, Vol. 1, ¶¶ 9.182–9.203 (3rd ed., New Delhi: Universal Law Publishing 1983). In the fourth and final edition of the book, Mr Seervai declined to discuss *Thomas* in any detail, on the basis that Justice Krishna Iyer, who had 'tipped the balance' in *Thomas* on the question of Article 16(4) being a facet of 16(1), subsequently retracted his views. See H.M. Seervai, *Constitutional Law of India*, Vol. 1, ¶9.272 (4th ed., New Delhi: Universal Law Publishing 2015). Interestingly, *N.M. Thomas*'s argument would be adopted by the Constitutional Court of South Africa, twenty-nine years later. See *Minister of Finance v. Van Heerden*, 2004 (11) BCLR 1125 (CC), ¶30: '... our constitutional understanding of equality includes what Ackermann J. in *National Coalition for Gay and Lesbian Equality and Another v. Minister of Justice and Another* calls "remedial or restitutionary equality". Such measures are not in themselves a deviation from, or invasive of, the right to equality guaranteed by the Constitution ... they are integral

to the reach of our equality protection.' See also, R v. Kapp (2008) SCC 41 (Supreme Court of Canada). The argument would also be accepted by the High Court of Justice in the United Kingdom, thirty-three years later. See R v. London Borough of Ealing (2008) EWHC 2062 (Admin) (High Court of Justice [QBD]). See also, Fredman, *Discrimination Law*, supra, 240: 'The growth of such exceptions to the principle of formal equality may signal a change in the underlying conception of equality itself.'

62. See Owen Fiss, 'Groups and the Equal Protection Clause' (1976) 5 *Philosophy and Public Affairs* 107.
63. See, e.g., N.D. Majumdar's formulation in the Planning Commission, that [the Commission] '… cannot recognize individual backwardness … backwardness must be collective'. Cf. Galanter, *Competing Equalities*, supra, 169.
64. Another slightly different argument is that well-organized groups are best positioned to benefit from affirmative action *for* the members of those groups. See, e.g., the discussion in K. Ahmad, 'Towards Equality: Consequences of Protective Discrimination' (14 January 1978) 13(2) *Economic and Political Weekly* 69, 71.
65. As is often pointed out, Ambedkar himself wanted reservations to 'sunset' in ten years' time.
66. N.M. Thomas, supra, ¶52 (majority opinion of Justice Mathew).
67. N.M. Thomas, supra, ¶113 (majority opinion of Justice Mathew).
68. As Sandra Fredman points out, conceptually the phrase 'equality of opportunity' is consistent with visions of both formal equality and an equality of results. Fredman, *Discrimination Law*, supra, 2.
69. Galanter, *Competing Equalities*, supra, 15.
70. Eleanor Zelliot, *Doctor Ambedkar and the Mahar Movement* (PhD Dissertation, University of Pennsylvania 1969), cf. Marc Galanter, *Competing Equalities*, supra, 20.
71. See the discussion in Anupama Rao, *The Caste Question: Dalits and the Politics of Modern India* (Berkeley: University of California Press 2009).
72. J.H. Hutton, *Census of India, 1931: Vol. 1* (Government of India, Manager of Publications 1933), available at https://ia802506.us.archive.org/14/items/CensusOfIndia1931/Census%20of%20India%201931.pdf.

73. See Government of India, *Report of the Franchise Committee* (2nd ed., Government of India Central Publication Branch 1932).
74. For a chronology of events and a critique of the Congress, see B.R. Ambedkar, *What Congress and Gandhi Have Done to the Untouchables*, Chapter One, available at http://www.satnami.com/WHAT%20CONGRESS%20AND%20GANDHI%20HAVE%20DONE%20TO%20THE%20UNTOUCHABLES.pdf.
75. 'The Nehru Report, 1928', *The Framing of India's Constitution: Select Documents, Vol. 1*, 58, 60 (B. Shiva Rao ed., New Delhi: Universal Law Publishing 1966).
76. Resolution of Congress on Fundamental Rights, 1931 (The Karachi Resolution), cf. *The Indian Nationalist Movement 1885–1947: Selected Documents*, 67 (B.N. Pandey ed., New Delhi: Macmillan 1979). At the time, the word 'disability' was used to refer to 'disadvantages'. I, therefore, use the two words interchangeably through the course of this chapter.
77. Galanter, *Competing Equalities*, supra, 39. Galanter cites the work of M.N. Srinivas.
78. Draft Report of the Sub-Committee on Fundamental Rights, 3 April 1947, *The Framing of India's Constitution: Select Documents, Vol. II*, supra, 137-38.
79. Interim Report of the Advisory Committee on the Subject of Fundamental Rights, 23 April 1947, *The Framing of India's Constitution: Select Documents, Vol. II*, supra, 294, 296.
80. Parliament of India, *Constituent Assembly Debates, Vol. VII*, 30 November 1948 (speech of B.R. Ambedkar), available at http://parliamentofindia.nic.in/ls/debates/vol7p16b.htm.
81. Ibid. See also B.N. Rau's response to a suggestion to drop the word 'backward' during the Comments phase of the Draft Constitution in early 1948. 'Comments and Suggestions on the Draft Constitution' in *The Framing of India's Constitution: Select Documents, Vol. 4*, supra, 3, 31.
82. The Bombay Depressed Classes and Aboriginal Tribes (Starte) Committee, 1929–30.
83. Marc Galanter, 'Who Are the Other Backward Classes? An Introduction to a Constitutional Puzzle' (28 October 1978) 13(43/44) *Economic and Political Weekly* 1818.

84. Parliament of India, *Constituent Assembly Debates, Vol. VII*, supra 30 November 1948 (speech of Chandrika Ram).
85. In fact, during the debates around the introduction of Article 15(4) into the Constitution through the First Amendment, specifically on the issue of what 'backwardness' meant, Prime Minister Nehru categorically stated: 'We want to put an end to … all those infinite divisions that have grown up in our social life … we may call them by any name you like, the caste system or religious divisions, etc. There are of course economic divisions but we realize them and we try to deal with them. … But in the structure that has grown up … with its vast number of fissures or divisions …' Cf. Galanter, *Competing Equalities*, supra, 66. Galanter points out that the purpose of Article 15(4), as revealed from the Parliamentary Debates, was to ensure 'special treatment to offset and remedy specifically those social inequalities of caste and community which were seen as underlying and compounding economic differences'. Galanter, 'Who Are the Other Backward Classes', supra, 1816. Indeed, a proposal by K.T. Shah to replace 'classes' with 'individuals' during the debates on Article 15(4) was specifically rejected. See N. Radhakrishnan, 'Units of Social, Economic, and Educational Backwardness: Caste and Individual' (1965) 7(3) *Journal of the Indian Law Institute* 262, 270. This is fortified by the fact that suggestions to replace 'backward' and 'socially and educationally backward' classes with a purely economic consideration for reservations (which would ask only about an individual's financial status), have often been made, but never been incorporated into the Constitution. In fact, the decision *not* to base reservations on individual economic criteria is powerful evidence for the argument that the philosophy of equality at work must take into account group identity in order to achieve meaningful individual emancipation. But see, contra, the judgement in *Kesava Iyengar v. State of Mysore*, AIR 1956 Mys 20. See also, Galanter, 'Who Are the Other Backward Classes', supra, for an account of the importance of 'social hierarchy' as an identifying criterion in the work of the Backward Classes Commission; and Radhakrishnan, 'Units of Social, Economic, and Educational Backwardness', supra, on the work of the Backward Classes Commission.

86. This reading is also supported by the structure of Part III. As Galanter points out, where the framers intended to 'consolidate and protect' group identity, they made specific provisions to do so (Articles 26–30), guaranteeing to religious denominations the right to manage their own affairs in matters of religion (Article 26b), or to minorities to protect their language and culture (Article 29). Galanter, *Competing Equalities*, supra. See also Rochana Bajpai, *Debating Difference*, Ch. 4, supra, who argues that the Constituent Assembly made 'egalitarian individualism' the basis for its group-oriented safeguards, and specifically rejected an approach based on *preserving group identity*, in the context of affirmative action.
87. Mr Seervai, for one, finds Ambedkar's speech 'luminously clear' in its exposition of the scheme of Article 16 (the rule/exception model). Seervai, *Constitutional Law of India*, supra, ¶9.281. I am not so sure.
88. Interestingly, in *Indra Sawhney* and beyond, even after *N.M. Thomas*, the Court has kept the limit of reservations to 50 per cent. See, e.g., *M. Nagaraj v. Union of India* (2006) 8 SCC 212. This is clearly inconsistent with the holding of *Thomas* that 16(4) is a facet of 16(1). When the Court has tried to justify maintaining the cap, it has normally been with reference to the fact that the legitimate claims of the non-backward classes cannot be entirely overridden; furthermore, in judgements after *Indra Sawhney*, while the rule-exception language has no longer been used, the Court has talked about 'balancing' Articles 16(1) and (4), in what seems to be a halfway house between the pre-*N.M. Thomas* position and the formulation in *N.M. Thomas* itself. See, e.g., *Ashok Kumar Gupta v. State of UP* (1997) 5 SCC 201.
89. See, e.g., Parliament of India, *Constituent Assembly Debates, Vol. VIII*, supra, 30 November 1948 (Speech of Hriday Nath Kunzru).
90. See, e.g., Parliament of India, *Constituent Assembly Debates, Vol. XI*, supra, 14 November 1949 (Speech of Thakur Das Bhargava).
91. Article 37, Constitution of India.
92. *State of Kerala v. N.N. Thomas*, supra, ¶64 (majority opinion of Justice Mathew).
93. *State of Kerala v. N.M. Thomas*, supra, ¶134.
94. Parliament of India, *Constituent Assembly Debates, Vol. VII*, supra, 4 November 1948 (speech of B.R. Ambedkar).

95. Parliament of India, *Constituent Assembly Debates, Vol. VII,* supra, 19 November 1948 (speech of B.R. Ambedkar).
96. Seervai, *Constitutional Law of India, Vol. II,* 4th ed., supra, 1934–1940.
97. This and the succeeding paragraphs are drawn from my earlier work; see, 'Directive Principles of State Policy' in *The Oxford Handbook of the Indian Constitution* 644 (Sujit Choudhry et al. eds., OUP 2016).
98. Ibid.
99. N.G. Jayal, *Citizenship and its Discontents* 148 (Cambridge: Harvard University Press 2013).
100. Bhatia, 'Directive Principles of State Policy', supra.
101. Parliament of India, *Constituent Assembly Debates, Vol. VII*, supra, 19 November 1948 (speech of B.R. Ambedkar).
102. *State of Kerala v. N.M. Thomas*, supra, ¶64 (majority opinion of Justice Mathew).
103. LIC v. Manubhai D. Shah, 1992 (3) SCC 637, ¶7.
104. For a proto-version of this argument, see Raj Kumar Gupta, 'Justice: Unequal but Inseparate' (1969) 11(57) *Journal of the Indian Law Institute* 57, 83.
105. *Indra Sawhney v. Union of India* (1992) Supp. (3) SCC 217, ¶843 (plurality opinion of Justice Jeevan Reddy).
106. The Court, however, limited the operation of the doctrine only to OBCs (Other Backward Classes), and made it clear that it would not apply to Scheduled Castes and Scheduled Tribes. The reasons are slightly different, and need to be briefly discussed (although the Court itself did not justify the proposition). Going all the way back to the debates in the 1920s, one of the important markers of the communities known as the Scheduled Castes was social stigma, or social opprobrium (which, in turn, operated to deny them access to public goods and opportunities). It is clear that social or educational 'advancement' is independent of social stigma, whose cause was *exclusively* group membership or group identity, something impossible for group members to ever shed. Secondly, the application of the creamy layer doctrine to the Scheduled Tribes would make even less sense, because, unlike castes, in case of the tribes, the Constitution *is* committed to preserving their autonomy and integrity as groups, as Schedules V and VI demonstrate. Singling out 'advanced individuals' within tribes would defeat that other, equally important, constitutional purpose.

107. *R.K. Sabharwal v. State of Punjab* (1995) 2 SCC 745.
108. In an illuminating essay, Vinay Sitapati (with whose account of the evolution of reservations jurisprudence I am in broad agreement in this chapter) argues that the jurisprudence of the Supreme Court post-*Thomas* has retreated from the 'substantive equality' articulation of the Equality Code, and ended up with a vague language of 'balancing'. See Vinay Sitapati, 'Reservations' in *The Oxford Handbook of the Indian Constitution*, supra, 720, 741. Sitapati (ibid., 740) also argues that substantive equality is a normatively unsatisfactory approach to the Equality Code, with which, naturally, I disagree. My argument is that the Court's retreat is a mistake, and a full-blooded jurisprudence of substantive equality, faithful to *Thomas*, is truest to the constitutional vision. For a similar view of *Thomas*, and an incisive criticism of the Court's subsequent retreat in the context of prohibiting sub-classification within SCs, see K. Balagopal, 'Justice for Dalits among Dalits: All the Ghosts Resurface' (2005) 40(29) *Economic and Political Weekly* 3128.
109. *Sukhnandan Thakur v. State of Bihar*, supra.
110. Ibid.
111. Ibid., ¶50 (dissenting opinion of CJ Das).
112. *Jagdish Rai v. State of Punjab*, AIR 1977 P&H 56.
113. Ibid., ¶10.
114. See Balagopal, 'Justice for Dalits among Dalits', supra.
115. Galanter, *Competing Equalities*, supra.
116. Interestingly, when this specific claim for *inclusion* in a government List of Backward Classes was raised by various groups before the High Court of Karnataka in a pre-*N.M. Thomas* case, *S.A. Partha v. State of Mysore*, AIR 1961 Kant 220, the Court rejected it on the grounds that it was essentially a plea to enforce the Directive Principles of State Policy. This logic, of course, was impeccable for its time, and precisely what (by implication) the Supreme Court rejected in *N.M. Thomas*.
117. This was also understood by Galanter, who expressed the fear that the core guarantee under 16(4) would be diluted by an uncontrollable multiplicity of claims. Galanter, *Competing Equalities*, supra, 391–95. Galanter's fears cannot be dismissed out of hand, especially going by what has happened to Article 21 in the last three decades.

118. Galanter, *Competing Equalities*, supra.
119. *Ajit Singh (II) v. State of Punjab*, (1999) 7 SCC 209.
120. *National Legal Services Authority v. Union of India*, (2014) 5 SCC 438.
121. Ibid., ¶62.
122. Ibid., ¶135.3.
123. *State of Kerala v. N.M. Thomas*, supra, ¶75 (majority opinion of Justice Mathew): 'Equality of result is the test of equality of opportunity.'
124. As Sandra Fredman puts the point, in slightly different language: 'Under-representation of [target groups] is a sign that there might be a hidden obstacle to entry, which, unless justifiable, should be removed.' Fredman, *Discrimination Law*, supra, 181.
125. Ibid., 134.
126. See, e.g., *Griggs v. Duke Power Co.*, 401 U.S. 424 (1971) (Supreme Court of the United States).
127. *British Columbia (Public Service Employee Relations Commission) v. BCGSEU* (1999) 3 S.C.R. 3 (Supreme Court of Canada).

4: Civil Rights: *Indian Medical Association* and Horizontal Discrimination

1. Press Trust of India, 'Govt to Set Up Equal Opportunities Commission for Minorities', *The Times of India* (20 February 2014) and *The Hindu* (20 February 2014); Express News Service, 'Cabinet Clears Equal Opportunities Panel', *The Indian Express* (21 February 2014).
2. See, e.g., United States Equal Employment Opportunity Commission; the United Kingdom Equality and Human Rights Commission.
3. Prime Minister's High Level Committee, *Social, Educational and Economic Status of the Muslim Community of India: A Report* (New Delhi: Ministry of Human Resource Development, 2006), available at http://mhrd.gov.in/sites/upload_files/mhrd/files/sachar_comm.pdf.
4. Erwin Chemerinsky, 'Rethinking State Action' (1985) 80(3) *Northwestern University Law Review* 503, 536.
5. Smruti Koppikar, 'How bias against Muslim flat seekers came to be entrenched in India's most cosmopolitan city', *Scroll* (28 May 2015), available at http://scroll.in/article/730409/how-bias-against-muslim-flat-seekers-came-to-be-entrenched-in-indias-most-cosmopolitan-city.

6. Gujarat Disturbed Areas Act, 1991. For a discussion, see infra.
7. In India, housing societies set rules, formal and informal, for the use and transfer of flats, apartment complexes, or sets of residential buildings.
8. See, generally, Richard R.W. Brooks and Carol M. Rose, *Saving the Neighbourhood: Racially Restrictive Covenants, Law, and Social Norms* (Cambridge: Harvard University Press 2013).
9. As we shall see below, cases dealing with restrictive covenants have involved blacks in the US and South Africa, and Jews in Canada and the United Kingdom.
10. Stephen Gardbaum, '"The Horizontal Effect" of Constitutional Rights' (2003) 102(3) *The Michigan Law Review* 387, 417.
11. *Shelley v. Kraemer*, 334 U.S. 1 (1948).
12. Ibid., 13.
13. Under the US Constitution's Supremacy Clause, the Constitution binds State courts., Constitution of the United States, art VI. §1, Cl. 2.
14. *Shelley v. Kraemer*, supra, 19.
15. See, e.g., Duncan Kennedy, 'The Stages of Decline of the Public/Private Distinction' (1982) 130 *University of Pennsylvania Law Review* 1349, 1352.
16. Laurence Tribe, *Constitutional Choices* 259–260 (Cambridge: Harvard University Press 1985).
17. Re Drummond Wren (1945) O.R. 778 (Ont. HC).
18. Ibid., ¶ 20.
19. Ibid., ¶ 30.
20. Ibid., ¶ 31.
21. *Noble v. Alley*, [1951] S.C.R. 64.
22. Ibid., at 70, following Clayton v. Ramsden, [1943] 1 All E.R. 16.
23. *Curators v. The University of Kwa-Zulu Natal*, 2011 (1) BCLR 40 (SCA).
24. Ibid., ¶ 35.
25. Ibid., ¶ 36.
26. Ibid., ¶ 38.
27. See Ralf Brinktine, 'The Horizontal Effect of Human Rights in German Constitutional Law' (2001) *European Human Rights Law Review* 421. See the famous *Luth* case: BVerfGE 7, 198.

28. Curators, supra, ¶38.
29. *Vishaka v. State of Rajasthan*, JT 1997 (7) SC 384.
30. See, infra, Section II.
31. *R. Rajagopal v. State of Tamil Nadu*, (1994) 6 SCC 632.
32. *Zoroastrian Cooperative Housing Society Limited v. District Registrar Cooperative Societies* (Urban), (2005) 5 SCC 632.
33. Zoroastrian Cooperative, supra, ¶9.
34. Ibid., ¶10.
35. Ibid., ¶13.
36. Indian Contract Act 1872, §23.
37. See the observations in *Sargunam Ammal v. Jayarama Padayachi* (1994) 1 LW 139, following *Gobindaswami Dasi v. Radha Ballabha Dasi* (1910) 15 C.M.N. 205.
38. Held as early as *Bani Muncharam v. Regina Stanger*, I.L.R. 32 Bom. 581. The citation of these cases is not meant to be an endorsement of their reasoning.
39. *Delhi Transport Corporation v. DTC Mazdoor Congress*, AIR 1991 SC 101.
40. Zoroastrian Cooperative, supra, ¶15.
41. Ibid., ¶19.
42. Ibid., ¶33.
43. Ibid., ¶29.
44. These limits are restricted to the sovereignty and integrity of India, public order, and morality.
45. See, e.g., Parliament of India, *The Constituent Assembly Debates, Vol. II* (Wednesday, 22 January 1947), available at http://parliamentofindia.nic.in/ls/debates/vol2p3.htm.
46. See, e.g., *NAACP v. Patterson*, 357 U.S. 449 (1958).
47. See, e.g., *State of Madras v. V.G. Row*, AIR 1952 SC 196.
48. Zoroastrian Cooperative, supra, ¶29.
49. Ibid., ¶33.
50. Parliament of India, *Constituent Assembly Debates, Vol. VII* (8 December 1948), available at http://164.100.47.132/LssNew/constituent/vol7p22.html.
51. Ibid.
52. See, e.g., *Ahmedabad St Xavier's College v. State of Gujarat*, AIR 1974 SC 1389.

53. See Will Kymlicka, 'The Rights of Minority Cultures: Reply to Kukathas' (1992) 20(1) *Political Theory* 140.
54. *Samatha v. State of Andhra Pradesh* (1997) 8 SCC 191, ¶12.
55. *Indian Medical Association v. Union of India* (2011) 7 SCC 179.
56. Ibid., ¶113.
57. All these definitions may be found in the Merriam Webster Dictionary. See http://www.merriam-webster.com/dictionary/shop.
58. I thank Krishnaprasad K.V. for pushing me to ensure greater clarity on this point.
59. *Boy Scouts of America v. Dale*, 530 U.S. 640 (2000); *Gould v. Yukon Order of Pioneers* (1996) 1 S.C.R. 571.
60. See Tarunabh Khaitan, *A Theory of Discrimination Law* (Oxford: Oxford University Press 2015).
61. Ibid.
62. Parliament of India, *Constituent Assembly Debates: Vol. VII* (29 November 1948), supra.
63. Ibid.
64. Ibid.
65. Ibid.
66. Ibid.
67. Parliament of India, Constituent Assembly Debates: Vol. XI (22 November 1949), available at http://164.100.47.132/LssNew/constituent/vol11p8.pdf.
68. Clause 4, Report of the Sub-Committee on Fundamental Rights, 16 April 1947, in B. Shiva Rao, *The Framing of India's Constitution*, *Vol. II* 169, 171 (New Delhi: Universal Law Publishing 2015).
69. Minutes of the Sub-Committee on Minorities, 18 April 1947, in ibid., 203-04.
70. Proceedings of the Advisory Committee, 21–22 April 1947, in ibid., 210, 221. Now Article 30 of the Constitution.
71. This schema was originally proposed by Habermas. See Nancy Fraser, 'What's Critical about Critical Theory? The Case of Habermas and Gender' (1985) 35 *New German Critique* 97, 112.
72. See, e.g., Seyla Benhabib, *Situating the Self: Gender, Community and Postmodernism in Contemporary Ethics* (New York: Routledge 1992).
73. See, e.g., Thomas Hobbes, *Leviathan* (1660), available at http://oregonstate.edu/instruct/phl302/texts/hobbes/leviathan-contents.

html; Jean Bodin, *Six Books of the Commonwealth* (M.J. Tooley trans., Oxford: Basil Blackwell, 1955), available at http://www.constitution.org/bodin/bodin.htm. Jacques Maritain, 'The Concept of Sovereignty' (June 1950) 44(2) *The American Political Science Review* 343, 345–46.

74. See, e.g., Gordon Wood, *The Creation of the American Republic, 1776–1787* (Chapel Hill: University of North Carolina Press 1969).
75. Sudipta Kaviraj, *Trajectories of the Indian State: Politics and Ideas* (Ranikhet: Permanent Black 2010).
76. Ibid.
77. Tanika Sarkar, 'A Prehistory of Rights: The Age of Consent Debate in Colonial Bengal' (2000) 26(3) *Feminist Studies* 601, 606; see also Tanika Sarkar, 'Something Like Rights? Faith, Law and Widow Immolation Debates in Colonial Bengal' (2012) 49 *Indian Economic and Social History Review* 295.
78. 'The Constitution of India Bill, 1895', cf. B. Shiva Rao, *The Framing of India's Constitution: Select Documents, Vol. I*, supra, 5; 'Congress Resolution on Self-Determination', 1918, cf. ibid., 31; 'The Nehru Report', 1928, cf. ibid., 58.
79. Vidhu Verma, 'Colonialism and Liberation: Ambedkar's Quest for Distributive Justice', (1999) 34(39) *Economic and Political Weekly* 2804, 2806. For Gandhi's role, see Ramachandra Guha, *Gandhi: The Years That Changed the World, 1914–1948* (New York: Alfred A. Knopf 2018).
80. Eleanor Zelliott, *Ambedkar's World* 14 (New Delhi: Navayana 2012).
81. Ibid., 60. This was recognized by Gandhi, who actively campaigned against school segregation on caste lines. See, e.g., Ramachandra Guha, *Gandhi*, supra.
82. Interestingly, one of the recommendations of the Starte Committee was the enforcement of 'polite treatment' of Depressed Classes by government officials. This anticipated one of the key slogans of the US civil rights movement, three decades later: 'A man has the right not to be humiliated in front of his son.' For an account of spatial and social segregation, see Mark Juergensmeyer, *Religious Rebels in the Punjab: The Ad Dharm Challenge to Caste* 143 (New Delhi: Navayana 2009).
83. Ibid., 76.
84. Zelliott, supra.
85. Ibid.

86. See, e.g., Mrinalini Sinha, *Specters of Mother India: The Global Restructuring of an Empire* (Durham: Duke University Press 2006).
87. B.R. Ambedkar, 'Ambedkar's Memorandum' in Shiva Rao, *The Framing of India's Constitution, Vol. 2*, supra, 84, 105.
88. Ibid., 106.
89. Gail Omvedt, *Seeking Begumpura* (New Delhi: Navayana 2009).
90. The full name is: The Gujarat Prohibition of Transfer of Immovable Property and Provision for Protection of Tenants from Premises in Disturbed Areas Act, 1991.
91. It hardly needs to be said that separate is not equal, especially in a majoritarian context. For more background, see Nidhi Tambi, 'It's High Time the Gujarat Government Recognises the Communal Elephant in the Room', *The Wire*, 1 March 2018, available at https://thewire.in/communalism/its-high-time-gujarat-government-recognises-the-communal-elephant-in-the-room.

5: Religious Freedom and Group Identity: *Saifuddin* and the Anti-Exclusion Principle

1. *Dr Noorjehan Safia Niaz v. State of Maharashtra* (2016) 5 AIR Bom R 660. For an analysis, see Gautam Bhatia, 'Haji Ali Dargah: Bombay High Court Upholds Women's Right to Access the Inner Sanctum', available at https://indconlawphil.wordpress.com/2016/08/26/haji-ali-dargah-bombay-high-court-upholds-womens-right-to-access-the-inner-sanctum/.
2. PTI, 'Supreme Court starts hearing on women's entry into Sabarimala temple', *The Hindustan Times*, 17 July 2018, https://www.hindustantimes.com/india-news/supreme-court-starts-hearing-on-women-s-entry-into-sabarimala-temple/story-CHSUfVlSLsnFZNEBEASG6N.html.
3. *Sardar Syedna Tahir Saifuddin v. State of Bombay*, 1962 SCR Supl. (2) 496.
4. Ibid., ¶61 (concurring opinion of Justice Ayyangar).
5. Ibid., ¶19 (dissenting opinion of CJ Sinha).
6. Ibid., ¶23 (dissenting opinion of CJ Sinha).
7. See, e.g., Rajeev Dhavan and Fali Nariman, 'The Supreme Court and Group Life' in *Supreme But Not Infallible: Essays in Honour of the*

Supreme Court of India 256–87 (B.N. Kirpal et al. eds., New Delhi: OUP 2000); B.P. Rao, 'Matters of Religion' (1963) 5 *Journal of the Indian Law Institute* 509; Marc Galanter, 'Hinduism, Secularism, and the Indian Judiciary' (1971) 21(4) *Philosophy East and West* 467.

8. See, e.g., First Amendment, Constitution of the United States of America; Section 15, Constitution of South Africa.
9. A point made by Rao, 'Matters of Religion', supra; D.E. Smith, 'India as a Secular State', in *Secularism and Its Critics* 177 (Rajeev Bhargava ed., OUP, New Delhi, 1998).
10. Lloyd Rudolph and Susanne Rudolph, *In Pursuit of Lakshmi: The Political Economy of the Indian State* 33 (Chicago: University of Chicago Press 1987).
11. Marc Galanter, 'The Religious Aspects of Caste: A Legal View' in *South Asian Politics and Religion* 289 (D. Smith ed., Princeton: Princeton University Press 1966).
12. Will Kymlicka, *Multicultural Citizenship: A Liberal Theory of Minority Rights* (Oxford: OUP 1996), Ch. 3.
13. See, e.g., *Hosanna-Tabor Evangelical Lutheran Church and School v. EEOC*, 565 US 171 (2012) (US Supreme Court). For a summary of the opposing views, see Rajeev Bhargava, 'Introducing Multiculturalism' in *Multiculturalism, Liberalism, and Democracy* 1 (R. Bhargava et al. eds., New Delhi: OUP 2007) 1.
14. Saifuddin, supra, ¶33.
15. See, e.g., Suhrith Parthasarathy, 'The Flawed Reasoning in the Santhara Ban', *The Hindu*, 24 August 2015.
16. *Wisconsin v. Yoder*, 406 U.S. 275 (1972) (US Supreme Court).
17. *Multani v. Commissioner* (2006) 1 SCR 256 (Supreme Court of Canada).
18. *Leyla Sahin v. Turkey* (2007) 44 EHRR 5 (Grand Chamber) (European Court of Human Rights).
19. But see *MEC for Education v. Pillay* (2008) 2 BCLR 99 (CC) (South African Constitutional Court); *R(E) v. Governing Body of JFS* (2009) UKSC 15 (United Kingdom Supreme Court). Note, however, that the *JFS* case was decided under the UK Race Relations Act, which specifically prohibited discrimination and exclusion in certain aspects of the private sphere. The argument in this chapter will deal with how the Indian Constitution speaks to such issues.

20. Gary Jacobsohn, *The Wheel of Law: India's Secularism in Comparative Constitutional Context* 102 (Princeton: Princeton University Press 2003).
21. Parliament of India, *Constituent Assembly Debates, Vol. VII,* 2 December 1948 (speech of Dr B.R. Ambedkar), available at http://164.100.47.132/LssNew/constituent/vol7p18.html.
22. See also T.N. Madan, 'Secularism in Its Place' in *Secularism and Its Critics*, supra, 297, 302.
23. Ibid.
24. *The Commissioner, Hindu Religious Endowments, Madras v. Lakshmindra Swamiar*, 1954 SCR 1005, ¶20.
25. *Ratilal Panachand Gandhi v. State of Bombay*, 1954 SCR 1035.
26. *Ram Prasad Seth v. State of UP*, AIR 1957 All 411, ¶12, relying upon *State of Bombay v. Narasu Appa Mali*, AIR 1952 Bom 84.
27. *Mohd. Hanif Qureshi v. State of Bihar*, 1959 SCR 629, ¶13.
28. *Durgah Committee, Ajmer v. Syed Hussain Ali*, 1962 1 SCR 383, ¶33. An *obiter* is an observation by a judge that does not form part of the conclusion or the reasoning leading to the conclusion, and is, therefore, not binding upon future benches.
29. *Tilkayat Shri Govindlalji v. State of Rajasthan*, 1964 SCR (1) 561, ¶57.
30. *Sastri Yagnapurushadji v. Muldas*, 1966 SCR (3) 242.
31. Rajeev Dhavan, 'Religious Freedom in India' (1987) 35(1) *American Journal of Comparative Law* 209, 224.
32. For criticism, see Rao, 'Matters of Religion', supra.
33. *Seshammal v. State of Tamil Nadu* (1972) 2 SCC 11.
34. *Commissioner of Police v. Acharya Jagdishwarananda Avadhuta* (2004) 12 SCC 770. See also *Ismail Faruqui v. Union of India*, 1994 SCC (6) 360, holding that praying at a mosque was not an essential part of Islam.
35. *Commissioner of Police v. Avadhuta*, supra, ¶62 (dissenting opinion of Justice Lakshmanan) See also H.M. Seervai, *Constitutional Law of India, Vol. 2* 1268 (4th ed., New Delhi: Universal Law Publishing 1993).
36. *Adi Saiva Sivachariyargal Nala Sanga v. Govt of Tamil Nadu* (2016) 2 SCC 725.
37. Jacobsohn, *The Wheel of Law*, supra, 101.

38. H.E. Groves, 'Religious Freedom' (1962) 4 *Journal of the Indian Law Institute* 190.
39. Galanter, 'Hinduism, Secularism, and the Indian Judiciary', supra, 482–83.
40. Dhavan and Nariman, 'The Supreme Court and Group Life', supra, 260.
41. For a critique of how colonial scholars themselves approached the question of Indian religion through a set of established lenses, see Ronojoy Sen, *Articles of Faith: Religion, Secularism, and the Supreme Court* 5 (New Delhi: OUP 2013).
42. See, e.g., *Shilubana v. Nwamitva*, 2008 (9) BCLR 914 (CC) (South African Constitutional Court).
43. *Mohd Hanif Qureshi v. State of Bihar*, supra.
44. Sen, *Articles of Faith*, supra, 18; See also Jacobsohn, *The Wheel of Law*, supra 101.
45. J.D.M. Derrett, *Religion, Law and the State in India* (London: Faber & Faber 1968); see also Sen, *Articles of Faith*, supra. Indeed, this broad critique exposes striking similarities between the judicial analysis of the freedom of religion, and the colonial British view of religious groups in India. The use of textual sources of dubious variety over the lived practice of the constituents, and the imposition of an external point of view that runs contrary to how the believers themselves act, were best exemplified by the notorious *Aga Khan* decision in 1866, dealt with extensively by Teena Purohit in *The Aga Khan Case* (Cambridge: Harvard University Press 2012).
46. As Farrah Ahmed correctly notes, in the context of Indian personal law, 'if group autonomy means anything, it surely means that the group should decide for itself the norms by which it is governed'. Farrah Ahmed, 'Remedying Personal Law Systems', *International Journal of Law, Policy and the Family* (forthcoming); preprint available at <http://papers.ssrn.com/sol3/papers.cfm?abstract_id=2777337>. Ahmed is equally cognizant of the heterodox claims within the group, and the tension securing between group autonomy and such claims.
47. Galanter, 'Hinduism, Secularism, and the Indian Judiciary', supra, 482; see also Jacobsohn, *The Wheel of Law*, supra, 98.
48. Galanter, 'Hinduism, Secularism, and the Indian Judiciary', supra, 483.

49. See Jacobsohn, *The Wheel of Law*, supra.
50. Rajeev Bhargava, 'What Is Secularism For', in *Secularism and Its Critics*, supra.
51. A point made by both Galanter and Sen.
52. *Saifuddin v. State of Bombay*, supra, ¶11 (dissenting opinion of CJ Sinha).
53. Saifuddin, supra, ¶23 (dissenting opinion of Justice Sinha).
54. B.R. Ambedkar, *The Untouchables: Who Were They and Why They Became Untouchables*, available at http://www.ambedkar.org/ambcd/39A.Untouchables%20who%20were%20they_why%20they%20became%20PART%20I.htm. Seervai, for instance, denies the validity of the analogy. See Seervai, *Constitutional Law of India*, supra, 1278.
55. Article 17, Constitution of India.
56. Parliament of India, *Constituent Assembly Debates, Vol. VII,* 29 November 1948 (speech of Dr B.R. Ambedkar), available at http://164.100.47.194/loksabha/writereaddata/cadebatefiles/C29111948.html. The first official definition of 'untouchability', in 1931 by the British Census Commissioner, was a broad one, defining it as social segregation characterized by exclusion from public amenities. J.H. Hutton, *Caste in India: Its Nature, Function and Origins* 194 (3rd ed., New Delhi: OUP 1961).
57. Parliament of India, *Constituent Assembly Debates, Vol. VIII,* 29 November 1948 (speech of Naziruddin Ahmed), supra.
58. Parliament of India, *Constituent Assembly Debates, Vol. VIII,* 29 November 1948, supra.
59. Parliament of India, *Constituent Assembly Debates, Vol. III*, 29 April 1947 (speech of K.M. Munshi), available at http://164.100.47.194/loksabha/writereaddata/cadebatefiles/C29041947.html.
60. Parliament of India, *Constituent Assembly Debates, Vol. III,* 29 April 1947 (speech of Rohini Kumar Choudhury), supra.
61. Parliament of India, *Constituent Assembly Debates, Vol. VIII*, 29 November 1948 (speech of K.T. Shah), supra. During the Comments and Suggestions Phase of the framing, the Drafting Committee rejected multiple written submissions to define 'untouchability', noting that it would be Parliament's task to do so in a statute. That, however, does not make the *constitutional* clause empty of meaning. See 'Comments and Suggestions on the Draft Constitution' in Shiva Rao,

The Framing of India's Constitution, Vol. 4, supra, 3, 33. This is especially because the article authorizing Parliament to make laws to implement provisions such as the untouchability prohibition (Draft Article 27), which was the rationale for the Drafting Committee's refusal to define 'untouchability' with any degree of specificity, was ultimately dropped from the Constitution.

62. See Parliament of India, *Constituent Assembly Debates, Vol. III*, 29 April 1947 (speech of Promatha Ranjan Thakur), supra; Parliament of India, *Constituent Assembly Debates, Vol. V*, 27 August 1947 (speech of Monomohan Das), available at http://164.100.47.194/loksabha/writereaddata/cadebatefiles/C27081947.html. Parliament of India, *Constituent Assembly Debates, Vol. XI*, 21 November 1949, (speech of H.J. Khandekar), available at http://164.100.47.194/loksabha/writereaddata/cadebatefiles/C21111949.html.
63. Parliament of India, *Constituent Assembly Debates, Vol. III*, 29 April 1947 (speech of P.S. Deshmukh), supra; Parliament of India, *Constituent Assembly Debates, Vol. VII*, 29 November 1948 (speech of Shri Shibban Lal Saksena), supra.
64. Parliament of India, *Constituent Assembly Debates, Vol. III*, 29 April 1947 (speech of S.C. Banerjee), supra.
65. Parliament of India, *Constituent Assembly Debates, Vol. XI*, 19 November 1949 (speech of M. Ananthasayanam Ayyangar), supra.
66. Ibid., 23 November 1949 (speech of B.M. Gupta).
67. Parliament of India, *Constituent Assembly Debates, Vol. VII*, 29 November 1948 (speech of Santanu Kumar Das), supra.
68. Parliament of India, *Constituent Assembly Debates, Vol. XI*, 22 November 1949 (speech of Ajit Prasad Jain), supra.
69. Furthermore, scholars who accept group rights in liberal political theory are circumspect about the legitimacy of *imposing* liberal norms upon groups who might be following illiberal practices. See, e.g., Chandran Kukathas, 'Are There Any Cultural Rights?' (1992) 20(1) *Political Theory* 105; Will Kymlicka, 'The Rights of Minority Cultures: Reply to Kukathas', (1992) 20(1) *Political Theory* 140.
70. *IMA v. Union of India*, supra.
71. See Anupama Rao, *The Caste Question* (Ranikhet: Permanent Black 2010). Unsurprisingly, the draft bill of rights that Ambedkar presented to the Fundamental Rights Sub-Committee contained a lengthy

clause for the prohibition of social boycotts. The Sub-Committee did not, however, include it in its report. See 'Ambedkar's Memorandum' in Shiva Rao, *The Framing of India's Constitution*, *Vol. II*, supra, 84, 91–92.

72. See Rao, *The Caste Question*, supra, 165; see also, B.R. Ambedkar, *What Congress and Gandhi Have Done to the Untouchables*, <http://www.ambedkar.org/ambcd/41D.What%20Congress%20and%20Gandhi%20CHAPTER%20III.htm>
73. Rao, *The Caste Question*, supra, Chs. 1–2.
74. The link between secularism and equality has been suggested by Cossman and Kapur. Brenda Cossman and Ratna Kapur, 'Secularism: Bench-marked by the Hindu Right' (1996) 31(38) *Economic and Political Weekly* 2613.
75. Rao, *The Caste Question*, supra, 81.
76. Ibid., 81–85.
77. Ibid.
78. For an overlapping (but different) account, see Hugh Collins, 'Discrimination, Equality and Social Inclusion' (2003) 66 *Modern Law Review* 16.
79. Tarunabh Khaitan, *A Theory of Discrimination Law* (Oxford: OUP 2015).
80. For a version of this argument, see Amy Gutmann, *Identity in Democracy*, Ch. 2 (Princeton: Princeton University Press 2003).
81. Partha Chatterjee, 'Secularism and Tolerance' in *Secularism and Its Critics*, supra, 344, 375.
82. Akeel Bilgrami, 'Secularism, Nationalism and Modernity' in *Secularism and Its Critics*, supra, 380, 405.
83. Bhargava, 'What Is Secularism For?', supra.
84. See, e.g., *Hosanna Tabor v. Equal Opportunity Employment Commission*, supra.
85. See Gutmann, *Identity in Democracy*, supra, 98.
86. It might be argued that for internal dissidents, the religious context is always a 'thick' one. This is undoubtedly true, to a certain extent, as far as the basic good of cultural membership goes. However, 'thick' religious groups, in the sense that we are discussing here, have the ability to deny to their constituents more than just the good of cultural membership; they have the ability to block their access to other basic goods, including material and economic ones.

87. Kukathas argues, for instance, that groups can subordinate their members as long as there is an option to exit into the broader market economy. See Kukathas, 'Are There Any Cultural Rights?', supra. See also *Hofer v. Hofer*, [1970] S.C.R. 958 (dissenting opinion of Justice Pigeon) (Supreme Court of Canada). However, as Farrah Ahmed points out (with the specific example of India), the right to exit is often illusory. Farrah Ahmed, 'Personal Autonomy and the Option of Religious Law' (2010) 24(2) *International Journal of Law, Policy and the Family* 222.
88. For a detailed account of the interlinkages between the religious and the social in Indian group life, in the context of dissenting socio-religious movements, see Juergensmeyer, *Religious Rebels in the Punjab*, supra. For an examination of religious group membership *itself* being an important good, see Farrah Ahmed, *Religious Freedom under the Personal Law System* 60 (Oxford: OUP 2015).
89. Stuart Woolman, 'Seek Justice Elsewhere: An Egalitarian Pluralist's Reply to David Bilchitz on the Distinction between Differentiation and Domination' (2012) 28 *South African Journal of Human Rights* 273, 285.
90. Michael Walzer, *Spheres of Justice: A Defense of Pluralism and Equality* 19 (New York: Basic Books 1983).
91. Rao, *The Caste Question*, supra, 77.
92. Ibid., 82. Rao cites the example of how the right to access temples and water tanks ended up becoming part of the same campaign, because of the spatial proximity of the two.
93. See, e.g., Kukathas, 'Are There Any Cultural Rights?', supra; Avishai Margalit and Moshe Halbertal, 'Liberalism and the Right to Culture' (1994) 61(3) *Social Research* 491; *Santa Clara Pueblo v. Martinez*, 436 U.S. 49 (1978) (Supreme Court of the United States).
94. Section 31, Constitution of South Africa.
95. Article 27, International Covenant for Civil and Political Rights.
96. See *Christian Education South Africa v. Minister of Education* (2000) (10) BCLR 1051 (Constitutional Court of South Africa).
97. See e.g., Charles Taylor, 'The Politics of Recognition' in *Multiculturalism: Examining the Politics of Recognition* (Amy Gutmann ed., Princeton: Princeton University Press 1994); for instances of how religious groups can facilitate personal autonomy, see Ahmed, *Religious Freedom*

under the Personal Law System, supra, 62, 82. For a genealogy of this argument, especially in the context of British political theory, see Tim Rogan, *The Moral Economists* (Princeton: Princeton University Press 2017).

98. See Bhargava, 'Introducing Multiculturalism', supra, 38.
99. David Bilchitz, 'Should Religious Associations Be Allowed to Discriminate' (2011) 27 *SAJHR* 219; David Bilchitz, 'Why Courts Should Not Sanction Unfair Discrimination in the Private Sphere: A Reply', (2012) 28 *South African Journal of Human Rights* 296.
100. Partha Chatterjee, 'Colonialism, Nationalism, and Colonized Women: The Contest in India' (1989) 16(4) *American Ethnologist* 622.
101. Jacobsohn, *The Wheel of Law*, supra, 80.
102. Section 295A, Indian Penal Code. See also Sections 153A and 153B, Indian Penal Code.
103. *Hasanali v. Mansoorali* (1948) 50 BomLR 389, relied upon in *Saifuddin*. As discussed above, though, the colonial approach to determining the composition and character of religious groups was entirely external in nature. Purohit, *The Aga Khan Case*, supra.
104. Tanika Sarkar, 'Something Like Rights? Faith, Law and Widow Immolation Debates in Colonial Bengal' (2012) 49(3) *The Indian Economic and Social History Review* 295.
105. Tanika Sarkar, 'A Prehistory of Rights: The Age of Consent Debate in Colonial Bengal' (2000) 26(3) *Feminist Studies* 601.
106. Partha Chatterjee, 'Colonialism, Nationalism, and Colonized Women: The Contest in India' (1989) 16(4) *American Ethnologist* 622.
107. Mrinalini Sinha, *Specters of Mother India: The Global Restructuring of an Empire* (Durham: Duke University Press 2006).
108. In fact, the 1928 government report specifically stated that the social boycott was particularly 'dangerous', since it invoked the principles of freedom of contract as justification, and, notwithstanding that, deserved to be outlawed. B.R. Ambedkar, *What Congress and Gandhi Have Done to the Untouchables,* supra.
109. Parliament of India, *Constituent Assembly Debates, Vol. VII,* 4 November 1948 (speech of Dr B.R. Ambedkar), supra. Even before Ambedkar, as early as 1947, while moving the resolution to establish an advisory committee dealing with fundamental rights, Govind Ballabh Pant foresaw the dangers. He lamented, 'The individual citizen who

is really the backbone of the State ... has been lost here in that indiscriminate body known as the community ... it is after all citizens that form communities and the individual as such is essentially the core of all mechanisms and means and devices that are adopted for securing progress and advancement'. Shiva Rao, *The Framing of India's Constitution, Vol. 2*, supra, 63.

110. Parliament of India, *Constituent Assembly Debates, Vol. VII*, 2 December 1948 (speech of Dr B.R. Ambedkar), supra.

111. For a chronology of this failure, see Rochana Bajpai, *Debating Difference*, Ch. 4 (New Delhi: Oxford University Press 2011). In *Shayara Bano v. Union of India* (2017) 9 SCC 1, while deciding upon the validity of 'instant triple talaq', a dissenting opinion authored by CJI Khehar and Justice Nazeer made a breathtakingly disingenuous attempt to undo the consensus that had been achieved in the Constituent Assembly, by declaring through judicial fiat that the right to a personal law system was a part of Article 25(1)'s guarantee of the right to freedom of religion. Unsurprisingly, the dissenting opinion made no reference to the Constituent Assembly Debates, and we can count ourselves fortunate that this attempted judicial hijack found itself on the wrong side of a 3–2 split verdict.

112. *Indian Young Lawyers' Association v. Union of India*, W.P. (Civ.) 373/2006. For an analysis, see Gautam Bhatia, 'The Sabarimala Judgment—I: An Overview', *The Indian Constitutional Law and Philosophy Blog* (28 September 2018), available at https://indconlawphil.wordpress.com/2018/09/28/the-sabarimala-judgment-i-an-overview/.

113. See Gautam Bhatia, 'The Sabarimala Judgment—II: Justice Malhotra, Group Autonomy, and Cultural Dissent', *The Indian Constitutional Law and Philosophy Blog* (29 September 2018), available at https://indconlawphil.wordpress.com/2018/09/29/the-sabarimala-judgment-ii-justice-malhotra-group-autonomy-and-cultural-dissent/.

114. Indeed, Justice Chandrachud relied on an earlier, published version of this chapter to make the case for the anti-exclusion principle as a possible way forward. For an analysis, see Gautam Bhatia, 'The Sabarimala Judgment—III: Justice Chandrachud and Radical Equality', *The Indian Constitutional Law and Philosophy Blog* (29 September, 2018), available at https://indconlawphil.wordpress.

com/2018/09/29/the-sabarimala-judgment-iii-justice-chandrachud-and-radical-equality/

6: The Freedom to Work: *Peoples Union for Democratic Rights* and Forced Labour

1. See, e.g., Anupama Roy, *Gendered Citizenship* 194 (New Delhi: Orient BlackSwan 2005).
2. Karachi Resolution, 1931; available at http://cadindia.clpr.org.in/historical_constitutions/karachi_resolution__1931__1st%20January%201931.
3. B.N. Rau, 'Notes on Fundamental Rights', 2 September 1946, cf. B. Shiva Rao, *The Framing of India's Constitution: Select Documents, Vol. II*, 22, 33 (New Delhi: Universal Law Publishing 1967).
4. *PUDR v. Union of India* (1982) 3 SCC 235.
5. Ibid., ¶14.
6. The phrase is borrowed from James Gray Pope, 'Labor's Constitution of Freedom' (1997) 106 *Yale Law Journal* 941.
7. *PUDR v. Union of India*, supra, ¶4. The PUDR was an organization born during the Emergency, and soon evolved into one of the most significant civil, political, and economic rights organizations in the country.
8. Ibid., ¶8.
9. *S.P. Gupta v. Union of India*, AIR 1982 SC 149.
10. *PUDR v. Union of India*, supra, ¶9.
11. Ibid., ¶11.
12. Ibid., ¶13.
13. Ibid.
14. Ibid.
15. Ibid.
16. Ibid., ¶14.
17. Ibid.
18. This problem is, naturally, magnified in a society like India, where law enforcement is weak, and the informal sector is massive.
19. Ibid., ¶14.
20. Ibid., ¶12.
21. Whether I have been rightly or wrongly imprisoned is a separate issue.

22. For a prior discussion of this issue in the context of Indian constitutional law, see Gautam Bhatia, *Offend, Shock, or Disturb: Freedom of Speech under the Indian Constitution*, Ch. 11 (New Delhi: OUP 2015).
23. David Miller, 'Constraints on Freedom' (1983) 94(1) *Ethics* 66, 72.
24. Gerald MacCallum, 'Negative and Positive Freedom' (1967) 76(3) *The Philosophical Review* 312.
25. Eric MacGilvray, *The Invention of Market Freedom* 312, 314 (New York: Cambridge University Press 2011).
26. The word 'liberal' here does not refer to political liberalism.
27. See, e.g., Quentin Skinner, *Liberty Before Liberalism* (Cambridge: Cambridge University Press 1998). Henry Sidgwick, *The Elements of Politics* (2nd ed., London: Macmillan 1897), available at https://ia800207.us.archive.org/31/items/theelementsofpol00sidguoft/theelementsofpol00sidguoft.pdf. For a critical genealogy that traces it back to Hobbes, see Corey Robin, *The Reactionary Mind* (2nd ed., New York: OUP 2018).
28. Isiah Berlin, 'Two Concepts of Liberty' in *Four Essays on Liberty* (Oxford: Oxford University Press 1969), available at http://faculty.www.umb.edu/steven.levine/courses/Fall%202015/What%20is%20Freedom%20Writings/Berlin.pdf.
29. F. Hayek, *The Constitution of Liberty* 12 (Chicago: University of Chicago Press 1978).
30. Ibid.
31. Ibid., 13.
32. Ibid., 137. For a genealogy of the argument from 'naturalness' of private hierarchical orders, going back to Edmund Burke, see Robin, *The Reactionary Mind*, supra.
33. See, e.g., Alex MacGilvray, *The Invention of Market Freedom* 1 (New York: Cambridge University Press 2011). This was also the philosophy espoused by the US Supreme Court during the well-known 'Lochner era', where labour regulations were struck down on the grounds that they interfered with the 'freedom of contract' that existed between employers and employees. See, e.g., *Lochner v. State of New York*, 198 U.S. 45 (1905). Alex Gourevitch, *From Slavery to the Cooperative Commonwealth: Labor and Republican Liberty in the Nineteenth Century* (New York: Cambridge University Press 2015).

34. Berlin, *Four Essays on Liberty*, supra, liii. For inconsistencies in Berlin's thought on this point, see MacGilvray, *The Invention of Market Freedom*, supra.
35. John Rawls, *A Theory of Justice* 204 (Cambridge: Harvard University Press 1971).
36. For a defence of the analogy between the market and natural forces, see Hayek, *The Constitution of Liberty*, supra. See also Ripstein's description: 'Each individual faces the labor market in just the way an individual faces the weather. The market sets parameters within which one must operate. And the only way to turn those parameters to one's advantage is the same as the only way to turn the weather to one's advantage – by exploiting their very inexorability.' Arthur Ripstein, 'Commodity Fetishism' (1987) 17(4) *The Canadian Journal of Philosophy* 733, 746.
37. See the discussion of Berlin and Rawls in Gerald Cohen, 'Freedom and Money', available at http://www.howardism.org/appendix/Cohen.pdf; see also Jeremy Waldron, 'Liberal Rights: Two Sides of the Same Coin' in *Liberal Rights: Collected Papers 1981–1991* 1–34 (Cambridge: Cambridge University Press 1993).
38. Quentin Skinner, *Liberty Before Liberalism* (Cambridge: Cambridge University Press 1998); Quentin Skinner, 'A Third Concept of Liberty' (2002) 117 *Proceedings of the British Academy* 237–268.
39. Skinner, *Liberty Before Liberalism*, supra, 69.
40. Ibid., 70.
41. Philip Pettit, *Republicanism: A Theory of Freedom and Government* 22 (Oxford: Oxford University Press 1997).
42. Ibid.
43. Skinner, 'A Third Concept of Liberty', supra, 256.
44. Skinner, *Liberty Before Liberalism*, supra, 84.
45. See, e.g., Thomas Hobbes' famous argument that freedom has no relevance to the form of government, and Harrington's response to him, cf. Pettit, *Republicanism*, supra, 38.
46. Ibid.,72.
47. Ibid., 122.
48. Skinner, *Liberty Before Liberalism*, supra, 60. This is a familiar argument. See also Karl Marx, *The German Ideology* (Moscow: Progress Publishers 1968), available at https://www.marxists.org/archive/marx/works/

download/Marx_The_German_Ideology.pdf, visited on 31 December 2017: 'Individuals obtain their freedom in and through association.'

49. Pettit, *Republicanism*, supra, 22: 'Domination, as I understand it here, is exemplified by the relationship of master to slave or master to servant.' See also, William E. Forbath, 'The Ambiguities of "Free Labor": Labor and Law in the Gilded Age' (1985) 1985 *Wisconsin Law Review* 767, 784: 'Unfreedom inhered in the slave's legal bonds of personal dependence.'
50. Pettit, *Republicanism*, supra, 52–53.
51. Pettit, *Republicanism*, supra, 75. See also Philip Pettit, 'Freedom in the Market' (2006) 5(2) *Politics, Philosophy & Economics* 131–49; Skinner, 'A Third Concept of Liberty', supra.
52. For an early variant of the argument, see Adam Smith, *The Wealth of Nations*, Book III, Chapter IV, available at https://www.marxists.org/reference/archive/smith-adam/works/wealth-of-nations/book03/ch04.htm: '[e]ach tradesman or artificer derives his subsistence from the employment, not of one, but of a hundred or a thousand different customers … though in some measure obliged to them all … he is not absolutely dependent upon any one of them'. Or, as the Reconstruction US politician William Graham Sumner put it in the late nineteenth century, '… a society based on contract is a society of free and independent men, who form ties without favour or obligation, and cooperate without cringing or intrigue'. William Graham Sumner, *What the Social Classes Owe Each Other* 24 (Caldwell: The Caxton Printers 1974), available at https://mises.org/system/tdf/What%20Social%20Classes%20Owe%20Each%20Other_2.pdf?file=1&type=document; see also MacGilvray, *The Invention of Market Freedom*, supra; Ripstein, 'Commodity Fetishism', supra.
53. Pettit, 'Freedom in the Market', supra, 139.
54. William Clare Roberts, *Marx's Inferno: The Political Theory of Capital* 97 (Princeton: Princeton University Press 2016).
55. MacGilvray, *The Invention of Market Freedom*, supra, 102.
56. Pettit, 'Freedom in the Market', supra, 144.
57. Roberts, *Marx's Inferno*, supra, 98. MacGilvray calls this a 'conceptual sleight-of-hand'. See MacGilvray, *The Invention of Market Freedom*, supra, 172. As William Forbath puts the point in his account of US labour history, citing D.B. Davis, 'one could justify exploitation only

by making it impersonal'. Forbath, 'The Ambiguities of "Free Labor"', supra, 784.

58. Ripstein, 'Commodity Fetishism', supra, 747. In his analysis of *Capital*, William Clare Roberts points out that Karl Marx's project was, in part, to demonstrate that early socialist thinkers were mistaken in taking as their objects of criticism individual 'acts of force or fraud committed by the proprietors.' This mischaracterized the form of domination exercised under capitalism, which was social in character, and ended up trapping them within the 'very social system that they want to escape'. See Roberts, *Marx's Inferno,* supra, 53, 58, 82, 93, 95, 132. See also, ibid., 96: 'One might say that individuals are forced to be market agents *in general*, but not forced to make *any particular* market decisions.' In *The German Ideology,* Marx himself framed it thus: 'The social power, i.e., the multiplied productive force, which arises through the co-operation of different individuals as it is determined by the division of labour, appears to these individuals, since their co-operation is not voluntary but has come about naturally, not as their own united power, but as an alien force existing outside them, of the origin and goal of which they are ignorant, which they thus cannot control, which on the contrary passes through a peculiar series of phases and stages independent of the will and the action of man, nay even being the prime governor of these.' Marx, *The German Ideology*, supra. Further, for an account of the concept of social domination in German critical theory, see Moishe Postone, *Time, Labour, and Social Domination: A Reinterpretation of Marx's Critical Theory* 30 (Cambridge: Cambridge University Press 1993), available at http://www.urbanlab.org/articles/Time/Postone%201993%20-%20Time%20Labour%20and%20Social%20Domination.pdf; see also Chris O'Kane, 'Fetishism and Social Domination in Marx, Lukacs, Adorno, and Lefebvre', available at https://reificationofpersonsandpersonificationofthings.files.wordpress.com/2013/06/chris-okane-thesis-final.pdf; Julius Sensat, 'Exploitation' (1984) 18(1) *Nous* 21–38.

59. See, e.g., Michel Foucault, *Discipline and Punish: The Birth of the Prison* (New York: Pantheon Books 1977).

60. Sharon Krause, 'Beyond Non-Domination, Agency, Inequality and the Meaning of Freedom' (2013) 39(2) *Philosophy and Social Criticism* 187–208; see also Alex Gourevitch, *From Slavery to the Cooperative*

Commonwealth, Labor and Republican Liberty in the Nineteenth Century (Cambridge: Cambridge University Press 2014).

61. Ibid., 10.
62. Roberts, *Marx's Inferno*, supra, 23; see also Karl Marx, *Grundrisse* (Harmondsworth: Penguin Books 1973), available at https://www.marxists.org/archive/marx/works/1857/grundrisse/, visited on 30 December 2017.
63. Ripstein, 'Commodity Fetishism', supra, 747. In *The German Ideology*, Marx writes: 'In history up to the present it is certainly an empirical fact that separate individuals have, with the broadening of their activity into world historical activity, become more and more enslaved under a power alien to them (a pressure which they have conceived of as a dirty trick on the part of the so-called universal spirit, etc.), a power which has become more and more enormous and, in the last instance, turns out to be the world market.' Marx, *The German Ideology*, supra.
64. Gourevitch, *From Slavery to the Cooperative Commonwealth*, supra, 45.
65. Marx, *Grundrisse*, supra. Elsewhere, Marx calls this 'the violence of things'. Marx, *The German Ideology*, supra. Among the early thinkers, Max Weber, as well, identified the market as a source of domination as oppressive as personal dependence. See Max Weber, 'Domination and Legitimacy', in *Economy and Society: An Outline of Interpretive Sociology* (New York: Bedminster Press 1968), available at https://ia600305.us.archive.org/25/items/MaxWeberEconomyAndSociety/MaxWeberEconomyAndSociety.pdf, visited on 30 December 2017. See also, Max Horkheimer, *Eclipse of Reason* (New York: Continuum Books 2004).
66. Miller, 'Constraints on Freedom', supra; US labour-republicans characterized it as the product of 'human law'. See Gourevitch, *From Slavery to the Cooperative Commonwealth*, supra.
67. Ibid., 84, quoting a prominent labour republican.
68. 'Labour-republicanism' because it borrows from republican theory in understanding freedom in social terms, and also in terms of power and domination rather than interference. Ibid.
69. Ibid., 109.
70. Ibid., 111; the English philosopher Thomas Hobhouse made this specific argument in the context of minimum wage laws: because '... [t]he opportunities of work and the remuneration for work are determined by a complex mass of social forces which no individual,

certainly no individual workman, can shape … [t]he 'right to work' and the right to a 'living wage' are just as valid as the rights of person or property'. See L.T. Hobhouse, *Liberalism* (London: Oxford University Press 1911), available at https://www.gutenberg.org/files/28278/28278-h/28278-h.htm. See also, Nien-he Hsieh, 'Rawlsian Justice and Workplace Republicanism' (2005) 31(1) *Social Theory and Practice* 115–42.

71. Gourevitch, *From Slavery to the Cooperative Commonwealth*, supra, 69; see also, Karl Marx in his early writings, arguing that alienated labour, because it belongs to and is directed by another, 'is thus not voluntary, but compelled, *forced labour* [Zwangsarbeit]', cf. Roberts, *Marx's Inferno*, supra, 139.
72. Pope, 'Labor's Constitution of Freedom', supra; see also Forbath, 'The Ambiguities of "Free Labor"', supra.
73. Thirteenth Amendment, Constitution of the United States.
74. See, e.g., the account in Forbath, 'The Ambiguities of "Free Labor"', supra.
75. *Lochner v. New York*, supra.
76. It might be legitimately asked whether this is a purely verbal argument. After all, if both Berlin and Rawls agree that economic circumstances make freedom worthless, then there exists a strong case for intervention in order that freedom actually be meaningful. What is the point of freedom that people cannot use? However, while labour-republicans and Rawls/Berlin might agree on some economic policies, the framing remains important: if public intervention is treated as an infringement upon freedom (as non-interference), then it is the very fact of intervention that requires justification; and the argument is reduced to balancing freedom against other values (economic security, welfare, well-being, etc.) This already reduces the range of possible arguments and justifications, justifications that would be available on the labour-republican understanding of freedom.
77. As Pettit puts the point: 'I do not interfere with you just through happening, like a natural obstacle, to be in your way or just through doing something that has the unforeseen effect of hindering you. Nor do I generally interfere with you just through allowing such an obstacle to get in your way, or through allowing another person to interfere:

not, at any rate, unless contextual criteria give such an omission a positive interpretation.' Pettit, 'Freedom in the Market', supra, 135. Notice how the words 'unless contextual criteria' necessarily qualify the clean, analytic distinctions that precede them, and accurately classify the entire enterprise as a question of moral judgement.

78. MacCallum, 'Negative and Positive Freedom', supra, 325–26.
79. S.I. Benn and W.L. Weinstein, 'Being Free to Act and Being a Free Man' (1971) 80(318) *Mind* 194, 197–98; see also the examples in Philip Pettit, 'A Republican Right to a Basic Income' in *Basic Income: An Anthology of Contemporary Research* 26 (Karl Widerquist et al. eds., Malden: Wiley Blackwell 2013).
80. Benn and Weinstein, 'Being Free to Act and Being a Free Man', supra, 199.
81. Ripstein, 'Commodity Fetishism', supra, 747.
82. In the Indian context, the debate about the meaning of freedom becomes even more salient, because it marks the distinction between an enforceable fundamental right under Part III of the Constitution, and matters of policy, indicated by Part IV, but ultimately left to the discretion of the legislature.
83. Clause 4, Karachi Resolution, supra.
84. See Section III(B), infra.
85. Clause 3, Karachi Resolution, supra.
86. Clause 5, Karachi Resolution, supra.
87. Pope, 'Labor's Constitution of Freedom', supra.
88. Clause 1(ii), Karachi Resolution, supra.
89. Clause 1(v), Karachi Resolution, supra.
90. Clause 2, Karachi Resolution, supra.
91. Clause 11, Karachi Resolution, supra.
92. Preamble, Karachi Resolution, supra.
93. Pope, 'Labor's Constitution of Freedom', supra, 942. Interestingly, the term 'effective freedom' is also used by Quentin Skinner in his discussion of Isiah Berlin's example of the blind man who is 'free' to read, but 'unable' to do so. Skinner's gloss on this is that the blind man is 'formally free' to read, but *effectively* unfree. Skinner, 'A Third Concept of Liberty', supra, 245. If we replace 'effective' with 'real', we can see how the Karachi Resolution represented a serious riposte to

the view that treated freedom as non-interference and the absence of intentional coercion. It is also interesting to note that Berlin dismissed the concept of 'economic freedom'—the exact phrase used by the Karachi Resolution—as something bordering on a conceptual error. Berlin, *Two Concepts of Liberty*, supra.

94. See K.T. Shah, 'A Note on Fundamental Rights', 23 December 1946, cf. Shiva Rao, *The Framing of India's Constitution, Vol. II*, supra, 36, 53.
95. B.R. Ambedkar, 'Memorandum and Draft Articles on the Rights of States and Minorities', 24 March 1947, cf. Shiva Rao, *The Framing of India's Constitution, Vol. II,* supra, 84, 87.
96. Ibid., 100.
97. Notice Ambedkar's use of the words 'subject' and 'governed', borrowed from republican ideas of freedom and servitude.
98. B.R. Ambedkar, 'Memorandum', cf. Shiva Rao, *The Framing of India's Constitution*, *Vol. II*, supra, 100–01.
99. Ibid., 101–02.
100. See, infra.
101. Discussion of the Fundamental Rights Sub-Committee, 27 March 1947, cf. Shiva Rao, *The Framing of India's Constitution*, *Vol. II*, supra, 125–26.
102. Discussion of the Fundamental Rights Sub-Committee, 28 March 1947, cf. Shiva Rao, *The Framing of India's Constitution, Vol. II, supra*, 127-28; see also B.N. Rau, 'Notes on the Draft Report', 8 April 1947, cf. Shiva Rao, *The Framing of India's Constitution, Vol. II,* supra, 147, 149.
103. Draft Report of the Sub-Committee, 3 April 1947, cf. Shiva Rao, *The Framing of India's Constitution*, *Vol. II*, supra, 137, 140.
104. Thirteenth Amendment, Constitution of the United States.
105. See e.g., *Bailey v. Alabama*, 219 U.S. 219 (1911).
106. Parliament of India, *Constituent Assembly Debates, Vol. III*, 1 May 1947 (speech of K.M. Munshi), available at http://parliamentofindia.nic.in/ls/debates/vol3p4.htm, visited on 30 December 2017.
107. Ibid.
108. Ibid.
109. Ibid. (speech of B.R. Ambedkar).
110. Ibid.

111. Ibid. (speech of P.K. Sen).
112. Parliament of India, *Constituent Assembly Debates, Vol. VII*, 3 December 1948 (speech of Damodar Sarup Seth), available at http://parliamentofindia.nic.in/ls/debates/vol7p19.htm, visited on 30 December 2017.
113. Ibid. (speech of B.R. Ambedkar).
114. Ibid. (speech of Renuka Ray).
115. Parliament of India, *Constituent Assembly Debates, Vol. III*, 1 May 1947 (speech of Dakshayani Velayudhan).
116. See, infra.
117. See Parliament of India, *Constituent Assembly Debates, Vol. VII*, 22 November 1948.
118. Forbath, 'The Ambiguity of "Free Labor"', supra, 768.
119. Preamble, Slavery Convention of 1926.
120. Article 1, Slavery Convention of 1926.
121. Even the Slavery Convention, it is important to note, did not equate forced labour with the absence of compensation. Article 5(1) provided that in countries where forced labour continued to exist, it should 'always receive adequate remuneration'.
122. Article 2(1), ILO Forced Labour Convention, 1930 (No. 29); there were exceptions for military service, civic obligations, penal liability, and emergencies (Article 2[2]).
123. Article 1(b), Supplementary Convention on the Abolition of Slavery, the Slave Trade, and Institutions and Practices Similar to Slavery, 1956.
124. The running together of the words 'law, custom or agreement' is testament to this.
125. Article 6, Constitution of Malaysia.
126. Article 30, Constitution of Kenya.
127. Article 6, Constitution of Botswana.
128. Article 25, Constitution of Uganda.
129. Article 9, Constitution of Lesotho.
130. Article 6(1) of the Malaysian Constitution prohibits slavery, and 6(2) prohibits forced labour. Article 30(1) of the Kenyan Constitution prohibits slavery and servitude, while Article 30(2) prohibits forced labour. Article 6 of the Constitution of Botswana, Article 25 of the

Constitution of Uganda, and Article 9 of the Constitution of Lesotho are structured in exactly the same way, and all draw upon the ILO Conventions.

131. Although, of course, a social practice is constituted by an aggregate of individual acts, bound by a non-trivial unity of purpose.

132. *Poola Bhaskara Vijaykumar v. State of Andhra Pradesh*, AIR 1988 AP 295, ¶4.

133. *Express Newspapers v. Union of India*, AIR 1958 SC 578.

134. See ibid, for an extended discussion.

135. For example, if the State fixed an absurdly low amount, a court would have the power to review it on the touchstone of Article 23.

136. On 15 November 1948, while rejecting K.T. Shah's proposed amendment to include 'socialist' in the Preamble, Ambedkar stated: 'What should be the policy of the State, how the Society should be organised in its social and economic side are matters which must be decided by the people themselves according to time and circumstances.' In the course of the same speech, Ambedkar went on to argue that, in any event, the proposed amendment was 'unnecessary', because through the Directive Principles of State Policy, 'socialist principles are already embodied in our Constitution'. Parliament of India, *Constituent Assembly Debates, Vol. VII*, 15 November 1948 (speech of Dr B.R. Ambedkar). This is why, in my view, the articulation that I provided earlier in this book—that the Constitution authorized and encouraged socialism but did not mandate it—is the correct one, and it is within that intellectual framework that the Fundamental Rights chapter ought to be interpreted.

137. *Sanjit Roy v. State of Rajasthan* (1983) 1 SCC 525.

138. *Lingegowd Detective and Security Chamber (P) Ltd. v. Mysore Kirloskar Ltd.* (2006) 5 SCC 180.

139. Ibid., ¶10.

140. *State of Karnataka v. Uma Devi* (2006) 4 SCC 1, ¶50.

141. *Mukesh Chandra v. State of U.P.*, (2000) 85 FLR 317 (All), ¶7.

142. Ibid., ¶14.

143. Ibid., ¶17.

144. Ibid., ¶15.

145. An interesting application of *PUDR* took place in the context of prison labour. Soon after *PUDR*, the High Court of Kerala, applying

the logic of the judgement, held that the State could not exact unpaid labour from prison convicts. Noting specifically the vulnerable position in which prisoners were placed vis-à-vis the State, the Court held, 'the right not to be exploited in contravention of Article 23(1) is a right guaranteed to a citizen, and there is no reason a prisoner should lose his right to receive wages for his labour'. In the Matter of Prison Reforms, Enhancement of Wages of Prisoners etc., AIR 1983 Ker 261, ¶29. But see also, Poola Bhaskara Vijaykumar, supra, which disagreed with this view; and *State of Gujarat v. High Court of Gujarat*, (1998) 7 SCC 392, where the Supreme Court was unable to arrive at a consensus.

146. The ratio of *Uma Devi* has, indeed, been watered down in the years since the judgement was delivered. As recently as May 2018, the Delhi High Court delivered a judgement on the regularization of school teachers, consciously ignoring the legal form (that they were appointed on contract), and focusing upon the *fact* of exploitation. *Indu Munshi v. Union of India*, LPA 286/2015. For an analysis, see Gautam Bhatia, 'Round-Up: The Delhi High Court's Experiments with the Constitution', *The Indian Constitutional Law and Philosophy Blog*, 26 June 2018, available at https://indconlawphil.wordpress.com/2018/06/26/round-up-the-delhi-high-courts-experiments-with-the-constitution/.

147. Another abortive attempt to constitutionalize labour rights (although not in the context of Article 23) was in *Air India Statutory Corporation v. United Labour Union* (1997) 9 SCC 377. In *Air India Statutory Corporation*, the Supreme Court held that if the government abolished contract labour in any establishment (under the provisions of the Contract Labour Act), then the affected workmen would have a right to regularization, even though there was no specific provision expressly allowing for that. One particularly significant feature of *Air India Statutory Corporation* was its attempt to constitutionalize labour law by expressly using Part III as well as the Directive Principles as *interpretive aids* to determine questions left open by the Contract Labour Regulation Act. Implicit in the Court's analysis was the idea that imbalances of power *within the workplace* are of *constitutional concern*, and subject to the application of constitutional values. In fact, the Court specifically invoked economic and social democracy, channelling Ambedkar's speech in the Constituent Assembly, and

used impeccably labour-republican language in observing, 'permanent employment which is not a bounty of the employer nor can its survival be at the volition and mercy of the employer. Income is the foundation to enjoy many Fundamental Rights and when work is the source of income, the right to work would become as such a fundamental right. Fundamental Rights can ill-afford to be consigned to the limbo of undefined premises and uncertain application.' Ibid., ¶49. *Air India Statutory Corporation* was, however, overruled by the Supreme Court in *SAIL v. National Union of Waterfront Workers* (2001) 7 SCC 1.

Another judgement that applied labour-republican constitutional logic to issues of labour law was *Hussainbhai v. The Alath Factory Thozhilali Union, Kozhikode* (1978) 4 SCC 257, where the Court held that even in cases where the mode of employment was formally through contract labour (which had fewer rights), an 'employment relationship' (and, consequently, the application of the full labour law regime with all its attendant rights) existed where there was 'economic control': 'a worker or group of workers labours to produce goods or services and these goods or services are for the business of another, that other is, in fact, the employer. He has economic control over the workers' subsistence, skill, and continued employment.' The Court did not invoke Article 23, or any other provision of the Fundamental Rights chapter, but did invoke Part IV. It appears, however, that the thrust of *Hussainbhai* has subsequently been diluted by the Supreme Court in *Balwant Rai Saluja v. Air India* (2014) 9 SCC 407.

148. Susan Walzer, *Thinking About the Baby: Gender and Transitions into Parenthood* (Philadelphia: Temple University Press 1998); Arlie Hochschild and Anne Machung, *The Second Shift: Working Families and the Revolution at Home* (London: Penguin Books 2012).

149. UN Women, 'Equal Rights and Responsibilities in Marriage', available at http://www.endvawnow.org/en/articles/766-equal-rights-and-responsibilities-in-marriage.html. For more details, see ActionAid, 'Making Care Visible: Women's Unpaid Care Work in Nepal, Nigeria, Uganda, and Kenya', available at http://www.actionaid.org/sites/files/actionaid/making_care_visible.pdf; see also Anna Knox et al., 'Connecting Rights to Reality: A Progressive Framework of Core Legal Protections for Women's Property Rights', *ICRW*, available at https://www.icrw.org/wp-content/uploads/2016/10/Connecting-Rights-to-

Reality-A-Progressive-Framework-of-Core-Legal-Protections-for-Womens-Property-Rights.pdf.

150. Evelyn Nakano Glen, *Forced to Care: Coercion and Caregiving in America* (Cambridge: Harvard University Press 2010), available at https://caringlabor.files.wordpress.com/2012/05/forced-to-care.pdf, visited on 30 December 2017; Alice Kessler-Harris, *Women Have Always Worked: A Historical Overview* (New York: Feminist Press 2012).
151. See, e.g., Silvia Federici, *Wages Against Housework* (Bristol: Falling Wall Press 1975), available at https://caringlabor.files.wordpress.com/2010/11/federici-wages-against-housework.pdf, visited on 30 December 2017; see also, Article 88, Constitution of Venezuela: 'The state recognises work at home as an economic activity that creates added value and produces social welfare and wealth. Housewives are entitled to Social Security in accordance with law.' For a list of resources, see http://www.generation-online.org/h/wages-for-housework.htm, visited on 30 December 2017.
152. See, e.g., the judgement of the Supreme Court of California in *Meyer v. Kinzer and Wife*, 12 Cal. 247 (1859), where Chief Justice Stephen Johnson Field wrote, 'The marriage, in respect to property acquired during its existence, is a community of which each spouse is a member, equally contributing by his or her industry to its prosperity, and possessing an equal right to succeed to the property after dissolution, in case of surviving the other.' See also, the marital law of South Africa, where the default legal system governing marriages is that of community of property.
153. These are 'partial community of property regimes'. Complete community of property regimes include property purchased before marriage. For obvious reasons, this can perpetuate oppression within the family, rather than mitigate it.
154. Editorial, 'For Equality all the Way', *The Hindu*, 3 April 2012, available at https://www.thehindu.com/opinion/editorial/for-equality-all-the-way/article3273970.ece.
155. See, e.g., *S.R. Batra v. Taruna Batra*, (2007) 3 SCC 169.
156. See, e.g., *Agnes Nanjala William v. Jacob Petrus Nicolas Vander Goes*, Mombasa CA Civil Appeal No. 127/2011.
157. Ibid.

158. See, e.g., the judgement of the Nairobi High Court in *Federation of Women Lawyers Kenya (FIDA) v. Attorney-General*, Petition No. 164B of 2016, where the High Court described the evolution of law, and also upheld a provision of the Matrimonial Property Act of 2018, which acknowledged non-monetary contributions to the household, but also made recognition conditional by courts on a case-by-case basis. The Court seemed to adopt a position that what a spouse received on the dissolution of marriage would be determined on the basis of what they had contributed in monetary or non-monetary terms. Statutorily, the definition of 'non-monetary' included domestic work, childcare, companionship, farm work, and management of the matrimonial property.

7: Privacy beyond the Public/Private Divide: *Sareetha* and Freedom within the Family

1. Section 9, Hindu Marriage Act. While a decree for the restitution of conjugal rights cannot be enforced by *physically* forcing the recalcitrant party to cohabit with the other, it can be enforced by attaching their property.
2. *T. Sareetha v. T. Venkatasubbaiah*, AIR 1983 AP 356. Procedurally, *Sareetha* came before the single judge as a revision petition against an order of a subordinate judge, and not a writ petition; consequently, adjudicating upon constitutionality in such a situation was somewhat unconventional.
3. Sareetha, supra, ¶17.
4. *Dadaji v. Rukhmabai* (1885) ILR 9 Bom 529.
5. *Dadaji Bhikaji v. Rukhmabai* (1886) 10 I.L.R. (Bom) 301.
6. For a non-representative sample of academic literature on the *Rukhmabai* case, see Sudhir Chandra, *Enslaved Daughters: Colonialism, Law, and Women's Rights* (New Delhi: OUP 2008); Padma Anagol, 'Rebellious Wives and Dysfunctional Marriages: Indian Women's Discourses and Participation in the Debates over Restitution of Conjugal Rights and Child Marriage Controversy in the 1880s and 1890s' in *Women and Social Reform in Modern India* 282–313 (Sumit and Tanika Sarkar eds., Bloomington: Indiana University Press 2008); Meera Kosambi, 'Gender Reform and Competing State Controls

over Women: The Rakhmabai Case (1884–1888)' (1995) 29(1–2) *Contributions to Indian Sociology* 265.

7. Tanika Sarkar, *Hindu Wife, Hindu Nation* 150 (Bloomington: Indiana University Press 2010).
8. Parliament of India, *Constituent Assembly Debates, Vol. III*, 30 April 1947, available at http://parliamentofindia.nic.in/ls/debates/vol3p3.htm.
9. Parliament of India, *Constituent Assembly Debates, Vol. VII*, 3 December 1948, available at http://164.100.47.194/loksabha/writereaddata/cadebatefiles/C03121948.html.
10. Parliament of India, *Constituent Assembly Debates, Vol. XI*, 15 September 1949 (speech of Pandit Thakur Das Bhargava), available at http://164.100.47.194/Loksabha/Debates/cadebatefiles/C15091949.html.
11. *M.P. Sharma v. Satish Chandra*, 1954 S.C.R. 377.
12. *Kharak Singh v. State of UP* (1964) 1 S.C.R. 332.
13. Ibid., ¶28 (Justice Subba Rao, dissenting).
14. Ibid., ¶13.
15. Ibid., ¶15.
16. *Gobind v. State of MP* (1975) 2 SCC 148.
17. Ibid, ¶24.
18. It is also rather inapposite to the context of the case itself, which was about police surveillance. This might be because the statement is copied verbatim (without acknowledgement) from the US Supreme Court judgement of *Paris Adult Theatres v. Slaton*, 413 U.S. 49 (1973), which was a case about zoning for adult theatres.
19. Jeff Weintraub, 'The Theory and Politics of the Public/Private Distinction' in *Public and Private in Thought and Practice: Perspectives on a Grand Dichotomy* 1, 2 (Chicago: University of Chicago Press 1999). See also Lawrence E. Klein, 'Gender and the Public/Private Distinction in the Eighteenth Century: Some Questions' (1995) 29(1) *Eighteenth-Century Studies* 97–109, warning that a facile public/private binary is ahistorical.
20. J. Roy, 'Polis and Oikos in Classical Athens' (1999) 46(1) *Greece and Rome* 1.
21. Don Slater, 'Public/Private' in *Core Sociological Dichotomies* (Chris Jenks ed., London: Sage Publications 1998) 136–37.

22. See Hannah Arendt, *The Human Condition*, Part II (2nd ed., Chicago: University of Chicago Press 2013).
23. The Greek word for this was *isonomia*, which translates to 'equality of political rights'.
24. Arendt, *The Human Condition*, supra; Weintraub, 'The Theory and Politics of the Public/Private Distinction', supra, 12; Martha Nussbaum, 'Is Privacy Bad for Women?', *The Boston Review*, 1 April 2000, available at https://bostonreview.net/world/martha-c-nussbaum-privacy-bad-women, visited on 13 July 2017.
25. Gurpreet Mahajan, 'Introduction' in *The Public and the Private* 1, 10 (Gurpreet Mahajan and Helmut Reifeld eds., New Delhi: Sage Publications 2003). See also Jean Elshtain, 'Moral Woman and Immoral Man: A Consideration of the Public-Private Split and its Political Ramifications', (1974) 4 *Politics & Society* 453–73.
26. Slater, 'Public/Private', supra.
27. See Dieter Grimm, *Constitutionalism: Past, Present, and Future* (Oxford: OUP 2016).
28. Seyla Benhabib, *Situating the Self: Gender, Community and Postmodernism in Contemporary Ethics* 109 (Cambridge: Polity Press 1992).
29. Ibid. See also, Carole Pateman, *The Sexual Contract* (Stanford University Press 1988); Joan Landes, 'The Public and the Private Sphere: A Feminist Reconsideration' in *Feminism, The Public and the Private* 135–63 (Joan Landes ed., Oxford: OUP 1998).
30. Ann Hughes, 'Learning from the Levellers?' in Elizabeth Anderson, *Private Government: How Employers Rule Our Lives* 75, 87 *(and Why We Don't Talk About It)* (New Jersey: Princeton University Press 2009).
31. Samuel D. Warren and Louis D. Brandeis, 'The Right to Privacy' (1890) 4(5) *The Harvard Law Review* 193, 220.
32. *Olmstead v. United States*, 277 U.S. 438 (1928).
33. *Katz v. United States*, 389 U.S. 347 (1967).
34. The Fourth Amendment to the Constitution of the United States: 'The right of the people to be secure in their persons, houses, papers, and effects, against unreasonable searches and seizures, shall not be violated, and no Warrants shall issue, but upon probable cause,

supported by Oath or affirmation, and particularly describing the place to be searched, and the persons or things to be seized.'

35. Olmstead, supra.
36. Katz, supra, 351.
37. Ibid., 361 (concurring opinion of Justice Harlan).
38. See, e.g., *Griswold v. Connecticut*, 381 U.S. 479 (1965); *Roe v. Wade*, 410 U.S. 113 (1973).
39. *Kyllo v. United States*, 533 U.S. 27 (2001).
40. Ibid., 40.
41. Ibid., 37. See also Solove, 'A Taxonomy of Privacy' (2006) 154 *University of Pennsylvania Law Review* 477, demonstrating how the spatial conception continues to be the paradigm within which privacy/surveillance cases operate: pp. 496–99.
42. Article 8, European Convention of Human Rights: 'Everyone has the right to respect for his private and family life, his home and his correspondence.'; Article 13(1), Basic Law of the Federal Republic of Germany: 'The home is inviolable.'
43. *Bernstein v. Bester*, 1996 (4) BCLR 449.
44. Ibid., ¶67. See also *Port Elizabeth Municipality v. Various Occupiers* (2004) 12 BCLR 1268 (concurring opinion of Justice Sachs).
45. The classic statement of the issue is considered to be in Carole Pateman, 'Feminist Critiques of the Public/Private Dichotomy' in *Public and Private in Social Life* 281 (Stanley I. Benn and Gerald F. Gaus eds., New York: St Martin's Press 1983). See also Ruth Gavison, 'Feminism and the Public/Private Distinction' (1992) 45 *Stanford Law Review* 1.
46. Nussbaum, 'Is Privacy Bad for Women?', supra. See also, Catherine MacKinnon, 'Privacy v. Equality: Beyond Roe v. Wade' in *Feminism Unmodified* 93–102 (Cambridge: Harvard University Press 1987).
47. Anderson, *Private Government*, supra; Michael Walzer, 'Liberalism and the Art of Separation' (1984) 12(3) *Political Theory* 315, 325.
48. See, e.g., the essays in *Feminism, the Public and the Private*, supra; Nancy Fraser, 'What's Critical about Critical Theory: The Case of Habermas and Gender' (1985) 35 *New German Critique* 97–131. See also Herbert Marcuse, *An Essay On Liberation* (Boston: Beacon Press 1971).
49. John Gardner, 'Private Activities and Personal Autonomy: At the Margins of Anti-Discrimination Law' in *Discrimination and the Limits*

of Law 148–49 (Bob Hepple and Erika M. Szyszczak eds., London: Mansell 1992).

50. One good example of this is Jean Cohen's analysis of the US Supreme Court judgement in *Planned Parenthood v. Casey*, 505 U.S. 833 (1992), where the Court criticized abortion rules that required a wife to notify her husband in cases of abortion, on the basis that this would increase the likelihood of domestic violence. Cohen says the Court 'explicitly rejects the old common-law understanding of a woman's role in the family along with the view that entity privacy trumps individual privacy within the marital unit'. Cohen, 'Rethinking Privacy', supra, 142.
51. *Griswold v. Connecticut*, 381 U.S. 479 (1965).
52. Ibid., 484.
53. Cohen, 'Rethinking Privacy', supra, 145.
54. *McGee v. Attorney-General*, [1974] IR 284.
55. Ibid. At least in part, this decision was influenced by textual provisions of the Irish Constitution recognizing the family as a basic unit of society. See Article 41, Constitution of Ireland.
56. See, e.g., Rajeswari Sunder Rajan, 'Women between Community and State: Some Implications of the Uniform Civil Code Debates in India' (2000) 18(4) *Social Text*, 55.
57. See, e.g., Bernard Cohn, *Colonialism and Its Forms of Knowledge: The British in India* 31 (Princeton: Princeton University Press 1996). The word 'Gentoo' is an archaic term, referencing 'Hindu'.
58. For example, the similarly worded Bengal Regulation of 1793 was cited by the Privy Council in *Moonshee Buzloor Ruheem v. Shumsoonnissa Begum* (1867) 11 MIA 551, as authority for the proposition that a suit for restitution for conjugal rights 'must be determined according to the principles of the Mahomedan law … for … the rights and duties resulting from the contract of marriage vary in different communities'. Ibid., ¶41. Later, the Privy Council, which was then the highest court of appeal for India, noted that there would be, 'nothing more likely to give just alarm to the Mahomedan community than to learn by a judicial decision, that their law, the application of which has been thus secured to them, is to be over-ridden upon a question which so materially concerns their domestic relations'. Ibid., ¶48. See also In re Kahandas Narrandas, 5 B. 154 (application of religious personal law to

matters of succession). In 1927, the Privy Council drew an express link between 'religion' and 'personal laws', holding, 'the law of succession in the case of a Hindu or a Mohammedan depends upon their own personal law: it depends upon the law of their religion'. *Mitar Sen Singh v. Maqbul Hasan Khan*, AIR 1930 PC 251, ¶4. In 1930, the Bombay High Court expressly equated family and religion, holding, 'Europeans, Hindoos and Mahometans have their respective family or religious laws'. *Peter Philip Saldanha v. Anne Grace Saldanha* (1930) 32 BOMLR 17. See also, *State of Bombay v. Narasu Appa Mali*, AIR 1952 Bom 84, ¶12: 'it is an historic fact that both the Muslims and the Hindus in this country have their own personal laws which are based upon their respective religious texts ...'

59. Ibid. See also Madhu Kishwar, 'Codified Hindu Law: Myth and Reality' (1994) 29(33) *Economic and Political Weekly* 2145.
60. Rachel Sturman, *The Governance of Social Life in Colonial India: Liberalism, Religious Law, and Women's Rights* 6 (Cambridge: Cambridge University Press 2012).
61. Ibid., p. 8.
62. Amrita Shodhan, *A Question of Community: Religious Groups and Colonial Law* 69 (New Delhi: Samya 2001).
63. For an excellent account of the colonial insistence on pigeonholing communities within rigid, pre-defined labels ('Hindu' and 'Muslim'), even against their express, contrary self-identification, see Teena Purohit, *The Aga Khan Case: Religion and Identity in Colonial India* (Cambridge: Harvard University Press 2012). Sudipta Kaviraj uses the term 'fuzzy communities' to describe the pre-colonial situation. Sudipta Kaviraj, *The Imaginary Institution of India* (New York: Columbia University Press 2010).
64. Ibid. See also Neeladri Bhattacharya, 'Remaking Custom: The Discourse and Practice of Colonial Codification' in *Tradition, Dissent, and Ideology: Essays in Honour of Romila Thapar* 20–51 (R. Champakalakshmi and S. Gopal eds., New Delhi: OUP 1996).
65. Rosalind O'Hanlon, *A Comparison between Women and Men: Tarabai Shinde and the Critique of Gender Relations in Colonial India* 10 (New Delhi: OUP 1994).
66. Shodhan, *A Question of Community*, supra, 36.

67. Madhavi Sunder, 'Cultural Dissent' (2001) 54(3) *Stanford Law Review* 495. See also Tanika Sarkar, 'A Prehistory of Rights: The Age of Consent Debate in Colonial Bengal' (2000) 26(3) *Feminist Studies* 601.
68. Radhika Singha, *A Despotism of Law* 163 (New Delhi: Oxford University Press 1998).
69. For the specific link between the colonial move to reliance upon canonical texts to determine the content of 'personal laws', and the subordination of women as embodiments of an inner cultural tradition found within the space of the home, see Partha Chatterjee, 'Colonialism, Nationalism, and Colonized Women: The Contest in India' (1989) 16(4) *American Ethnologist* 622; Lata Mani, 'Contentious Traditions: The Debate on Sati in Colonial India' (1987) 7 *Cultural Critique* 118–56, citing, among others, the historian D.D. Kosambi. For an example of how this played out in judicial decisions, see *Sidlingapa v. Sidava*, (1878) ILR 2 Bom 624, where the Bombay High Court held that a wife's right to maintenance arose not out of the contractual relationship of marriage, but as a 'liability created by Hindu law in respect of the jural relations of the Hindu family'. Ibid., ¶8. See the discussion in Sturman, *The Government of Social Life*, supra, calling it a right arising out of marital status. For a similar argument in a more international context, see the essays in Nira Yuval-Davis and Floya Anthias eds., *Woman-Nation-State* (London: Palgrave MacMillan 1985).
70. O'Hanlon, *A Comparison between Men and Women*, supra, 12.
71. Anupama Roy, *Gendered Citizenship: Historical and Conceptual Explanations* 86 (New Delhi: Orient Longman 2005). Tanika Sarkar uses the words 'inviolate' and 'autonomous'. Sarkar, *Hindu Wife, Hindu Nation*, supra, p. 36. See also Charu Gupta, *Sexuality, Obscenity, Community: Women, Muslims, and the Hindu Public in Colonial India* 123 (New Delhi: Permanent Black 2001), citing Partha Chatterjee, *The Nation and its Fragments: Colonial and Postcolonial Histories* 120–21 (Princeton: Princeton University Press 1993). For an analysis of how this discourse continues today, see Nivedita Menon, 'State/Gender/Community: Citizenship in Contemporary India' (1998) 33(5) *Economic and Political Weekly*, PE3, 7.
72. Sarkar, 'A Prehistory of Rights', supra.

73. Flavia Agnes, 'Patriarchy, Sexuality, and Property' in *Family, Gender, and Law in a Globalizing Middle East and South Asia* 19, 22 (Kenneth M. Cuno and Manisha Desai eds., Syracuse, NY: Syracuse University Press 2009).
74. Partha Chatterjee, 'The Nationalist Resolution of the Woman Question' in *Recasting Women: Essays in Indian Colonial History* 306–34 (New Delhi: Zubaan Books 1989); Roy, *Gendered Citizenship*, supra.
75. Roy, *Gendered Citizenship*, supra, 135. But see the 18th Session of the Indian National Congress (1904), dedicated to 'women's issues' such as polygamy, child marriage, and education.
76. Chatterjee, 'The Nationalist Resolution of the Woman Question', supra. See also Uma Chakravarti, *Rewriting History* 94 (New Delhi: Zubaan 2013), for an account of a similar division between the 'political' and the 'social' within the reformist Poona Sarvajanik Sabha.
77. 'This notion of culture effectively erases the agency of those involved in such practices.' Mani, *Contentious Traditions*, supra, 151–52.
78. *Eisenstadt v. Baird*, 405 U.S. 438, 453 (1972).
79. *Roe v. Wade*, supra.
80. Sareetha, supra, ¶17.
81. Ibid.
82. Ibid.
83. Ibid.
84. Ibid.
85. Ibid., ¶18.
86. Ibid., ¶19.
87. Gobind, supra, ¶22.
88. Sareetha, supra, ¶23.
89. Ibid., ¶24.
90. Ibid.
91. Ibid., ¶27.
92. *Olmstead v. New York*, supra.
93. Ibid., 453 (Justice Brandeis, dissenting).
94. The word 'democratization' carries historical valence. For instance, Joan Scott cites an interesting example of Louis de Bonald, an early-nineteenth-century French legislator, who criticized the concept of divorce laws on the basis that it amounted to 'veritable domestic

democracy', and allowed the 'wife, the weak part, to rebel against marital authority...' Joan Scott, 'Gender: A Useful Category of Historical Analysis' (1986) 91(5) *American Historical Review* 1053, 1071. See also Kumkum Sangari and Sudesh Vaid, 'Introduction' in *Recasting Women: Essays in Colonial History* 1–27 (New Brunswick: Rutgers University Press 1989).

95. Sareetha, supra, ¶38.
96. The issues with S. 9 were exacerbated by judicial interpretation of the term 'reasonable cause', which was often read to *require* the wife to live in the 'matrimonial home' (i.e., the husband's home), notwithstanding the fact that her own professional career might have necessitated her living elsewhere. See, e.g., the discussion in Vimal Balasubrahmanyan, 'Conjugal Rights: Shift in Emphasis Needed' (1984) 19(35) 1510, 1510; Kusum, 'Wife's Right to Employment versus Husband's Conjugal Rights' (1977) 19(1) *Journal of the Indian Law Institute* 77; *Kailashwati v. Ayodhia* Prakash, (1977) *Punjab Law Reports* 216; but see, contra, *Radhakrishna v. Dhanalakshmi*, AIR 1975 Mad 331.
97. In fact, Justice Choudary's combination of privacy and equality is an (unintentionally) direct response to Catherine MacKinnon's critique of American abortion-privacy doctrine in *Roe v. Wade*, which, she argues, laid down a right of decisional privacy/autonomy *in the abstract*, without any consideration of whether such autonomy was real or effective within the familial or spousal relationship. MacKinnon, 'Privacy v. Equality', supra.
98. James Scott, *Domination and the Arts of Resistance: Hidden Transcripts* (New Haven: Yale University Press 1990).
99. See, e.g., Sudipta Kaviraj, *Trajectories of the Indian State* (Ranikhet: Permanent Black 2010).
100. Roy, *Gendered Citizenship*, supra, 45.
101. Padma Anagol, *The Emergence of Feminism in India, 1850–1920* 60 (London: Routledge 2006).
102. See, e.g., John Stuart Mill, *The Subjection of Women*, Ch. 2: 'The Laws Governing Marriage' (1869), available at http://www.earlymoderntexts.com/assets/pdfs/mill1869.pdf, visited on 21 July 2017. Mill did, however, advocate that married women should devote themselves to housework.
103. Ibid.

104. Soonderbai Powar, *The Bitter Fruits of Hinduism*, cf. Anagol, *The Emergence of Feminism*, supra, 30.
105. Ibid., 31; see also Krupabai Satthianadhan, *Miscellaneous Writings* (Madras: Srinivasa Varadachariar & Co. 1896). The word 'slavery' was used by more than one contemporary writer. See Padma Anagol, 'Rebellious Wives and Dysfunctional Marriages', supra, 437. See, as well, the writings of Vidyasagar, and the analysis in Sumit Sarkar, 'Vidyasagar and Brahmanical Society' in *Women and Social Reform in India* 118–46, supra.
106. See Mahua Sarkar, 'Rokeya Sakhawat Hossain and the Gender Debate among Muslim Intellectuals in Late Colonial Bengal' in *A Feminist Foremother: Critical Essays on Rokeya Sakhawat Hossain* 25, 31 (Mohammad A. Quayum and Md. Mahmudul Hasan eds., New Delhi: Orient BlackSwan 2017), as well as the accompanying essays in the volume.
107. Satthianadhan, 'Home Training of Children' in *Miscellaneous Writings*, supra, 9.
108. Gail Omvedt, *Cultural Revolt in a Colonial Society: The Non-Brahmin Movement in Western India* 113 (New Delhi: Manohar Publishers 2011).
109. Pandita Ramabai, *The High Caste Hindu Woman* (Bombay: Maharashtra State Board for Literature and Culture 1981).
110. The most radical movement for democratizing the private sphere, and, in particular, the marital relationship, was birthed in South India, under the leadership of Periyar. See, e.g., S. Anandhi, 'Women's Question in the Dravidian Movement c. 1925–1948' (1991) 19(5/6) *Social Scientist* 24–41; V. Geetha, 'Periyar, Women, and an Ethic of Citizenship' (1998) 33(17) *Economic and Political Weekly* 9–15. See also, the institution of 'satyashodhak weddings' created by Jyotirao Phule, where wedding vows expressly required the groom to state that the bride would have 'full rights' within marriage. Uma Chakravarti, *Rewriting History: The Life and Times of Pandita Ramabai* 88 (New Delhi: Zubaan 2013).
111. 'Letters from a Hindu Lady', *The Times of India* (1885), cf. Anagol, 'Rebellious Wives and Dysfunctional Marriages' in *Women and Social Reform in Modern India*, supra.

112. Sudhir Chandra, *Enslaved Daughters* 112 (New Delhi: Oxford University Press 2008).
113. A point made by T.N. Madan. See T.N. Madan, 'Of the Social Categories of "Private" and "Public": Considerations of Cultural Context' in *The Public and the Private*, supra, 95: '... [Rukhmabai] invited the intrusion of public institutions into the Hindu home'.
114. See, e.g., O'Hanlon, *A Comparison between Women and Men*, supra, 17.
115. See, e.g., Mahavir Prasad Dwivedi, *Rachnavali*, *Vol.* 7, cf. Gupta, *Sexuality, Obscenity, Community*, supra, 126.
116. Article 41(1), Constitution of Ireland.
117. Kharak Singh, supra, ¶28.
118. Ibid.
119. Neil Richards, 'Intellectual Privacy' (2008) 87 *Texas Law Review* 387; Margot Kaminski and Shane Witnov, 'The Conforming Effect: First Amendment Implications of Surveillance, beyond Chilling Speech' (2014) 49 *University of Richmond Law Review* 465.
120. Ibid.
121. Kharak Singh, supra, ¶29 (Justice Subba Rao, dissenting).
122. Ibid.
123. Kharak Singh, supra, ¶30 (Justice Subba Rao, dissenting).
124. Gobind, supra, ¶28.
125. *Justice K.S. Puttasawamy v. Union of India*, supra, 'Order of the Court'.
126. Fourth Amendment, Constitution of the United States.
127. Article 41, Constitution of Ireland.
128. See, e.g., Parliament of India, *Constituent Assembly Debates*, , *Vol. III*, 30 April 1947 (speech of Somanth Lahiri), supra.
129. Akhil Amar, 'Fourth Amendment First Principles' (1994) 107 *Harvard Law Review* 757.
130. See, especially, *Justice K.S. Puttaswamy v. Union of India*, supra (concurring opinion of Justice Nariman; plurality opinion of Justice Chandrachud).
131. *Harvinder Kaur v. Harmander Singh Choudhry*, AIR 1984 Del 66.
132. Ibid., ¶9; later, he noted that 'a disproportionate emphasis on sex, almost bordering on obsession, has coloured the view of the learned judge [i.e., Justice Choudary]'. Ibid., ¶47.
133. Ibid., ¶12.

134. Ibid.
135. Ibid., ¶34, This observation, however, is particularly difficult to parse. Whatever the temperature of the principles of constitutional law, the remedy of restitution of conjugal rights was itself the creation of a law—Section 9 of the Hindu Marriage Act (HMA), a statute. Was it Justice Rohatgi's contention that cold constitutional law had no place in the intimate and delicate sphere of the home, but that cold statute law could be let in? Or was it his case that Section 9 of the HMA was warmer than Articles 14 and 21 of the Constitution? We do not know.
136. Ibid., ¶35.
137. Ibid., ¶36.
138. *Saroj Rani v. Sudarshan Kumar Chadha*, AIR 1984 SC 1562, ¶14.
139. Ibid., ¶16.
140. *Justice K.S. Puttaswamy v. Union of India*, supra, ¶40 (concurring opinion of Justice Chelameswar).
141. Ibid., fn. 61.
142. *Justice K.S. Puttaswamy v. Union of India*, supra, ¶140 (plurality opinion of Justice Chandrachud).
143. Ruth Vanita, 'The Special Marriage Act: Not Special Enough' (1990) 58 *Manushi* 14–15.
144. Section 13A, Hindu Marriage Act.
145. Flavia Agnes, 'Reforms As If Women Mattered', available at http://www.indiatogether.org/manushi/issue119/reforms.htm, visited on 14 July 2017.
146. Explanation, S. 375, Indian Penal Code; Sir Mathew Hale, *History of the Pleas of the Crown* (1736), available at https://archive.org/details/historiaplacitor01hale, visited on 14 July 2017.
147. Melisa J. Anderson, 'Lawful Wife, Unlawful Sex—Examining the Effect of the Criminalisation of Marital Rape in England and the Republic of Ireland' (1998) *Georgia Journal of International and Comparative Law* 139.
148. Jahnavi Sen, 'Maneka Gandhi's Altered Stance on Marital Rape Angers Activists', *The Wire*, 12 March 2016, available at https://thewire.in/24649/activists-angered-by-maneka-gandhis-altered-stance-on-marital-rape/, visited on 14 July 2017.
149. In the immediate aftermath of *Sareetha*, one scholar wrote that the judgement 'tacitly' admitted that 'there *is* such a thing as rape within

marriage'. V. Balasubahmanyan, 'Conjugal Rights v. Personal Liberty: Andhra High Court Judgment' (1983) 16(29) *Economic and Political Weekly*.

150. *State of Bombay v. Narasu Appa Mali*, AIR 1952 Bom 84.
151. See A.M. Bhattacharjee, *Matrimonial Laws and the Constitution* (New Delhi: Eastern Law House 2017).
152. See also, Tanika Sarkar, 'Something Like Rights? Faith, Law and Widow Immolation Debates in Colonial Bengal' (2012) 49 *Indian Economic & Social History Review* 295, 303.
153. See, e.g., Cohn, *Colonialism and Its Forms of Knowledge*, supra.
154. This point is not new. See, e.g., Frances E. Olsen, 'The Family and the Market: A Study of Ideology and Legal Reform' (1983) 96(7) *Harvard Law Review* 1497, 1505–06. Catherine MacKinnon also makes this argument while criticizing the US Supreme Court's abortion jurisprudence, which located the right to abortion within the right to privacy, while also holding that the State was under no obligation to 'facilitate' abortion, and could withhold funds accordingly. MacKinnon, 'Privacy versus Equality', supra, pp. 99–100.
155. See Flavia Agnes, 'Personal Laws' in *The Oxford Handbook of the Indian Constitution* 903 (Sujit Chaudhry et al. eds., New Delhi: Oxford University Press 2016). There is widespread scholarly consensus on this issue. See Sturman, *The Governance of Social Life*, supra; Shodhan, *A Question of Community*, supra, 8: 'Personal law was thus construed at once as an integral part of the colonial legal system, adjudicated in colonial courts by colonial legal personnel, and as an arena of non-intervention by the colonial state.' Marc Galanter, 'The Displacement of Traditional Law in Modern India' (1968) XXIV(4) *Journal of Social Issues* 65; Kishwar, 'Codified Hindu Law', supra, 2145. In the words of the early nineteenth-century colonial administrator, Mountstuart Elphinstone, 'We ought not to be guided by Hindu law, which is a new introduction of our own.' Mountstuart Elphinstone, 'Report on the Territories' in *Selections from the Official Writings of Mountstuart Elphinstone, Governor of Bombay* 252, 330 (Cambridge: Cambridge University Press 2011).
156. See Patricia Uberoi, 'Feminism and the Public-Private Distinction' in *The Public and the Private*, supra, 205–29.
157. Slater, 'Public/Private', supra, 139.

158. Seyla Benhabib, 'Models of Public Space: Hannah Arendt, the Liberal Tradition, and Jurgen Habermas' in *Habermas and the Public Sphere* 73, 92 (Craig Calhoun ed., Cambridge: MIT Press 1992).
159. For an analysis of how *Puttaswamy* implicitly commits to prioritizing decisional privacy over spatial and relational privacy, and therefore impacts the issues discussed in this section, see Gautam Bhatia, 'The Supreme Court's Right to Privacy Judgment – II: Privacy, the Individual, and the Public/Private Divide', 28 August 2017, available at https://indconlawphil.wordpress.com/2017/08/28/the-supreme-courts-right-to-privacy-judgment-ii-privacy-the-individual-and-the-publicprivate-divide/.

8: Speech, Association, Personal Liberty, and the State of Exception: *Jyoti Chorge v. State of Maharashtra*

1. *Shreya Singhal v. Union of India* (2015) 6 SCC 1.
2. S. 2(o)(ii), UAPA.
3. S. 3, UAPA.
4. S. 10, UAPA.
5. S. 20, UAPA.
6. *Jyoti Babasaheb Chorge v. State of Maharashtra* (2012) 6 AIR Bom R 706; see also *Dhawala Rama Dhengale v. State of Maharashtra*, Crl. Bail. Application No. 1536/2012.
7. *Sagar Tathyaram Gorkhe v. State of Maharashtra*, Crl. Bail Application No. 1657/2014.
8. Giorgio Agamben, *State of Exception* 2 (Chicago: University of Chicago Press 2005). Agamben writes: '… the voluntary creation of a permanent state of emergency has become one of the essential practices of contemporary states, including so-called democratic ones'.
9. Article 19(1)(a), Constitution of India: 'All citizens shall have the right to freedom of speech and expression.'
10. Article 19(1)(b) (freedom of assembly) and 19(1)(c) (freedom of association) are structured similarly.
11. The next two paragraphs present, in compressed form, a more detailed argument made in Gautam Bhatia, *Offend, Shock, or Disturb: Freedom of Speech under the Indian Constitution* (New Delhi: Oxford University Press 2015).

12. The fact that executive authorities, including the police, honour this more in the breach is a different matter.
13. Betwa Sharma, 'One Year After His Arrest, Chandrashekhar Azad is a Prisoner of the Yogi Adityanath Government', *The Wire*, 7 June 2018, available at https://www.huffingtonpost.in/2018/06/07/one-year-after-his-arrest-chandrashekhar-azad-is-a-prisoner-of-the-yogi-adityanath-government-without-trial-or-bail_a_23452448/.
14. Upendra Baxi, *The Crisis of the Indian Legal System* 30 (New Delhi: Vikas Publishing House 1982); see also, Ujjwal Kumar Singh, *The State, Democracy, and Anti-Terror Laws in India* 68 (New Delhi: Sage Publications 2007).
15. Article 22(3), Constitution of India.
16. Article 22(4), Constitution of India.
17. Article 22(7), Constitution of India.
18. *A.K. Gopalan v. State of Madras*, 1950 SCR 88.
19. See, for example, the analysis in *K.S. Puttaswamy v. Union of India*, (2017) 10 SCC 1. See also Anup Surendranath, 'Life and Personal Liberty' in *The Oxford Handbook of the Indian Constitution*, 756-57 (Sujit Chaudhry et al. eds., New Delhi: Oxford University Press 2016). H.M. Seervai, however, rejects this reading of *Gopalan*. See infra.
20. *R.C. Cooper v. Union of India*, 1970 SCR (3) 530.
21. *Haradhan Saha v. State of West Bengal* (1975) 3 SCC 198.
22. Ibid., ¶31.
23. Most famously, *Maneka Gandhi v. Union of India* (1978) 1 SCC 248.
24. See *A.K. Roy v. Union of India* (1982) 1 SCC 271, which rejected a challenge to the National Security Act on the grounds that *Haradhan Saha* had upheld a law that was largely similar.
25. *State of Punjab v. Sukhpal Singh* (1990) 1 SCC 35.
26. Ibid., ¶9.
27. The specific preventive detention orders in this case were ultimately quashed on a technicality.
28. *State of Punjab v. Sukhpal Singh*, supra, ¶9.
29. Ibid., ¶72.
30. Ibid., ¶57.
31. Ibid., ¶61.
32. *Dropti Devi v. Union of India* (2012) 7 SCC 499.
33. COFEPOSA, 1974.

34. Dropti Devi, supra, ¶69.
35. Ibid., ¶70.
36. See Carl Schmitt, *Political Theology* (Chicago: University of Chicago Press 2006). It is important to note that in Kashmir, the state of exception was *literally* made permanent by an amendment to the Constitution that insulated preventive detention from fundamental rights review, and lasted twenty-five years. The situation has scarcely improved under laws such as the Jammu and Kashmir Public Safety Act. The virtual absence of constitutionalism as a constraint on State power and coercion in Jammu and Kashmir would require, of course, a book in its own right. For a summary, see Ghazala Peer, 'Preventive Detentions in Kashmir: Still a Lawless Law', *Journal of Indian Law and Society Blog*, 9 March 2013, available at https://jilsblognujs.wordpress.com/2013/03/09/preventive-detentions-in-kashmir-still-a-lawless-law/.
37. The present language is more restrictive than the original, and is the result of the 44th Amendment.
38. Article 359, Constitution of India; also, a result of the 44th Amendment.
39. See, infra.
40. Agamben, *State of Exception*, supra, 4.
41. Article 352, as it stood at the time, allowed for the imposition of Emergency on account of 'internal disturbance'.
42. *ADM, Jabalpur v. Shivakant Shukla* (1976) 2 SCC 521.
43. See, e.g., H.M. Seervai, *Constitutional Law of India, Vol. 2*, 2205–40 (4th ed., New Delhi: Universal Law Publishing 1993).
44. *Justice K.S. Puttaswamy v. Union of India*, supra.
45. With the rider that, after the 44th Amendment, Articles 20 and 21 may not be suspended even during an Emergency.
46. ADM Jabalpur, supra, ¶255 (concurring opinion of Justice Beg).
47. Ibid., ¶129 (concurring opinion of CJI Ray).
48. Ibid., ¶130 (concurring opinion of CJI Ray).
49. Ibid., ¶418 (concurring opinion of Justice Chandrachud). See also, ¶36, where CJI Ray accused critics of painting 'diabolic distortion and mendacious alignment'.
50. Ibid., ¶226 (concurring opinion of Justice Beg)
51. Ibid., ¶324-A (concurring opinion of Justice Beg).

52. As Ujjwal Kumar Singh points out, the court has been habituated to deciding cases of this kind within an overarching 'reasons of State' framework. Singh, *The State, Democracy, and Anti-Terror Laws*, supra.
53. *Liversidge v. Andersen* (1941) UKHL 1.
54. ADM Jabalpur, supra, ¶230 (concurring opinion of Justice Beg).
55. 'Liberty is itself the gift of the law and may by the law be forfeited or abridged.' Ibid., ¶35 (concurring opinion of CJI Ray).
56. The Ninth Schedule of the Constitution contains laws that are immunized from fundamental rights review.
57. In 2017, the Supreme Court singled *ADM Jabalpur* as one of the two discordant notes in its history. *Justice K.S. Puttaswamy v. Union of India*, supra.
58. Kalyani Ramnath, 'ADM Jabalpur's Antecedents: Political Emergencies, Civil Liberties, and Arguments from Colonial Continuities in India' (2016) 31(2) *American University International Law Review* 209. For a comprehensive survey of the various special laws passed by the Indian Parliaments, see Singh, *The State, Democracy, and Anti-Terror Laws in India*, supra.
59. *Makhan Singh v. State of Punjab* (1964) 4 SCR 797.
60. Ibid., ¶47. See also *Ghulam Sarwar v. Union of India*, AIR 1967 SC 1335.
61. It is also rather unreasonable to expect vocal public opinion, whether enlightened or otherwise, to issue forth from a jail cell.
62. Venkat Iyer, *States of Emergency: The Indian Experience* (Delhi: Butterworths India 2000).
63. Singh, *The State, Democracy, and Anti-Terror Laws in India*, supra. As Gunther Frankenberg astutely points out, the normalization of the state of exception is designed to 'shake off or ease the burden of justification', which would apply if a formal Emergency was declared. G. Frankenberg, *Comparative Constitutional Studies: Between Magic and Deceit* 286 (Cheltenham: Edward Elgar Publishing 2018). See also, ibid., pp. 285–89, for a comparative account of the methodologies by which the state of exception is normalized.
64. See, e.g., K.G. Kannabiran, *Wages of Impunity: Power, Justice and Human Rights* (Hyderabad: Orient Longman 2004). See also, Mrinal Satish and Aparna Chandra, 'Of Maternal State and Minimalist

Judiciary: The Indian Supreme Court's Approach to Terror-Related Adjudication' (2009) 21(1) *National Law School of India Review* 51. Indeed, in *Krishna Mochi v. State of Bihar* (2002) 6 SCC 81, the Court expressly inverted the innocent-until-proven-guilty principle on the basis of the unique nature of terrorism. See also, Shylashri Shankar, *Scaling Justice: The Supreme Court, Social Rights and Civil Liberties in India* (New Delhi: Oxford University Press 2009).

65. *Kartar Singh v. State of Punjab* (1994) 3 SCC 569, ¶22.
66. Ibid., ¶32.
67. As the Italian oral historian, Alessandro Portelli, writes in his study of terror trials in 1970s Italy, the judicial process reduces what is a complex phenomenon (in that case, left-wing terrorism, as defined by the State) with a number of causes and consequences, into a series of discrete, self-contained events. The task, which involves an assessment of both historical and political considerations, is performed without historians or politicians. Portelli points out that 'the magistrates [are] involved in reconstructing the past, redefining its meaning, and attempting an overall interpretation. These are historical tasks, and it is appropriate to examine the way they were performed from the point of view of the theory and method of history, oral history specifically, given the nature of most sources used', Alessandro Portelli, 'The Oral Shape of the Law' in *The Death of Luigi Trastulli and Other Stories: Form and Meaning in Oral and Public History* 241, 246 (Albany: State University of New York Press 1991). Beyond this, a close scrutiny of the court's method is particularly important, because unlike the work of historians, the judicial narrative acquires *force*. In many cases, it is literally a matter of life and death; and in all cases, by virtue of the courts' position as the supreme arbiter of the Constitution, it acquires a normative valence and salience that far outlives the specific details of the individual case. It is for this reason that the long prefatory comments in *Kartar Singh* and *PUCL*, which, in the form of seemingly self-evident factual statements, actually smuggle in a set of historical, political, moral, and ethical assessments, need to be critiqued in their turn.
68. Kartar Singh, supra, ¶145.
69. Ibid., ¶253.
70. *PUCL v. Union of India*, (2004) 9 SCC 580, ¶4.

71. Ibid., ¶9.
72. Ibid., ¶13, quoting the home minister's speech while piloting the Bill; see also, *Devendar Pal Singh v. State of NCT of Delhi*, (2002) 5 SCC 234, where similar reasons were invoked to uphold the death penalty under TADA.
73. *Naga People's Movement for Human Rights v. Union of India* (1998) 2 SCC 109.
74. Under the colonial Code of Criminal Procedure (1898), the concept of separation between the executive and the judiciary was severely diluted. One of the features of the new Code of Criminal Procedure, enacted in 1973, was to follow through on the constitutional mandate for the separation of powers, contained in Article 50. To this end, the powers of the executive magistrates were circumscribed, defined in the Code itself, and broadly limited to executive functions (such as passing prohibitory orders in cases of disturbances to public order). *Kartar Singh*'s sophistry that, because a central government nominee was exercising judicial functions, she was holding judicial office is particularly grating when placed within this historical context—a core purpose of the 1973 CrPC was exactly to *prevent* judicial powers from being conferred on executive officials. In his dissenting opinion, Justice Ramaswamy pointed out that this, effectively, 'polluted the stream at its source'. Kartar Singh, supra, ¶399 (dissenting opinion of Justice Ramaswamy). See also the judgement of the Andhra Pradesh High Court in *V. Mohan Ranga Rao v. State of Andhra Pradesh* (1985) 2 AP LJ 361 (AP).
75. Kartar Singh, supra, ¶365.
76. Naga People's Movement for Human Rights, supra, ¶61.
77. Abhinav Sekhri, 'Reversing the Presumption of Innocence – Part III', *Proof of Guilt*, available at https://theproofofguilt.blogspot.in/2015/05/reversing-presumption-of-innocence-part_9.html.
78. See, e.g., S. 43D(5) of the Unlawful Activities Prevention Act; see also Abhinav Sekhri, 'Reversing the Presumption of Innocence – Part II', *Proof of Guilt*, supra.
79. Abhinav Sekhri points out that such provisions were simply borrowed from colonial-era laws, which were enacted at a time when the 'presumption of innocence' was not as fundamental to criminal

jurisprudence as it is now. Abhinav Sekhri, 'Reversing the Presumption of Innocence – Part I', *The Proof of Guilt*, supra.

80. Kartar Singh, supra, ¶351; this was replicated in *PUCL v. Union of India*, supra, where the Court upheld an identical provision by referring to how offences under the POTA were more 'complex' than ordinary offences. See also Naga People's Movement for Human Rights, supra.
81. *PUCL v. Union of India*, supra, ¶42.
82. Ibid., ¶43.
83. Kartar Singh, supra, ¶328; see also *Krishna Mochi v. State of Bihar*, supra.
84. *PUCL v. Union of India*, supra, ¶22.
85. Naga People's Movement for Human Rights, supra, ¶¶43–44.
86. *ADM Jabalpur*, supra, ¶529 (dissenting opinion of Justice Khanna).
87. Mathew Arnold, writing about Percy Bysshe Shelley.
88. See Portelli, 'The Oral Shape of the Law', supra. For an example of a contrary judgement, see *Nandini Sundar v. State of Chhattisgarh* (2011) 7 SCC 547, where the Court held that a State-backed private militia, armed to fight the Naxalites, was unconstitutional.
89. Agamben, *State of Exception*, supra.
90. *Dhawala Rama Dhengale v. State of Maharashtra*, Crl. Bail. Application No. 1536/2012, ¶12.
91. *Jyoti Chorge v. State of Maharashtra*, Crl. Bail Application No. 1020/2012, ¶4.
92. Ibid., ¶8.
93. Ibid., ¶18.
94. Ibid., ¶21.
95. This writer has heard the expressions 'contagion' and 'quarantine' used in court by a judge of the Supreme Court in early 2018 in order to distinguish between the bail provisions of the Prevention of Money Laundering Act from the bail provisions of anti-terror statutes. There is no transcript of the hearing.
96. *Arup Bhuyan v. State of Assam* (2011) 3 SCC 377.
97. *Indra Das v. State of Assam* (2011) 3 SCC 380.
98. *State of Kerala v. Raneef* (2011) 1 SCC 784.
99. Jyoti Chorge, supra, ¶29.
100. Ibid., ¶33.

101. Ibid., ¶27, cf. Arup Bhuyan, supra.
102. As Ujjwal Kumar Singh writes of TADA, 'Most movements of ethnic self-determination in their various manifestations were subsumed under the generic label "terrorist" and "disruptive". The explanations of both these labels within the text of TADA reduced these struggles to acts designated as terrorist and disruptive. These descriptions, as the pattern of detentions under TADA would show, depoliticized identity struggles dismembering them into specific acts of violence, demanding extraordinary legal solutions, procedures, and punishments.' Singh, *The State, Democracy, and Anti-Terror Laws*, supra, 52.
103. Jyoti Chorge, supra, ¶32.
104. Kartar Singh, supra, ¶406 (dissenting opinion of Justice Ramaswamy).
105. Kartar Singh, supra, ¶450 (dissenting opinion of Justice Sahai).
106. Perhaps unsurprisingly, Justice Sahai prefaced his short opinion with the observation, 'If the State adopts indiscriminate measures of repression resulting in obliterating the distinction between the offender and the innocent and its measures are repressive to such an extent where it might not be easy to decipher one from the other, it would be totally incompatible with liberal values of humanity, equality, liberty and injustice.' Kartar Singh, supra, ¶442 (dissenting opinion of Justice Sahai).
107. *State of Exception*, supra, 1.
108. Anil Kalhan et al., 'Colonial Continuities: Human Rights, Terrorism, and Security Laws in India' (2006) 20(1) *Columbia Journal of Asian Law* 93, 126.
109. Ibid.
110. The Bengal State Prisoners Regulation (Regulation III of 1818).
111. Kalhan et al., 'Colonial Continuities', supra.
112. Criminal Tribes Act, 1871. See Meena Radhakrishna, *Dishonoured by History: Criminal Tribes and British Colonial Policies* (New Delhi: Orient BlackSwan 2001); Dilip D'Souza, *Branded by Law* (New Delhi: Penguin 2001).
113. For a historical account of the criminalization of communities—with the attendant vagueness of 'membership'—in colonial jurisprudence through the nineteenth century, which was accompanied by collective punishment, see Radhika Singha, *A Despotism of Law* (New Delhi: Oxford University Press 1998).

114. Cf. Sanjay Nigam, 'Disciplining and Policing the "Criminals by Birth", Part 1: The Making of a Colonial Stereotype—The Criminal Tribes and Castes of North India' (1990) 27(2) *The Indian Economic and Social History Review* 131, 140.
115. Ibid., 141.
116. The Reception Committee, *Report of the 34th Session of the Indian National Congress: Presidential Address*, 8, 18 (Amritsar: 1922).
117. Ibid.
118. Ibid., 33.
119. C.R. Das, 'Freedom Through Disobedience', *Presidential Address at the 37th Session of the Indian National Congress* (Delhi: Arka Publishing House 1922), available at https://www.gutenberg.org/files/35349/35349-h/35349-h.htm, visited on 1 April 2018.
120. Ibid.
121. Ibid.
122. Nehru spoke about the CTA during a speech in 1936.
123. Srinivasa Sastri, *The Indian Citizen: His Rights and Duties* 29 (Delhi: Hind Kitab Limited 1948).
124. See Kannabiran, *The Wages of Impunity*, supra, 22–23.
125. Hansa Mehta, 'Civil Liberties', *Presidential Address at the All India Women's Conference, 1945* 10 (Aundh: Aundh Publishing Trust 1945).
126. In the Constituent Assembly, there was a train of thought that argued for the continuation of colonial-era powers on the specific basis that the new government, being of the people, would never misuse them. See, e.g., Parliament of India, *Constituent Assembly Debates, Vol. V*, 22 August 1947 (speech of Pandit Lakshmi Kanta Maitra), available at http://164.100.47.194/loksabha/writereaddata/cadebatefiles/C22081947.html.
127. Kannabiran, *The Wages of Impunity*, supra, 51.
128. Sastri, *The Indian Citizen*, supra.
129. See, e.g., Parliament of India, *Constituent Assembly Debates, Vol. V*, 22 August 1947, supra (speech of Mr Hussain Imam, pointing out that other countries allowed for preventive detention only during times of war; speech of Mahboob Ali Baig Sahab Bahadur); Parliament of India, *Constituent Assembly Debates, Vol. IX*, 29 August 1949 (speech of Shri Shibban Lal Saksena), available at http://164.100.47.194/loksabha/

writereaddata/cadebatefiles/C29081949.html; and 15 September 1949 (speech of Bakshi Tek Chand), available at http://164.100.47.194/loksabha/writereaddata/cadebatefiles/C15091949.html.

130. Parliament of India, *Constituent Assembly Debates, Vol. IX*, 16 December 1949, supra, available at http://164.100.47.194/loksabha/writereaddata/cadebatefiles/C16091949.html.

131. For a quick, accessible summary, see Abhinav Sekhri, 'Preventive Justice Part I – The History Behind Article 22', *The Proof of Guilt*, available at https://theproofofguilt.blogspot.in/2016/12/preventive-justice-part-1-history.html.

132. See e.g., Parliament of India, *Constituent Assembly Debates, Vol. VII*, 6 December 1948 (speech of K.M. Munshi), available at http://164.100.47.194/loksabha/writereaddata/cadebatefiles/C06121948.html.

133. As B.N. Rau noted in his initial note on fundamental rights as early as 2 September 1946, the more conservative framing was 'really meaningless as a guarantee against oppressive laws after enactment'. B.N. Rau, 'Notes on Fundamental Right', cf. B. Shiva Rao, *The Framing of India's Constitution: Select Documents, Vol. II* 21, 32 (New Delhi: Universal Law Publishing 1967); the issue was also discussed in the Sub-Committee on Fundamental Rights on 26 March 1947, where the concern was raised that a 'due process' clause would impede the legislature's ability to carry out land reform. Minutes of the Meeting of the Sub-Committee on Fundamental Rights, 26 March 1947, cf. Shiva Rao, *The Framing of India's Constitution*, supra, 121–22. The first internal draft Fundamental Rights chapter did contain a due process clause (Clause 11), and also a clause prohibiting prolonged detention before trial and unreasonable refusal of bail (Clause 29), based on Hersch Lauterpacht's International Bill of Rights. Commenting on Clause 11, B.N. Rau noted that it would be a safeguard against 'predatory legislation' but might also 'stand in the way of beneficent social legislation'. Note by the Constitutional Adviser (B.N. Rau) on the Effect of Some of the Proposed Clauses, cf. Shiva Rao, *The Framing of India's Constitution*, supra, 151. Due process remained in the Constitutional Adviser's draft Constitution, prepared after the first round of debates, in October 1947 (Article 16), but the detention provision had gone. 'Due process' then remained in the Drafting

Committee's draft Constitution until as late as 22 January 1948, but was dropped in the February draft that was presented to the Assembly, with the footnote that the phrase 'procedure established by law' was more 'specific'. This was draft Article 15. Shiva Rao, *The Framing of India's Constitution, Vol. III*, supra, 523.

134. For example, Alladi Krishnaswami Ayyar, who supported dropping 'due process', did so on the grounds that a due process clause would *preclude* preventive detention laws. Parliament of India, *Constituent Assembly Debates, Vol. IX,* 15 September 1949 (speech of Alladi Krishnaswami Ayyar); see also 16 September 1949 (speech of Shri B.M. Gupte).
135. See Parliament of India, *Constituent Assembly Debates, Vol. VII*, 13 December 1948 (speech of Dr B.R. Ambedkar), supra. Ambedkar said, with something of a flourish, that leaving the final word on liberty to a legislature 'packed by party men' or to 'five or six gentlemen sitting in the ... Supreme Court' was like sailing between Scylla and Charybdis.
136. Parliament of India, *Constituent Assembly Debates, Vol. IX,* 15 September 1949 (speech of Shri H.V. Pataskar), supra. The fact that the *purpose* of (what became) Article 22 was to compensate for what was not given under Article 21 ('procedure established by law') was agreed on by both supporters and opponents of preventive detention. The opponents only argued, further, that Article 22 failed miserably to achieve that purpose. See ibid.
137. Parliament of India, *Constituent Assembly Debates, Vol. IX,* 16 September 1949 (speech of Ananthasayanam Ayyangar).
138. Ibid. (speech of Shrimati G. Durgabai).
139. Article 22(3), Constitution of India. See Parliament of India, *Constituent Assembly Debates, Vol. IX,* 15 September 1949, supra.
140. Ibid., 16 September 1949 (speech of Dr B.R. Ambedkar). Ambedkar then went on to note that through its specific language, clause (3) was meant to *curtail* the otherwise unbounded power of the legislature to pass preventive detention laws. However, as Thakur Das Bhargava correctly noted, this argument was rather disingenuous: the legislature's power to pass preventive detention laws flowed from the Lists of the Seventh Schedule which Ambedkar himself had drafted. To this, Ambedkar only replied: 'I made it. You passed it.'
141. The argument that the Constituent Assembly ultimately adopted the 'liberty perspective' as opposed to the 'public order perspective', and the

view that it has been the courts that have subsequently misinterpreted the Constitution by giving primacy to the public order perspective, is supported by Aparna Chandra and Mrinal Satish. See 'Criminal Law and the Constitution' in *The Oxford Handbook of the Indian Constitution*, supra, 794, 798.

142. *R.C. Cooper v. Union of India* (1970) 1 SCC 248.
143. Seervai, *Constitutional Law of India*, *Vol. 2*, supra, 969–1014. Seervai also argues that *Gopalan* did not endorse the silos theory either: it only made the limited, and correct, point that Articles 19 and 21 operated in different spheres.
144. *A.K. Gopalan v. State of Madras*, supra, ¶26 (opinion of CJI Kania).
145. In *Justice K.S. Puttaswamy v. Union of India*, supra.
146. *A.K. Gopalan v. State of Madras*, supra, ¶103 (dissenting opinion of Justice Fazl Ali) Article 19(5) allows the State to impose reasonable restrictions on the freedom of movement. See also Abhinav Sekhri, 'Preventive Justice Part 2: Looking Inside Pandora's Box', *The Proof of Guilt*, available at https://theproofofguilt.blogspot.in/2016/12/preventive-justice-part-2-looking.html.
147. Parliament of India, *Constituent Assembly Debates, Vol. IX*, 15 September 1949 (speech of Dr B.R. Ambedkar), supra.
148. *A.K. Gopalan v. State of Madras*, supra, ¶93 (dissenting opinion of Justice Fazl Ali).
149. Parliament of India, *Constituent Assembly Debates, Vol. IX*, 16 September 1949 (speech of Dr B.R. Ambedkar), supra.
150. This argument has an important corollary. In *Maneka Gandhi v. Union of India* (1978) 1 SCC 248, the Supreme Court held that Article 21 *did*, in fact, include a 'due process' requirement. As a matter of constitutional text and history, this is indefensible. As we have seen above, the Constituent Assembly consciously adopted the phrase 'procedure established by law' and not 'due process', and despite fierce disagreement about the merits of this choice, there was consensus about its *consequences*: 'procedure established by law' required only a validly enacted law, which stipulated a procedure. *Maneka Gandhi* performed an entirely unpersuasive sleight of hand by holding that the word 'law' itself entailed a substantive requirement that what was enacted be 'just, fair, and reasonable'. This effectively turned the text of

Article 21 on its head, and judicially resurrected the argument that had been made, and lost, in the Constituent Assembly.

In other words, in *Gopalan*, the Supreme Court wrongly adopted the silos theory; and then in *Maneka*, it applied the wrong corrective by expanding Article 21, and making the phrase 'procedure established by law' bear the burden of a full-blown theory of constitutional liberty.

Perhaps for this reason, there has been almost no serious attempt to defend *Maneka Gandhi* on *constitutional* grounds. The defences have largely been consequential: 'Think of the peril the citizen would be in if there was no substantive check on the government's power to deprive individuals of their life or personal liberty.'

But the argument above should make it clear that consequential position is also flawed. Once it is established that the silos theory had no support in the text or history, and once it is established that Article 22 was never meant to be a complete code (quite the opposite), the corollary is that in adjudicating Part III violations, the Court would necessarily have to read Articles 14, 19, and 21 together, and, therefore, the proportionality standard under Article 14, and the proximity standard under Article 19, would apply to determine the constitutional validity of these impugned laws that violated personal liberty.

However, not only was *Maneka Gandhi* unnecessary to achieve greater freedom under the Constitution, its impact, if any, has been damaging. *Maneka Gandhi* became the trigger for the Court to expand Article 21 of the Constitution to a point where the 'right to life and personal liberty' has lost all meaning and, as a result, has become severely diluted. Moreover, the Court's cavalier approach to the constitutional text and history would have long-term consequences upon constitutional interpretation as a whole, sacrificing constitutional fidelity to the ideological predilections of individual judges, characterized most vividly in the public interest litigation regime. See Anuj Bhuwania, *Courting the People* (New York: Cambridge University Press 2017).

While I cannot develop this argument further here, the point is this: if *Maneka Gandhi* is indefensible as a matter of constitutional interpretation, unnecessary for achieving substantial safeguards on personal liberty, and damaging in other respects, then perhaps, instead of granting it an uncritically canonical status, it ought to be better understood as a well-intentioned, but misguided, wrong turn. One does not need to smuggle in due process into Article 21 to protect liberty: the Constitution, as interpreted correctly, protects it. *Maneka Gandhi* is incorrect, and ought to be overruled.

151. See e.g., Akhil Amar, *The Bill of Rights: Creation and Reconstruction* (New Haven: Yale University Press 2000), demonstrating that the phrase 'the freedom of speech' acquired a different connotation due to a shift from a political system in which Parliament was deemed supreme, to one in which 'The People' were deemed supreme.
152. See, Gautam Bhatia, 'Transformative Constitutional Amendments' (2015) XIII (1) *Dartmouth Law Journal* 1, 22; Amar, *The Bill of Rights*, supra, 224.
153. Kannabiran, *The Wages of Impunity*, supra.
154. Ornit Shani, *How India Became Democratic* (New Delhi: Penguin 2018).
155. The phrase 'culture of justification' was used by the South African constitutional scholar Etienne Mureinik to describe the transition from the apartheid regime to a constitutional democracy. See Etienne Mureinik, 'A Bridge to Where? Introducing the Interim Bill of Rights' (1994) 10 *South Africa Journal of Human Rights* 31.
156. Mehta, 'Civil Liberties', supra.
157. *Justice K.S. Puttaswamy v. Union of India*, supra.
158. See the highly deferential approach adopted by the Supreme Court in *Attorney-General for India v. Amratlal Prajivandas*, AIR 1994 SC 2179.
159. Kalyani Ramnath, 'The Other Criminal Codes: Crises, Excesses and the Goondas Acts in Indian Legal Imagination', unpublished manuscript on file with the author.
160. The Karnataka Prevention of Dangerous Activities of Bootleggers, Drug-Offenders, Gamblers, Goondas, (Immoral Traffic Offenders, Slum Grabbers and Video or Audio Pirates) Act, 1985.
161. 2013 Amendments to this Act bizarrely state that audio and video piracy is prejudicial to the maintenance of public order.
162. Section 8, Karnataka Goonda Act, supra.
163. Gautam Bhatia, *Offend, Shock, or Disturb*, supra, 81.

164. There is also an argument to be made that, insofar as the non-speech offences are concerned, they fail the proportionality standards under Articles 14 and 21.
165. For other laws authorizing preventive detention, see e.g., Amnesty International's work, available at https://amnesty.org.in/news-update/3200-held-administrative-detention-lawless-laws-must-scrapped-india-2/.
166. S. 2(e)(vi), Chhattisgarh Vishesh Jan Suraksha Adhiniyam, 2005.
167. S. 8, ibid.
168. See the Jammu and Kashmir Public Safety Act, 1978.
169. Chhattisgarh Special Public Safety Act, supra.
170. Usha Ramanathan, 'Ostensible Poverty, Beggary, and the Law' (2008) 43/44 *Economic and Political Weekly* 33. The article deals in some detail with the impact of the law. Vijay Raghavan and Mohammed Tarique, 'Penalising Poverty: The Case of the Bombay Prevention of Begging Act, 1959' (2018) LIII(22) *The Economic and Political Weekly* 26. But see *Ram Lakhan v. State*, 137 (2007) DLT 173, where the Delhi High Court explicitly 'read down' the provisions of the Act in order that it might conform to constitutional standards, in a manner very similar to what *Jyoti Chorge* would do seven years later. For an analysis, see Ashish Goel, 'Indian Anti-Beggary Laws and their Constitutionality through the Prism of Fundamental Rights, With Special Reference to *Ram Lakhan v. State*' (2010) 1 *Asia-Pacific Journal on Human Rights and the Law* 23–38. On 8 August 2018, the Delhi High Court became the first state to strike down the Act. See *Harsh Mander v. Union of India*, W.P. (C) 10498/2009 (High Court of Delhi). However, because of concessions by the state government, the decision was based on narrow grounds, limited to a distinction between 'voluntary' and 'involuntary' begging. See Gautam Bhatia, 'Something of Freedom Is Yet to Come: The Significance of the Delhi High Court's Decriminalisation of Beggary', *The Indian Constitutional Law and Philosophy Blog*, 10 August 2018, https://indconlawphil.wordpress.com/2018/08/10/something-of-freedom-is-yet-to-come-the-significance-of-the-delhi-high-courts-decriminalisation-of-beggary/.
171. S. 2(d), Bombay Prevention of Beggary Act, 1959.
172. S. 5, ibid.

173. S. 9, ibid.
174. There is also the Bombay Habitual Offenders Act of 1959, ostensibly a 'successor legislation' to the Criminal Tribes Act, and which was meant to mark a shift to the concept of 'individual responsibility'. While it partially does so, the Act allows for compulsory fingerprinting and registration of individuals even after they have been convicted *and served their time*. The Act also allows the state government to restrict the movements of 'registered offenders', and one of the circumstances that the government is expected to take into account is whether the individual follows a lawful occupation that is conducive to an 'honest and settled way of life'. Here again, the punishment is not for what is *done* but for who the person *is*. The Act also provides for 'corrective settlements'. The less said about those, the better.

9: Privacy and the Criminal Process: *Selvi v. State of Karnataka*

1. Stephen David, 'The Bangalore lab where India's most high-profile criminals cough up the truth', *India Today*, 22 May 2006, available at https://www.indiatoday.in/magazine/offtrack/story/20060522-bangalore-lab-where-criminals-of-india-cough-up-the-truth-783015-2006-05-22, visited on 19 April 2018.
2. Rakesh Prakash, 'Dr Narco and Ms Hide', *Bangalore Mirror*, 28 February 2009, http://bangaloremirror.indiatimes.com/opinion/sunday-read/dr-narco-and-ms-hide/articleshow/22204505.cms, visited on 19 April 2018.
3. Arun Ferreira, 'My Tryst with Narco-Analysis', https://www.countercurrents.org/Narco_Experiences_1_.pdf, visited on 19 April 2018.
4. 'To detect lies, FSL doctors truth', *Bangalore Mirror*, 26 June 2008, http://bangaloremirror.indiatimes.com/bangalore/cover-story/to-detect-lies-fsl-doctors-truth/articleshow/22463752.cms, visited on 19 April 2018.
5. Ibid.
6. Arun Ferreira, *Colours of the Cage* (New Delhi: Aleph Book Company 2014). Arun Ferreira was re-arrested in August 2018, and was under house arrest at the time that this book was sent to the publisher.

7. See, infra, Section II.
8. S. 93, Code of Criminal Procedure.
9. S. 53, ibid.
10. See, e.g., the concept of 'pre-cogs' in the novels of Philip K. Dick.
11. *Feldman v. United States*, 322 U.S. 487, 490 (1944).
12. See Andrew Ashworth QC, *The Hamlyn Lectures: Human Rights, Serious Crime and Criminal Procedure* 12–13 (London: Sweet & Maxwell 2002).
13. *Rochin v. California*, 342 U.S. 165 (1952).
14. Herbert Packer, 'Two Models of the Criminal Process' (1964) 113 *University of Pennsylvania Law Review* 1; Mirjan R. Damaska, 'Evidentiary Barriers to Conviction and Two Models of Criminal Procedure: A Comparative Study' (1972–73) (121) *University of Pennsylvania Law Review* 121. For a more updated version, see Erik Luna, 'The Models of Criminal Procedure' (1999) 2(2) *Buffalo Criminal Law Review* 389. Scholars have also proposed models that take into account a greater number of values than just accuracy and concern for rights. See, e.g., Ashworth, *The Hamlyn Lectures*, supra. Other scholars have rejected this framework altogether. See, e.g., John Griffiths, 'Ideology in Criminal Procedure or a Third "Model" of the Criminal Process', (1970) 79(3) *The Yale Law Journal* 359. For a nuanced application of this approach to Indian law (while also differing from), see Aparna Chandra and Mrinal Satish, 'Criminal Law and the Constitution' in *The Oxford Handbook of the Indian Constitution*, 794 (Sujit Chaudhry et al. eds., New Delhi: Oxford University Press 2016).
15. Ibid., 10.
16. Ibid., 13.
17. Ibid., 16.
18. Ibid.
19. For an alternative approach, based on law's need to balance factual accuracy and moral and expressive authority, see Ian Dennis, 'Instrumental Protection, Human Right, or Functional Necessity? Reassessing the Privilege against Self-Incrimination' (1995) 54(2) *Cambridge Law Journal* 342, 352.
20. See, e.g., *Mapp v. Ohio*, 367 U.S. 643 (1961); but see also *Hudson v. Michigan*, 547 U.S. 586 (2006).

21. *R v. S.A.B.* (2003) 2 S.C.R. 678; Chandra and Satish, 'Criminal Law and the Constitution', supra, 795. See also the proposals of the Criminal Law Revision Committee and the Royal Commission on Criminal Procedure, discussed in Dennis, 'Instrumental Protection, Human Right, or Functional Necessity?', supra, 347, fn. 22: '... a combination of reliability, disciplinary and protective principles'. There are, of course, other values as well, that may not always be reducible to these two: for example, the criminal law's expressive function.
22. See, e.g., Amar and Lerner, who argue, though with qualifications, that 'reliability' is the central value underlying the guarantee against self-incrimination. Akhil Amar and Renee Lerner, 'Fifth Amendment First Principles: The Self-Incrimination Clause' (1995) 93 *Michigan Law Review* 857.
23. See, e.g., *Ferreira v. Levin* (1996) 1 BCLR 1, where the Constitutional Court of South Africa articulated a due process justification for a right against self-incrimination.
24. *R v. S.A.B.* (2003) 2 SCR 678, 703.
25. *M.P. Sharma v. Satish Chandra*, 1954 SCR 1077, ¶10.
26. Ibid., ¶17. As the Canadian Supreme Court put it, 'the principle of self-incrimination imposes limits on the extent to which an accused person can be used as a source of information about himself'. *R v. B*, supra, 693. See also *R v. Jones* (1994) 2 S.C.R. 229.
27. Twenty-five years later, the Court narrowed this down still further in *V.S. Kuttan Pillai v. Ramakrishnan* (1980) 1 SCC 264.
28. But see, e.g., Redmayne, drawing a distinction between processes that do or do not 'involve co-opting the suspect'. Mike Redmayne, 'Rethinking the Privilege against Self-Incrimination' (2007) 27(2) *Oxford Journal of Legal Studies* 209, 215. See also *Fisher v. United States* 425 U.S. 391 (1976).
29. Ibid.
30. Ibid., ¶4.
31. Ibid., ¶8.
32. This reasoning of *M.P. Sharma* was overruled in 2017 in *K.S. Puttaswamy v. Union of India*, supra.
33. There is, intuitively, an internal contradiction here: while there may be reliability concerns with compelled oral self-incriminating testimony, the same fears are unlikely to apply to documents, because *at the time*

they were written (with the self-incriminatory content), there was no compulsion. See, e.g., Dennis, 'Instrumental Protection, Human Right, or Functional Necessity?', supra. For a contrary view, see Amar and Lerner, 'Fifth Amendment First Principles', supra, pointing out that, as a matter of fact, documents written in the form of confessionals often contain exaggeration and hyperbole and that, therefore, even a theory of self-incrimination founded on reliability may exclude self-incriminating documentary evidence.

34. See Abhinav Sekhri, 'From "Bully Boys" to "Willing Servants"?' Police, the Third Degree, and Indian Courts, 1861–1961', SSRN (2018), available at https://papers.ssrn.com/sol3/papers.cfm?abstract_id=3174042.
35. *State of Bombay v. Kathi Kalu Oghad* (1962) 3 SCR 10.
36. S. 73, Evidence Act.
37. S. 27, ibid.
38. State of *Bombay v. Kathi Kalu Oghad*, supra, ¶11.
39. Id., ¶¶11–12.
40. Id., ¶31 (concurring opinion of Justice Das Gupta).
41. Incidentally, *Kathi Kalu*'s logic provides a stronger justification for including documentary evidence within the scope of the right against self-incrimination. Documents *once written* (and then seized) cannot be changed.
42. For a contemporary critique, see K.R. Dixit, 'Protecting Against Self-incrimination', (1962) 4(1) *Journal of the Indian Law Institute* 144.
43. Ibid., ¶10.
44. Ibid., ¶32 (concurring opinion of Justice Das Gupta).
45. Ibid., ¶10.
46. Ibid.
47. *State of Gujarat v. Shyamlal Mohanlal Choksi* (1965) 2 SCR 457, ¶16 (dissenting opinion of Justice Shah).
48. In fact, Justice Shah expressly noted: 'but the hypothesis that our Legislature has accepted wholly or even partially the rule of protection against self-incrimination is based on no solid foundation'. Ibid., ¶5. The irony of calling the colonial legislature 'our Legislature' was apparently lost on him.

49. For an account of how the courts have privileged the crime control model across domains of criminal law, see Chandra and Satish, 'Criminal Law and the Constitution', supra, 798–812.
50. *Schmerber v. California*, 384 U.S. 757 (1966), noting that:

    ... There will be many cases in which such a distinction is not readily drawn. Some tests seemingly directed to obtain 'physical evidence', for example, lie detector tests measuring changes in body function during interrogation, may actually be directed to eliciting responses which are essentially testimonial. To compel a person to submit to testing in which an effort will be made to determine his guilt or innocence on the basis of physiological responses, whether willed or not, is to evoke the spirit and history of the Fifth Amendment.

    In his dissenting opinion, Justice Black criticized the normative foundations of the distinction itself, wondering what was it about a blood sample that lacked a 'communicative nature'. Black went on to note, persuasively, 'It is a strange hierarchy of values that allows the State to extract a human being's blood to convict him of a crime because of the blood's content, but proscribes compelled production of his lifeless papers.' *Schmerber v. California*, supra, p. 775 (dissenting opinion of Justice Black). Nonetheless, the testimonial/physical evidence dichotomy was a staple part of US self-incrimination jurisprudence in the mid-twentieth century. See Amar and Lerner, 'Fifth Amendment First Principles', supra. It was also a feature of Canadian self-incrimination jurisprudence.
51. *Horvath v. The Queen* (1979) 2 S.C.R. 376, 377.
52. Ibid., 401.
53. Ibid., 425.
54. The Canadian Supreme Court borrowed this phrase from the US Supreme Court judgement in *Townsend v. Sain*, 372 US 293 (1963).
55. Ibid., 426. See also, *Saunders v. The United Kingdom* (1996) ECHR 65: '... in defiance of the will of the accused'.
56. The trademarked version of the anaesthetic sodium thiopental.
57. *Selvi v. State of Karnataka* (2010) 7 SCC 263, ¶8.
58. Ibid., ¶14.
59. Ibid., ¶72.
60. For a critique of this framing, see the observations of Judge Friendly, quoted in Amar and Lerner, 'Fifth Amendment First Principles',

supra, 887: '[u]se of a suspect's answers "merely to find other evidence establishing his connection with the crime ... differs only by a shade from the permitted use for that purpose of his body or his blood"'.

61. S. 53, CrPC.
62. See, e.g., *Ferreira v. Levin* (1996) 1 BCLR 1: 'The more that self-incrimination takes the form of oral communication, the more compelling will the protection be; the more objective or real the existence of the incriminating material, on the other hand, the more attenuated.' (Concurring opinion of Justice Sachs, ¶259).
63. Ibid., ¶181.
64. Ibid., ¶184.
65. See, e.g., the observations of the Canadian Supreme Court in *R v. S.A.B.*, supra, p. 694, noting how in previous judgements, 'no distinction was drawn between products of the mind and products of the body with respect to the principle against self-incrimination'.
66. Ibid., ¶185.
67. A point noted by Justice Black in his dissenting opinion in *Schmerber*. See infra. See, however, *Saunders v. UK*, supra, ¶69: '[the right against self-incrimination] does not extend to the use in criminal proceedings of material which may be obtained from the accused through the use of compulsory powers but which has an existence independent *of the will of the suspect*'.
68. Ibid., ¶¶224–26.
69. *Horvath v. The Queen*, supra, ¶433. In discussing the constitutionality of a DNA bank, the Court later framed the issue as 'the rights of individuals to control the release of personal information about themselves'. *R v. S.A.B.*, supra, p. 701.
70. *Justice K.S. Puttaswamy (Retd.) v. Union of India*, supra.
71. The Court's framing in *Selvi*, and the distinction between physical and mental privacy, has been debated across jurisdictions, in judgements of constitutional courts, and in academic writing. It has been both defended and criticized. See, e.g., Mike Redmayne, 'Rethinking the Privilege against Self-Incrimination' (2007) 27(2) *Oxford Journal of Legal Studies* 209. Gerstein puts the point thus: '[G]overnmental authority is being used for the express purpose of shaping the conscience of the individual. Nothing could be more repugnant to the principle with which we are concerned.' Robert S. Gerstein, 'Privacy and Self-

Incrimination' (1970) 80(2) *Ethics* 87, 98–99. Galligan links the 'zone of privacy' to autonomy and identity. D.J. Galligan, 'The Right to Silence Reconsidered' (1988) 41(1) *Current Legal Problems* 69. In *Saunders v. United Kingdom* (1996) ECHR 65, a majority of the European Court of Human Rights drew a distinction between evidence dependent on the 'will' of the subject, and evidence independent of it—a distinction that was criticized as incoherent by Judge Martens in his dissenting judgement, who pointed out:

> Why should a suspect be free from coercion to make incriminating statements but not free from coercion to cooperate to furnish incriminating data? The Court's newly adopted rationale does not justify the distinction since in both cases the will of the suspect is not respected in that he is forced to bring about his own conviction … [and] what about a PIN code or a password into a cryptographic system which are hidden in the suspect's memory? (*Saunders v. UK*, supra, ¶12 dissenting opinion of Judge Martens).

Ian Dennis also points out that on the 'will of the subject' theory, there is no reason documents should fall within the privilege against self-incrimination, because, after coming into existence, their contents continue to exist independent of the will of the subject. Dennis, 'Instrumental Protection, Human Right, or Functional Necessity?', supra.

72. See also *Nandini Satpathy v. P.L. Dani* (1978) 2 SCC 424.
73. *R v. S* (R.J.) (1995)] 1 S.C.R. 451, 605 (concurring opinion of Justice L'Heureux-Dubé).
74. Cf. *Ahmed Mahomed Jackariah v. Ahmed Mahomed* (1888) ILR 15 Cal 109.
75. Shyamlal Mohanlal, supra, ¶11 (dissenting opinion of Justice Shah).
76. Fifth Amendment, Constitution of the United States of America.
77. R.H. Helmholz, 'Origins of the Privilege against Self-Incrimination: The Role of European Ius Commune' (1990) 65 *New York University Law Review* 962.
78. John H. Langbein, 'The Historical Origins of the Privilege Against Self-Incrimination at Common Law' (1994) 92 *Michigan Law Review* 1047; Eben Moglen, 'Taking the Fifth: Reconsidering the Origins of the Constitutional Privilege against Self-Incrimination' (1994) 92(5) *Michigan Law Review* 1086; *Ferreira v. Levin*, supra.

79. *R v. S.* (R.J.) (1995) 1 S.C.R. 451, ¶107.
80. In his draft notes on Fundamental Rights, B.N. Rau noted that it was borrowed from the Fifth Amendment to the US Constitution. B.N. Rau's 'Notes on the Draft Report', Shiva Rao, *The Framing of India's Constitution*, *Vol. II*, supra, 147, 149.
81. For example, in K.M. Munshi's Draft Bill of Rights, the guarantee against self-incrimination is found under the heading *Special Rights*, and apart from the section dealing with the core freedoms. Shiva Rao, *The Framing of India's Constitution, Vol. II,* supra, 69, 79. In the Fundamental Rights Sub-Committee's first draft bill of rights, it came under the title *Miscellaneous Rights*. Draft Report of the Sub-Committee, 3 April 1947, ibid., 137, 141. The provisions were shifted by the Drafting Committee from the *Miscellaneous Rights* sub-section on 3 November 1947, although the reasons are not specified. Ibid., 334.
82. Interestingly, in the Draft Constitution that he compiled out of the work of the different sub-Committees, and placed before the Drafting Committee in October 1947, the Constitutional Adviser B.N. Rau *added*, before the self-incrimination clause, the following words: *save as provided in Section 132 of the Indian Evidence Act, 1872 as in force at the commencement of this Constitution*, [shall any person be compelled in any criminal case to be a witness against himself]. Recall that Section 132 of the Evidence Act denies extending the privilege against self-incrimination to witnesses on the stand. In his Notes, B.N. Rau observed that this was 'new' and the purpose was to 'prevent a failure of justice'. However, this addition was dropped by the Drafting Committee, on the grounds that Article 20(3) clearly intended to apply to an accused and, therefore, the addition was unnecessary.
83. For a more detailed foray into colonial jurisprudence, and how the constitutional text marked a break with the past, see Abhinav Sekhri, 'From "Bully Boys" to "Willing Servants"?', supra.
84. Dennis, 'Instrumental Protection, Human Right, or Functional Necessity?', supra, 344.
85. Ibid.
86. For a proto-version of this argument, see K.S. Sharma, 'Law and Order and Protection of the Rights of the Accused in United States and

India: A General Framework for Comparison' (1972) 21 *Buffalo Law Review* 361, 406.

87. Courts across jurisdictions have held this.
88. This standard, of course, is not free from difficulty. A pending case before the Supreme Court involves the questions of whether *voice samples* fall within the scope of the self-incrimination guarantee. From one perspective, speaking involves a *mental* act, and, therefore, the physical evidence has its root in mental processes, in the words of *Selvi*. On the other hand, what is being analysed is not the *content* of the speech, but its *physiological* characteristics, which are entirely 'innocuous' in themselves, like blood or fingerprints. See Gautam Bhatia, 'The Gujarat High Court's Voice Spectrography Judgment, and the Limits of *Selvi v. State*', *Indian Constitutional Law and Philosophy Blog*, 15 February 2017, available at https://indconlawphil.wordpress.com/2017/02/15/the-gujarat-high-courts-voice-spectrography-judgment-and-the-limits-of-selvi-v.-state/.
89. *Justice K.S. Puttaswamy v. Union of India*, supra.
90. *Selvi v. State of Karnataka*, supra, ¶¶119, 246.
91. See, e.g., Abhinav Sekhri, 'From "Bully Boys" to "Willing Servants"?', supra.
92. *M.P. Sharma v. Satish Chandra*, supra, ¶10.
93. *Raja Narayanlal Bansilal v. Maneck Phiroz Mistry*, AIR 1961 SC 29.
94. Abhinav Sekhri, 'Confessions, Police Officers and Section 25 of the Indian Evidence Act, 1872' (2014) 7 *National University of Juridical Sciences Law Review* 1.
95. *Directorate of Enforcement v. Deepak Mahajan* (1994) 3 SCC 440. See Abhinav Sekhri, 'Detention, Deepak Mahajan, and Self-Incrimination', *The Proof of Guilt*, 3 March 2016, available at https://theproofofguilt.blogspot.in/2016/03/aprevious-version-of-this-post-appeared.html. The Court's gradual move in this direction was perceived as early as 1972. See K.S. Sharma, 'Law and Order and Protection of the Rights of the Accused in United States and India', supra.
96. Abhinav Sekhri, 'The Right against Self-Incrimination: Re-Defining Minimums, *The Proof of Guilt*', 13 March 2016, available at https://theproofofguilt.blogspot.in/2016/03/the-right-against-self-incrimination-re.html.

97. Chandra and Satish, 'Criminal Law and the Constitution', supra. For an early version of this argument, see K.K. Nigam, 'Due Process of Law: A Comparative Study of Procedural Guarantees against Deprivation of Personal Liberty in the United States and India', (1962) 4(1) *Journal of the Indian Law Inst.* 99.

Epilogue: 'Something of Freedom Is Yet to Come': The Aadhaar Case, Technological Self-Determination and the Future of Transformative Constitutionalism

1. Many of these days were truncated, however, so the Attorney-General's assessment may not have been entirely accurate.
2. An informal record of all thirty-eight days of the oral arguments—'live-tweeted' from the courtroom—can be accessed here: https://docs.google.com/document/d/1H-zGU3yIt6fKLxfrAKXI2EsievolyaFA3PO3jDv8cQM/edit?usp=drivesdk. This record was prepared by myself, Prasanna S., and the Software Freedom Law Centre (SFLC). All of us represented the petitioners, and the record should, therefore, be filtered for bias.
3. See: https://uidai.gov.in/component/fsf/?view=faq&catid=31.
4. *Justice K.S. Puttaswamy v. Union of India*, 2018 SCC Online SC 1642.
5. For analysis, see Gautam Bhatia, "The Aadhaar Judgment: A Round-Up", *The Indian Constitutional Law and Philosophy Blog*, 5 October 2018, available at https://indconlawphil.wordpress.com/2018/10/05/the-aadhaar-judgment-a-round-up/.
6. Virginia Eubanks, *Automating Inequality: How High-Tech Tools Profile, Police, and Punish the Poor* 3, 5 (New York: St Martin's Press 2017). For the first comprehensive account at the turn of the century (that is relevant today), see Simson Garfinkel, *Database Nation: The Death of Privacy in the 21*st *Century* (Sebastopol: O'Reilly 2000).
7. Reuben Binns, 'Fairness in Machine Learning: Lessons from Political Philosophy' (2018) 81 *Journal of Machine Learning* 1, 3.
8. See, e.g., Frank Pasquale, *The Black Box Society: The Secret Algorithms That Control Money and Information* (Cambridge: Harvard University Press 2015). 'Automation bias' was visible, in particular, during the Aadhaar arguments, when the State repeatedly claimed that biometric

authentication was the most accurate identification technology available.

9. Anand Murali, 'The Big Eye: The tech is all ready for mass surveillance in India', *FactorDaily*, 13 August 2018, available at https://factordaily.com/face-recognition-mass-surveillance-in-india/.
10. As Virginia Eubanks notes, in a slightly different context: 'The integration of policing and homelessness blurs the boundary between the maintenance of economic security and the investigation of crime, between poverty and criminality, tightening a net of constraint that tracks and traps the unhoused. This net requires data-based infrastructure to surround and systems of moral classification to sift.' Eubanks, *Automating Inequality*, supra, 180.
11. See, e.g., (albeit in a slightly different context), Solon Barocas & Andrew D. Selbst, 'Big Data's Disparate Impact', (2016) 104 *California Law Review* 671, 699, asking us to imagine 'the *model* as the decision-maker'.
12. The DNA Technology (Use and Application) Regulation Bill, 2018, available at http://www.prsindia.org/uploads/media/DNA/DNA%20Bill,%202018.pdf.
13. See, e.g., Suraj Yengde, 'There's a caste bias in our prison system—And we need to talk about it now', *Huffington Post*, 23 March 2017, available at https://www.huffingtonpost.in/suraj-yengde/theres-a-caste-bias-in-our-prison-system-and-we-need-to-talk-ab_a_21662007/. The National Crime Records Bureau publishes prison statistics on an annual basis. See, e.g., http://ncrb.gov.in/statpublications/psi/Prison2015/PrisonStat2015.htm.
14. Sheldon Krimsky & Tania Simoncelli, *Genetic Justice: DNA Data Banks, Criminal Investigations and Civil Liberties* 152 (New York: Columbia University Press 2011).
15. For a set of examples demonstrating the link between methods of data collecting and processing, and substantive equality, see Barocas & Selbst, 'Big Data's Disparate Impact', supra.
16. Ibid., 153.
17. Eubanks, *Automating Inequality*, supra, 153. It is also argued that using DNA profiling to predict *racial* characteristics (of, say, a suspect) will only reify the concept of 'race', which has no independent existence

outside of being a social construct. See Krimsky & Simoncelli, *Genetic Justice*, supra, 273.

18. See, e.g., Gaurav Bhatnagar, 'Aadhaar and hunger: Second Jharkhand woman starves to death after being refused rations', *The Wire*, 2 January 2018, available at https://thewire.in/food/aadhaar-hunger-jharkhand-starvation-death-rations.
19. Alok Pandey, 'Homeless in UP denied night shelters without Aadhaar, "What do we do?", they ask', *NDTV*, 13 January 2018, available at https://www.ndtv.com/india-news/homeless-in-up-denied-night-shelters-without-aadhaar-what-do-we-do-they-ask-1799513.
20. Eubanks, *Automating Inequality*, supra, 195.
21. Akshay Deshmane, 'The Dalit Identity Dilemma', *Frontline*, 28 April 2017, available at https://www.frontline.in/cover-story/the-dalit-identity-dilemma/article9629313.ece.
22. Vance Packard, 'Don't tell it to the computer', *The New York Times Magazine*, 8 January 1967, available at http://simson.net/ref/1966/Packard_Privacy_Stuff.pdf.
23. The Genetic Information Non-Discrimination Act, 2008.
24. *United India Insurance Co Ltd v. Jai Prakash Tayal*, RFA 610/2016 (High Court of Delhi). The judgement was inexplicably stayed on appeal by the Supreme Court without any reasoned order, and has not (to the author's knowledge) been decided yet.
25. Eubanks, *Automating Inequality*, supra, 194.
26. Anand Venkatanarayanan, 'Fingerprints, Aadhaar and Law Enforcement – A deadly cocktail is in the making', *The Wire*, 16 August 2018, available at https://thewire.in/tech/aadhaar-fingerprints-ncrb-police-investigations.
27. See, e.g., written submissions on behalf of K.V. Viswanathan, available at www.livelaw.in.
28. Anand Venkatanarayanan, 'Fingerprints, Aadhaar and Law Enforcement – A deadly cocktail is in the making', supra.
29. Id.
30. Id.
31. Id.
32. Towards the end of August, it was announced by the UIDAI that facial recognition would be introduced in a 'phased manner' from the middle of September, starting with mobile phone companies.

33. Eubanks, *Automating Inequality*, supra, 122.
34. Krimsky & Simoncelli, *Genetic Justice*, supra, Ch. 2.
35. Id., for an account of US case law on the subject. The fact that many modern algorithms are based on extracting sensitive information from publicly available data suggests that the underlying assumption is that we do not retain our privacy rights over such data, which is, of course, contrary to the right-to-privacy judgement of the Supreme Court in *Justice K.S. Puttaswamy v. Union of India*, (2017) 10 SCC 1.
36. Eubanks, *Automating Inequality*, supra, 195. See also Lilian Edwards & Michael Veale, 'Enslaving the Algorithm: From a "Right to an Explanation" to a "Right to Better Decisions"?', (2018) 16(3) *IEEE Security and Privacy* 46: 'Because algorithms are trained on historical data, they risk replicating unwanted historical patterns of unfairness and/or discrimination.'
37. Cynthia Dwork et al., 'Fairness through Awareness', arXiv:1104.3913 [cs.CC] (2011).
38. See, for example, the provisions of the EUGDPR.
39. Edwards & Veale, 'Enslaving the Algorithm', supra.
40. Gaurav Bhatnagar, 'Javadekar's 80,000 "Ghost" teachers: Activists, MHRD, Dispute Status of Probe', *The Wire*, 13 May 2018, available at https://thewire.in/education/no-probe-on-javadekars-claim-that-80000-ghost-teachers-detected-in-higher-education.
41. Eubanks, *Automating Inequality*, supra, 77.
42. Cynthia Wong, 'We underestimate the threat of facial recognition technology at our peril', *The Guardian*, 17 August 2018, available at https://www.theguardian.com/commentisfree/2018/aug/17/we-underestimate-the-threat-of-facial-recognition-technology-at-our-peril.
43. *Justice K.S. Puttaswamy v. Union of India*, supra, ¶263 (dissenting opinion of Justice Chandrachud).
44. Edwards & Veale, 'Enslaving the Algorithm', supra.
45. Frank Pasquale, *The Black Box Society: The Secret Algorithms That Control Money and Information* (Cambridge: Harvard University Press 2015).
46. Edwards & Veale, 'Enslaving the Algorithm', supra.
47. See, e.g., Cathy O'Neil, *Weapons of Math Destruction: How Big Data Increases Inequality and Threatens Democracy* (New York: Crown 2016).

48. For a summary of the debate, with citations to the relevant scholarship, see Vidushi Marda, 'Machine Learning and Transparency: A Scoping Exercise' (22 November 2017), available at SSRN: https://ssrn.com/abstract=3236837.

    For a detailed and technical account, which focuses as well on the broader issue of the limits of transparency in solving algorithmic discrimination, see Joshua A. Kroll et al., 'Accountable Algorithms', (2017) 165 *University of Pennsylvania Law Review* 633, 647–650, 657–660.
49. Solon Barocas & Andrew D. Selbst, 'Big Data's Disparate Impact', (2016) 104 *California Law Review* 761.
50. *Justice K.S. Puttaswamy v. Union of India*, supra, ¶3 (dissenting opinion of Justice Chandrachud).
51. *Common Cause v. Union of India*, WP (Civ) No. 215/2005.
52. Id., ¶153.
53. See Gautam Bhatia, 'Under a Humane Constitution', *The Hindu*, 12 March 2018, available at https://www.thehindu.com/todays-paper/tp-opinion/under-a-humane-constitution/article23043291.ece; see also Gautam Bhatia, 'Round-Up: Constitution Bench Judgments on Assisted Dying and Parliamentary Standing Committee Reports', *Indian Constitutional Law and Philosophy*, 29 June 2018, available at https://indconlawphil.wordpress.com/2018/06/29/round-up-constitution-bench-judgments-on-assisted-dying-and-parliamentary-standing-committee-reports/.
54. Walter Benjamin, 'On the concept of history', I:2 *Gesammelte Schriften* (Frankfurt: 1974), available at http://members.efn.org/~dredmond/ThesesonHistory.html.

Index

About the Author

GAUTAM BHATIA GRADUATED FROM the National Law School of India University in 2011. He read for the BCL and the MPhil at the University of Oxford (on a Rhodes scholarship), and the LLM at Yale Law School. At Oxford, he won the Herbert Hart Prize for writing the best essays in Jurisprudence and Political Theory, and a chapter of his MPhil (on the jurisprudence of Ronald Dworkin) was published as a standalone article in the peer-reviewed *Australian Journal of Legal Philosophy*. He is now a DPhil (Law) candidate at the University of Oxford.

He has been a practising lawyer in New Delhi, and visiting faculty at various law schools. His practice has seen him involved in some important contemporary constitutional cases, such as the challenge to criminal defamation, and the nine-judge bench right to privacy case (where one of his articles was cited by the plurality judgement). His scholarship has appeared in the *Oxford Handbook for the Indian Constitution*, *Max Planck Encyclopedia of Comparative Constitutional Law*, and in peer-reviewed journals such as *Constellations* and *Global Constitutionalism*. His first book, *Offend,*

Shock, or Disturb: Freedom of Speech under the Indian Constitution, was published in 2015. His work has been cited by the Supreme Court of India and by numerous high courts. His first science fiction novel, *The Wall*, was published by HarperCollins in 2020.